Sustainable Management, Wertschöpfung und Effizienz

Reihe herausgegeben von
Gregor Weber, Breunigweiler, Deutschland
Markus Bodemann, Warburg, Deutschland
René Schmidpeter, Köln, Deutschland

In dieser Schriftenreihe stehen insbesondere empirische und praxisnahe Studien zu nachhaltigem Wirtschaften und Effizienz im Mittelpunkt. Energie-, Umwelt-, Nachhaltigkeits-, CSR-, Innovations-, Risiko- und integrierte Managementsysteme sind nur einige Beispiele, die Sie hier wiederfinden. Ein besonderer Fokus liegt dabei auf dem Nutzen, den solche Systeme für die Anwendung in der Praxis bieten, um zu helfen die globalen Nachhaltigkeitsziele (SDGs) umzusetzen. Publiziert werden nationale und internationale wissenschaftliche Arbeiten.

Reihenherausgeber
Dr. Gregor Weber, ecoistics.institute
Dr. Markus Bodemann
Prof. Dr. René Schmidpeter, Center for Advanced Sustainable Management, Cologne Business School

This series is focusing on empirical and practical research in the fields of sustainable management and efficiency. Management systems in the context of energy, environment, sustainability, CSR, innovation, risk as well as integrated management systems are just a few examples which can be found here. A special focus is on the value such systems can offer for the application in practice supporting the implementation of the global sustainable development goals, the SDGs. National and international scientific publications are published (English and German).

Series Editors
Dr. Gregor Weber, ecoistics.institute
Dr. Markus Bodemann
Prof. Dr. René Schmidpeter, Center for Advanced Sustainable Management, Cologne Business School

More information about this series at http://www.springer.com/series/15909

Jan Kopia

Effective Implementation of Management Systems

Management Systems as a
Success Factor for the Efficiency
of Organizations

 Springer Gabler

Jan Kopia
Berlin, Germany

Dissertation, The Bucharest University of Economic Studies, Bucharest, Romania, 2018

ISSN 2523-8620   ISSN 2523-8639   (electronic)
Sustainable Management, Wertschöpfung und Effizienz
ISBN 978-3-658-26508-3   ISBN 978-3-658-26509-0   (eBook)
https://doi.org/10.1007/978-3-658-26509-0

Springer Gabler
© Springer Fachmedien Wiesbaden GmbH, part of Springer Nature 2019

This Springer Gabler imprint is published by the registered company Springer Fachmedien Wiesbaden GmbH part of Springer Nature
The registered company address is: Abraham-Lincoln-Str. 46, 65189 Wiesbaden, Germany

Dedication

To my loved family

To my dear wife Vanessa and my precious children Desmond, Darrion and Fionella who were so supportive and patient with me while working on this research.

And to my parents, Marion und Heino, without whom this project ever would have been worked on.

Table of Contents

List of Abbreviations

BPM	Business Process Management
BSC	Balanced Scorecard
COSO	Committee of Sponsoring Organizations
ERM	Enterprise Risk Management
EU	European Union
EFQM	European Foundation for Quality Management
KM	Knowledge management
PMS	Performance Management System
IMS	Integrated Management System
ICM	Intellectual Capital Management
RO	Risk Officer
CRO	Chief Risk Officer
EI	Emotional Intelligence
EVA	Economy Value Added
HCE	Human Capital Efficiency
HLS	High-Level structure
IC	Intellectual Capital
ISO	International
JIT	Just in Time
KPI	Key Performance Indicator
MSS	Management System Standard
PDCA	Plan-Do-Check-Act
RIMS	Risk and Insurance Management Society
M & A	Mergers and Acquisition
OC	Organizational Culture
OEMs	Original
OHSAS	Original Equipment Manufacturer
VAIC	Value Added Intellectual Coefficient

| VUCA | Volatile, Uncertain, Complex, Ambiguous |
| TQM | Total Quality Management |

List of Figures

List of Tables

Abstract

This PhD-thesis assesses the problems of the evaluation of integrated management systems in the context of sustainability business processes and risk management. Based on a literature research the author evaluated the current trends and known knowledge in this research field and, within the last three years, conducted his personal empirical studies. Several areas were the focus of these studies, which are closely related to the research topic. One aspect is the organizational performance and its measurement, including its shift from purely financially measured methods to multidimensional approaches, which also include sustainability dimensions required by the EU. Additional aspects are success factors of integrated management systems and its entanglement with risk management. Enterprise-wide risk management concepts offer viable solutions for enterprise-wide management systems and their measurement. Another focus is the importance of the strategic linkage of management systems toward the top level of the organization.

Within this thesis, the author places special emphasis on problems in the research field he identified during many management systems audits he conducted and the evaluation of viable solutions.

With the development of a model to evaluate integrated management systems by taking sustainability and risk management into account the applicability of it to link the results for strategic usage was focused upon. The model includes the extended use of a balanced scorecard together with a strategic map-process, the execution premium and the plan-do-check-act-cycle of management systems. In addition, it presents an approach for scientists and practitioners to further test and deepen the understanding of related topics.

Keywords:

Integrated Managament System, Organizational Performance, Evaluation, Sustainability, Risk Management, Leadersthip Style, Management System Standards, Organizational Cultural, Enterprise Risk Management, Knowledge Management, Intellectual Capital, Managerial Culture, Organizational Effectiveness and Efficiency, Performance Measurement, Cultral Communication, Business Processes, Agility, Lean Management, Total Quality Management, ISO norms, Kaizen

Rezumat

Prezenta teză de doctorat analizează dificultățile evaluării sistemelor integrate de management în contextul proceselor sustenabilității în afaceri şi managementului riscurilor. Pe baza cercetării aprofundate a literaturii în domeniu, autorul a evaluat tendințele actuale şi cunoştințele disponibile în acest domeniu de cercetare şi a formulat propriile sale studii empirice pe parcursul ultimilor trei ani. În centrul acestor studii s-au aflat mai multe domenii ce au strânsă legătură cu subiectul cercetării.

Un prim aspect esențial îl reprezintă performanța organizațională şi măsurarea acesteia, vizând trecerea ei de la metodele măsurate strict financiar la abordările multidimensionale, incluzând de asemenea, dimensiunile de sustenabilitate cerute de Uniunea Europeană. Alt aspect se referă la factorii de succes ai sistemelor integrate de management şi legătura lor cu managementul riscurilor. Managementul riscului la nivel de întreprindere oferă soluții posibile pentru sistemele de management implementate în cadrul companiei şi pentru evaluarea lor. Un aspect sensibil se referă la importanța legăturii strategice a sistemului de management cu decidenții de la nivelul de conducere al organizației.

În cuprinsul prezentei teze, autorul a pus accentul, în mod deosebit, pe problemele practice din domeniul cercetării, identificate pe durata unor numeroase audituri ale sistemelor de management, pe care le-a desfăşurat şi pe evaluarea unor posibile soluții.

Dezvoltarea unui model de evaluare a sistemelor integrate de management, prin luarea în considerare a sustenabilității şi a managementului riscurilor, dar şi utilizarea acestuia în vederea interconectării rezultatelor, a permis evidențierea aplicabilității şi utilizării lui strategice. Modelul include posibilitatea utilizării extinse a balanced scorecard-ului, împreună cu procesul strategic de acțiune Execution Premium, precum şi ciclul plan-do-check-act ale sistemelor de management reprezentând astfel, o nouă direcție de abordare pentru cercetători şi practicieni în vederea continuării testării şi aprofundării înțelegerii subiectelor aflate în raport direct cu acestea.

cuvinte cheie

sistem integrat de management, performanța organizațională, sustenabilitate, managementul riscurilor, stil de conducere, standarde pentru sistemul de management, management organizational şi cultural, managementul cunostintelor, capital intelectual, cultura managerială, evaluarea performantei, procese de afaceri, agilitate, managementul calitatii totale

Introduction

The nature of most businesses is to exchange goods or services for money. Even though certain organizations with different objectives, such as social enterprises and NGOs, have different goals than merely increasing their monetary value, they also exchange good or services to reach their defined targets. Seen from a business process perspective, it can be said, that the core competence of organizations is to reach their defined targets by transforming inputs to outputs. This is reached by the execution of organizational processes which connect the various parts of the organization and, in turn, steered by the execution of management practices. The management of all parts of an organization can be complex since it includes different targets depending on the levels of the processes (e.g. operational processes, strategic processes etc.). It is also complex due to the diverse business functions and the complexity of the environment with different stakeholders having varied expectations. Considering these aspects, it becomes clear that there are different goals to be reached simultaneously. For example, the management of the production sector of the business wishes to achieve a high quality and a low defect rate. The sales management, on the other hand, wants to achieve high sales growths, the human resources department wants to recruit the right people, the environmental managers want a low rate of environmental pollution, the top management wants to please stakeholders and customers, and the legal department puts emphasis on laws and regulations. New social and political developments also focus on the topic of sustainability and defines the requirements for organizations which further places pressure on management regarding the focus of organizational targets and the definition and evaluation of goals and strategies. Managing all these different targets in an efficient and effective manner is typically done through the separation of management tasks within different organizational levels and functional areas. Top management defines generic goals and strategies which must be transferred into detailed executable tasks and processes within the functional areas or business units.

Management systems could be a key component within this complex field since they operate on all levels of an organization. Management system standards offer possibilities to manage these various aspects based on best-practice approaches. They define a set of requirements for different aspects of the operation of sustainable business processes and assist the management in doing so. International standards for management systems exist in different areas, focusing certain aspects of an organization, such as:

© Springer Fachmedien Wiesbaden GmbH, part of Springer Nature 2019
J. Kopia, *Effective Implementation of Management Systems*, Sustainable Management, Wertschöpfung und Effizienz, https://doi.org/10.1007/978-3-658-26509-0_1

- Quality management,
- Environmental management,
- Energy (consumption) management,
- Information security management,
- Risk management,
- Business continuity management,
- Crisis management,
- Health and safety management and so on.

Most standards were established by standardization bodies, such as ISO (International Organization for Standardization), BSI (British Standard Institution) and alike. They also serve as the central part for the accreditation of such standards. In addition to these standards there are best practice approaches without certification bodies but from industry associations, researchers, individual companies or federations which publish approaches, such as Total Quality Management, the EFQM Excellence Model, lean management, KAIZEN, agile principles etc. Many companies are adopting such standards enhancing their sustainable business processes and fulfilling requirements of laws and stakeholders. Many of them also acquire a certification based on these standards proofed by an external auditing process. This requires these companies to continuously evaluate and improve the management system on a regular basis. The implementation of management systems and the certification process of international standards are similar all over the world and therefore a comparable approach to implementing standardized processes within businesses.

Besides these general positive aspects, companies are facing various problems regarding management systems. One problem raises the question, which management system standards should be implemented (and whether this system should be officially audited through a certification process). Another problem is the integration of multiple management systems. Many organizations already use more than one management system, integrating them into a combined management system to use synergies and possible benefits. An integrated management system is one management system managing different focus areas. ISO makes integration easy by the definition of a similar structure in all of their newest editions of the management systems. This structure is called the "high-level structure" (HSL). This high-level structure also requires that management systems must use a risk-based approach to define plans and goals. Besides the obvious benefits of integration, no clear statement in scientific literature exists that integration is always beneficial. Also, there is no standardized approach to integration. Other problems are related to the question whether management systems inhibit or enhance organizational processes since they require the organization to set up tasks and processes which seem overwhelming at first.

Measuring the effectiveness and efficiency of management systems and the general evaluation of the performance are aspects, which need to be considered. Each management system must deal with risks. Risk management approaches are a crucial element of management as well. Based on a risk management process, which includes at least risk identification, ratings, and the definition of mitigations, measures are defined that act as the operational part and central aspects of each management system. The management of risks and opportunities is vital for organizations to survive and an essential process for all organizations regardless of a possible existing management system. Analyzing and acting based on risk and opportunities is an important management task in each organization. A concise organization-wide risk management (sometimes using a standard, such as an enterprise risk management based on COSO or ISO 31000) should include the risk management processes of management systems.

Organizations need to consider many aspects when adapting management system standards. Whether their use is beneficial for an organization has been for many years a matter of scientific research. Despite industry-wide usage, the scientific research in the management systems' topics remains scattered. This begins with the question of the definitions of integrated management systems and continues with an examination of the way to evaluate benefits. Most scientific authors identify benefits of integrated management systems for the organization. The following list presents an excerpt of some of these benefits (Wilkinson & Dale, 2002; W.M. To et al., 2012; Bernardo et al., 2015):

- An improvement in the efficiency and effectiveness of the organization by avoiding the duplication of effort
- A reduction of bureaucracy by eliminating the duplication of policies, procedures, and registers
- The alignment of goals, processes, and resources
- A reduction in the costs of internal and external audits, and
- the availability of joint training and improved communication between all organizational levels
- A similar structure in the standards, based on the continuous improvement cycle.

Organizations need to answer many questions before implementing a management system. Besides the basic fulfillment of requirements of laws, regulations and the expectations of stakeholders (e.g. by requiring specific management systems because of the industry or geographic region the company is operating in), there are other important aspects to consider in the context of management system implementation. The following list is an excerpt of important questions, which are scientifically assessed in this thesis:

- Is it useful to integrate the management systems into an integrated management system?
- Are there enough resources for the implementation and the operation of a management system?
- The project phase of implementation requires different people and other resources as in the operational phase.
- Is there enough management attention for the management system?
- Many standards require the involvement of the management, which shows in the defined goals, the set resources, the strategic relevance of the management system etc.
- Is the organizational culture and leadership methodology suable for the required aspects of the management system?
  Different management systems require different philosophies in regard to leadership and organizational culture for a successful operation of a management system.
- How can an organization evaluate the management system?
  Assessing the maturity and performance of the management systems is necessary for the continuous improvement process.
- How does the management system influence the performance of the business?
  The goal of management systems is to improve certain parts of the organization by applying principles, which are being integrated into the business processes. This improvement in sustainable business processes should be evaluated with regularity and reported for the decision-making process.

To answer these questions, the author assessed these topics in different studies during his PhD-program. The basis for the thesis topic was defined during projects the author was involved in over the last five years. Throughout his work, the author gained valuable insights into the problematics in the area of management system implementation and certification by running external audits as well as by introducing management systems within companies in consulting projects in different management systems, industries, and geographic regions. Within the last years, the author was concerned with these problems and collected data and ideas about possible solutions. In order to understand the problems more clearly and in order to develop valuable and long-lasting solutions based on scientific research, the author is using his PhD-thesis to assess the topic in greater detail and to develop a model for the evaluation of integrated management systems based on his experiences, pool of ideas, data and learnings to:

- further research the context and effects of integrated management systems for businesses worldwide,
- developing a solution to evaluate the performance of management systems for organizations,
- finding better approaches for his work and for the work of others in the field of consulting of companies during implementation and improvement projects of management systems and related business processes,
- emphasis the connection of management systems and aspects of sustainability business processes and their strategic importance,
- identifying aspects to create better auditing capabilities in management system audits.

The evaluation of the effects of a management system is discussed in the scientific literature without a clear consensus. The problem seems to be the definition of the word "effect" or "performance" in the context of organizations, management systems, and organizational processes. According to some scientists, performance can be interpreted not only on the financial perspective but in a different way depending on the assessment and goals. Measuring performance for management systems using only financial values does not seem to be the right way since management systems deal with many different topics, which are sometimes not related to the core business and value creating processes (e.g. information security management or environmental management). Other aspects of performance are important as well. These features include organizational culture, leadership, capability of innovations, knowledge management, organizational learning, risk management, process effectiveness and efficiency etc. Sustainability, as required by certain governments, is important for the operations of a company and has to be considered in performance evaluation of some management systems that are related to sustainability aspects. The evaluation of multiple dimensions becomes important. These dimensions have to be seen in relationship to business targets and the strategy defined by the management. They should be used to steer the organization in the right direction.

This thesis is structured in two parts:

The first part identifies current scientific research in areas related to the research topic. This part serves as the basis for the identification of current trends and knowledge as well as research gaps to create concrete studies and a research plan presented in part two of this thesis. Part one is important as a theoretical basis for the development of the models the author develops in conclusion of this thesis.

The second part takes the results of the identified knowledge gaps and fields of interest of part one and carry out several empirical studies to elaborate on the relevant topic in a scientific manner. All study results are important parts to develop a thesis, which is presented as a model for the evaluation of the performance of management systems in the context of sustainable business processes and knowledge management.

The first chapter of part one focusses on the definition and understanding of "organization" and "business processes" in the context of performance. Using a literature research, influence factors on sustainable business processes are identified as well as possibilities to measure the effect using measurements in respects to effectiveness and efficiency. Chapter one presents an insights into existing models and frameworks to evaluate organizational effectiveness and efficiency. These models use different approaches to assess the topic of the performance within business processes analyzing various aspects and assessing multiple dimensions. This includes aspects of knowledge, learning, and leadership. The balanced scorecard method as a well-known and established way to evaluate performance is introduced as well as its current extensions. Furthermore, recent developments in the management of business processes are presented including principles of lean and agile management. Studies in knowledge and organizational learning and their influence on performance are summarized in the last part of chapter one. This portion also includes the effects of different leadership styles and organizational cultures that put different emphases on knowledge creation, transferring, sharing, and maintaining, and the motivational effects of these leadership styles.

Chapter two gives insights into diverse scientific studies on the connection between risk management and sustainable business processes because risk management is a central topic in management systems and a natural process within all organizations. Since risk management models and methodologies are required in management systems on the one hand and for strategic use on the other, the research of its underlying principles and evaluation methods are introduced. Suggestions by scientists who investigated the connection between enterprise risk management and the performance of organizations showing its importance are demonstrated. The last part of chapter two focusses on performance indicators in the field of risk management, its multiple dimensions and serves as an example to assess related aspects in the organizational context offering a valuable insight into evaluation approaches for management systems.

In chapter three, the author identifies the relationship between sustainable business processes and integrated management systems based on existing research in the field. Recent developments in management systems and modern approaches and methodologies are compared. This involves the comparison of models and methodologies, such as Total Quality Management, the EFQM excellence model, ISO-based international standards and the evaluation of its effects on business processes. The answers to questions about success factors of integrated management systems are presented with a special focus on:

- aspects of leadership styles
- organizational culture
- knowledge management
- effects of the high-level structure of integrated management systems within different industries and geographic regions.

The last part focusses on measurement approaches of management systems and their relevance to organizational outputs in the context of risk management.

The second part of the thesis is the research portion of this PhD-candidate. It summarizes various research projects the author of this thesis conducted over the last three years in his field of study. The researche include different methodologies, qualitative and quantitative studies, as well as empirical evaluations tentatively answering the hypotheses in the relevant fields within the scope of this thesis.

Chapter four starts with the research objective to investigate possible connections between defined targets of organizations and reported organizational performance. The focus is on the analysis of the type of targets especially in the field of sustainability, organizational learning and knowledge management and their effects on a firm's performance. Quantitative sales targets, as well as generic statements regarding goals within a production industry, are compared to existing figures and reports. The second part of the study focusses on the connection between business process performance evaluation and enterprise risk management. For this research, a meta-analytic approach is used to evaluate studies in the field of enterprise risk management and existing evaluation models. In his research, the author presents a framework on assessing enterprise risk management using multiple dimensions serving as a basis for the suggested model of the management system performance evaluation in chapter six. A case study approach is used to test this risk management assessment model. The authors continue on the research path to study the importance of knowledge management by performing a quantitative study based on a correlation analysis of values for intellectual capital and a firm's performance within the automotive business environment. The final part of chapter four is concerned with the evaluation of the effects of methodologies to manage an organization based on agile or lean principles. This aspect is of importance to further elaborate ways to understand the influencing factors and evaluation methods of the performance of management systems and useful approaches for their evaluation. The goal is to identify reasons why lean and agile methodologies are creating better results in some circumstances than other tactics do.

Chapter five expands on the topic of management systems in general. The first study evaluates the advantages of the high-level structure and its effect on integrated management systems. Using an empirical evaluation of the collected data, the author proves and disproves hypotheses within this topic. One such topic is the success factors of integrated management systems and the question of how these factors are defined and evaluated. The second study considers the question of how leadership influences the performance of management systems. A quantitative analysis of data is used to identify favorable leadership styles and its influence on management systems. To identify relationships between management systems and knowledge management, another study elaborates on the results of established management systems in a certain industry and its development over time. This study also compares the development of intellectual capital as the measurable value of knowledge and organizational learning during the introduction and operation of management systems over a period. The last part of chapter five studies common assessment methods for management systems in the service sector. Based on existing management systems within selected companies, survey results are analyzed using qualitative and quantitate comparisons.

In chapter six the author develops a holistic model to evaluate the performance of integrated management systems in the context of business processes and enterprise risk management based on the before mentioned studies, new EU requirements in the context of sustainability, and data collected during work projects by the author. Using the knowledge gained from his projects, as an auditor and consultant for management systems and a selection of collected data, the author identified knowledge gaps and general problems using observation and by applying qualitative and quantitative analyses. The author develops a solution based on the findings and proves them within the thesis to improve his own work, and future works of scientists and practitioners. One aspect of this solution is supported by the investigation of the requirements given by the EU in regard to sustainability reporting which forces organizations to report their performance using multiple dimensions.

Research methodology	Research objectives	Chapters and fields of research
Part I: Literature review		
Theory	The theoretical framework for this thesis is developed using an exhaustive literature research.	Chapters 1, 2, and 3: • Performance evaluation in sustainable business processes • Integrated management systems • Knowledge management and organizational learning • Risk management
Hypotheses	Based on the literature research results, knowledge gaps are identified and hypotheses are formulated	
Part II: Own contribution		
Empirical analyses	Empirically analysis through quantitative and qualitative analyses.	Chapters 4 and 5: • Evaluation of performance within sustainable business processes • Influence of integrated management systems
Implementation	Development of a model to evaluate the performance of integrated management systems.	Chapter 6: • Knowledge gaps and practical problem in management systems • Performance evaluation model development • Empirical testing of the model
Empirical evaluation	Verification of the developed model using quantitative analyses	

Figure 1: Structure of research and thesis
(Source: by author)

The holistic model to evaluate the performance of integrated management systems in the context of business processes and enterprise risk management is tested in the last part of this thesis using quantitative analyses and correlations between core elements of the developed model and results from surveys and interview results from organizations. The research methodology is presented in figure 1.

This research was created with the assistance of different individuals who were inspiring and supportive as well as critical and provided valuable feedback at any stage of the research project. During the creation process, my scientific coordinator and supervisor Prof. Univ. Dr. Pamfilie Rodica was available for all my questions. Another person I must thank is Prof. Univ. Dr. Marieta Olaru, who answered many of my questions regarding the organization of the PhD-program as well as questions regarding my studies. In addition to that, I am grateful for all organizations which were willing and able to answer my questions or were part of surveys. I must also thank all partners, colleagues, and people involved in discussions during conferences and research initiatives.

Finally, I need to thank my family for all the support they gave me during the time of the development of this thesis. Without their help, there wouldn't have been enough time to manage the workload during the research and simultaneously working on other projects. This thesis is dedicated to them.

Part I: Current State of Scientific Knowledge in the Field of Research

1 Building up the concept of organisational performance

1.1 Performance evaluation - main target of organization aiming to create competitive advantage

The word "organization" is defined in different ways in scientific literature and has been discussed at length by thousands of scientists. Over the years organizations are being studied using different points of view. To give an excerpt of the length of time this topic is being studied, some authors are cited as follows. Several decades ago the context of the decision-making process was studied (Reitzel, 1958) focusing on the way individuals work together, how command and control can be achieved and executed, and what types of organizational processes are necessary for that context. Years later, scientists continued discussing the definition of organizations. According to Morin (1977), an organization can be defined as a group of people who work together to reach a goal. This group of people shares common goals which they are working on in a specific environment over a certain period. Two decades later, Olmstead (2002) suggested a definition which emphases the goal of an organization to produce something. According to him, this is being achieved through a network of relationships between individuals (or components in general). The authors identify several characteristics of organizations, e.g. the need to operating in a changing environment with the necessity to adapt to these changing circumstances (Duncan, 1972), the distributed activities which range from local management and knowledge to global interaction and the global integration of cultures and processes. The complexity behind the word "organization" makes it necessary to separate the studies, breaking into subjects which can be assessed more easily depending on the area of research and the study method.

If not operated as social enterprise and entrepreneurship (Dees et al., 2006; Nyssens, 2006) or any form of non-profit organization, most companies will be involved in commercial or economic activities with the goal to increase profit. But there is more to it than profit. Simon (1959) included behavioral aspects into that thought and differentiated the profit-maximizing strategy toward a more profit-satisfactory strategy. These aspects were further interpreted by different economists, e.g. by Williamson's utility maximization (Curwen, 1976), and Cyert et al. (1992) who emphasizes the distinction between several individuals (Shareholders, managers, owners etc.) within the organization and the manner market companies are operating in. Also, Drucker stated that entrepreneurs seek opportunities not only in commercial but also in goals of a social nature (1985).

© Springer Fachmedien Wiesbaden GmbH, part of Springer Nature 2019
J. Kopia, *Effective Implementation of Management Systems*, Sustainable Management, Wertschöpfung und Effizienz, https://doi.org/10.1007/978-3-658-26509-0_2

Nevertheless profit, as financial value, is still a commonly referred value for the performance of a company. Therefore, a specific area to study, regarding organizations, is the topic of organizational performance. Performance plays a significant role for organizations considering the basic definition that performance of an organization means to fulfill all tasks which are necessary to reach its goal (e.g. increasing profit). This is true not only for for-profit organizations since even the non-profit sector can be assessed and compared stating the word "performance" – most likely profit won't be the indicator in this case.

Measuring, performance is important in order to make progress. Organizations need to know their status to define targets for the future. Increasing performance is the goal of most organizations as it is required by the market. Performance evaluation in general and the measurement in specific is an endeavor which is discussed in the scientific literature and in applied management for years (Richard et al., 2009). It is also a multi-disciplinary topic since performance can be assessed on various levels. According to So and Durfee (1998), organizational performance is based on three factors: task-environmental factors, structure, and behavior. Focussing on the behavioral-science approach, organizations can be seen as a triangle between structure, processes, and people (see figure 2). Behaviors are strongly related to human resource management, psychology and leadership aspects (Mintzberg, 1998; Wai et al., 2015). With behavioral aspects, organizational culture comes into place and defines various features, such as norms and regularities, but also dominant values which influence the organizational climate (Campbell, 1977). According to Pugh (1990) organizational structure is defined as the way

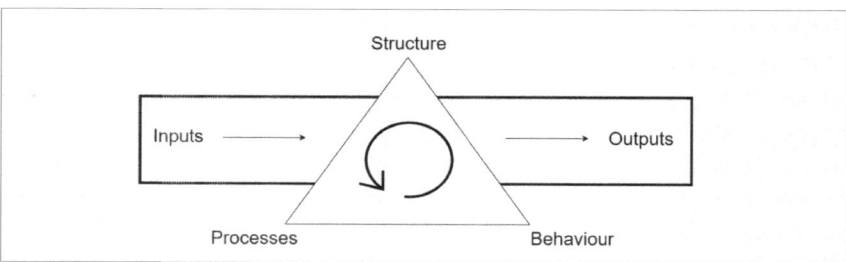

Figure 2: Structure of an organization from a behavioral-science perspective
(Source: own interpretation of the organizational triangle)

organizations realize task allocation, coordination between people and management tasks to succeed in reaching its goals. This mainly involves the levels of hierarchies, mostly named by descriptive words such as:

- bureaucratic structures
- functional structures
- divisional structures
- Matrix structure
- etc.

Adding a market and environment perspective to the logic presented in figure 2, it seems reasonable to assume that the influence of the market and the environment the company is operating in, influences the organization. Main influencing factors are (McGee et al., 2010; Maidenhead.Sammut-Bonnici et al, 2015):

- economic situation
- social and demographic development
- political and legal aspects
- technological development

The economic dimension involves aspects, such as inflation, unemployment rates, and interest rates which affect the demand and product prices (Griffin, 1997). The economic perspective is also related to the availability of money to invest and therefore the possibility of companies to execute strategic decisions (as investing in innovations, buy-or-make-decisions, purchasing machinery and technology etc.).

The socio-cultural dimension includes for example demographic development, the role of the customer, etc.

Political and legal restrictions influence an organization based on policies, rules, and laws but also lobbying, corruption etc.

Technological development is a strong influencing factor in many industries particularly considering the fact of increased automation (Chui et al., 2015). The rapid development of new materials, machinery, and the quickly evolving hardware and software that optimizes and improve business processes makes it necessary for organizations to constantly monitor this dimension.

Besides the four basic dimensions other elements to consider can be added, e.g. the ecologic perspective, social responsibility, and sustainable business (Amato et al., 2009) etc.

The fact that organizations need to survive within the competitive landscape makes them similar in certain ways, such as the ability to deal with resources and capabilities (Prahalad et al., 1990; Kompalla et al., 2016a). Capabilities is another used idiom in the literature within the context of organizational studies. Teece et al. (1997) suggested the concept of dynamic capabilities and the ability for organizations "[...] to integrate, build, and reconfigure internal and external competencies to address rapidly changing environments." The authors stated that the ability to gain and use the knowledge necessary for developing products and services became a dominant topic at the end of the 19th century. Cordes-Berszinn et al. (2013) suggested that especially intangible goods (in contrast to the traditionally seen value-improving tangible goods in an organization) must be seen as the predominant paradigm for the explanation of competitive advantages. The authors also stated that the measurement of such intangible goods – mainly the organizational knowledge – is not an easy task.

1.1.1   Aspects of performance measurement

A common statement is: what you can't measure, you cannot manage. The measurement of organizational performance is a natural act since companies, on the one hand, need to identify their own situation to be able to set goals and to improve, and on the other hand, organizations need to be "measurable" by stakeholders (including banks etc.). If nothing is measured, it would not be possible to get an idea of the status, the quality, the success, and the financial situation etc. of a company.

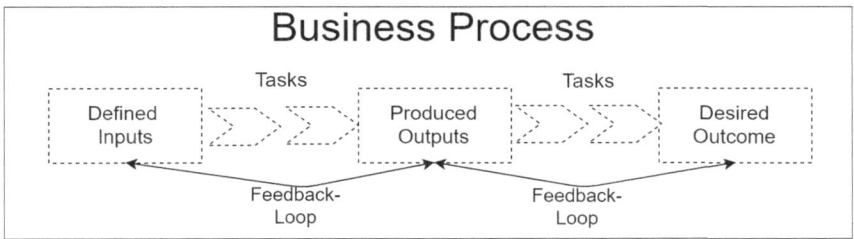

Figure 3: Definition of a business process
(Source: own elaboration based on Zairi M. (1997), Business process management: a boundaryless approach to modern competitiveness, business process Management Journal, Vol 3 No. 1, pp. 68-80)

Schiuma (2009) pointed out that literature and scientific research of business administration and managerial topics emphasize the measurement aspect with a focus on identifying the right quantitative and/or qualitative parameters that influence the performance of the processes of a business. A business process turns an input into an output (see figure 3) and therefore is the core element of creating value for a company using information or material (Zairi, 1997; Osterloh & Frost, 2006; Becker & Kahn, 2011). The term business process has a long tradition and evolved over the last decade as a new concept. Smith & Fingar (2003) defined three different stages of development of the idea of business process. The beginning of the 20th century where the focus was on measuring and analyzing procedures, the second stage with the business process re-engineering-concept (BPR) in the 1990s, and the third stage with the melting of several concepts into business process management (BPM).

Measuring performance by applying these components seems logical. This is the reason why the measuring of performance can be defined as an accomplishment of a task measured against a certain standard, a level of evaluation of dimensions such as speed, quality, cost, accuracy etc. (Bierbusse & Siesfeld, 1997).

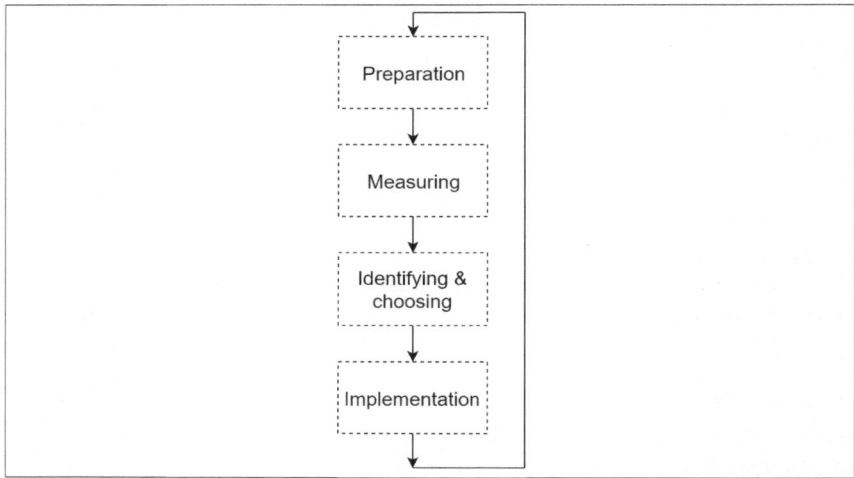

Figure 4 Improvement process: constant organizational performance measurement
(Source: own elaboration based on Buble, M., Dulčić, Ž., Pavić, I. (2001), Methodological approach to organizational performance improvement process. Management: Journal of Contemporary Management Issues, 6(1-2), 1-15)

After measuring, performance can be improved. The development of an improvement process and correct measuring is the starting point for any improvement process (see figure 4). To measure performance, the goals must be defined. Performance indicators can be used to either measure efficiency (e.g. time-based indicators) or to use effectiveness (e.g. through performance reviews).

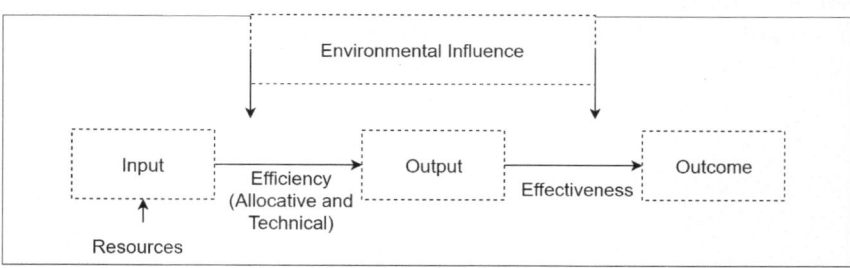

Figure 5 The difference between effectiveness and efficiency

(Source: own elaboration based on Mandl U., Dierx A., Ilzkovitz F., (2008), The effectiveness and efficiency of public spending, European Commission, Directorate General for Economic and Financial Affairs, pp. 3-4)

The differentiation between operational performance and organizational performance has to be considered. As shown in figure 5, influencing factors include inputs, outputs, and outcomes but also factors emerging from the environment. This includes all influencing factors stated above. Contrasting measurements of the inputs to the outputs can be one way to assess performance. The difficulty is to measure the right issues and to draw the right conclusions. For example: a company measures the amount it spends for recruitment for new personnel for a certain project (input value) and compares this value to the results of the projects measured in project time invested (output value) and finally return on invest of the product (outcome as market value). There is no proven correlation between the input and the output. Many different parameters must be considered in order to get a better understanding of the nature of performance.

Organizational performance, in the form of an output, can be measured using the "traditional" financial perspective (Digalwar & Sangwan, 2011), e.g. measuring the perspective of the market through total sales, market share or the perspective of shareholder return by calculating total shareholder return, economic value added, etc. (Richard et al., 2009). Measuring organizations based only on these indicators was common between 1880 and 1980. After the 1980th the competitive landscape changed, and the emphasis was put on quality and efficiency. Systems as total quality management (TQM), supply-chain-management (SCM), just-in-time (JIT)-production, as well as an increased use of technologies changed the way performance of organizations were seen. As remarked in the previous section, measuring intangible assets through non-financial values became important as well. These mainly included the dimension of cost, time, value, and other efficiency indicators (Goldratt, 1990; Sullivan, 1986; Noble and Lahay 1994).

Different methodologies are suggested to measure efficiency factors or intangible goods. Besides time-, and cost-based indicators, the effects of the employees and their knowledge and capabilities were realized as key factors. This was the starting point for performance measurement frameworks which do not explicitly measure only the time or cost-perspective but connect them to operational outcomes and create a better understanding of the correlations of performance with the organization.

1.1.2   Frameworks to evaluate organizational effectiveness

Performance measurement is a widely discussed topic (Van Looy et al., 2016) and in general not an easy but very challenging topic (Sidrova & Isik, 2010). According to Digalwar & Sangwan (2011) studies in performance measurement can be categorized in three ways: traditional performance measures, non-traditional performance measures, and integrated frameworks (see section above).

Measuring the effectiveness of an organization is one possible way to identify values for organizational performance. Assessing the effectiveness of organizations evolved over time. Different performance measurement approaches and frameworks were developed by practitioners and scientists, many of them focusing on financial values. Key performance indicators such as market share, turnover, cash flow, gross profit, return on equity, return on investment, debt to equity ratio, revenue growth rate, earnings before tax, etc.

Starting at first from goal-oriented perspectives and developing toward the inclusion of external effects such as the environment of external constituencies, context, boundaries, organizational culture, and team development (Campbell, 1977; Penning et al., 1977; SundStrom et al., 1990; Kennerley & Neely, 2002; Janićijević, 2010).

The competing values model (Quinn et al., 1983) suggested using three dimensions of competing for the measurement of values: focus (internal-external), structure (control-flexibility), outcomes (means-ends).

Lynch and Cross developed a measurement system which takes non-financial perspectives into consideration, the performance pyramid (McNair et al., 1990). It defines a causal relationship between strategic and operative performance indicators (see figure 6).

Figure 6 Finding a definition using the Performance Pyramid
(Source: own elaboration, adapted from Digalwar, Abhijeet & Sangwan, Kuldip Singh. (2011), An overview of existing performance measurement frameworks in the context of world class manufacturing
performance measurement. Int. J. of Services and Operations Management. 9. 60 - 82.)

Including non-financial values into performance management changed the perspectives of performance measurement since it connected the strategic level of a company to the operative perspective.

1.1.3 The balanced scorecard and other methods to assess organizational perfor-
mance

In the 1990s Kaplan & Norton (1992) developed the balanced scorecard (BSC) using
four different perspectives to assess performance: the financial, customers, internal,
and learning perspective (see figure 7). It demonstrates that performance is a complex
topic which must be interpreted and measured from several different perspectives.
The balanced scorecard is one of the most used measurement frameworks (Van Looy
& Shafagatova, 2016).

A similar approach as the balanced scorecard is the French "tableau de bord" (Chiapello et al., 1996; Epstein et al., 1997; Bessire, 2000). It is older than the balanced
scorecard and originated in France.

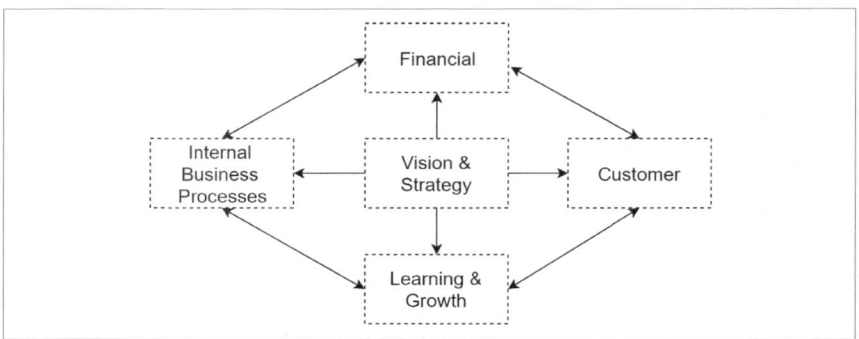

Figure 7 The dimensions of the balanced scorecard
(Source: own elaboration based on the results of own research)

Neely et al. (1996) developed the Cambridge performance measurement design process which also emphasizes several dimensions of performance. It includes the elements internal, external, financial and non-financial and links them to strategies. In this manner it can be used as a coherent performance measurement system (PMS). PMS is important to organizations for the success of the company (Najmi et al., 2005). A PMS can be used to examine the situation in an organization by including multiple dimensions in the measurement. This includes the financial aspects but also new approaches toward the inclusion of other dimensions starting from activity-based management (ABM), activity-based costing (ABC) and also including indicators of different management systems. Neely et al. (2005) suggested the term PMS in the context of the definition of efficiency and effectiveness of actions. Many different PMS-models or PMS-concepts have been suggested. Tatitcchi et al. (2010) lists over 20 PMS models in their research which were developed between 1980 and 2007 For instance, Castell (1996) proposed the network enterprise model, highlighting the fact that companies are highly dependent on a constant flow of information, capital, and cultural communication requiring network-structures to be efficient. These networks consist of autonomous units which are simultaneously dependent on each other and their performance can be measured through the "connectedness" and consistency of these networks.

The EFQM Excellence Model (2010) is another approach which can be used to measure performance since it defines a model which connects different organizational levels and tasks as a non-prescriptive framework. It was introduced in 1992 as a framework for assessing organizations for the European Quality Award (Hossaini et al., 2004;

Javidi, 2006; Uygur et al, 2013). Using a self-assessment approach, improvement activities are identified against certain excellency criteria.

Neely et al. (2002) who are known for the Cambridge performance measurement design process, developed the Performance Prism in 2002. The prism shows the following dimensions:

- Stakeholder satisfaction
- Stakeholder contribution
- Processes
- Strategies
- Capabilities

Performance is interpreted using stakeholder satisfaction, which is represented as the top of the prism. Stakeholder satisfaction is the result of other elements, mainly the contribution of the stakeholder (e.g. in the form of requirements, goal settings, management etc.) and the way these goals are orchestrated applying the three elements: processes, strategies, and capabilities.

The idea is that satisfaction of the stakeholders is directly correlated to organizational performance. The core questions, therefore, are what strategies, processes, and capabilities are necessary and how are they implemented to support stakeholder satisfaction.

Data-Envelopment-Analysis (DEA) is also an often-cited term in the context of performance measurement (Charnes et al., 1978). DEA measure the efficiency of decision-making units (Zhu, 2014). It is a methodology for modeling operational processes to evaluate performance using linear programming techniques. DEA can be used to measure the efficiency of an organization considering a certain group relative to the best possible output within that group (Thanassoulis et al., 2016). There are different concepts of efficiency, so it is important to consider these differences. The efficiency can be a technical efficiency, an allocative efficiency, or a cost efficiency (Steering Committee for the Review of Commonwealth/State Service Provision 1997).

Looking at the capability-aspects of a knowledge-driven environment where the competitive landscape is highly dependent on technology and knowledge, more measurement methods of performance in that area are suggested. Some of them explicitly measure knowledge using approaches such as intellectual capital (IC) (Stewart, 1997;

Pulic, 2008; Bontis et al, 2001). Measuring knowledge is a topic which will be discussed in the next chapter.

Intangible assets also include diverse stakeholder expectations using an external and also an internal perspective. This may also include ecological or environmental requirements, corporate social responsibilities (CSR) or regulations as defined by management system standards (MSS).

Before deciding what performance, measurement to use, it is important to be sure what to measure and how the data can be interpreted.

The above-cited performance measurement frameworks have their benefits and limitations (Digalwar & Sangwan, 2011). Digalwar & Sangwan (2011) conducted a meta-analysis identifying several limitations of this existing research between the years 2012 and 2014. Their use should be well analyzed based on the required results. It is also important to know that there is neither a clear definition of performance, performance management nor of (key) performance indicators in the scientific literature.

Uzun (2007) stated the following problems of performance measurement mentioned by Steers (1976) already in 1976:

1. The organizational performance itself is abstract
2. Performance changes over time which is a dynamic and unstable element
3. The interrelation between evaluation criteria is complex
4. The reliability and validity of the measurement itself
5. The relevance of the measurement method and criteria for the organizational environment and characteristics
6. The contribution of the chosen criteria to the dynamics of the organization
7. The consideration of individual measurement as well as and in contrast to organization-wide measurement

Similar problems were suggested by Hilal et al. (2009).

According to Tseng (2010), performance can be measured with an internal perspective and measures, such as cost, product quality, and profit. Performance can also be measured with an external perspective and a benchmark against the market using measures such as quality, customer satisfaction etc. Tseng also highlights the fact that performance is not purely measurable using financial indicators but other factors as well, e.g. motivation of employees, quality, focus on training and development, knowledge and knowledge sharing (see table 1).

Table 1 Measurement criteria for organizational performance

1.Total effectiveness	11. Motivation	21. Technical abilities of executives
2. Efficiency	12. Morale	22. Information management and communication
3. Productivity	13. Control	23. Preparedness
4. Profit	14. Conflict	24. Utilization of environment
5. Quality	15. Planning and objective setting	25. Evaluations by externals
6. Occupational accidents	16. Flexibility/Adaptation	26. Stability/Determination
7.Growth	17. Goal consensus	27. Value of human resources
8. Absenteeism	18. harmony between role and norm	28. Sharing of participation and authority
9. Employee turnover rates	19. Internalisation of organisational objectives	29. importance attached to training and development
10. Job satisfaction	20. Social abilities of executives	30. Importance attached to success

(Source: Robbins, S. P, and Barnwell, Neil, (2002), Organisation Theory: Concepts and Cases. Prentice Hall, (2002), cited by Samuel et al., 2017).

The above-stated fact that performance should be measured in multiple dimensions that include internal and external perspectives were also highlighted by Kennerley & Neely (2002). They developed a framework for the measurement of organizational performance which

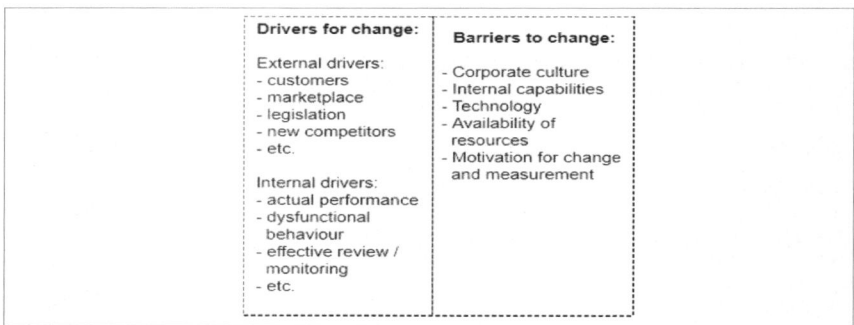

Figure 8 Drivers for change and barriers to change
(Source: own, based on Kennerley Mike, Neely Andy, (2002) A framework of the factors affecting the
evolution of performance measurement systems, International Journal of Operations & Production
Management, Vol. 22 Issue: 11, pp.1222-1245)

is based on these two perspectives which influence each other through triggers and
are mandatory in the change process (see figure 8). The authors acknowledge that
change is a very important aspect since the capability to change and to adapt to a
constantly changing environment and the marketplace is very important (see next section). The ability to change is dependent on:

1. Corporate culture
2. Internal capabilities
3. Technology
4. Availability of resources
5. Motivation of the employees

These aspects are discussed in the next chapter.

Kennerley & Neely (2002) also suggested a framework for the manner external triggers are causing a reaction within the organization resulting in internal triggers. These
internal triggers are reflected and determined by the organizational culture, the people, the processes, and the systems in use. In relation to the performance measurement framework, the authors suggested the measurement framework must be
adapted on a regular basis depending on the external triggers and the subsequently
following internal triggers. The internal triggers initiate internal changes which must
be reflected in the performance measurement system. This cycled approach is a continues improvement process.

There are more performance measurement frameworks, tools, and approaches, however, the goal of this chapter is to give an overview of the most commonly used frameworks, of which some of them will be further elaborated on in this paper.

1.1.4   Summary of frameworks and current status of performance measurement

This section will present a summary of scientific research and practical usage within the scope of performance measurement. It is notable that typical terms in that context (e.g. organization, organizational performance, performance in general, performance measurement, and performance indicators) are not clearly defined and may have different interpretations. Many different approaches and frameworks were developed since this field started to become the focus of scientific research. Since the 1990s the emphasis from purely financial oriented performance measurement has changed toward the inclusion of other dimensions. Measuring performance involves the measuring of efficiency of organizational units and effectiveness of business processes, and it additionally includes all stakeholder expectations as well as political, ecological, environmental, and social aspects.

To measure performance in multiple dimensions measurement frameworks which were recommended by scientists are applied. This are also more or less adapted by practitioners. Considering the fact that the BSC indorsed by Kaplan & Norton (1992) is the most used framework in this context (Van Looy et al., 2016; Bain Company, 2015) The measuring multiple dimension approach seems to in great demand. This is also related to the question of what exactly can be measured. Van Looy et al. (2016), identified 140 performance indicators commonly used in scientific research. The authors also identified a gap in scientific research regarding the existence of a "comprehensive measurement framework" that includes concrete performance indicators, and process-driven. To be useful for practitioners, such a framework must offer specific performance indicators and in a defined context. Homburg et al. (2012) refer to a performance measurement system as a "comprehensive performance measurement systems (CMPMS)". The authors suggest that such a system must fulfill requirements which coming from three areas: the breadth, the strategic fit and the cause-and-effect relationship between the information and the strategic goals. The "breadth" is necessary to gain a broad view of the aspects that should be measured and mast include recent and historical data as well as a performance indicator in multiple dimensions. "Strategic fit" refers to the idea that the measurement system must fit the overall strategy of the organization in the sense of defined strategic targets. The "cause-and-effect relationship" is necessary for analyzing the relationships of processes within the value chain of the organization since there are many different types of organizations and markets operating differently and should be measured differently as well. Useful performance measurements include the accurate goal setting, the collecting of the precise data, and the correct understanding of the developed data through analyzing, interpreting, reviewing and appropriate action (Smith & Bititci, 2016).

Performance plays a key role for organizations all over the world since performance is mostly connected to financial success and the (financial) survival of the firms. Performance measurement and assessment concepts and frameworks such as BCM, TQM, BPR, BPM, EFQM, management system standards (MSS) etc. earned recognition over the last years and will further serve as the basis for research and practical use. Despite the considerable importance of a comprehensive methodology to measure (process) performance, little research exists on concrete performance indicators. This might be because performance and the selection of indicators are strongly dependent on the organization. Nevertheless, selecting the right indicators is essential for a beneficial measuring of performance. One way to do this is to use a diagnostic model from the research field of organizational diagnosis and Organizational Change Management as proposed by Janićijević (2010) and Kennerly & Neely (2002). Such a model can be used to assess an organization from various perspectives, e.g. by analyzing processes by using hard- and soft as well as static and dynamic components (see table 2).

Table 2 Analyzing organizations based on their components

Components	Hard component	Soft component
Static component	Organizational structure (hierarchies etc.)	Organizational behavior (culture, power structure etc.)
Dynamic component	Business processes	Interpersonal processes (Leadership, flow of communication, team-communication etc.)

(Source: own elaboration, based on Janićijević Nebojša, (2010), business process in origanizational diagnostics Management, Vol. 15, 2, pp. 85-106)

Organizational change management involves all necessary dimensions, from structural aspects and strategy to personnel-related aspects, leadership styles, and motivation. To view business performance, it is also necessary to look at business processes. Related and derived concepts linked to the business process will be discussed in the following section.

1.2 Performance in sustainable business processes considering management- and leadership aspects

The Organizational performance which was summarized in the last section is related to process performance. The theory and practice of organizational processes originated in early management studies (Taylor, 1919; Drucker, 1954; Davonport, 1993). Since Porters Value Chain (1985) they developed to related concepts, such as business process Re-engineering (BPR), business process Management (BPM) and further into areas as knowledge management, TQM etc. It can be said that the role of business processes plays a role in all contemporary organizational structure (Harmon, 2014).

Processes present the core of the transformation of input to output within an organization. Effectiveness of the business processes is the goal of any improvement process (Škrinjar et al., 2008). In relation to PMS the term Process Performance Measurement System (PPMS) was suggested which emphases the process orientation (Kueng, 2000).

The re-engineering of processes was suggested by Hammer (1990) as a core principle for organizations to analyzing and improving their processes instead of just using technology to automate the same existing processes. According to him the goal is to use technology – and especially information technology – to improve business processes and to create a better outcome („Don't automate, obliterate"). It became a widely used concept in the 1990s but also gained critique of being used to emphasize the use of technology and the disregard of people (Davenport, 1993). The BPR-process is following a constantly repeated improvement process (Hammer & Champy, 1995) consisting of:

1. Renewing: Through training the employees will be better prepared for their work tasks and can better be integrated into the organizational processes.
2. Revitalizing: A re-organization of the business processes helps to improve the processes.
3. Reframing: Existing ways of thoughts are being discarded and new methods and methodologies are being introduced.
4. Restructuring: All activities which are in the scope of the re-engineering process will be changed and newly designed.

The primary goal in re-engineer the processes is to improve the customer expectations. This form of process optimization was mainly aimed to optimize the value chain by improving quality, time, cost, or service. BPR is a radical approach (Hammer & Champy, 1993) since it the goal is to dramatical improve the performance based on the before mentioned dimensions of time, cost, quality, or service. The concept was widely adapted by businesses and a matter of scientific research since then. Ramirez et al. (2012) studied 228 firms with the focus on BPR and information technology and found evidence of significant improvements. Other scientists suggested minor adjustments to the original BPR, e.g. Kontio (2007) who emphasized the operational part of BPR to maximize the potential of processes. Organizational change (Kennerly & Neely, 2002) and the term change management is related to BPR in that sense that the core of BPR is to change organizational processes. Driven by the market forces, a constant organi-

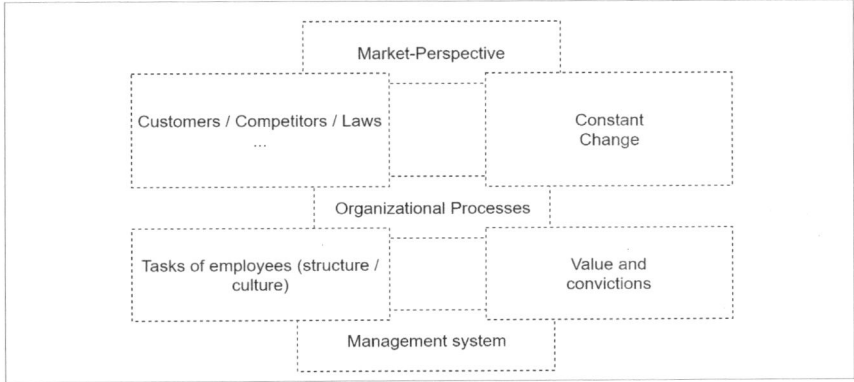

Figure 9 The rhombus-model of economic processes
(Source: Own elaboration based on Luca Magdalena, (2014), Risk in Contemporary Economy International Conference ISSN-L 2067-0532 ISSN online 2344-5386 XVth Edition, 2014, Galati, Romania, Dunarea de Jos, University of Galati – Faculty of Economics and Business Administration)

zational change process is necessary (see figure 9). These changes have to be applied on different levels, e.g. on organizational procedures, the use of technology or machinery, required skills of employees etc. Al-Mashari et al. (2001) developed a holistic BPR-framework which is based on a change management process involving benchmarking and Total Quality Management parts as aspects of measurement. TQM helps to identify problematic areas and benchmarking assists to measure the efforts and compare them strategically. Some success factors of BPR are (Hussein & Dayekh, 2014; Sorunke & Nasir, 2016):

- A commitment of the organization: Organizational change lead to changes in processes, tasks, job descriptions, responsibilities, technology etc., and can only be successful if there is a commitment to realize these changes.
- BPR team composition: A competent team must be selected to manage the BPR-process since the change process mostly concerns different levels of the organizational structure with deep effects. This involves a well selected group from the top management as well from the business units, a useful decision-making process and a good communication.
- Business needs analysis: Every change of processes is only successful if the change fits to the strategic goals. This requires an analysis of the business needs.

- Adequate IT infrastructure: One core element of BPR is the automation through technology. Therefore, it is important to assess existing technologies and infrastructures with the question whether to adapt them or not.
- Effective change management: Change management is a complex topic (Kondalkar, 2009) which involves many different aspects from organizational to behavioral science. This is also expressed in the model of Kennerley & Neely (2002) in regards to external and internal organizational drivers and barriers related to organizational culture, capabilities, technology, and motivation. This complex topic needs to be realized carefully but effectively in order to be successful.
- Ongoing continuous improvement: changes made to processes should be continuously improved.

Nevertheless the authors also identified that these tools are not very well integrated into the BPR-process. The authors also try to discover reasons why many BPR-initiatives fail. Important aspects in this sense are related to the change management process which involves cultural and structural changes and is not easily accomplished. It is also criticized that BPR-models have limits regarding the fact that many models only focus on one single process and do not

Table 3 Comparison between production principles

Category	Fordism	Post-Fordism	Toyotism
Production principles	- Standardization of products - Special-Purpose tools and equipment - Assembly line - Division of labor	- Specialized products and jobs - Multi-Purpose Equipment - Flexible Specialization - New technologies	- Elimination of waste - Automation - „Heijunka"
Organizational culture	- Workers are paid with higher wages - Economic of scale - Mass products for mass market	- Service and the white-collar worker - Economy of scope - Small-batch production	- Kaizen, 5S etc. - Economy of scope - Kanban principles

Category	Fordism	Post-Fordism	Toyotism
Supply chain	- Push system - Just in Case - Fully integrated supply chain	- Pull system - JIT - Individual specialized firms as suppliers	- Pull system - JIT - Individual specialized firms as suppliers

(Source: Turi A, Mocan M, Ivascu L, Goncalves G, Maistor S, (2015), From Fordism to Lean management: Main shifts in automotive industry evolution within the last century, MakeLearn International Scientific Conference on Management of Knowledge and Learning, pp 25-27)

take effects on a more global perspective into consideration (Hussein et al., 2013). The authors list 17 limitations of BPR models based on BPR researches starting from the limited practicability with a too generic point of view, the lag of the employee perspective, the missing analytical process, to the exclusion of cultural issues (especially outside of western countries). Methodologies and tools used for BPR are also a limitation point. Other scientists stated that TQM is the origin of BPR and not a separate concept (Kock, 2005). BPR is more a specific shaping of TQM or other concepts, especially other long existing concepts as lean practices (Womack, 1990), „Fordism", and Toyotism (Turi et al., 2015). There is no common agreement which of the concepts influenced which. Nevertheless, the ideas behind Fordism and Toyotism existed long before. Dioguardi (2010) showed the influence of Fordism toward Toyotism and all related terms and ideas, such as Just-in-Time-production (JIT) and lean production principles and Kaizen (see table 3), all elements which are necessary for a concise BPR-process. In this context a similar methodology was developed which were already mentioned above. One of them is the „theory of constraints" (Goldratts, 1990) which takes the perspective that each process has at least one constraint which prevent the process from being limitlessly effective and/or efficient. The goal is to identify and optimize the constraints that way that the process becomes more efficient or effective. This also includes that dimensions of existing policies, existing equipment, and problems with people. In Germany a similar concept was developed by Mewes (1971) called Energo-Kybernetic System (EKS) in which the analysis of the constraint is a central aspect since – according to Mewes - the constraints are the limiting factors of every organization which need to be overcome in order to successfully increase performance.

1.2.1 The shift from structure to behavior and the importance of the leadership style

Even though scientists and practitioners such as Fayol, who suggested the 14 principles (Rodrigues, 2001), Weber with his Bureaucracy theory (Weber, 1978), and Taylor's Piece Rate System (Taylor, 1896), the human aspect of organization was recognized. In 1965 Tuckman introduced the "Five Stage Model of Group Development" (Forsyth, 2006) which focused the performance of teams.

The idea that changes in the organizational processes also involves changes to people brought new insides into management literature and science. Classical managerial theories were mostly based on structural changes coming from theories of organizational design which emphasis the coordination and control of activities (Mintzberg, 1979; Child, 1977). Despite the fact that organizational commitment is also being studied for a longer time (Mowday et al., 1979), the focus on organizational culture and behavior was a new trend in the 1980s and 1990s which explores the human behavior within organizational context (Denison, 1990). New concepts of process optimization were suggested which also included elements from behavioral science. Looking at production processes the concepts of Fordism and Toyotism were mentioned. Principles, such as lean manufacturing and lean production gained popularity (Wilson, 2009) and were extended to a management principle in many industries, e.g. the automotive industry, the steel- and electrical manufacturing industry. "Lean" has many aspects (tools) of the Toyotism (see table 4), such as JIT-systems, Jidoka (Coetzee et al., 2016), Kaizen, 5S, Kanban, integrative supplier management, work teams etc. (Komus & Kamlowski, 2014) and is also related to the term Toyota Production System. The focus lays on waste elimination in that way that the production becomes as efficient as possible. It includes the analysis and identification of waste and the optimization of the identified bottlenecks (Shah &Ward, 2012). A constantly ongoing improvement processes and a perfect system is the goal (see table 4). This way performance can be raised (Lander & Liker, 2007). The central element of the house of

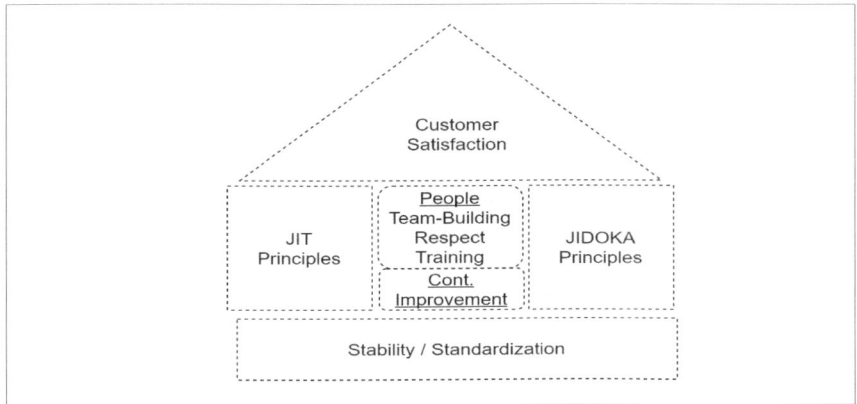

Figure 10 House of Lean – Customer satisfaction with lean principles
(Source: own elaboration based on Kim Christopher S., Spahlinger David A., Billi John E., (2009) Creating Value in Health Care: The Case for Lean Thinking, JCOM December Vol. 16, No. 12, pp. 557-562)

lean (See figure 10) is people and topics related to behavioral science. Effective team-building, team-management, training, and creating a fitting culture are important and presented in the used methodologies and tools (see table 4). Kaizen as the central way of thinking empowered employees to work in small teams which efficiently create new ideas for improvement (Maurer, 2014) and uses several techniques and tools as Kanban. Kanban helps teams to see work tasks and progress through visualization (Sugimori et al., 1977). Gemba as part of Kaizen to enable employees to walk around and inspect processes (Suárez-Barraza et al., 2012). The 5S relate to general principles of Kaizan. According to the authors Kaizen and 5S are the foundation of principles such as JIT, TQM and Total Productive Maintenance (TPM).

Another central element for lean methodologies and tools is continues improvement (Liker & Franz, 2011). Seen from this perspective all methodologies can be summarized under have a close relationship to each other (see table 4).

Table 4 Difference between methodologies and tools from the perspective of continuous improvement

Continuous improvement methodologies						
Theory of constraints	TQM	Lean production	Six Sigma	balanced scorecard	BPR	TPM
Tools						
Kaizen, 5S, JIT, Kanban, JIDOK, Value Stream Mapping, Gemba...						

(Source: own elaboration based on Coetzee R., van der Merwe & L. van Dyk, (2016), Lean implementation strategies: how are the Toyota way principles addressed? South African Journal of Industrial Engineering, Vol 27(3) Special Edition, pp 79-91)

Another possibility to summarize the methodologies and tools as well as the importance

Table 5 The Toyota Way and the 14 management principles

Continues improvement	Cultural aspects (respect for people)	- Long-term philosophy - Create flow - Use a pull system - Level out the workload - Stop and fix the problem - Standardize tasks - Use visual control - Use reliable, tested technology - Continual organizational learning through kaizen
Challenge & Kaizen	Genchi genbutzu, Respect, & Teamwork	- Go and see for yourself to understand the situation - Make decisions slowly by consensus - Grow leaders who live the philosophy - Respect, challenge, and help your suppliers - Respect, develop, and challenge your people and teams

(Source: Coetzee R., van der Merwe & L. van Dyk, (2016), Lean implementation strategies: how are the Toyota way principles addressed? South African Journal of Industrial Engineering Vol 27(3) Special Edition, pp 79-91)

of cultural aspects can be done using the Toyota way as seen in table 5. The Toyota way consist of 14 principles which are related to Kaizen-principles.

1.2.2   Current status of business process management

Improving performance of processes is sometimes called business process management (BPM). Process orientation was already mentioned in literature in 1934

(Nordsieck, 1934). Nevertheless, the term BPM came up after the 1990s and the development of BPR (see section above). After the criticism of BPR mentioned above, the concept of processes as the central element which can be measured, managed, and improved manifested in new terms. One of such term is BPM which has no clear definition nor a clear methodology. In BPM processes or parts of processes are being focused mostly to (continuously) improve those (Dumas et al., 2013). But BPM is more than only improvement. Despite a clear definition of BPM in scientific literature there are common elements to BPM. Elzinga et al. (1995) defined BPM as a systematic approach to analyze, improve, control, and manage business processes. The final goal behind these steps is to improve the outcome for the customer (e.g. through increased quality or services). Zairi (1997) uses this definition but defines the improvement aspects regarding all fundamental aspects of an organization, as manufacturing, marketing, communication etc. It can be seen that this doesn't seem to be a new idea compared to the existing idea before that (and mentioned in the sections before). BPM methodologies focus on two objectives: to capture and evaluate existing business processes by analyzing their elements and to create and challenge new business processes in order to improve (Davenport, 1993; Kettinger et al., 1995).

But with BPM the process orientation in contrast to strong functional hierarchies became the focus. The functional organizational structure was criticized in favor of a constantly improved process approach with the focus on the customer and the involvement and responsibility of the employees (DeToro &McCabe, 1997; Zairi, 1997; Lee & Dale, 1998). This process-orientation (which is called business process Orientation – BPO) is the main driver of the term BPM and the idea to manage entire chains of evens, activities and decisions (also automatically using technology) (Dumas et al., 2013). Around 2000 with the start of the new millennium and the increasing use of technology the philosophy of process orientation gain importance. Vertical and horizontal flow of information were overall goals (Daft, 2004). Even though BPO is not an independent discipline it is a concept used in BPM and other areas to improve business performance (Lindfors, 2003). McCormack's and Johnson's (2001) saw in BPO the new way to define organization process-oriented as opposed to the „old" view of Porter, Deming, Drucker, Davenport etc. who did not emphasize a horizontal and process oriented structure. BPM together with BPO focusses on a strategic fit (Benedict et al, 2013) which was already mentioned in previous concepts (see above sections). Gardner (2004), Reijers (2006), Hammer (2007) agreed on the idea that BPO is an organizational effort to make business processes the platform for organizational structure and strategic planning. In 2010 Kohlbacher (2010) showed that organizational performance can be increased through process orientation. He suggested a conceptual model of a PPMS (see figure 11). The focus on strategic aspects and stakeholder is in alignment with

Kuengs et al., (2001) definition of PPMS who see the multiple dimensions (Kung & Hagen, 2007) which need to be measured in the following aspects (and are similar to the Balanced Score-Card dimensions mentioned above):

- The investor perspective: financial values
- The employee perspective: employee engagement and satisfaction
- The customer perspective: customer satisfaction
- The societal perspective: societal values
- The innovation perspective: different values

Most important aspects of the conceptual PPMS-models in figure 11 is the idea to measure processes and not organizational units using multiple dimensions.

The process orientation is a mandatory aspect of BPM. Modern technologies are used to support the BPM idea. New technologies help to assists in process optimization. New

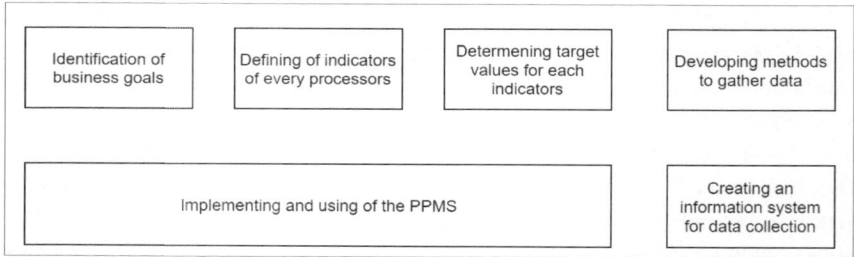

Figure 11 Conceptual models of a Process Performance Measurement System
(Source: own elaboration, based on Kohlbacher M. (2010), The effect of process orientation: a literature review, business process Management Journal, Vol 16 No. 1, pp. 135-152)

technology help model, execute, analyze and measure, communicate, and improve processes (e.g. by using workflow-management systems (van der Aalst & van Hee, 2004; Jablonski & Bussler, 1996; Leymann & Roller, 1999). In times where efficiency and effectiveness (including saving money) becomes vital for organizational results, automation can be a valuable asset. The area of business process modelling through the use of technology and information systems is a scientific topic by itself (sometimes seen as part of Software Engineering). It is an intensively studies topic within the last 10 years (van der Aalst, 2013). Several different BPM methodologies have been invented which can be clustered into three categories (Harmon & Wolf, 2014):

1. Top-down, large scale improvement of the entire organization
2. Bottom-up approach, improve individual activities through methodologies and tools such as six sigma, lean six sigma etc.
3. Information technology usage, focusing on automation through tools such as ARIS, Rational Unified Process etc.

The authors of this study also conclude that a big part of the organizations use the bottom-up approach and deal with individual activities with the focus on business process improvement using the PDCA-cycle (Plan-Do-Check-Act) invented by W.E. Deming. According to Lahajnar & Rožanec (2016) the focus changed from single processes to the business process management of large-scale process architectures in the 21th century using the top-down approach and new developed methodologies by organizations, scientists, or brands such as BP-Trends methodologies (Harmon, 2014), Rummler-Brache (Rummler & Brache, 2013), and 7FE BPM (Jeston & Nelis, 2013). It is suggested by Lahajnar & Rožanec (2016) that each organization needs to identify its own methodology or approach to use BPM for its best by starting from one of the suggested versions and the use of their evaluation framework to make a selection. Other authors come to a similar conclusion. Since there is no clear definition and little guidance on how to choose which indicator for performance measurement (Heckl and Moormann 2010) and under what circumstances (Shah et al. 2012) it is necessary to analyze the situation individually.

Compared to BPR there are some differences to BPM. BPM usually involves continuous improvement processes, BPR focusses on one big change. This big change is usually more risky and more expensive than the changes created through BPM. Bigger changes usually involve more manpower and more problems regarding cultural or human aspects regarding the work place and work processes. Seen from this perspective, BPM and BPR are complimentary rather than a substitute to each other, in spite of the fact that scientist also state that BPM is a successor of BPR (Curbera et al., 2008).

Another topic which is being studied by scientists is the maturity of BPM. Maturity models improve the BPM initiatives of companies through improving the capability of the models. This usually involves the three steps (Iversen et al., 1999):

- Assessing the current situation
- Guiding improvement indicatives
- Controlling progress

Röglinger et al. (2012) identified several maturity models and categorized them into basic models, descriptive models, and prescriptive models suggesting a better integration and consolidation of the several different models and a more practical approach. Rosemann & vom Brocke (2010) identified six core elements in that context (based on existing maturity models of scientists suggested between 1997 and 2009). These six elements are:

- Strategic alignment: The BPM needs to be aligned with the organizations strategy by a close link between the organizational goals and its processes and measures.
- Governance: The organizational governance in terms of roles and responsibilities and governance structure has to support the BPM-approach.
- Methods: BPM-Methods have to be established and should support BPM (e.g. a method as Six Sigma)
- Information technology: The technology should work as enabler for BPM and act toward process improvement.
- People: As core elements within BPM, people have to be trained, and knowledge has to be shared.
- Culture: A process-centered culture has to be developed which helps to develop an open-minded culture which is open to change and improvement.

1.2.3 Industry-wide applied agile methodologies

BPM methodologies as discussed in the last section also involve agile methodologies as methods and implementation concepts. Methodologies and tools, such as the Kaizen-aspects, Kanban, Lean, team work, etc. mentioned before, are closely linked to agile methodologies. The term agile refers to the ability to quickly respond to market needs and was originally used in software development. The agile principles were defined in the so-called agile manifesto[1] which describe the common goals of agile methodologies from the perspectives of the inventors. These core goals are:

- Individuals and interactions over processes and tools
- Working software over comprehensive documentation

---

1   http://agilemanifesto.org/, accessed 11.11.2017

- Customer collaboration over contract negotiation
- Responding to change over following a plan

It is about the creation of products with the focus on the expectations of the stakeholder by creating simple designs in a step-by-step incremental approach. The focus in on creation and realization. A constant communication between all involved people and the empowerment of the team is one principle. Simple and lean processes is another and minimal formal processes (Cockburn, 2007). Lee & Xia (2010) emphasize the team's capability to efficiently and effectively respond changing circumstances of the project life cycle. Flexibility is an important factor. As seen in table 5 (see above) several of these aspects are based on the Toyota Way and the 14 management principles. In addition to the agile principles several agile methods have been developed which support the core ideas presented above, e.g. extreme programming (Auer, K., Miller, R. Extreme Programming Applied. Addison-Wesley, 2002, Scrum (Schwaber & Beedle, 2001) and Angile Unified Process (Lisana, 2014), Scaled Agile Framework (Hayes et al., 2016). Before 2005 there was a lag in in research in that field (Dybå and Dingsøyr, 2008). After 2005 the number of publications increased and include diverse topics, e.g. success factors of adoption and post-adoption issues (Mangalaraj et al., 2009; Cao et al., 2009). The fact that the goal of agile development is strong customer focus and a rapid adaption of the product development to the circumstances Highsmith & Cockbum (2001) highlights aspects which were not only interesting to the software development focused industry but to many other organizations as well. Many projects planned traditionally fail (Budzier & Flyvbjerg, 2015), which might be one reason for new approaches to project management using agile methodologies. By keeping up a constant communication and feedback-loop with the customer enables to project team to work more effectively toward the project goal. The previously more often use project management methodologies based on a waterfall-model-method (Kaur & Sengupta, 2013) has the disadvantage of a missing constant interaction toward the customer which makes projects based on this methodology problematic for certain kinds of projects where this feedback-loop is necessary (see table 6).

Table 6 Some of the typical differences between agile and traditional project methodologies

Project Characteristics	Agile Methodology	Traditional Methodology
Customer / Stakeholder interactions	Often / Constant Feedback-Loops	Rare / Milestone-based

Team responsibility	Empowerment of team and team decision making, intrinsic motivation of team members	Usually low, responsibility lays in management
Planning	Based on self-managed teams and incremental short sprints, experimentation	Complex project planning, estimations, and requirement documents
Learning	Constant learning of new methods, technologies, exchange	Learning is secondary and behind defined project goals
Time for delivery	Rapid Prototyping, quick working parts /products as early as possible	Long delivery time after finishing the production

(Source: own elaboration based on the results of own research)

Scientific authors also suggest agile principles in the context of BPM (Rito-Silva et al., 2009) embracing the specifics of the agile approach as short feedback-cycles, people-empowerment, technology-integration into business processes design, or agile business process Modeling (Paschek et al., 2016). Since the agile methodology is generic other industries and business area trying to adapt the agile approach as well. Figure 12 shows other aspects in comparison to traditional based methodologies which show that the benefits of agile methods can be used in other industries as well.

In the last section the way of thought of Kaizen including methods and tools, such as Lean production, JIT etc. were mentioned. These principles have their origin in the automotive industry which were always forced to improve their supply chain in order to survive in the competitive landscape (Howard et al., 2006; Mintzberg, 1994). The automotive industry is facing a constant and world-wide competition – in 2017 not only by other established automotive brands but even from competitors of other markets, such as the IT-industry which enter the market through their technological competence. This competence is demanded by the customer because of newly developing idea, such as electric engines, self-driving cars, etc. The drastic change and the increasing market diversity, the demand for environmental and social awareness are strong aspects forcing the automotive sector (Howard et al., 2006) to become

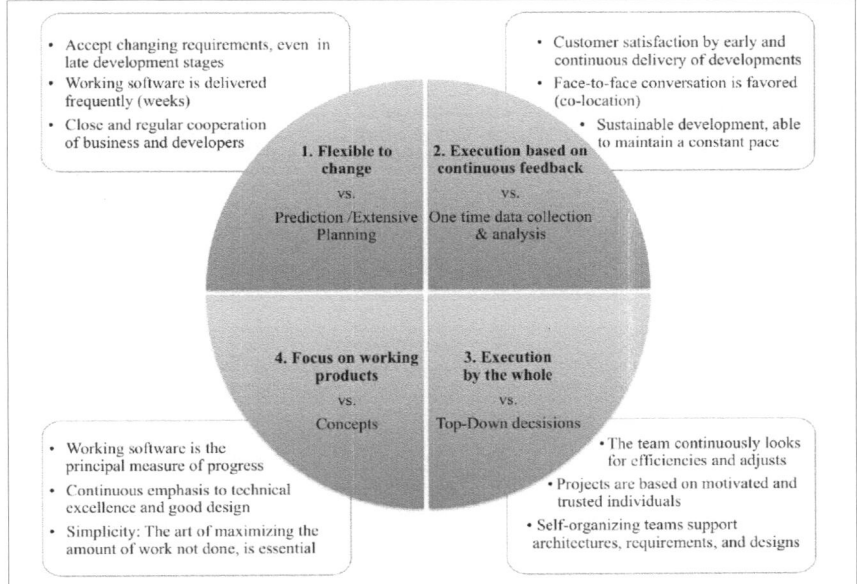

Figure 12 Contrasting agile and classic project management principles
(Source: Own representation based on Beck, K. et al. (2001), Principles behind the agile Manifesto. Agile Alliance. http://agilemanifesto.org/., 1 January 2016; Highsmith, J. (2001), History: The agile Manifesto. agilemanifesto.org, 04.04.2016)

more flexible, e.g. by adapting agile methodologies in their value creation process.

Under the term "lean" automotive manufacturer optimize their supply chain using lean manufacturing principles / methodology (Womack et al., 1990) introduced by Toyota and its the Toyota Production System (TPS). Lean processes are also an element of agile methodologies. Nevertheless, there is a basic different between lean production and agile production (Groover, 2000):

- The focus of lean production is on the elimination of waste and also on the reduction of cost. This is done through optimizing of the production processes.
- Agile production is a wider term which opens the mindset of the culture of the organization toward a "change culture" where the importance is the satisfaction of the customers' needs.

Table 7 shows the differences between a lean manufacturing logistics and an agile manufacturing logistics.

Table 7 Lean manufacturing versus agile manufacturing

Factors	Lean logistics / manufacturing	Agile logistics / manufacturing
Objectivity	Efficiency	Flexible to meet demands
Methodology	Remove all waste	Satisfy customers
Constraint	Customer service	Cost
Rate of change	Long-term and stable	As fast as necessary according to the customers requirements
Performance measurement	Productivity, utilization	Lead times, service level
Type of work	Uniform, standardized	Variable, adaptive
Way of control	Formal planning cycles	Less structured by empowered staff

(Source: Own representation based on Waters, D. (2003), Logistics-An Introduction to Supply Chain Management)

Lean production principles are commonly used within the automotive industry and industries with similar mass production and assembly lines. TQM, as another method-ology already mentioned above, is coming from the automotive field as well. Together with lean production these two methodologies have the roots in that industry and are being used globally.

The reason has to do with the constantly increasing demand of customers and re-tailers worldwide which have much more choices than ever before not only between many different options related to the product but also between competition through brands producing and selling worldwide. It is important to understand the marketplace and to optimize the supply chain toward new conditions. This is the reason why supply chain strategies are part of the business strategies (Cohen, Rousell, 2005). Agile strat-egies play a major role in that context since flexible reaction regarding customer de-mands becomes vital. Globalization makes comparison between competitors easier, deregulation forces organizations to follow certain rules, the technological develop-ment creates possibilities for companies (especially startups) to enter the market quickly, etc. – the pressure for organizations is growing. This very volatile, uncertain, complex and ambiguous environment (VUCA) needs an organizational structure which supports it. Therefore, innovations become important and the processes to support them. This means flexible processes which are open for changes. But lean principles focus constant processes without change (see above). It is necessary for organizations in that industry to identify the point between the flexible agile manufacturing and the cost sensitive planned optimized manufacturing process. This point is called Decoupling Point (see figure 13). A constant innovation requires an organization which is open for change, learning, and knowledge sharing. These are principles of Kaizen and TQM as well as of the agile principles. It requires

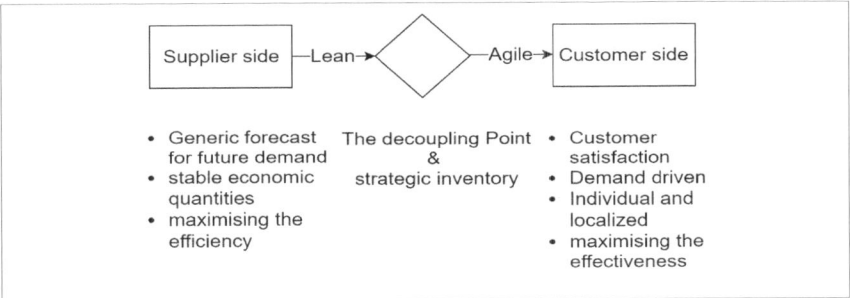

Figure 13 How agile and lean manufacturing is connected through the decoupling point

(Source: Own representation based on Christopher, M. (2005), Logistics and supply chain management: Creating value-added networks. Harlow, England: Prentice Hall, 2005; 21. Amir, Faiza. (2011), Significance of Lean, Agile and Leagile Decoupling Point in Supply Chain Management. Journal of Economics and Behavioral Studies. Database for Advances in Information Systems, Vol. 30, No. 2, 66-81.)

not only the right organizational structures and information technology but also the right mindset and culture to adapt these principles. In fact, scientific research showed that the change toward agile processes mostly failed due to people and not processes (Andraski, 1994).

1.3 Connections between performance of business processes and knowledge management

1.3.1   Organizational culture and the effect on processes

As seen in the last chapter a culture of innovation, learning, and knowledge sharing is important for organizations to survive in the competitive landscape. The influence of organizational culture on organizational processes and performance has been studied since the 1960s in which influencing books such as "The Social Psychology of Organizations" (Katz & Kahn, 1967) were published. The book is based on researches going back to the 1940s in which the survey research center (SRC) and researchers such as Rensis

Likert investigated the influence of human relations within organizations in 1947 (Newton, 1995; House et al., 2004). Organizational culture as a term was mentioned in 1979 according to Hofstede et al. (1990). Already in the 1930 authors as Mead (1934) and Weber (1930) developed theories about behavior patterns, communication, and organizational actions.

It is being studied for a long time already but there is still no scientific consensus about the exact meaning due to several reasons (Ogbonna & Harries, 2000):

- Culture is very complex and cannot be reduced easily and used as a analytical tools
- Culture cannot be used for assessing organizational aspects, such as power, politics, and climate since it is a different context
- It is unclear whether organizational culture can be changed at all

A cultural network consists of the following elements which are connected to each other and in constant stages of development showing the complexity of the topic (Johnson et al., 2012):

- The general values and beliefs (paradigm)
- Control Systems
- Ritual and Routines
- Organizational structures
- Stories
- Symbols
- Power structures

Different definitions were suggested over time. Robin (1999) defined organizational culture as "system of common sense that members have regarding their organization and this feature distinguishes two organizations". Schein (2010) defines organizational culture as "series of basic assumptions a group makes in a specific order in order to solve the issues of external adaption and internal integration". Another definition focusses on the mental, structural, and human behavioral elements (see also 1.1.2) of the organization as well as social aspects and aspects of integration (Dolatabadi et al., 2010; Meyerson & Martin, 1987).

Cameron & Quinn (2005) presented four types of organizational culture using two dimensions: one is flexibility against control and another shows control orientation inside and outside of the organization (Cameron & Quinn, 2005). In difference to the national level, organizational culture result in organizational practices (de Hilal et.al., 2009).

Despite the problematic definition of organizational culture, there is scientific some research on the effects of organizational culture on business performance. Kilic (2015) summarized the two approaches of Kotter & Heskett (1992) and Deal & Kennedy (1982). The first scientists consider shared values as an important elements of an organization which sustain a performance culture. Deal & Kennedy the organizational culture impacts success of the business because of the fact that there is a learning curve from past experiences. Organizational culture can be analyzed at three levels (Schein, 1995):

1. artifacts
2. values and norms
3. basic assumption and premises

Artifact are visible through organizational structure and processes. Even though they are visible, they are complex and include the internal language, symbols, and technologies. Values and norms are represented by the chosen strategies of the organization and define the framework in which employees are working with. The last point is about unconscious conceptions which are being taken for-granted and serves as the basis for the first two. It is also suggested that organizational culture is not static but changeable over time (Beugelsdijk et al., 2006).

1.3.2 The importance of knowledge management and leadership styles aiming to the performance of business processes

As seen in the chapters above, an open culture which is based on improvement, change, and knowledge sharing are elements of management concepts, such as TQM, Kaizen, agile methodologies etc. The market pressure forces companies to innovate, knowledge becomes an important part of the day by day business (Tseng, 2009; Chattopadhyay, 2007). Peter Drucker stated in 2001 that knowledge and the management of that knowledge is a vital component of an organization as an important driving factor which even replaces assets as machineries, capital, human beings etc. (Drucker, 2001) therefore becoming a necessity (Seyyed, 2012). Considered as an intangible (Jones & Hill, 2009) good (see chapter above) knowledge is one of the components which enables organizations to keep the competitive advantage by creating valuable goods or services which are rare and costly to imitate or substitute (often called "Resourced Based View"). As other non-physical assets such as brand names, reputation, and intellectual property, also knowledge develops through time (Schein, 1995) and has a strong link to the organizational culture and social development within companies (Makhija, 2003). Knowledge management deals with (James et al., 2005):

1. Knowledge creation
2. Knowledge transfer
3. Knowledge sharing
4. Knowledge maintainance

Knowledge can be created and converted in four different stages which Nonaka (1994) suggested in a model called SECI (see below) as a cycling and spiral process of transforming knowledge between one form to the other. Nonaka also suggested that knowledge can be tacit and explicit. The first is subjective, context-specific, and experience-based and cannot be expressed in a written form (e.g. believes, mental models etc.). Explicit knowledge is more generic, not specific to a certain context, and expressible through words or in written format (e.g. theoretical models etc.). SECI stands for the conversion of one of these knowledge form into the other or into the same form with new content:

1. Socialization means the conversion of the tacit knowledge into new tacit knowledge
2. Externalization means to articulate tacit knowledge and converting it into explicit knowledge
3. Combination converts explicit knowledge into more complex explicit knowledge
4. Internalization converts explicit knowledge into tacit knowledge

Tseng (2010) researched on this effect and analyzed the effect of organizational culture and corporate performance through the different aspects of knowledge conversion (see figure

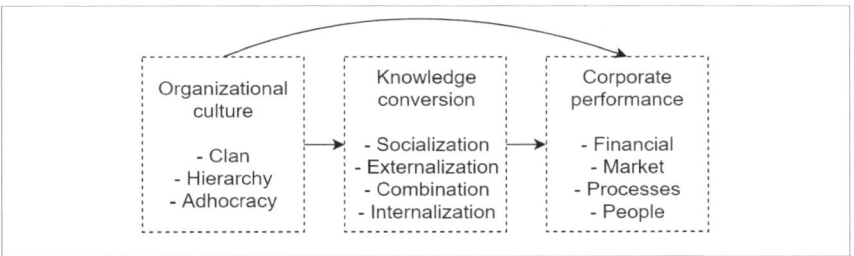

Figure 14 The correlation between OC and KC on corporate performance
(Source: own elaboration based on Tseng, S.M. (2010), The Correlation between organizational culture and Knowledge Conversion on Corporate Performance. Journal of Knowledge Management, 14, 269-284)

14). Besides organizational culture which the authors differentiates in clan culture, hierarchy culture, adhocracy culture, and market (Quinn & Cameron, 2005), knowledge conversion is a social process which highly depends on individuals who are the core element of creating and converting tacit and explicit (Nonaka, 1994; Nonaka & Takeuchi 1995; Sanchez & Palacios, 2008). Tseng (2010) identified a direct correlation between organizational culture and corporate performance as well as a correlation between Externalization, Combination, and Internalization and corporate performance. The authors also conclude that the best organizational form for knowledge conversion is the form of adhocracy culture which is no surprise considering that this culture is agile, open to change, it values innovation and a knowledge sharing culture.

Another model of knowledge management was suggested by Choo (1998) called Sense-Making knowledge management model. This basis of this model was the idea that there is cyclic connection between sense making processes, knowledge creation, and decision making. Knowledge creation is reached through sense making (which itself is related to streams of experiences) and through external information and knowledge. The scientist highlighted the fact that the strategical use of knowledge involves mainly a sense making aspect of knowledge, a creation aspect, and a decision-making aspect based on that knowledge.

Wiig (1993) suggested a model based on the organization of knowledge (Dalkir, 2011). According to the author, knowledge can only be useful, it if is organized depending on the context it is used. He suggested several dimensions such as completeness (the amount of available knowledge), connectedness (relations between knowledge objectives), congruency (consistence between all knowledge objectives), and perspectives and purpose (the point of view people see and use the knowledge). He also categorized knowledge into the categories form: public, shared, personal and type: factual, conceptual, expectational, and methodological.

Boisot's I-Space model (Boisot, 1998) defined information and data in that context. Information is this content which the user is extracting from the data. Boisot defined a three dimensional cube as information space (I-Space) in which information can be describes in levels of codification (and uncodification), abstraction (and Concretion), and level of diffusion (and undiffusion). Information in this space cycles through the dimensions in the following ways:

- From the uncodified to the codified form
- From the concrete to the abstract form
- From the undiffused to the defused form

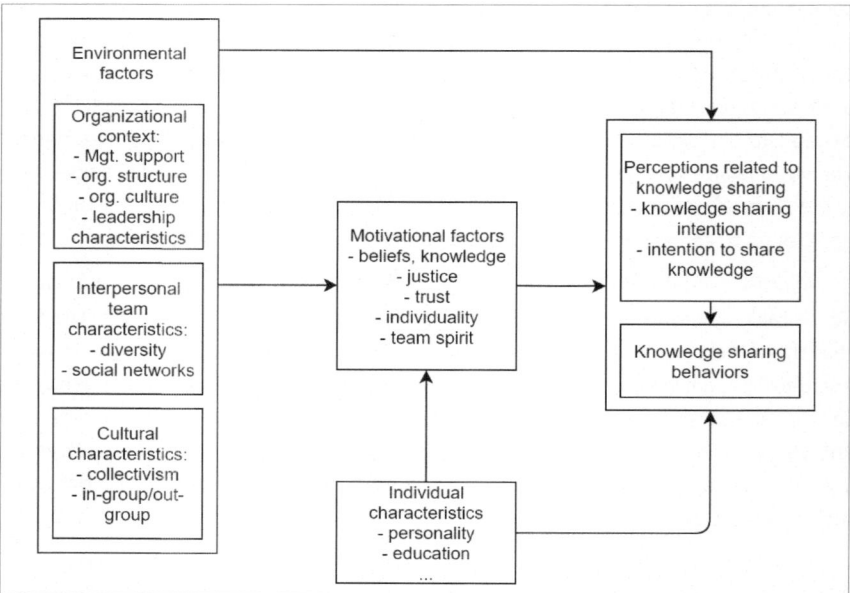

Figure 15: The context of knowledge sharing in scientific literature

(Source: own interpretation based on Wang, S., & Noe, R. A. (2010), Knowledge sharing: A review and directions for future research. Human Resource Management Review, 20(2), 115-131)

The result of this model is the transformation of knowledge in a cycle, e.g. from common sense (cultural knowledge) to personal (tacit knowledge) to proprietary (explicit knowledge) and finally to public (explicit knowledge) which is then again transformed into common sense. This flow was described by Boisot (1998) and is known as the Boisot knowledge management model.

Wang and Noe (2010) analyzed research within scientific papers regarding knowledge management and knowledge sharing. The authors stated that knowledge sharing is the basis for knowledge creation and therefore a very important aspect in the area of knowledge management (the results of their research can be seen figure 15). They suggest that external factors (which mean factors within the organization, the cultural context, related to interpersonal / team and cultural characteristics), motivational factors, and individual characteristics leads to perceptions which are related to knowledge sharing. Knowledge sharing as important aspect was also confirmed by other authors (Brčić & Mihelič, 2015).

The EFQM KM Model (for more information of EFQM Model please see chapter 1.1.3) highlights several aspects of knowledge management to achieve organizational goals (Dalkir & Liebowitz, 2011). Martín-Castilla & Rodríguez-Ruiz (2008) suggested that the EFQM model uses intellectual capital (IC), a form to measure knowledge. The authors demonstrated that the links between IC-components and EFQM framework.

Markos & Sridevi (2010) and Domniku (2014) showed the influence of employee engagement and motivation on performance suggesting different strategies to strengthen employee engagement which is related to the culture of the company. Golafzani & Chirani (2016) analyzed the relationship between different cultured and financial performance in manufacturing firms and concluded that there is a strong connection between the type of culture and the financial performance starting from a market culture, the clan-culture, the adhocracy culture, and the hierarchy culture. This is confirmed by other scientists, such as Jacobs et al. (2013) who also identified a positive relationship between a clan culture and financial performance. Authors such as Hogan & Coote (2014) and Zafar et al. (2016) also identified such influence regarding adhocracy and market culture. The fact that knowledge conversion and the general effect of knowledge has a positive impact on performance of a company was also the result of a research which measured performance in the dimensions of (Kinyua et al., 2015):

- Newly developed products
- Increase of the speed of the response to crises

- Product improvements

- Process implementations based on new ideas and improvement initiatives
- Focusing on customer retention

Kinyua et al. (2015) concluded in their research that knowledge conversion and knowledge application positively impact the performance of organizations within the banking industry.

Different authors mention the importance of organizational culture and the effects on the above stated SECI-areas of knowledge management. Creating and sharing of knowledge has to do with the willingness of the employees which is related to psychological dimensions and mental capabilities. Scientists suggested connections to fields like emotional intelligence (EI) and motivation as well as violation to these aspects (Zavareghi, 2008). This is also related to the behavior of the management, executed through the leadership style (Kopia, 2016 and chapter 5.2). These psychologic aspects of human behaviors are suggested to be factors which are mostly ignored by scientific research in the field of knowledge management (Trentin & McKeran, 2008; Zavareghi 2008). Especially the elements of EI together with the willingness and capabilities of employees effect knowledge management. Figure 16 shows the connection between the fields of EI (based on Goleman, 1996), organizational culture, leadership style, and knowledge management.

Figure 16 The connection between EI, OC, leadership and KM
(Source: own elaboration based on the results of own research)

It must be stated that there is a connection between the organizational culture and leadership (Ogbonna & Harris, 2000) which at the end is related to the performance of an organization (see figure 17).

In literature review in the area of process management and organizational culture, Grau & Moormann (2014) discovered that the academic literature concerning the relation of BPM and organizational culture is limited because the organizational psychology aspects are mostly ignored in BPM-studies and empirical studies in that field are almost not existing. The authors identified 26 studies between 1997 and 2012 in the pre-selected 450 journals which focusses on the selected topic. Most recent studies reveal that there is a correlation between corporate culture and knowledge conversion and process management, process orientation and process optimization and the cultural aspects are one important success factors in that regard (Kohl-

Figure 17 How leadership-style effects performance

(Source: own, based on Ogbonna, E. and L. C. Harris (2000), Leadership style, organizational culture and performance: empirical evidence from UK companies. International Journal of Human Resource Management, 11(4), 766-788).

bacher & Gruenwald, 2011; Sidorova & Isik, 2010). Skrinjar et al. (2008) identified a connection between process orientation and the performance of a company also stating that the organizational culture impacts the company's performance. Baird et al. (2011) analyzed the relationship between organizational culture, Total Quality Management, and performance showing that several elements of organizational culture is a success factor for TQM. TQM is positively related to profit, hence financial performance of companies.

Tacit and explicit knowledge influences the way how processes are designed, how companies are managed, and how the organization deals with external triggers. Knowledge is an important asset for many companies, especially those which have a strong need for innovation, such as the field of high-technology-products (Kimizm, D., 2005). The management of knowledge is an area called knowledge management and a topic in scientific research since the 1990s (McInerney, 2002). The importance of knowledge is also reflected in the EUROPE 2020 initiative in which knowledge and innovation play a vital role for the growth within the EU.

In the last chapter was shown, that knowledge is important for innovation and the conversion of knowledge (Nonaka and Takeuchi, 1995) between tacit and explicit knowledge as a cyclic process depends on the organizational culture. Knowledge management therefore is the system used to facilitate the creation, transformation, sharing, and organization of knowledge. Transforming knowledge from individuals into organizations and vice versa is a core element of the knowledge management cycle (see figure 18). Besides the already stated scientists, different approaches to knowledge management cycles were suggested (Dalkir, 2017). Such approaches include models from Meyer & Zack (1996), Bukowitz & Williams (2000), McElroy (1999), Wiig (1993), Carlile & Rebentisch (2003) etc. The concepts are

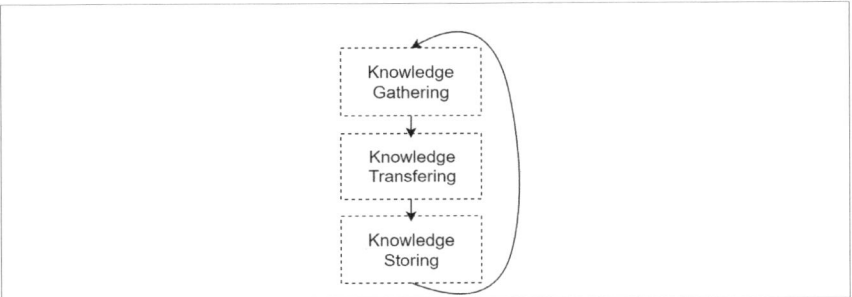

Figure 18 A knowledge management cycle
(Source: Own interpretation based on the results of own research)

comparable since they all have typical elements of creating / gaining / collecting knowledge, transforming, shaping, sharing, using, and storing it. Dalkir (2011) developed an integrated

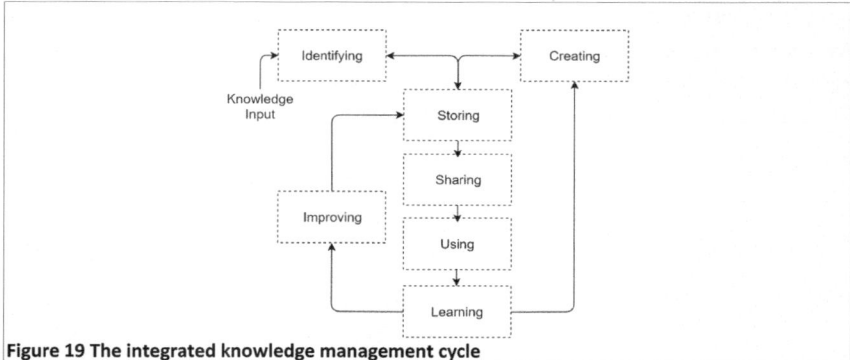

Figure 19 The integrated knowledge management cycle
(Source: own representation based on Evans, M.M.; Dalkir, K. and Bidian, C. (2014). A Holistic View of
the Knowledge Life Cycle: The Knowledge Management Cycle (KMC) Model, The Electronic Journal of
Knowledge Management, 12(2): 85–97.)

approach using some of the suggested models by other scientists (figure 19).

The integrated approach emphasizes the aspect of learning (more exact "double
loop learning" (Berta et al., 2015)) since the aspect of a continuous improvement is
important (Evans et al, 2014). Figure 19 represents the idea of the integrated
knowledge management cycle based on Evanset et al (2014).

1.3.3   Evaluating knowledge management and organizational learning through intellectual capital

In the last section the importance of knowledge and different approaches and definitions in that context were discussed. Some of the mentioned approaches contain
elements to measure knowledge. This chapter identifies scientific suggestions on how
to measure knowledge.

The question behind the measurement of knowledge for organizations is the question of the Return-on-Invest (ROI) of knowledge. If there is a clear ROI of "knowledge",
knowledge management will become more important for organizations since they can
see the benefit of their knowledge management initiatives. In the last chapter it was
shown that knowledge is a complex topic involving different forms of knowledge and
a dependency to aspects such as organizational culture, interpersonal elements, psychological aspects etc. Knowledge itself is intangible and therefore difficult to measure
(Milan, 2005; Yallwe & Buscemi, 2014). Despite the problem to measure knowledge,

organizations increasingly recognize the potential of knowledge and knowledge management to innovate and to create new products and services. Scientific literature presents some approaches to measuring the ROI of knowledge.

The importance of knowledge was already recognized in the form of intellectual
assets in production firms which using JIT (see last section) (Steward, 1991). According
to the author, content analyses and cost-benefit analyses should be used to value each
element of knowledge. This intellectual capital (IC) measures the intellectual assets of
an organization. The idea is that this value is at least as high as it would cost to recreate
that knowledge. IC consists of human capital, relational capital, and structural capital
(See figure 20). The market value of a firm is

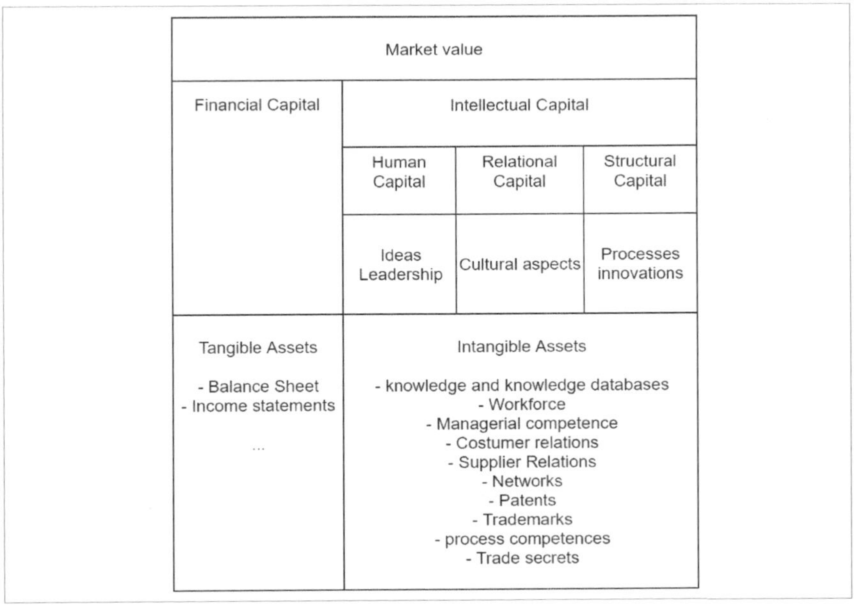

Market value		
Financial Capital	Intellectual Capital	
	Human Capital	Relational Capital	Structural Capital
	Ideas Leadership	Cultural aspects	Processes innovations
Tangible Assets - Balance Sheet - Income statements ...	Intangible Assets - knowledge and knowledge databases - Workforce - Managerial competence - Costumer relations - Supplier Relations - Networks - Patents - Trademarks - process competences - Trade secrets	

Figure 20 The intellectual capital framework

(Source: Johnson, H.A., W. (1999), An integrative taxonomy of intellectual capital: Measuring the stock
and flow of intellectual capital components in the Firm, International Journal Technology Management, Vol.18, Nov. 5/6/78, pp. 562-575).

the sum of its financial capital and the intellectual capital (Johnson, 1999). Different
views on IC were developed over time. The knowledge management cycles cited in the
last section had the goal to increase intellectual capital (Bukowitz & Williams, 2000).

Knowledge is the basis for IC (Ramezan, 2011) and intellectual capital Management (ICM) becomes an important part of the strategical management within organizations. Performance of organizations are consequences of the organizational strategies and they are bound to the capacity to manage knowledge. Knowledge therefore is an important aspect in business strategy (Choo & Bontis, 2002).

Knowledge management and organizational learning are closely linked (Vera, 2001). In figure 21 it is visible that organizational learning presented in the last section is linked to knowledge management. Both areas have elements which involve the static and dynamic aspect of knowledge which can be expressed as IC.

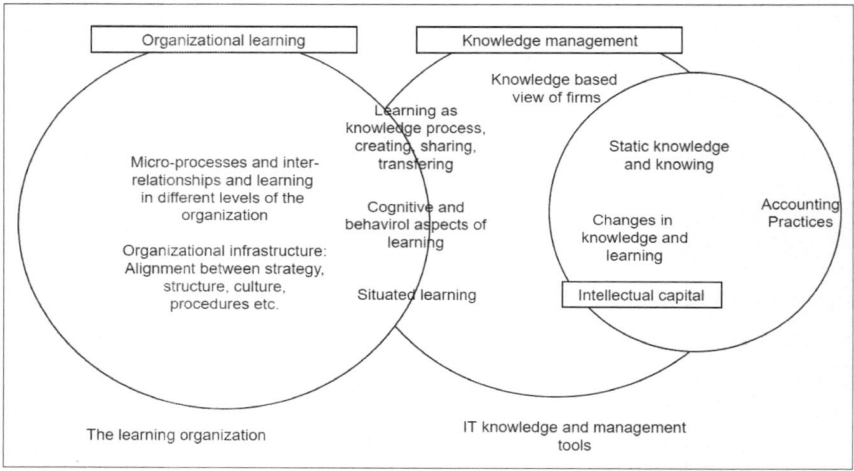

Figure 21 The differentiation between organizational learning, knowledge management, and intellectual capital fields
(Source: own, based on Vera, D. and Crossan, M. (2001), Organizational learning, knowledge management, and IC: an integrative conceptual model, Organizational Learning and Knowledge Management. New Directions 4th international conference, pp. 616-634)

Scientific researchers suggested several models for intellectual capital. Sveiby (2010) lists over 35 measurement models for IC which were developed between the years 1950 and 2009. Sveiby clustered them into a matrix which differentiates whether the model results in a financial value and whether it uses an organizational level only in contrast to single component (see figure 22).

1.3.4   Measuring of intellectual capital as an essential element of evaluating performance

According to Ståhle et al. (2011), the intellectual capital can be measured using the Value-Added Intellectual Coefficient (VAIC) with the following formula:

VAIC = CEE + HCE+ SCE (1) (or: ICE + CEE)

(CEE capital employed efficiency calculated as CEE = VA/CE (2))

(HCE human capital efficiency calculated as HCE = VA/HC (3)

(SCE structural capital efficiency calculated as: SCE = SC/VA (4)

(CE = Capital employed)

(HC = Human Capital)

(SC = Total assets minus Total current liabilities)

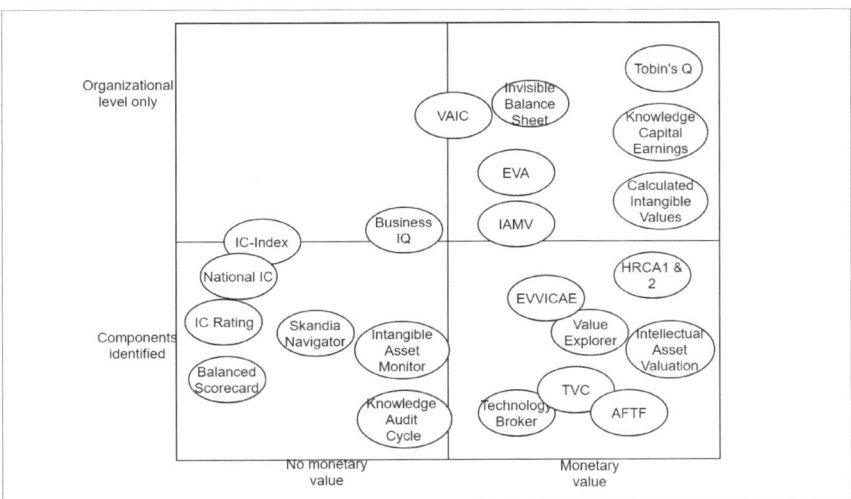

Figure 22 Measurement models for intellectual capital

(Source: own presentation based on Sveiby, K. E. (2010) Methods for Measuring Intangible Assets. Available: http://www.sveiby.com/files/pdf/intangiblemethods.pdf, accessed 05.10.2017).

The scientific literature comes to a different conclusion whether VIAC is useful for assessing IC or not (Svanadze & Kowalewska, 2015; Ståhle et al., 2011; Volkov, 2012; Arenas, 2012; Mondal & Ghosh, 2012; Bontis, 2001).

Some other methods to measure IC are (van der Berg, 2002):

- Tobin's Q Ratio is a measurement of ratio between the market value of physical assets and the value for their replacement. It includes aspects such as technology and human capital.

Table 8: Indicators of Skandia Navigator Model

Customer focus	Process focus	Human focus	Renewal & Development focus
Market share	Administrative expense	Leadership index	Competence development expenses
Number of customers	Process time	Motivation index	Training expenses
Sales	PCs per employee	Employee turnover	Average customer age
Customer rating	IT expenses	Number of managers	Business development expenses
Field sales management	Admin expenses	Training days	Share of development hours
Customers lost		Average Age of employees	Investment in product support

(Source: own elaboration based on the work of Edvinsson & Malone (1997), intellectual capital: Realizing Your Company's True Value By Finding Its Hidden, Brainpower, New York: Harper Business)

- Skandia and it's IC Navigator is known to be the first bigger organization which used IC. They model defines IC as the difference between market and book value of an organization (see figure 23 and table 8).

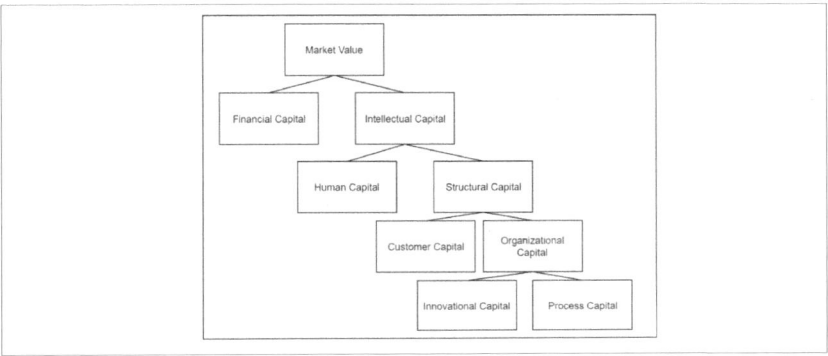

Figure 23 Skandia IC Navigator
(Source: own, based on Edvinsson & Malone (1997), intellectual capital: Realizing Your Company's True Value By Finding Its Hidden, Brainpower, New York: Harper Business)

- The Balanced Scorecard (see chapter 3.3.3) measures different dimensions and includes aspects such as learning and growth.
- Economic Value Added (EVA): Steward (1997) suggested EVA as an approach to measure a company's value closer to the cash value.
- The Technology Broker's IC Audit (Brooking, 1998) includes the dimensions of market assets, human-centered assets, intellectual property assets, and infrastructural assets and rates a value in the given time ignoring future development.

Some other known models are the Market Value Added (MVA), intellectual capital Services' IC-Index, Sveiby's The Intangible Asset Monitor (IAM) etc. One method to measure knowledge can be realized by using an audit as suggested by Brooking's Technology Broker's IC Audit (Brooking, 1998) or the 10-step knowledge management roadmap (Tiwana, 1999).

Maturity models are another way to measure knowledge (Lahti et al., 2009) which show relevant aspects on how to assess knowledge in order to measure it. Maturity models exist for all kinds of organizational aspects. They describe the development in the context of maturity over time and identify rating-methods to assess this "level of maturity". Maturity generally can be defined as a complete state of development and as a set of capabilities of an organization expressing its competencies to realize excellent processes (Van Looy, De Backer, & Poels, 2011) – see also chapter 3. Diverse models to evaluate knowledge management models were suggested over time (see below) with different approaches, dimensions and assessment methodologies. They have common elements. Most models contain three generic perspectives:

- Maturation time as the development of the maturation over time (Souza & Voss, 2001; Fraser et al., 2002);
- Capability as the progress toward a level of completeness or perfection (Urdang & Flexner, 1968),
- Evolution as the connection to the development of business processes (Lahti et al., 2009)

Some of the models are based on the Capability Maturity Model (CMM) developed by the Software Engineering Institute (SEI) and around original thoughts of Crosby (1979). It includes five levels of maturity (Initial, Managed, Defined, Quantitatively Managed, Optimized/ing).

Examples of maturity models based on CMM include

- the Siemens knowledge management maturity model (Ehms, 2001)
- the Paulzen & Perc's knowledge process quality model (KPQM) (Paulzen & Perc, 2002)
- Infosys' knowledge management maturity model (Kochikar, 2000)
- Pee & Kankanhalli (2009) developed a model with five stages (G-KMMM) and an objective assessment methodology using processes, people, and technology
- The KMMM for the nuclear industry by Boyles et al (2009)

Despite the number of suggested models, the way to assess maturity is not clearly defined in scientific literature (Pee et al: 2006). Baykiz (2014) lists 20 maturity models and suggested an integrated approach of maturity model measurement for knowledge management. It contains the three dimensions of Pee & Kankanhalli (2009) People, Process, and Technology and uses an assessment methodology based on questionnaires. Sajeva & Jucevicius (2018) assess knowledge management maturity using the dimensions: Strategic leadership, knowledge management process, knowledge culture, organizational learning, technological infrastructure, and organizational infrastructure based on questionnaires.

Kuriakose et al. (2010) developed a morphological framework for knowledge management maturity models to solving the problem of the diversity of existing models by evaluating 15 models and capturing the essentials.

To summarize this chapter the following can be said: The identified method for assessing and measuring knowledge usse different approaches such as measurement models and maturity models. In order to calculate a ROI it is necessary to establishing a methodology to assessing knowledge and knowledge management which based on a chosen knowledge management model and measurement approach. Scientific research does not give a clear condense so far about the right model or the right usage of a model depending on the situation.

2 The connection of risk management and sustainable business process performance

2.1 Enterprise risk management and applied operational frameworks

This paper aims to provide a review on the topic of risk management within organizations with a special focus on enterprise risk management systems and the challenges of measuring effectiveness and efficiency. Common frameworks of such risk management systems like the COSO ERM and the ISO 31000 will be introduced together with some background on their development.

According to the institute of risk management (2006) it is necessary to minimize the threat and potential of risks by managing risks within organization which includes the first important step of identifying them. Several frameworks for risk management were developed over time. Most known is the ISO 31000 risk management principles and guidelines which define risks as an unexpected situation which leads to uncertainty. It is references by many different ISO standards for risk management methodologies. Looking at a broader perspective, such as ERM, known principles were defined by the Committee of Sponsoring Organizations of the Treadway Commission's (COSO). COSO (2004) highlights the importance of identifying and assessing risks on all levels of the organization as well as the strategic relevance of risk management. Kopia et al. (2017a) defined risks as an event that adversely affect the outcome of a business or a business objective. These risks can appear in different dimensions, such as the financial dimensions or in the operational dimension etc. Risks can be measured by using the calculation to multiply the likelihood of the occurrence with the impact of the risk event. Risks can also be having positive impact and interpreted as chances for the organization to benefit from it (Anderson, 2005).

As will be shown, risk is playing a central role to organization especially in the current environment and outside factors are hereby driving the design of risk management systems to be more integrated. Hereby, the philosophy and understanding of risk is twofold. While risk usually entails the notion of losses or negative events, risk can also be understood as a change when viewed as uncertainty about future developments. In this respect, risk is deeply integral to the role of performance and value maximization within organizations. Therefore, management may consider risk in the business strategy in order to enhance effectiveness and efficiency. Hereby, effectiveness

© Springer Fachmedien Wiesbaden GmbH, part of Springer Nature 2019
J. Kopia, *Effective Implementation of Management Systems*, Sustainable Management, Wertschöpfung und Effizienz, https://doi.org/10.1007/978-3-658-26509-0_3

targets the selection of the best possible course of action for the respective organization while efficiency targets the best possible way of how to do the things after they
have been selected.

Central to the functioning of ERM systems is the aspect of measurement of effectiveness and efficiency, which will be discussed in more detail in this paper. Hereby,
the concept of the balanced scorecard is useful to consider as it includes measures of
performance in different perspective that include financial and operational measures.
However, there is still a strong need to customize this framework to the respective
organization with individual metrics, e.g. with relevant key performance indicators that
will also be discussed later. Organizations are best prepared to achieve their selected
goals when they are able to design and implement mature systems relevant to the
organization that are flexible enough to consider outside development relevant to
their performance.

The next chapter will entail in more detail the relevant understanding of risk and
the role and development of risk management within organizations. The frameworks
of the COSO ERM and ISO 31000 will be described here. Chapter 3 focusses on the
aspect of measurement of effectiveness and efficiency, showing relevant aspects as
well as some selected metrics and current issues like key performance indicators.
Chapter 4 contains a discussion on the topic of measurement where the role of maturity is especially highlighted. Chapter 5 provides a short outlook and discusses current developments.

2.1.1   Traditional and enterprise risk management and existing frameworks

This chapter entails the basics of the understanding of risk and risk management in
relation to organizations. After having laid the fundamentals on the notion of risk, its
impact on organizations and the respective management tasks resulting from it, a discussion on traditional risk management will be provided to serve as the fundament to
better understand the enterprise risk management frameworks that are central to the
review provided in this paper. These frameworks are going to be described in more
detail and two fundamental frameworks, the COSO ERM and the ISO 31000 will be
investigated specifically. Finally, a short note on some other enterprise risk management frameworks is intended as well as a short summary of the chapter.

The issue of dealing with risk has always been central to any human endeavor.
However, with the increase in technologically driven connectivity that is coming long

the forces of digitalization and by an increase in the disruption of business models, risk has become ever more central. Currently, not only chances are more connected but risk as well. This increase in connectivity does bring systemic risks, whereby risks of large companies can spread quickly onto other actors (Romeike, 2018). A recent example that shows the issue of systemic risks in relation to the financial markets has been the last financial crisis that has also brought many questions in relation to weakness and flaws within corporate governance principles (Kirkpatrick, 2009).

Organizations that are facing a diverse set of risks in their activities can deal with these demands by establishing risk management practices. Risk management is nowadays central and considered as a necessity in many organizations. Two reasons can be pointed out for this development. First, the need to comply with existing regulations, which is called reactive risk management, and second, the need or goal to use risk management in order to assist management achieving their strategic objectives. By applying modern methods of data analysis within an environment characterized by digitalization and connectivity, risk management may help recognize risks early which may then trigger an optimal response by the respective organization (Romeike, 2018). Risk management methods differ and as a result of the already mentioned financial crisis, existing methods of dealing with risk have been criticized heavily from a number of directions and alternative methods have been proposed. There has been a push observed for the development and application of so-called enterprise management systems (ERM) that can deal with risks in a holistic, consolidated and strategic way by using a more structured and integrated approach (Lundquist, 2015).

Frameworks like COSO ERM or ISO 31000 will be shown in more detail. These approaches promise to deal with risk in a better way than traditional risk management practices that are considered in the next paragraph of this paper.

As has been shown above, risk is a central issue for people and organizations since a long time where it was especially important within the fields of military, policy making, maritime shipping, and gambling etc. (Romeike, 2018). The relevant question in this respect is, in what ways can risks be managed? To answer this question and to show traditional methods of managing risk, it must be made clear, what should be understood under the term "risk".

Usually, risk is defined as a negative outcome from a specific situation, e.g. the impact of a natural disaster, workplace injuries etc. Hereby, the probability of the occurrence of the bad outcome as well as the magnitude of the loss suffered is of relevance and must be taken into account. Situations are considered riskier the higher the difficulty to predict the outcome or the higher the volatility. Therefore, risk if often measured using the standard deviation (Niehaus, 2017). However, a more modern and general notion of risk does also entail the notion of chance, which describes a positive deviation from the expected outcome of a risky situation (Romeike, 2018).

Traditional techniques of managing risk can encompass single strategies like hedging or using corporate insurance. It can also entail single activities like tracking workplace injuries (Lundquist, 2015). Risk management is also of high importance within the financial market. Here, a number of risk measures exist, that help risk managers to quantify and hereby assess risk (Albrecht & Maurer, 2005).

What is key to the understand of traditional risk management, especially when compared to enterprise risk management systems is that a traditional risk management process is set up to identify, measure, monitor and perhaps report risk only individually and disintegrated from other risk factors relevant to the organization. It does so with little structure, formality or centralization (Lundquist, 2015). A more thorough understanding and managing of risk within organizations can be performed using modern ERM systems that are covered in detail in the next paragraph.

As the call for ERM is being observed in the literature as a way to more effectively deal with risks that organizations face has been made, motivated by observed failures of risk models applied (Kirkpatrick, 2009), it must be asked what does exactly constitute an ERM and what is the difference to traditional methods of managing risk.

ERM systems or frameworks do not totally discard traditional methods of risk management like dealing with potential accidents or assuming product liability. However, what is central to the concept of an ERM is that these management systems do also incorporate other

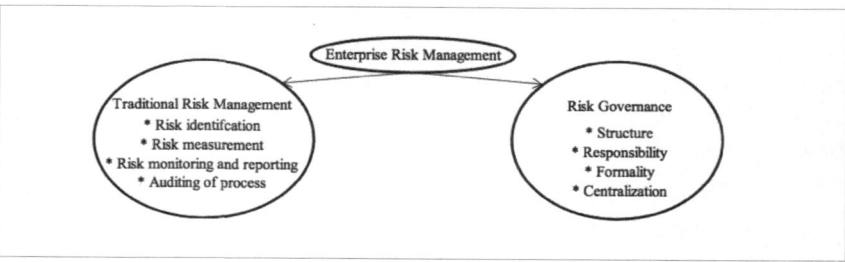

Figure 24 Conceptualization of enterprise risk management

(Source: Lundquist, S. A. (2015), Why firms implement risk governance – Stepping beyond traditional risk management to enterprise risk management, J. Account. Public Policy, 34, pp. 441-466)

important risks. These can include strategic risks like activities from competitors or product obsolescence (Bromiley et al., 2015). Basically, an ERM is combining the traditional methods of managing risk with risk governance, using an integrated approach (Lundquist, 2015). This approach of a combination of traditional methods with risk governance is shown below in figure 24. Risk governance as the second and new part that constitute an ERM generally deals with providing direction and control of the entire risk management system. This entails the provision of the entire risk management structure, including the assignment of responsibilities, accountability and authority as well as the establishment of rules and procedures for decision-making (Lundquist, 2015).

ERM systems are a relatively new concept and discussion and clarifications about its meaning and scope are manifold and sometimes conflicting. Bromiley et al. (2015) provide a literature review that includes an overview of ERM definitions from academic journals (Bromiley et al., 2015).

Of high importance in relation to ERM is the focus an organization has onto different classes of risks. There are generally three risk classes of relevance: 1) strategic risks, 2) operating risks, and 3) financial risks. These are risk classes were all individual risks can be aggregated into. Developments in recent years have shown that most companies focus on financial risks. This is fundamentally not in line with the basic assumptions of an ERM and probably caused by an increase in the discussion related to financial risks in the wake of the last financial crisis that brought many regulations specific to the risks of financial institutions. However, studies show that financial risks usually do not cause the largest risks onto institutions but that strategic risks are having the largest impact in terms of its potential magnitude of experiencing losses. Therefore, a successful ERM approach shall target risk in its entirety by implementing an equal identification, assessment and management of all risk relevant for the organization (Hunziker, 2018). A correct focus on the right risks may lead to a risk management approach that is effective in the sense that it is useful for managing the risks the organization faces. An incorrect focus on a risk of comparatively lower importance may lead to an efficient management of this specific kind of risk, but through neglecting the most important things, this approach may cause problems.

When implementing a ERM within an organization, it needs to be clarified, which ERM framework or which norm for a ERM system should be used that is efficient as well as effective for the specific type of organization. There is a number of potential ERM frameworks available. However, two frameworks are considered to be the most prevalent ones in terms of discussion and dissemination in practice. These two frame-works, which should be discussed in more detail in the following paragraphs are 1) the COSO ERM and 2) the ISO 31000 norm (Hunziker, 2018).

COSO ERM

The COSO ERM framework serves as a guideline in the field of risk management. It was originally formulated by the Committee of Sponsoring Organizations of the Tread-way Commission (COSO) and looks back on a comparatively long history as an interna-tional standard for company-wide risk management. The COSO ERM was heavily prop-agated by accounting firms and it was largely applied in the US but also in Europe in conjunction with the internal control mechanism ("Internes Kontrollsystem"). Because of its inherent complexity, experts generally agree that the COSO ERM is best suited to large corporate groups (Romeike, 2018).

The COSO ERM is not meant to be a one-size-fits-all approach to risk management within organizations but instead calls for individual adjustments and customizations. Of importance is the support by top management and the risk culture within an organ-ization. This risk culture can be positively influenced by respective and repeated com-munication and provision of information across organizational hierarchies (Hunziker, Meissner, 1997).

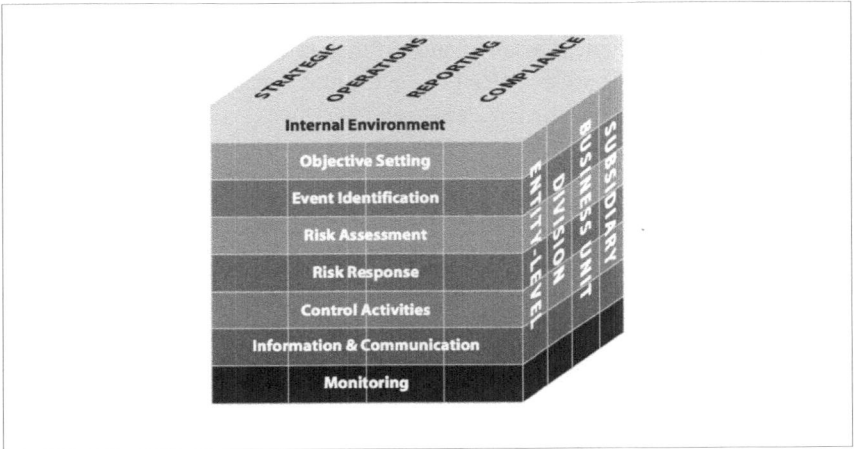

Figure 25 COSO ERM framework

(Source: Committee of Sponsoring Organizations of the Treadway Commission (COSO) (Hrsg.), (2009), http://www.coso.org/IC-integratedFramework-summary.htm, Internal Control— integrated Framework, Retrieved March 23, 2011)

The central understanding of risk within the COSO framework relates to its role in conjunction with shareholder value maximization. This value maximization goal is understood as the fundamental objective of companies and the challenge and task to management is simply to determine the correct amount of uncertainty, an organization should take. Specifically, company value is maximized in this tradeoff situation "when management sets strategy and objectives to strike an optimal balance between growth and return goals and related risks, and efficiently and effectively deploys resources in pursuit of the entity's objectives." (COSO, 2004). This definition clearly shows the issue of targeting efficiency and effectiveness as two separate but important goals. Later in this paper, a discussion on these two aspects in relation to the problem of measurement will be provided.

COSO ERM entails four objectives relevant for any organization that is applying the standard. In addition to these objectives there are eight components of relevance. These components are interrelated and integrated within the management process. Figure 25 shows the COSO ERM framework.

The goals of the respective entity that is trying to manage its risks should be described and discussed in more detail because of their relevance to the topic of measurement related to efficiency and effectivity in the next chapter. The goals, as shown in figure 25 can be described in more detail as (COSO, 2004):

- Strategic – These are high-level goals in alignment to the central mission and objective of the organization.
- Operations – This relates to the effective and the efficient use of the company's resources.
- Reporting – This includes the reliability of the reporting.
- Compliance – This relates to fulfillment of applicable laws and regulations.

Of central interest in this paper is the notion of the strategic goals as well as the goals related to operations. While strategic goals are thought to include mostly the issue of doing the right things, goals related to operations show both aspects relevant to the discussion in this paper. On the one hand, management may need to decide on the course of action within operations, which relates to the effectiveness and is generally comparable to the strategic goals when viewed in this way. On the other hand, operational goals also target the efficiency aspect. That means, that process should be made as efficient as possible and resources shall be used as efficient as possible. These issues will be investigated in more detail in the next chapter on the measurement of efficiency and effectiveness.

ISO 31000

The second ERM framework that is considered to be of high importance is the ISO 31000. This standard has been developed as a top-level approach to risk management. In recent years, many companies disregarded the COSO ERM in favor of the ISO 31000. This approach aims at combining risk management with existing management systems in order to establish an active risk control system characterized by its ability to prevent risks in the first place. In theory this should lead to an integrated management system were existing borders between issues like work safety, quality management, risk management and other management systems may disappear in favor of a more integrated approach to managing organization-wide risk properly (Romeike, 2018).

The combination of risk management systems intended by the ISO 31000 may encompass systems like quality management that are also targeted by other ISO norms like the ISO 9000 and the related ISO norms to quality management. Also, systems specific to certain industries may be integrated as well to serve as a part of the ISO 31000. Examples include norms relevant for the automobile industry, medicine, telecommunication, air travel etc. (see Schlosske & Thieme, 2017, for more details to these norms). Potential integrations may also include other risk management norms, e.g. the ISO 27005 that is relevant for dealing with information security risks by providing relevant guidelines (ISO, 2011). This kind of customization of the ERM is probably necessary to build a useful and working system within the specific organization of relevance.

As a general proposition, the ISO 31000 is criticized in the literature because of its generic approach that does not take into account the specifics of the individual company and the industry sector. However, it must be questioned, whether an all-encompassing standard is even possible to design because it must theoretically capture the entire heterogeneity of all industry segments and companies of any size (Romeike, 2018). Therefore, the individual customization of the ISO 31000 framework is considered to be necessary and the integration of other established norms related to specific areas, like other ISO norms etc., onto the basic framework of the ISO 31000 seems promising but does also pose demands and challenges to the management of the organization. Generally, the customization of an ERM is relevant to other ERM frameworks as well, which has been shown above for the case of the COSO ERM where individual customization is also being proposed.

The ISO 31000 has features that also deviate from other ERM systems. The deviations to the second framework of high importance, the COSO ERM should be displayed in the following table 9. Contrasting the features shall give a better understanding on the framework. It should also serve to provide necessary input for the question on measurement in the subsequent chapter of this paper.

Table 9 Factors that show deviations of ISO 31000 and COSO ERM

Factor	ISO 31000	COSO ERM
Assessment of chances of risky events	Events with positive consequences are considered equally	Focus on negative consequences of events to be considered for further evaluation
Methods to risk management	Broad set of measure including what to do with positive deviations	Four methods possible: 1) prevention, 2) reduction, 3) risk sharing, 4) risk acceptance
Evaluation of risks	Sophisticated evaluation related to the consequences of the event	Evaluation only related to the specific events (probability and magnitude)
Understanding of the concept or framework	Instruction for implementation of a risk management process with a very generic nature	Flexible standard useful for the evaluation of existing risk management processes
Instructions and scope for action	As mentioned very generic with a lot of scope for actions by the organization	Very detailed instruction with less scope for action

(Source: Own presentation based on Hunziker, S., Meissner, J. O. (2017), Risikomanagement in 19 Schritten. Wiesbaden: Springer Gabler)

The ISO 31000 therefore characterizes itself as a framework for dealing with risk in a more general sense that can explicitly include positive deviations and therefore chances to the organization. This makes it useful as a more general tool of management that tries to increase the value of the firm. However, to apply this norm correctly, it must be properly customized. Management needs to put more effort and resources into the development of an ISO 31000 framework which may also lead to failure and misspecification. The COSO ERM however is useful to provide a detailed check of existing systems already in place.

Currently, the ISO 31000 norm is in the process of being renewed. The goal of the revision work is the make this standard easier und clearer by using simple language and resort to the fundamentals of risk management. Hereby, it is challenging to find a good balance between the provision of detailed guidance and the sheer volume of the relevant ISO 31000 document (ISO, 2017).

2.1.2 Limitations of enterprise risk management within existing frameworks

The two most important ERM frameworks that are currently relevant, the COSO ERM and the ISO 31000, have been described in the preceding paragraphs of this paper. Despite of the fact that these two frameworks seem to be well established, with the ISO 31000 becoming, as has been shown, a little more relevant at the expense of the COSO ERM, it must be asked whether there are good alterative ERM frameworks that are promising to be of relevance in the near future.

To answer this question, it must be remembered that the definition, scope and meaning of an ERM is generally not clearly established in the relevant literature. Hereby, distinctions of different questions have to be considered. Especially what goals should be thought of in general and how the distinction between risks and chances are being made (Bromiley, 2015). These differences in the fundamental understanding and approach of an ERM have yet been observed in the preceding remarks on the differences of the COSO ERM in relation to the ISO 31000. Arena et al. (2010) show in relation to data obtained from three different companies that their approach to risk management differed significantly and ranged from an approach to fulfill its compliance duties to an approach that include encompassing corporate governance approaches for increasing company value.

Another issue that should be mentioned is the need to customize even the two most relevant ERM frameworks mentioned in the relevant literature. Therefore, it seems unlikely that the search for another fundamental ERM framework may yield results that are worthy. From this respect, it seems to be the best way to look at the specific features of an ERM, especially with regards to the operationalization of efficiency and effectiveness and potential key performance indicators that can be integrated and applied within a customized ERM for the benefit of the respective organization.

2.1.3 Summary of the usage and principles of operational and enterprise risk management

Enterprise risk management (ERM) can be seen as an enterprise wide risk management practice implementing all of the above cited process on different levels of the organization. It is the try to prevent adverse situations of the entire organization by a concise risk management process (Institute of risk management, 2016). The goal of ERM is to apply risk processes within the day-to-day business which is the reason why all risk related processes should be integrated and aligned with the business processes (e.g. the Internal Control System, Quality Management, project management methodologies, operational and strategic planning etc.). The goal is to achieve a high transparency of the risk situation which is partially required by laws and regulations (e.g. in the financial area) but also useful for creating value for the organization. Ideally the risk situation can be aggregated to the top management where strategic decisions can be made based on that up-to-date situation of the company. This way risks and opportunities can be wisely treated (Anderson, 2005).

Existing approaches and frameworks to risk management

There are different standards, best-practices, and frameworks for risk management. In the above chapters ISO 31000 and COSO were mentioned as very commonly used risk management frameworks. These frameworks also highlight the importance of measurement,

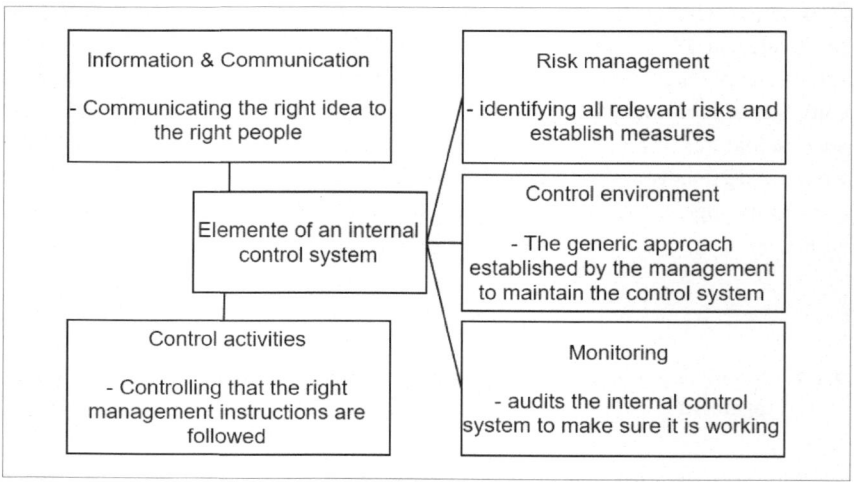

Figure 26 Internal Control System of the COSO-framework

(Source: own, based on Kaplan, (2012), Internal control systems, http://kfknowledgebank.kaplan. co.uk/KFKB/Wiki%20Pages/Internal%20control%20systems.aspx, accessed 10.07.2016)

e.g. using key performance indicators (KPI). In COSO it is suggested to establish an internal control system to make regular evaluations of the risk management process. This internal control system consists of the following components: COSO also highlights the importance of roles and responsibilities and the human factor (Brünger, 2009).

Based on that COSO defines specific responsibilities of roles which have to be present within the enterprise risk management process (see figure 26).

It must be noted that the human factor is a critical component in the risk management process since many decisions, evaluations, executions etc. are based on the behavior of human beings. These factors are difficult to consider in every theoretical framework (Brünger, 2009). In contrast to COSO, ISO 31000 is a collection of risk management guidelines which are required by diverse ISO standards. ISO based management system require a constant risk management approach. Therefore, ISO 31000 requires to establish a generic risk management commitment, a design of a risk process which fits to the company, the correct implementation, monitoring, and improvement of the risk management (see figure 27).

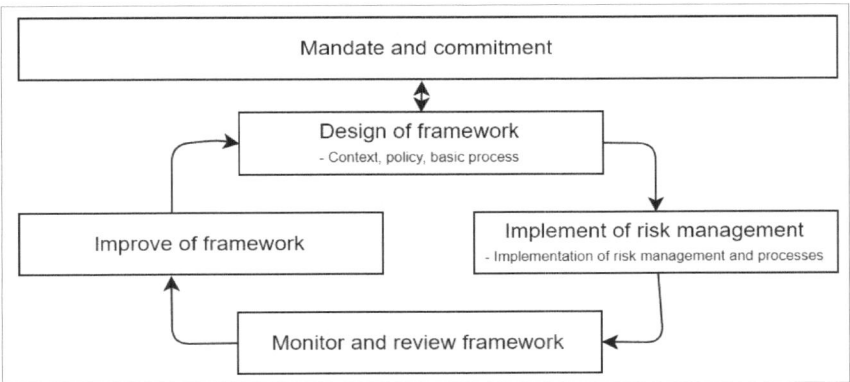

Figure 27 Risk management framework based on ISO 31000

(Source: own, based on AIRMIC, Alarm, IRM: (2010), A structured approach to Enterprise risk management (ERM) and the requirements of ISO 31000, https://www.theirm.org/media/886062/ISO3100_doc.pdf, accessed 03.02.2018, p.8)

The aspect of monitoring and reviewing of the risk management framework, which is required by ISO 31000 is not answered concisely neither within scientific literature nor in practice. An internal control system as suggested by COSO needs to assess measurement practices. One way to approach this is to use the balanced scorecard method. The BSC can serve as an instrument to measure the progress over time. The advantage of the BSC to measure multiple dimensions is a necessity in ERM since ERM also deals with risk management related tasks on all levels and diverse dimensions with the goal to present an aggregated view for the top management. The BSC might include the use

of economic value added (EVA) as it is an established way of measuring the value creation of a company (Hawawini et. al., 2003). Comparing the approaches of ERM and
the BSC it can be seen that there are similarities (Beasly et al., 2006):

- Both are using an enterprise-wide approach to assess its underlying question
- Both are useful to assess multiple dimensions, business areas, and factors
- Both have a top-down approach, which is continuously and holistically

Beasly et al. (2006) developed a model of using ERM and BSC together in the context of a supply chain process. This example as well as the approaches of other authors
(Nagumo et al., 2006; Saeidi et al., 2014) was a starting point of the model developed
by the authors of this research. This way a risk scorecard can be developed which contains financial and non-financial indicators. Acharyya (2008) suggested to combine the
EVA method with the BSC-method to have a multi-dimensional approach also using
traditional methods. This is also the opinion of other scientists, who highlight that EVA
is an instrument which is useful for evaluating ERM (Hawawini et. al., 2003; Woods,
2007).

Measuring ERM and risk management in general by using indicators cannot be easily defined for all organizations alike. Each organization needs to define their own
measurement approaches which should be aligned with the processes and strategic
objectives. An instrument which might be helpful is the maturity level evaluation. Risk
management maturity (RMM) is an important aspect when assessing the level of risk
management. The maturity of the process can be assessed using approaches, such as
the RIMS (The Risk and Insurance Management Society, 2016), "Aon ERM Risk Maturity
Model" (Aon, 2016), "RIMS" – the Risk Maturity Model for Enterprise risk management
(RIMS 2016), and other maturity models developed mainly by practitioners. However,
since there is a constant need to improve the risk management process organizations
never really reach a "full maturity" (Hillson, 2010). The following questions are not answered clearly yet but are essential in order to efficiently and effectively use ERM
within organizations:

- How can ERM (or risk management in general) be measured in order to constantly
  improve the process and in order to evaluate the maturity of the risk management
  process?
- How can the effects of ERM (or risk management in general) on performance of
  the organization be measured?

Several authors studied the topic of the effects of ERM on performance, e.g. Kraus & Lehner (2012) who created a cause-and-effect-diagrams as can be seen in figure 28.

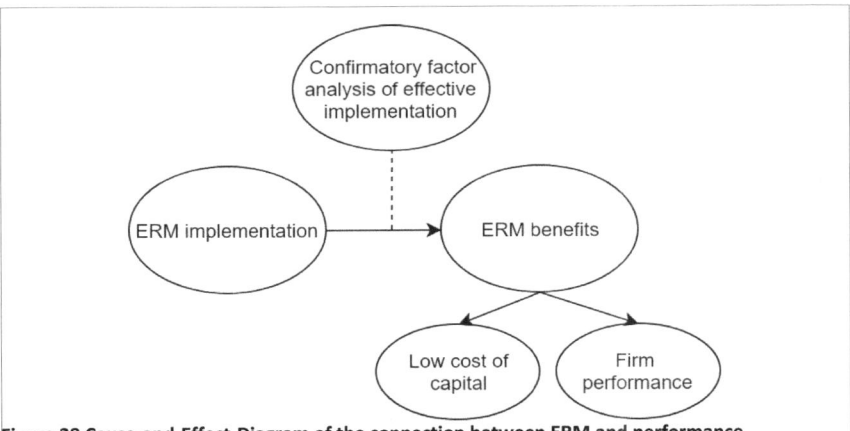

Figure 28 Cause-and-Effect-Diagram of the connection between ERM and performance

(Source: own interpretation based on Kraus, V., Lehner, O.M., (2013), The nexus of enterprise risk management and value creation: Connecting the Dots and Finding the Blind Spots, Journal of Finance and Risk Perspectives, Vol. 1, No. 1, pp. 230-261; 577; Woods, M., (2007), Linking risk management to strategic controls: a case study of Tesco plc. International. International Journal of Risk Assessment and Management, 7(8), pp. 1074-1088)

This chapter provided an introduction to the understanding of risk and the role risk is playing within organizations. As a central concept to any business activity, risk is central for management to consider, which shows the importance of risk management. Risk management has evolved from a more isolated traditional approach to a more integrated approach considering organizational goals.

Central to such systems is the understanding of risk not only containing the notion of negative developments and losses but also the role of chances that uncertain development may bring to organizations and that can be used opportunistically by management in order to foster organizational goals. ERM systems may provide management with a guide to find ways to increase organizational performance and increase value. Such a philosophy is basically part of the frameworks that have been described in this chapter, the COSO ERM and the ISO 31000.

These systems are however only considered as providing general frameworks, so there is a strong need to customize these systems to the respective organization, e.g. by integrating some other ISO norms onto the ISO 31000 framework. The next chapter entails the topic of measurement that is relevant for ERM systems, focusing on the aspects of effectiveness and efficiency. Indicators referred to under the term key performance indicators will also be discussed in the light of ERM systems.

ERM systems are not static but evolve due to the complexity of the business environment, technological developments and evolution as well as due to the emergence of new risks relevant to the organization (PwC, 2017). So, companies are best positioned to recognize such developments with respect to their organizations and design their ERM systems in a way to foster their organizational goals.

2.2 Measuring efficiency and effectiveness within risk management frameworks

Even though, ERMs have been welcomed by a number of actors like legislative bodies, rating agencies, stock exchanges, and professional associations etc., academic research related to this subject is still in its early stages. Research into ERM is also relatively scattered amongst a variety of disciplines with a large part of accounting and finance journals covering the subject while ERM is comparatively neglected in management journals (Bromiley et al., 2015). In addition, the problem intensifies somehow, when trying to understand and correctly describe an ERM in the first place. As was mentioned already in the last chapter, ERM call for individual customization and individual features which are expected to deviate in a material way amongst different companies. Therefore, a specific aspect of an ERM that is of relevance to a financial institution may be irrelevant or at least not very important to a mining company or another firm from a different industry sector.

However, despite the individual aspects that need to be taken into account here, an ERM shall help to achieve efficiency and effectiveness. Those aspects had been mentioned already in the last chapter as a fundamental part of the COSO ERM and should be stated even more clearly at the beginning of this chapter to serve as a basis for the following investigation.

Fundamentally, effectiveness describes the relation of current output to the output that is desired by the decision-maker or management. Effectiveness relates to doing the right things in a long-term approach. Efficiency on the other hand relates not to the right things but onto the way of doing things right. In that sense, efficiency is of a more short-term nature and it target the relation of current output to current input (Bea & Haas, 2016). While strategic goals are mainly relevant for the effectiveness aspect, operating goals are relevant for effectiveness and efficiency.

In this sense, Callahan, Soileau (2017) characterize an effective ERM as a tool to manage downside risk as well as upside risks, where downside risk refers to the frequent notion of risk as something negative that must be insured against or that needs to be hedged in order to reduce potential financial losses or to mitigate regulatory risk. Upside risk on the other hand focusses on the enhancement of firm value by critically analyzing business opportunities. Hereby, elements of firm strategy, investment activities as well as innovation activities and questions of efficiency become relevant to investigate. This understanding of risk, containing potential positive and negative aspects of risk shall be especially analyzed within the current paper as it seems to provide the most useful notion in order to support management decision making.

As systems for management become ever more relevant for management practice, which for example includes the ISO 9001 norm that is related to quality management (Aba et al., 2016), the question of managing risks within such integrated frameworks shall becoming of more interest to researchers and practitioners. Given this background, Barafort et al. (2017) investigate how the topic of risk management is addressed within the wide variety of ISO norms and how the issue of managing risk can be adequately deployed within the IT settings of management systems. Overserving these individual aspects is expected to be useful for organizational risk management.

A framework to address and measure efficiency and effectiveness is the balanced scorecard that includes a number of performance measures that consist of some more traditional and financial measures of success while also containing operating measures of relevance to the company or organization. These can include metrics like customer satisfaction or measures in relation to internal processes (Banker et al., 2004). The balanced scorecard is in addition a flexible tool that can be adjusted and potentially integrate new measures specifically tailored to the business model of the organization in question. In addition, the balanced scorecard also includes measures that target the aspects of learning and growth that can be used to make an evaluation in order to foster continuous improvement of the organization (Banker et al., 2004). These may include areas that relate to the topic of risk inherent in the business that is critical to evaluate and manage well. It is obvious that the balanced scorecard approach has many similarities to the ERM frameworks discussed above as strategic and operational issues are addressed within an integrated framework.

Measures that can potentially be included within the balanced scorecard approach can be referred to under the term key performance indicators that may include innovative and critical new measures. Such measures must be identified by management as well as regularly evaluated and also potentially adapted to changing circumstances (Schmutte, 2007). Such measures shall be explored in more detail in paragraph 2.2.3 after discussion the measurement of effectiveness and efficiency.

2.2.1   Measuring effectiveness of risk management

Effectiveness has been described above in the introductory remarks to this paragraph. The notion of effectiveness basically describes the claim onto management to do the right things instead of doing the things right, which is the hallmark of efficiency. Therefore, effectiveness must be even be considered as primary to efficiency. This is also evident within the COSO ERM framework. The philosophy behind this framework is to achieve value for the group of stakeholders relevant to the organization. This goal is therefore deeply related to the strategy of the firm and its objectives in alignment to the risk appetite and the respective decisions. Reducing risks from undertakings while striving for growth opportunities and deploying the firm's capital accordingly are key aspects in this regard (COSO, 2004).

Fundamental to this objective is the optimal selection of available business opportunities in comparison to other potential ways to capital allocation. A measure to obtain such a comparison is the Economic Value Added (EVA) that compares different investment opportunities within a firm to alternative investment opportunities. The concept of the EVA hereby demands for management to choose the best possible investment option by explicitly considering the opportunity cost of capital in the investment decision making process. This measure can be applied across divisions of a company (Schmutte, 2007). Hereby the element of risk must be understood in the light of all potential opportunities available to choose from. If a company for example regularly chooses second best investment options, competitors that are better in the evaluation of business opportunities may get stronger which in turn increases the general risk of the company. The co-founder of the technology firm Apple describes this in relationship to the role of focus within innovation, where it is necessary to "saying no to 1,000 things" (CNN, 2016).

As such, an ERM can be considered as a control system for strategic management, whereby activities of a value-based approach is fundamental to its nature and tools like the balanced scorecard are useful to apply (Mikes, 2009). Integrating the ERM with business planning is recommended for all business units to enhance resource allocation and to focus on the most critical aspects of risk. The types of relevant risks may vary across different companies, so the role of risk should be aligned with the fundamental business strategy of the respective organization (Fraser, Simkins, 2016).

As already mentioned, the concept of the balanced scorecard is thought to be of high relevance in determining strategic measures. It was originally intended as a tool to better measure company performance in the face of critique of existing performance measurement systems that generally focused either on financial or on operating metrics (Kaplan, Norton, 1992). As a result of that, the balanced scorecard integrated a diverse set of perspectives fundamental to the respective organization in four different dimensions or perspectives that include several metrics for measurement. Table 10 shows these dimensions together with relevant metrics for measurement in respective categories as applicable.

Table 10 Measures within the balanced scorecard

Perspective	Potential Measures
Financial	• Value: Share Price, Return on Capital Employed • Revenue: Revenue from new sources, customer profitability • Productivity: Operating cost per unit, asset utilization • Survive: Cash Flow
Customer	• New products: percentage of sales of proprietary products • Supply response: On-time delivery • Supplier: Key account market share, key account ranking • Other: Customer acquisition, retention, satisfaction
Internal Business	• Manufacturing: Unit cost, cycle time • Innovation: Plan vs. actual innovation time, number of innovations • Other: operational excellence, compliance to regulatory and environ-mental processes
Innovation and Learning	• Employee competencies • Technology • Corporate Culture

(Source: Own presentation in adaptation from Kaplan, R.S. and Norton, D.P., (1992), The balanced scorecard--Measures That Drive Performance. Harvard Business Review, 70(1), pp.71-79; Kaplan, R. S., Norton, D. P. (2000), Having Trouble with your strategy? Then Map it., Harvard Business Review, 78 (5), pp. 3-11)

The metrics shown in the table above are not meant to be understood as a set of all-inclusive metrics possible because there are a number of other criteria possible, which are for example mentioned by Kaplan, Norton (1992). In addition, the balanced scorecard should be adjusted to the respective firm or sector, comparable to the ERM to be of proper use. While some measures are of obvious and general nature and there-fore relevant to companies irrespective of their individual characteristics like for exam-ple the share price or the corporate culture, other measures that target the environ-ment may be of more relevance to certain industries like the aviation industry or oil & gas etc. when compared to sectors like healthcare, education etc.

The relevant question in this paper is the relation of metrics from the respective four perspectives in the balanced scorecard to the issue of risk and to the central no-tion of this paragraph that focusses on the measurement of effectiveness.

The topic of risk is inherent within all perspective. Financial risks can include a de-crease in revenue or an increase in costs, while from the perspective of the customer, risk may result from low quality customer services or products that fail to meet market demand. The operational aspect of the internal business perspective also entails no-tions of risk as ineffective production processes may lead to higher costs and lower

quality. Also, the perspective of learning is prone to fundamental business risks as learning entails the important aspect of employee qualifications and the corporate culture is fundamental to the understanding of quality inside an organization (Bright, Cooper, 1993) as well as to the implementation of quality management systems (Gimenez-Espin et al., 2012).

Aspects of effectiveness can also be observed when analyzing metrics from the balanced scorecard. Similar to the concept of the EVA, the concept of the Return on Capital Employed can be measured for different investment scenarios to provide management with a better information basis for decision making with regard to foster effectiveness inside the organization. Besides these metrics mentioned so far, a number of other metrics can also be included within an ERM system. Mike (2009) mentions several metrics that are applied and relevant for banks. These include the metric of value-at-risk that measures the unanticipated loss that is derived from the loss distribution of different risk types and which can be applied for credit losses, market losses or operational losses. This metric may also be used to compare different alternatives in order to enhance the effectives within organizational risk management. The economic capital or economic risk capital is another measure. It is used to calculate the amount of capital needed to cover liabilities in the case of unexpected losses from market, credit or operational as well as insurance losses (Mikes, 2009). Related to effectiveness, economic risk capital may be used to assist in the comparison of different alternatives or environments in order for management to take this information into account when formulating the strategy of the institution. As such, the concept of economic capital can be applied to compare and aggregate risks and to limit the capacity for risks of relevant business initiatives or profit centers to serve as tool of setting limits and control (Mikes, 2009).

As effectiveness is fundamentally dependent on the context the organization is operating in because of its deep relation to strategy formulation, variables that are surrounding the organization are of high interest and should be critically analyzed related to their impact on choosing the best course of strategic action. Gordon et al. (2009) provide a framework of such contextual variables that shall be considered within an ERM systems. The following figure (29) shows these variables form their study:

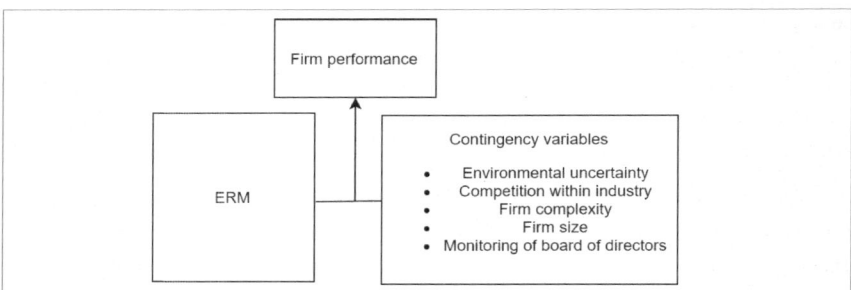

Figure 29 Contextual variables relevant for matching firm performance and enterprise risk management

(Source: own, based on Gordon, L.A., Loeb, M.P., Tseng, C-Y. (2009), Enterprise risk management and firm performance: A contingency perspective, J. Account. Public Policy, 28, pp. 301-327)

Similar to what was pointed out to be relevant for the balanced scorecard is also be of relevance in the study of Gordon et al. (2009). This is the fact that measures potentially relevant for use in measuring the effectiveness of strategy in the face of organizational uncertainty shall be carefully selected taking the relevant environment as well as the specific characteristics of the firm and the sector into account.

2.2.2   Measuring efficiency of risk management

As described above, the notion of efficiency relates to doing the things right, where it is generally irrelevant whether these things are effective. Therefore, efficiency relates to a higher degree on the internal side of the organization and is, for example relevant for designing processes. However, efficiency and effectiveness cannot be clearly separated because of the interaction between both concepts. As mentioned by Kaplan, Norton (2000), faster process-cycle times or enhanced capabilities of employees can lead to an increase in revenue. If the company can anticipate such an increase in efficiency, it is possible that this may influence investment decision-making, hereby showing an impact on the effectiveness.

Examples for concrete metrics to use within the balanced scorecard approach that also relate to the aspect of efficiency can be found in table 10. These include amongst others, the operating cost per unit that can be improved by making the process more efficient or the on-time delivery of supply. However, the aspect of risk is relevant when looking at the areas these metrics target. For example, the decrease in the time to delivery may increase the risk to the business in case of interruptions. As the risk of supply interruptions is currently evaluated as a critical concern amongst businesses worldwide (Kumar et al., 2018) emphasizing the relevance of this problem.

Risks from operations are manifold and the operational risk is regarded as the most challenging kind of risk to quantify and manage. Within the banking sector, operational risk is addressed by banking regulations under the Basel II norms, hereby providing incentives to banks in their risk modelling for operational risks specifically. However, the large majority of institutions is still in the early stages of establishing relevant databases and to learn about operational risks. Frequently, only the most commonly observed operational risks are possible to get modelled and hereby measured (Mikes, 2009). The sheer number of risk detected may cause problems in this regard. Fraser & Simkins (2016) provide the example of a company that had a total number of 700 different risks detected, which were then recorded within a risk register and subsequently updated. However, this approach is being considered as impractical and as an administrative burden and not as a relevant and practical approach in order to assist management in the decision-making process. The authors conclude that a total of 10 to 20 risk factors that are being assessed as the most relevant to the company should be monitored and reported upon.

Renault et al. (2016) provide a short literature review on the drivers and obstacles to ERM implementation within the construction sector. Similar to the results from Mikes (2009) they report frequent problems in relation to the difficulties of quantifying the risks as well as problems in relation to the lack of reliable and qualitative data as well as access restriction and proper risk language. Furthermore, they evaluate ERM implementation as positive and call for management to evaluate the efficiency of the metrics employed.

Potential ways to improve this current situation in relation to the modelling and measurement of risks shall be subject to further evaluation in the next paragraph discussing key performance indicators. Remarks on the operationalization of measurement are also being provided by Fraser & Simkins (2016) who propose the categorization of risks for 1) the velocity and 2) their resilience. They also propose the use of a risk calendar. Velocity hereby describes the interval between the event and the peak impact of this event to the business and resilience contains the ability to detect and employ respective resources and plans as well as the availability of such resources. The risk calendar keeps track of important events that may positively or negatively affect the organization in the future and shows potential impacts that may be addressed by management.

2.2.3   Key performance indicators within enterprise risk management

Key performance indicators (KPIs) are measuring the performance of an organization in relation to its objectives in order to enable corrective actions in case of deviations observed. To support decision makers with relevant information, these indicators
need to be regularly checked and evaluated to consequently target the relevant aspects they are intended to measure and also be applied within an integrated setting
instead of a manual integration that is frequently observed (Schmutte, 2007; Mate,
2017). The following figure 30 shows different ways to measure performance within
the dimension of their complexity and importance. As can be seen, KPIs themselves
are neither important nor quite complex. However, frameworks that combine them
are very important but also challenging in terms of their complexity. Key performance
indicators are not useful on a stand-alone basis. Tubis & Werbińska-Wojciechowska
(2017) provide an example of KPIs that are used at transportation companies that include such metrics like turnover rate, profitability of connections, global cost of business activity, maintenance cost per vehicle or the average takings per connection. In
an isolated consideration, these indicators may not be improper to use, given the sector in question. However, they generally

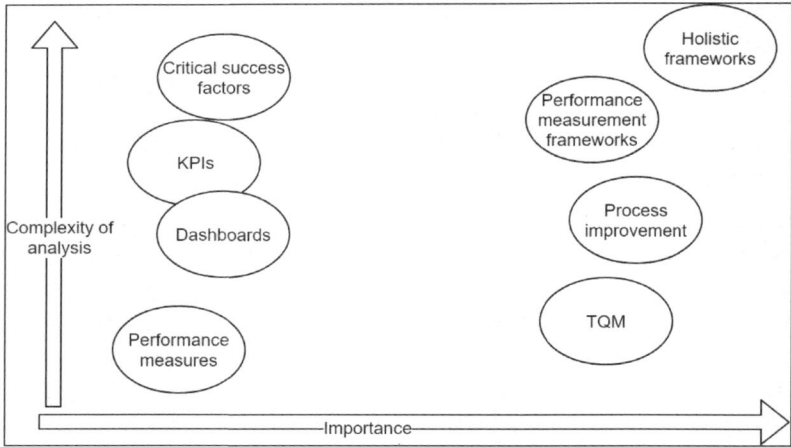

**Figure 30 Different ways to measure performance across the dimensions of complexity and im-
portance**

(Source: own presentation based on Matthews, J.R. (2011), Assessing Organizational Effectiveness: The
Role of Performance Measures, The Library Quarterly: Information, Community, Policy, 81 (1), pp. 83-
110)

lack the level of efficiency, logistics and processes and are therefore not suited for management to base their decision on. The authors propose the use of a number of KPIs within the balanced scorecard in order to align the individual indicators with the detailed objectives of the firm in order to assist management. The list of metrics shows clearly the relevance for performance and risk as well. This is evident for the KPI "punctuality". While a company that scores low on this KPI can improve performance and potentially profitability by being more punctual, a company that already scores high must consider this KPI more in a typical risk-based view in the sense that a decrease in punctuality may lead to a loss of confidence amongst customers. For example, the famous Shinkansen train measures the punctuality in seconds and is 100 percent on time when measured in French standards, while the French TGV train is way ahead from such high scores (Japan Today, 2015). This example clearly shows the dual side of KPIs when looked at from a perspective of performance and risk.

In order for KPIs to be successfully applied within an ERM system, they should be clearly evaluated in relation to their relevance to risk management (Wisutteewong, Rompho, 2015). That also contains the influence of the individual industry sector as mentioned in paragraph in relation to the integration of ISO norms for respective sectors and other topic addressed by these standards. Key performance indicators must therefore be tailored to the organization as their relevance differs across them (Matthews, 2011).

Summary and outlook to discussion

Measurement is central to managing risk within organizations as it relates to central aspects of potential losses as well as to performance. This chapter provided a review on the measurement of effectiveness as well as to efficiency while also addressing the topic of KPIs that can be used to measure specific aspects relevant to the business and combined to form a more integrated approach of managing risk and increasing performance. Hereby, the concept of the balanced scorecard was discussed specifically and the usefulness of this approach to deal with the issues of effectiveness and efficiency had been pointed out.

As has been shown, effectiveness should be measured and evaluated, taking contextual variables and alternative in the form of opportunity costs into account. There are financial measures like the EVA available that can be used to judge alternative in-vestment opportunities and such measures are of a more general nature and need not be customized to the respective industry.

Efficiency on the other hand is more related to the internal side of the business, e.g. to processes. As such, it is necessary to customize relevant measures to the indus-try segment in order to best assess relevant factors for risk and performance. The mod-elling of such operational metrics and risk has been shown to be more challenging due to their size and data availability issues. This problem is also highly relevant for the concept of the key performance indicators that need to be carefully selected and up-dated.

The next chapters will shed some more light on these issues as maturity models, the role of risk culture and the influence of developments in the analysis of data will be discussed.

2.2.4   Discussing on the problems of measuring risk and performance within enter-prise risk management frameworks

This chapter aims to provide some more general and current remarks on issues related to the measuring of risk and performance inside ERM systems used to manage organizational risk across organizations in general.

Within the framework of the ISO 31000, risk management shall be integrated into the totality of the systems applied within any organization. This includes overall gov-ernance, planning and strategy, management, reporting and policies as well as values and organizational culture. The topic of risk shall be given high priority. Strong commit-ment is needed at the level of leadership as well as on other levels to implement such a risk policy framework (Barafort et al., 2017). In this sense, measuring risk as well as performance must be seen from the individual area of application within the organiza-tion as has been shown within the thesis with regards to customization of KPIs and the inclusion of industry specifics. Furthermore, influences are coming from a wide field that includes soft criteria like the organizational culture mentioned above.

For risk management systems to work well, the maturity of these systems needs to be considerd as the aspect of maturity may have consequences for the relevant topics of efficiency and effectiveness, which are relevant within this paper. There are factors driving the maturity of risk management systems that can and should be considered by organizations aiming to increase performance and decrease risk. Reports issued from management to a board

Figure 31 Maturity level of enterprise risk management

(Source: Own presentation in relation to Oliva, F.L. (2016), A maturity model for enterprise risk management, Int. J. Production Economics, 173, pp. 66-79)

level committee that contain the top risk exposures are advancing the maturity as do clearly articulated risk appetite statements that are integrated in the strategic plan of the organization.

In addition, formal training of senior management and the creation of risk committees at the management level also strongly correlate with ERM maturity (Beasley, 2006).

A relevant aspect to include into this topic are so-called maturity models that are able to compare different sets of integrated management systems and that show the relative stage of evolution for such systems. Domingues et al. (2016) provide such a maturity model that consists of six different maturity levels which can be applied across different contexts as well as companies.

However, the topic of risk management is only a part of such a maturity model for integrated management systems if the maturity model is not specified to explicitly relate to risk management. Yeo, Ren (2009) provide such a specified maturity model in the context of Complex Product Systems which they call risk management Capability Maturity Model. Another maturity model is proposed by Oliva (2016) which is shown in figure 31.

The different levels in the model of Oliva (2016) show the maturity or the sophistication of the ERM applied (see figure 31). This ranges from a low level with little sophistication and structure to a systematic level with the highest sophistication that is characterize by its conscious, organized and transparent design. In between is the contingency level where there is some general awareness of risks, the structural level that contains a more intensive application of available tools and methods and the participative level where a general high level of awareness can be observed and communication is integral and present as is the participation of employees (Oliva, 2016). The model clearly shows the relevance of the people and the commitment of leadership and employees necessary for an ERM to be of use to manage organizational risk that is part of the COSO-ERM framework (COSO, 2004).

2.2.5 Current tendencies within the theory and practice of enterprise risk management

The last chapter aims to provide some outlook and description of current development within the large field of ERM systems. As has been shown already, there is an extensive body of issues relevant to this field, so the outlook does not aim to be encompassing but should try to give an indication on some actual topics of interest.

The ISO 31000 norm is constantly being revised and there is a discussion that involves the meaning and definition of risk in an international environment as the understanding differs across countries. There are currently other discussions that relate to the suggestion to transform the ISO 31000 into a general management standard (Barafort et al., 2017).

The discussion on the understanding of risk in general revolves around the question whether the notion of risk shall include opportunities or if it shall focus on the negative deviations. For example, in the UK, the understanding of risk generally includes the opportunity aspect while in France, risk is generally viewed for the aspect of danger or prevention, which can also be observed in Germany (Barafort et al., 2017). This is a fundamental issue for the understanding and managing of uncertain future events relevant to the organization. This shows the relevance of culture within the management of organizational risk. The consulting firm McKinsey is mentioning the term "risk culture", which seems to be relevant to this aspect. It can be described as the "norms of behavior for individuals and groups within an organization that determine the collective ability to identify and understand, openly discuss and act on the organization's current and future risks" (McKinsey, 2016). As such, cultural characteristics are of fundamental importance.

Besides these human and soft factors that are relevant to consider, there are other more technical issues of high relevance. As mentioned in the paper, the balanced scorecard is useful to apply as a tool for measuring and subsequently managing performance. This approach had been characterized as flexible and in the need to adapt to the industry segment and current external forces that should be identified and considered by management. Currently, there are suggestions in the academic literature to integrate a number of important factors. These include the aspect of sustainability within the balanced scorecard. Concretely, sustainability entails the consideration of environmental and social aspects in the organization's objectives in a systematic way (Hansen & Schaltegger, 2012; Asif et al., 2011).

To systematically integrate such perspectives, data needs to identified and respective measures or key performance indicators must be defined and implemented. However, companies are facing problems to operationalize and to measure corporate social activities well (Kalender & Vayvay, 2016). This is causing problems with regards to firms in practice and to researchers as well because of data availability issues. Hansen & Schaltegger (2012) suggest to compile large lists of environmental and social criteria or indicators and to address the impact level for measurement. They suggest to extend the usually small measurement period and to obtain third party support.

Kucukaltan et al. (2016) suggest to incorporate other non-financial aspects within the balanced scorecard approach to target the relevance of several stakeholders relevant to the organization for firms in the Turkish logistics industry. They mention the role of social media usage for brand building as well as a number of other items like government satisfaction, community satisfaction or non-government organization satisfaction. It seems to be that these specific suggestions to Turkish firms in the logistics industry may also be relevant for other countries and sectors to consider. However, the relevance is probably not equal and shall differ across organizations.

The current environment is characterized by a strong inflow and importance of data and an increased role of technology and connectivity that is generally affecting the business environment. Therefore, ways to use new technologies to incorporate more data into the measurement of performance and risk may seem useful to investigate. This is especially useful given the role of individual characteristics of firms and industry sectors and the need for customization of ERM systems. Peral et al. (2017) propose the application of data mining techniques to find out which key performance indicators shall be used within organizations in order to best associate with the respective business goals. These techniques include for example the forecasting of relevant trends or the visualization of data correlations. The application of big data technologies that make such an application possible is currently regarded to bring a profound influence to business management and is considered to be a key technology (Raguseo, 2018).

3 Influence of integrated management systems on sustainable business processes

3.1 The relationship between sustainable business processes and integrated management systems

This part of this thesis is reviewing the current state of management systems and integrated management systems. Driven by current trends and forces, the application of management systems is of high interest, which raises questions related to their design and the relevant success factors for those systems.

The development experienced within the last years shows an increase in the role of quality management and an increase in the sophistication of relevant management systems. This sophistication is especially observable when it comes to the question of integration. As will be shown in this paper, there is a general trend observable that contains the integration of sub-concepts into larger management frameworks. An example, which will be discussed in more detail in this paper is the balanced scorecard that contains several metric relevant to a set of different areas of interest within a company.

In order for management systems to function well, several success factors need to be mentioned that influence these systems, hereby showing their relevance. Out of these aspects, the human element is of a special concern, which contains the influences of leadership, employees and the organizational culture. As will be shown, these influences are key to the workings of management systems today. As management systems need to react to decreases in innovation cycles and increases in demands from customers (Rothlauf, 2014), the role of measurement is of further relevance. This includes the measurement of effectiveness and efficiency by management systems in order to execute a useful strategy and create optimized sustainable operational processes. Other topics of interest include the discussion on differences in management systems due to differences in the relevant industry sector and geography as well as the role of certifications to achieve operational excellence and foster organizational performance as well as managing the relevant risks inherent to the business model.

The paper aims to include a variety of authors on the chosen subjects in order to show the current discussion in the field. However, the discussion can only touch the surface of the discussion due to the extensive field of literature and the high number of areas investigated.

© Springer Fachmedien Wiesbaden GmbH, part of Springer Nature 2019
J. Kopia, *Effective Implementation of Management Systems*, Sustainable Management, Wertschöpfung und Effizienz, https://doi.org/10.1007/978-3-658-26509-0_4

The following chapter provides an overview of the history of management systems and a description of some systems of relevance, including the role of ISO standards.

3.2 Sustainable business processes and integrated management systems

3.2.1   Overview of management systems

Motivated by increasing demands from forces like globalization, turbulent markets and ever-increasing complexity of products, the leadership of companies need to strengthen the structures and transparency of their organizations. Management systems are hereby considered as useful tools to provide such kind of stabilization. Their application can lead to continuous improvement of organizational processes which also includes aspects of a sustainable management. Management systems can therefore help increase profitability (Schlosske, 2017). This dynamic environment is expected to even intensify, forcing companies to recognize important trends and developments early in order to use them to fulfill their objectives (Rothlauf, 2014). There are currently six trends that are shaping the environment of companies, which are shown in figure 32. These trends shall be considered when analyzing and evaluating management systems.

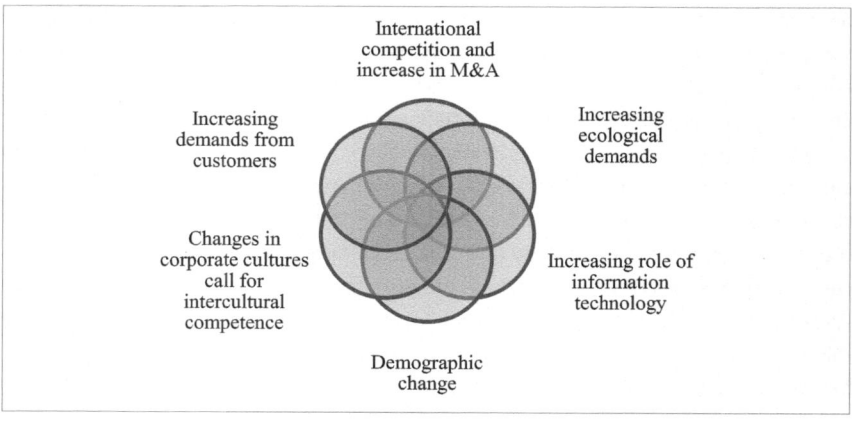

Figure 32 Six trends shaping business environment

(Source: Own presentation based on Rothlauf, J. (2014), Total Quality Management in Theorie und Praxis: Zum ganzheitlichen Unternehmensverständnis, 4th edition, Berlin: De Grypter)

Within the last couple of years, management discussion focused on a variety of isolated concepts. Key concepts hereby included lean management, Kaizen, benchmarking, Just-in-Time, Kanban, balanced scorecard as well as a number of additional concepts. These concepts had one thing in common: they either provided a sole focus on one area of interest, e.g. procurement, sustainable production processes, quality control etc. or they proclaimed an orientation on employees or on competitors that are considered as best in class. What has been lacking in that discussion was a comprehensive and thorough approach that combined all groups of actors relevant for the supply chain. One such system which shall be explained in more detail in this chapter is Total Quality Management (TQM). TQM provides a comprehensive approach to give answers to the demands of modern company leadership and it can hereby include important sub-concepts already mentioned, for example Benchmarking or Six Sigma etc. (Rothhaus, 2014).

Another important tool is the EFQM model. This model integrates a number of criteria to evaluate the maturity level of an organization. It does not relate to a single focus but covers the organization as a whole and hereby enables comparisons amongst different companies to find the best practice within a sector (Schlosske & Thieme, 2017). Companies applying the criteria of the EFQM model show better results in relation to their product quality, flexibility and innovative abilities (Lay et al., 2009).

The development and application of such management systems must be understood along the developments of quality management through history. Until 1950, quality control of products mainly consisted of finally checking the product produced and hereby evaluating whether the product passes the quality test or if the product should be disposed of or reworked on. Measures to improve quality were mostly absent. This method was costly with respect to time and resources. Increasingly, management recognized factors that are influencing product quality like packaging, storing etc. With an increase in competition that brought a strong focus on costs in the 1970s and 1980s, companies were forced to increase their efficiency. This development led to the emergence of norms for quality management like the ISO norms of the 9000 family that relate to processes within companies in order to improve the respective organization (Schlosske & Thieme, 2017).

Popular management systems like Total Quality Management or the EFQM model are going to be described in more detail below. In addition, the role of the ISO norms is going to be evaluated in the context of management systems and quality control.

Quality management systems can support company leadership significantly (Schlosske & Thieme, 2017). In this paragraph, the focus will be set on two important management systems, the Total Quality Management and the EFQM model. In addition, an overview of the role of the ISO norms will be given.

Total Quality Management (TQM)

Total Quality Management (TQM) is a process-related method of management that is focused on quality originally introduced to production facilities by E. Deming, J. Juran, A. Feigenbaum, and P. Crosby. It encompasses a wide range of elements within a company and aims at the improvement of internal processes as well as on establishing a superior product quality. As a concept to foster economic profitability, TQM serves as a tool to add value and to increase revenue and profitability by applying a customer-centered focus. There are two key assumptions behind this concept (Schwawel & Billing, 2018):

1. The improvement of process quality is going to decrease costs and increase productivity, and
2. The improvement of product quality will increase revenue and hereby the market share of the company.

Despite its focus on processes and products, TQM also recognized the influence of leadership and employees within the company, where direct and indirect effects are of importance. Hereby, knowledge management must be pursued, and resources must be dedicated to the people involved. As a tool for long-term success, TQM requires an adjustment of structure and processes in line with the TQM requirements (Schwawel & Billing, 2018). As mentioned in the introduction to this chapter, TQM can include sub-concepts that only focus on specific aspects of the value chain. These sub-concepts can improve TQM by allowing for the consideration of issues not yet covered by this concept. An example for this is employee satisfaction that may be of relevance for a continuous improvement. This is not covered by TQM but by the concept of the Balance Scorecard. Therefore, combining TQM with the Balance Scorecard approach can subsequently foster management objectives by improving company performance (Hoque, 2002). TQM uses eight elements illustrated in figure 33.

Figure 33 The eight elements of Total Quality Management

(Source: own elaboration based on EDUCBA, (2016), https://www.educba.com/the-8-crucial-tqm-elements/, accessed 08.07.2016)

Companies that aim to implement TQM can proceed by relying on three fundamental stages (Schwawel & Billing, 2018) that are shown below in figure 34.

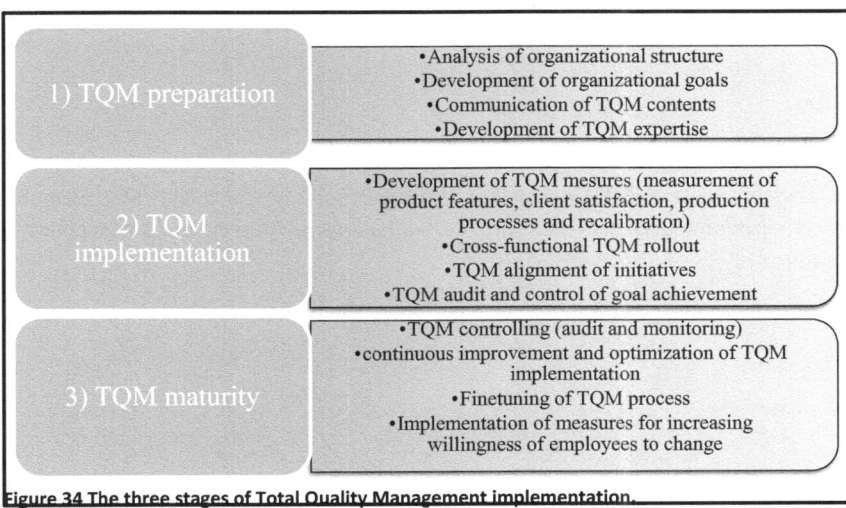

Figure 34 The three stages of Total Quality Management implementation.

(Source: Own presentation based on Schwawel, C. and Billing, F. (2018), Top 100 Management Tools, 6th edition, Wiesbaden: Springer Gabler)

TQM can be implemented using different approaches:

- The definition of quality teams or cycles
- Quality enhancing programs with zero defect rates
- Methods of quality control
- Frequent customer surveys and feedback
- Benchmarking
- Diverse QM-systems, such as ISO based management systems (ISO 9001)
- Continuous improvement programs

The concept of TQM is broad and cannot be described in its entirety in this paper. Of importance is the approach of Deming that encompasses a set of 14 criteria that essentially describe a strong goal orientation, a focus on quality and not necessarily on costs only, a commitment to improvement as well as a strong call to good leadership practices and employee involvement (Rothlauf, 2014). In addition to Deming, companies in Japan started to develop their own TQM-approach mainly driven by Kaoru Ishikawa (Ishikawa, 1985).

EFQM

The abbreviation EFQM stands for European Foundation for Quality Management, an organization founded in 1988 with it's headquarter in Brussels and partnerships in a number of

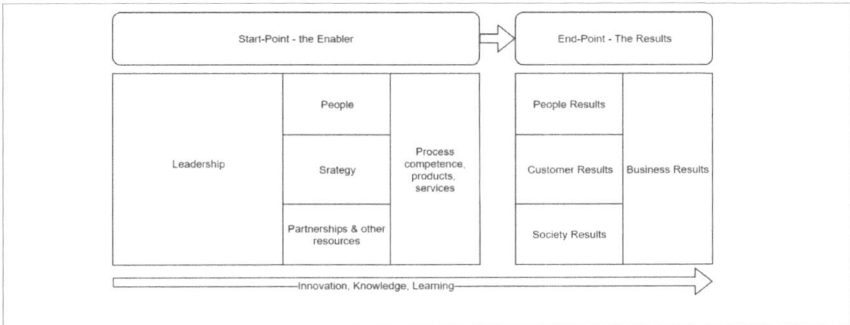

Figure 35 The EFQM Excellence model
(Source: own interpretation based on EFQM (2017), An Overview of the EFQM Excellence model, re-trieved: http://www.efqm.org/sites/default/files/overview_efqm_2013_v2_new_logo.pdf, 22.01. 2018.)

other countries. EFQM is a European institution, originally founded to increase com-petitiveness of European companies that is now promoting quality management. Key to this goal is the EFQM model that consists of 9 criteria and 32 sub criteria that can be applied to measure and hereby assess the maturity level of an organization. Currently 30.000 companies are using this tool. These companies are characterized by 1) good and sustainable results (in all required dimensions of a sustainable development), 2) high demands to its corporate culture, and 3) being a perceived role model for others (Schlosske & Thieme, 2017).

The 9 criteria mentioned, can be classified into the two segments of "enabler" and "results". Weights can be assigned to the criteria accordingly (Lay et al., 2009). The five "enabler" criteria show what needs to be developed while the four "results" criteria show the results of the organization in accordance to the strategic goals (EFQM, 2017). The model is shown in figure 35.

3.2.2   The role of international norms in integrated management systems

There is a variety of ISO norms related to management systems and quality control. Especially the ISO norms of the 9000 family of norms need to be mentioned here as these norms provide help and guidance since many years to establish and maintain quality within organizations (Schlosske & Thieme, 2017). The most central ISO norm related to quality management is ISO 9000. This norm encompasses the key foundations and terms and can be used as a practical guidance for ISO 9001 that relates to the requirements for the certification of the company's management system (Schlosske & Thieme, 2017). The following table 11 shows a number of key ISO norms relevant for this paper with a short description.

There seems to be a general alignment of the use of ISO audits and the use of quality

Table 11 Selection of important international standards

ISO Norm	Description
ISO 9000	Key foundations and terms of quality management (customer orientation, leadership, relationship management, improvement, process orientation etc.)
ISO 9001	Requirements for certifications of quality management systems
ISO 9004	Guidelines for quality management systems that surpass the requirements of ISO 9000
ISO 19011	Guidelines for proper execution of audits
ISO 14001	Criteria for environmental management systems
ISO 50001	Criteria for efficient use of energy in order to decrease costs and foster the conservation of resources
ISO 27001	Requirements for security of information management systems

(Sources: Schlosske & A., Thieme, P. (2017), Qualitätsmanagementsysteme, in: Spath, D., Westkämper, E., Bullinger, H.-J., Warnecke, H.-H. (eds), Neue Entwicklungen in der Unternehmensorganisation. Berlin Heidelberg: Springer; ISO 50001 Energy management, retrieved, https://www.iso.org/iso-50001-energy-management.html, ISO 14000 family – Environmental management, https://www. iso.org/iso-14001-environmental-management.html, ISO/IEC 27000 family – Information security management systems, https://www.iso.org/isoiec-27001-information-security.html, 22.01.2018)

management systems. For example, the ratio of companies that had an environmental audit in line with DIN ISO 14001 is much higher amongst companies that apply the EFQM model than other firms that do not use EFQM (Lay et al., 2009). The ISO norms can also be included in the TQM framework. Here, a mayor goal may be to obtain the certification in line with ISO 9001 (Schwawel & Billing, 2018). ISO norms usually (this is no requirement anymore) follow a PDCA-cycle (Plan-Do-Check-Act) which can be seen in figure 36 and originated in 1987 as

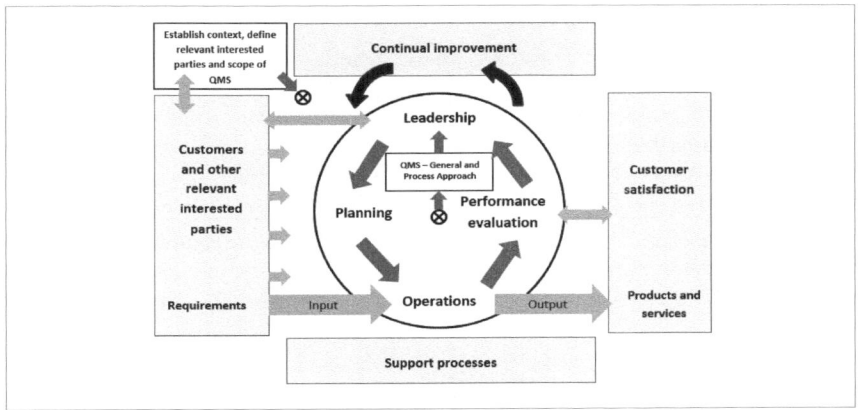

Figure 36 The Plan-Do-Check-Act-cycle in international management systems

(Source: ISO/DIN 9001(en), (2015), https://www.iso.org/obp/ui/#iso:std:iso:9001:dis:ed-5:v1:en , accessed 27/10/2016)

the year the ISO (International Organization for Standardization) was established. This standard had their origins in the BS 5179 (British Standard published by the British Standards Institute, BSI). There is a globally operating business to certify management systems, especially ISO in the context of ISO standards. There are official certification bodies which are eligible to perform audits at companies to certify an ISO based management system. Similar to other management system, ISO management systems focus on a continuous improvement process and a risk-based process which should identify risks and opportunities as early as possible in order to define measures to react effectively and efficiently. In contrast to ISO 9001 where official documents and best practice in the form of requirements exist, does EFQM focus on "excellence" which is self-assessed by the companies itself. In order to successfully certify according to an ISO based management system, the requirements defined in the high-level structure (see table 12) have to be fulfilled (see also 3.3.4).

Most ISO standards are based on a high-level structure (HSL or Annex SL) which makes it easier to use more than one management system within a company (see table 12). Several aspects within that structure are similar in each system and must therefore only be implemented once. Each chapter of the HLS has a specific and different focus within each management system.

Table 12 The high-level structure of international management systems

Main part	Detailed part
1. Scope	6. Planning
2. Normative references	7. Support
3. Terms and definitions	8. Operation
4. Context of the organization	9. Performance evaluation
5. Leadership	10. Improvement

(Source: own elaboration based on ISO HLS, (2015), http://www.iso.org/iso/home/standards/management-standards/mss-list.htm, accessed 08/08/2016)

3.2.3 Comprising the study of the relationship between sustainable business processes and management systems

Shaped by current megatrends, management systems seem to be of more relevance than ever. These systems can be used to evaluate and even improve product quality and processes and hereby achieving company objectives. This current situation has been developed, as has been shown, out of a historical quest for improvements of product quality that has shaped and influences many of the processes related to that.

Popular management systems that aim to combine some of the existing and isolated features relevant to the supply chain of the company have been shortly introduced and discussed. These include the TQM and the EFQM. In addition, the relevance of the ISO norms has also been described as they have the potential to be included within management systems for providing a more comprehensive approach.

The general purpose of management systems is to improve products, services as well as to increase the efficiency of internal processes. However, there are not only questions related to efficiency that are relevant to the company. There are also questions in connection to the effectiveness. Hereby, effectiveness shall be understood as a measure for long-term planning and acting. This basically includes a strategic approach related to the decision of what should be done. Efficiency on the other hand relates more to the issue of how things should be done properly and in a more short-term fashion (Bea, Haas, 2016). This two-fold way is showing in the EFQM model, where the "enablers" encompass for example strategy and leadership as being relevant for targeting effectiveness and processes, products & services that are in a material way related to the impact of efficiency.

The success factors of management systems will be discussed in the next chapter. It should be interpreted in context of their relevance to achieving the company's objective of increasing value by targeting effectiveness and efficiency by characterizing its integrative nature. This discussion shall serve to provide more insight into the relevant details of the more general frameworks analyzed and described in this chapter.

3.3 Influence factors for performance in integrated management systems

3.3.1   The balanced scorecard and the execution premium as strategic link

As companies use management systems and systems become integrated, a general complexity of those systems is to be expected. Furthermore, as has been shown in the introductory remarks of the last chapter, current mega trends are very much influencing the business environment and management should be ready for this challenge by using properly adjusted management systems as support devices to make their companies effective and efficient.

To achieve these goals, several success factors should be evaluated. These include the more human element of leadership, corporate culture and the influence of employees as well as more technical issues related to measurement or differences in industry segments as well as geography. Furthermore, the role of certifications of management systems should be described and analyzed critically.

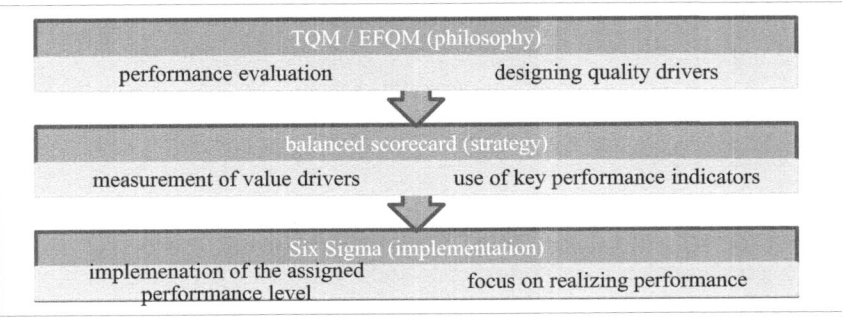

Figure 37 Interlinkage of TQM / EFQM with BSC and Six Sigma

(Source: Own presentation based on Schmutte, A. M. (2007), Six Sigma im Business Excellence Prozess – Wertorientierte Unternehmensführung mit balanced scorecard, EFQM und Six Sigma bei Siemens, in: Töpfer, A. (eds), Six Sigma – Konzeption und Erfolgsbeispiele für praktizierte Null-Fehler-Qualität. 4th edition, Berlin Heidelberg New York: Springer, pp. 384-396)

As mentioned in chapter 3.1.1 of this paper, several sub-concepts or sub-systems can be integrated within TQM. Out of many possible sub-systems that can be thought off, two shall be mentioned as of having a high relevance. These are the concepts of Six Sigma and the balanced scorecard. Figure 37 shows the interlinkage of these concepts.

Hereby, the balanced scorecard can help the company to operationalize the business strategy by focusing on the relevant drivers of value that are specific to the company. This is being done by dedicating resources and by prioritizing the measures that are being planned. A consequent measurement is hereby necessary for managing increase and improvement of performance. In contrast to the balanced scorecard, Six Sigma is characterized by a strict concentration on the implementation side. By providing concrete goals and milestones, a realization of the level of value that is originally targeted is intended (Töpfer, 2007). This interlinkage between the management system and the strategy is highlighted by the research of Kaplan and Norton (2004) who suggested to create a "strategic management system". They called their solution "Strategic Map" and connect strategic elements with the performance measurement aspect using the balanced scorecard. Management systems operate on the business process level in various business units. This strategic mapping will help to create synergies and transparency within the organization. Generally, the balanced scorecard was a matter of analyses in many studies (Speckbacher et al., 2003; Assiri et al., 2006; Chi & Hsu-Feng, 2011; Habidin et al., 2012; Madsen, 2014; Braam, 2012; Madsen et al., 2015), most of them confirm the benefits of this method. Capelo & Ferreira (2009) concluded that BSC creates a mental business models "that resemble reality, enabling them to make good decisions". De Geuser et al. (2009) also confirms the alignment of processes, competences, and services including business units by making strategy a continuous process. Besides strategic map there is another important link to be highlighted. The "Execution Premium" suggested by Kaplan & Norton (2008) in the same context implements a cyclic approach which orders the strategic alignment time-wise. It consists of six stages:

1. Development of the strategy with 3 inputs: internal context, external context, existing strategy.
2. Planning the strategy. This step involved the actual development of the BSC (individually for each organization) and the Strategy Map.
3. Alignment of the organization with its strategy.
4. Planning of the necessary operations. This also includes a financial perspective.
5. Monitoring of the results and the learning and knowledge perspective.

6. Continuously improvement by testing of the results. If results are not positive or in disharmony with the set strategy, change of the results by adapting the operational procedures – returning to step 1, or 4 respectively.

It can be summarized that the use of an evaluation system, such as the balanced scorecard, and a strategic link in regards to the use of a management system are vital components for organizations. In this thesis, a recourse to these concepts will be made with a specific emphasis on the concept of the balanced scorecard with regard to its role in measuring performance.

3.3.2 The contribution of leadership, organizational culture and influence of employees

Leadership is having a central role within the topic of management systems. This is relevant for example in the case of TQM. Here, the stage in the development of the TQM contain an increase in the role of leadership. Sustaining quality within a company is not only relevant to specialists and isolated by an only focus on the product but with an increase in the maturity of the TQM system, quality issues are being characterized by a more visionary and pragmatic approach pursed by management (Rothlauf, 2014). Also, within the EFQM model, leadership is one of the "enabler" criteria and can therefore considered to be of a central importance. Leadership with in the EFQM model is ideally described as shaping the future and make things happen by using a flexible and enabling approach for sustained success of the organization while simultaneously complying to values and ethics at all times (EFQM, 2017).

However, leadership is not only relevant for the superordinate concepts of TQM and EFQM but also for the sub-concepts as well. For example, Six Sigma requires management to have specific competencies in order to lead continuous improvements of processes successfully. At Siemens, leadership is required to 1) identify and select projects for improvement, 2) assign resources and communication structures needed, and 3) evaluate and assess progress within organizations (Kleemann et al., 2007). Leadership training is applied at Siemens and implemented at each division of the company. Hereby, an integrated understanding of the interrelations of EFQM, balanced scorecard and Six Sigma should be developed. Checklists and question catalogues are used (Schmutte, 2007). This example shows two issues of relevance for this paper. First, the critical role of leadership for management systems to manage effectively and second, the fact that sub-concepts of a wide variety serve to design a company-wide integrated management system.

In addition to the role of leadership, the organizational culture is of further relevance for the management of quality as seen from a standpoint of total quality management. Hereby the culture determines the view of what is understood by the term "quality" and how it is interpreted within the respective organization (Bright, Cooper, 1993). Organizational culture is in this respect regarded as a key element relevant for the implementation of TQM (Gimenez-Espin et al., 2012).

Having stated that organizational culture is a relevant factor for the management of quality and respective systems of management, it should be examined what is understood by the concept of organizational culture and which aspects of organizational culture are fostering these processes or are detrimental to their success. Considering this aspect, the concept of organizational culture doesn't seem to be a concept with a clear scientific consensus because it's high fragmentation (Yildiz, 2014; Bright, Cooper, 1993). Some authors even assume that the concept is impossible to define unambiguously (Lapina et al., 2015).

Organizational culture is generally considered as encompassing the general pattern of beliefs, behavior as well as values that are shared by the members of the organization (Bright, Cooper, 1993; Lapina et al., 2015). As such a concept does not only contain the visible characteristics like the layout or design of the organizations offices or its headquarter but also other invisible elements like rituals, symbols, language etc., which are relevant for shaping attitude, communication and behavior. These individual factors are in addition unique to the respective organization (Yildiz, 2014), which makes the analysis on their impact on issues of quality management systems even more challenging.

Gimenez-Espin et al. (2012) show on the basis of their analysis of 451 Spanish companies that companies that adhere to the beliefs and values of the clan and the adhocracy culture are generally promoting a quality orientation and hereby increasing their business performance. This result coincides with their review of the relevant literature. A clan culture hereby includes, amongst others, employee engagement, internal guidance and senior management support while an adhocratic culture is characterized by continuous innovation, an orientation towards customer needs, management by facts etc. (Gimenez-Espin et al., 2012; Lagrosen, 2003).

In addition to that, by commencing international activities, the environment the company is dealing with becomes ever more diverse and complex and intercultural competencies are required because of the influences from people with a different cultural background and a divergent set of thinking and acting (Rothlauf, 2014). These differences in cultural norms manifest themselves in a unique approach of dealing with risk and chances (Romeike, 2018).

However, it is not mandatory that culture is shaping the understanding and role of quality management within a specific organization. It is also possible that the implementation and application of tools like TQM is changing the culture which in turn brings more participation in the teams. As such, management and employees are considered to have a strong influence on building the organizational culture (Yildiz, 2014). This was also shown above in the critical role of leadership related to the compliance to ethics within the framework of the EFQM. The influence of employees as a success factor for management systems shall be evaluated in the next paragraph of this paper.

As shown above, employees are considered to be of influence for the organizational culture, which in turn influences the understanding and the perceived importance of quality management. As such, employees should be considered as vital success factors for the mentioned aspects of management systems, for example regarding their knowledge of internal processes, ways of communication etc. Considering the importance of employees in achieving the organization's objectives, it should be asked what factors are influencing performance, satisfaction and commitment. These factors are key to the company culture and should be recognized by management (Lund, 2003).

Companies employing the EFQM model seem to give employees a greater importance. Empirical data show that companies using this model are regularly assessing employee satisfaction und are measuring respective indicators. In contrast to other companies, these companies stand out with a higher ratio of applying such measures. Job satisfaction in these organizations is much higher while sickness levels are lower, albeit only marginally (Lay et al., 2009). An increase in employee satisfaction after the implementation of TQM has also been observed by Buch & Rivers (2001).

Within the TQM, an orientation to employees is considered as a basic element in order to increase the capacity of employees for finding solutions and creative insights. This requires a set of measures for selecting, choosing and developing employees and to encourage them to competently apply their skills within the organization. Hereby, effective communication channels are also being needed (Rothlauf, 2014). Therefore, the role of leadership is considered as vital for fostering employee development as employees who are perceiving management as more committed and supportive do also perceive the TQM values as being more integrated within the culture of the organization (Buch & Rivers, 2001).

The role of employees, leadership and culture seems to be interrelated to a high degree, whereby the corporate cultures of adhocracy and clan cultures seem to benefit quality management systems the most in contrast to other cultures like the market culture and the hierarchy culture (Lund, 2003; Gimenez-Espin et al., 2012). The following table 13 shows the corporate cultures mentioned and shows their key characteristics:

Table 13 Characteristics of different corporate cultures

	Clan culture	Adhocracy culture	Hierarchy culture	Market culture
Attributes	Participation and team work, sense of family	Creativity and entrepreneurial approach	Uniformity, role and regulations	Competitiveness, goal achievement
Leadership style	Mentor, parent-figure	Innovator, risk taker, entrepreneur	Administrator, coordinator	Achievement-oriented and decisive
Bonding	Tradition, loyality	Flexibility, risk	Rules, policies, procedures	Competition, production
Strategic emphasis	Commitment, morale	Innovation, growth	Stability, predictability	Market superiority, competitive advantage
Characterization	Internal maintenance coupled with flexibility	Competition and differentiation coupled with flexibility	Internal maintenance, control, order	Competition and differentiation coupled with control and order

(Source: Own presentation based on Lund, D.B. (2003), Organizational culture and job satisfaction, Journal of Business & Industrial Marketing, 18 (3), pp.219-236)

3.3.3   The issue of measurement of success in the context of management systems

This paragraph relates to the measurement of the success of management systems. As mentioned in chapter 3.2.1 of this paper, the management system TQM centers on either a decrease in costs or an increase in productivity as well as on increasing overall profitability indicated by an increase in revenue and market share. So, the issue of measurement should center on these indicators and show the impact of the management systems applied within the organization.

The fundamental approach behind this topic of measurement is the management approach that is driven by facts, which is integrated within the adhocratic culture (Lagrosen, Lagrosen, 2003) and, as shown above, is having a positive influence in the sense that it fosters quality management within organizations. Measurement of success is therefore considered to be key to the achievement of a value-based management. This method should evaluate every division of a company and align it with fostering shareholder value. One method of measuring such a value-based contribution is the Economic Value-Added approach which evaluates the results of a division in relation to their opportunity costs and can serve as a fundamental instrument for measuring and steering the company in the right direction (Schmutte, 2007).

However, management systems like the TQM relate to the aspect of efficiency as well as to effectiveness. This has also been pointed out in paragraph 3.2.3 in relation to the EFQM model. Therefore, measurement should center on those two aspects in order to provide the value intended. One such approach is the balanced scorecard, which provides a framework to select several performance measures in order to supplement some more traditional financial measures of success and also operating measures of relevance to the company or organization like customer satisfaction, learning or measures with regard to internal processes (Banker et al., 2004). The balanced scorecard can therefore be assessed as being flexible in the integration of potentially new measures that can be integrated and tailored to the specific business model. These can include critical new measures that can be summarized by the term key performance indicators. These indicators need to be identified, regularly evaluated and potentially adapted (Schmutte, 2007). Furthermore, as businesses need to adapt and change through time, the balanced scorecard is of use because it can provide relevant measures of learning and growth to evaluate and drive continuous improvement (Banker et al., 2004).

Critical to the functioning of the balanced scorecard as a tool for strategy execution is the way of communication from senior management to lower-level employees (see chapter 2.2.1). Within the four BSC-perspectives, several individual metrics of measurement can be applied which include some more general ratios and measures proposed by Kaplan, Norton (2000). These can include, amongst others, customer profitability or operating costs per unit for the financial perspective and customer acquisition, retention and satisfaction for the customer perspective as well as some other general metrics for the perspectives of internal processes as well as for learning and growth. However, as will be shown in the next paragraph 3.3.4, there are individual metrics or key performance indicators proposes for certain industry sectors. Examples include Dincer et al. (2017) and Tubis, Werbińska-Wojciechowska (2017) that provide individual measures for the aerospace sector.

The relevance of the individual metrics depends on the sector or the individual business model. Hereby, the real value of measuring performance within an organization by relying on metrics is the alignment of the performance measures with the goals, visions and objectives of that organization. Hereby, it is irrelevant, whether the metrics can be easily collected or hard to obtain (Matthews, 2011). Therefore, it is important to identify the role of the measurement in its context. This also involves the industry and size of the specific sector.

3.3.4 Differences within industrial segments and their geographical position

As TQM practices have been applied in different kinds of organizations, it seems relevant to investigate whether those practices differ in relation to a variety of industry segments. While TQM practices are generally contributing to the performance within organizations, the application of TQM applications has been reported to differ across sectors. Panuwatwanich & Nguyen (2017) mention several examples in this regard. According to the studies mentioned by these authors, TQM serves as a successful management philosophy in the sectors of manufacturing and service but its benefits to the construction sector is not yet clear. In addition, the actual usage of TQM also varies across industry sectors as reported by Terziovski & Samson (1999) for companies in Australia.

Table 14 Examples of industry specific ISO norms

Industry sector	Quality norm(s) and short description
Automobile	QS 9000 in North America; ISO 16949 (technological specifications), other norms of the Verband der Automobilindustrie e.V. (VDA)
Medicine	ISO 13485 and ISO/TR 14969 as a guideline to apply the ISO 13485; ISO 15189 for medical laboratories
Aerospace	EN 9100 which is based on ISO 9100
Telecommunication	TL 9000 which is based on the ISO 9000
Test laboratories	ISO 17025 contains requirements for competencies

(Source: Schlosske, A., Thieme, P. (2017), Qualitätsmanagementsysteme, in: Spath, D., Westkämper, E., Bullinger, H.-J., Warnecke, H.-H. (eds), Neue Entwicklungen in der Unternehmensorganisation. Berlin Heidelberg: Springer)

As described in paragraph 3.2.2 of this paper, there are several ISO norms available that can also be integrated within the TQM framework. This integration can be designed with the specifics of the relevant industry in mind as there are a lot of ISO norms or similar relevant quality norms specific to certain industries. Table 14 entails some examples for such norms and industry sectors (Schlosske & Thieme, 2017).

In addition to the norms mentioned above that relate to the specifics of the industry, there are also industry specific measurements possible that can for example be applied within the balanced scorecard approach. Tubis & Werbińska-Wojciechowska (2017) for example mention several key performance indicators that can be applied within a balanced scorecard approach that is especially tailored to the Polish passenger transport sector. These indicators include amongst others relevant industry-specific metrics for example the profitability of the connections or the maintenance costs per vehicle. These authors then develop a set of indicators for all four levels of the balanced scorecard with regard to this industry segment and country. Similarly, Dincer et al. (2017) provide an overview of the literature on relevant performance measures for the four levels of the balanced scorecard with regard to the European aerospace industry. The key factors encompass several sector-specific ratios like number of flights or number of passengers but also some general ratios especially within the financial perspective of the balanced scorecard like the return on equity or the debt ratio etc.

Their results show that tools for quality management systems like the balanced scorecard are best designed when they include several sector-specific ratios relevant to the business model. In addition, applicable norms and regulations within an industry seem to be of value for inclusion in the management system. The relevance of TQM also seems to differ as their dissemination is not equal amongst sectors. Terziovski & Samson (1999) even assume that the innovation activities in relation to new products is not explained by TQM application but by the type of industry. Therefore, TQM is expected to benefit industry sectors differently because of unique aspects of these industries.

Besides the differences in industry sectors, there may also be differences in relation to the geography of the business. Hereby, it is expected that differences can arise due to different regulations as well as differences in costs or other relevant market factors. For example, Tubis & Werbińska-Wojciechowska (2017) mention that the development of skills and qualifications is currently a priority as they report a declining trend at the market for drives in Poland. This may not be the case in any geographical environment, so this aspect may have a unique evaluation tailored to the specific situation. In addition, differences in regulations convey the application of specific regulations within a regional market, like the application of QS 9000 in the North American automobile sector (Schlosske & Thieme, 2017).

On the basis of international standards, such as those from ISO, organizations can get a certification by an accredited certification body. Organizations can obtain a certification as a result of an external audit conducted by independent auditors that are evaluating whether the organization is in compliance to the norms. In Germany, these auditors are required to verify their special capabilities in order to perform such audits (Schlosske & Thieme, 2017).

Terziovski, Samson (1999) show that the status of being certified with regards to ISO 9000 has little to no power of explanation in relation to organizational performance. However, the authors assume that the ISO 9000 certification can help to foster a climate of change within the organization that in turn may have positive effects on the management of quality. A study on small and medium-sized companies in Australia confirms this result. Here, Rahman (2001) could not obtain a positive relationship between the organizational performance and the certification for ISO 9000.

A study by Aba et al. (2016) on the contrary shows a positive relationship regarding certification. For US firms, that have obtained a certification with regard to ISO 9001, financial operating performance improved over a period of five years compared to firm without certification. The authors assume that factors like quality improvement, cost reduction, increases in sales and employee productivity, better data management and control etc. are contributing factors for this result.

Therefore, the role of certification for achieving organizational performance is mixed but generally, a positive relationship is very likely. As discussed in the paragraph dealing with the role of employees as success factors, job satisfaction has been increasing in firms applying the EFQM model, so certification may at least have no negative effects. Further research is encouraged in the literature that uses larger time frames for the empirical data. In addition, investigations on the impact of other ISO standards and certifications are recommended (Aba et al., 2016).

3.3.5   Summary of influence factors for performance in integrated management systems

In this chapter, a variety of success factors for management systems have been discussed. This paragraph summarizes the results obtained from the review of the relevant literature. Furthermore, an outlook shall be given on current issues of interest.

Since management system operate on the business process level it important to assess their effectiveness and efficiency with a measurement system using different dimensions. Such a measurement system is the balanced scorecard. Besides the evaluation of the performance results have to be used on the strategic level. Therefore, it link between the operational level and the strategic level should be defined. One suggested for that is the strategic mapping and the execution premium developed by Kaplan & Norton.

The role of leadership has been given a strong emphasis for the working of management systems. Leadership is considered as one of the "enabler" criteria from the EFQM model, confirming this strong role. Despite the weaknesses in the understanding and the clearness of definition of organizational culture, emphasized by Yildiz (2004) and Lapina et al. (2015), organizational culture is considered as absolutely vital. In that sense, a "[...] successful interaction between the "organizational culture" and "quality management" is a key factor in the achievement of the organization's performance excellence" (Lapina et al., 2015). In that sense, corporate cultures like the clan and the adhocracy culture have shown to support quality management systems especially well, while the hierarchy and the market culture are not considered supporting. Similar to leadership, employees are also considered vital for organizational excellence. Factors like satisfaction and commitment are of influence here.

With management systems becoming more integrated, the measurement of success needs to target the effectiveness and the efficiency. Systems like the balanced scorecard or the balanced scorecard Strategy Map proposed by Kaplan, Norton (2000) can be considered of use to achieve this goal. However, in order to be properly adjusted, sector specific metrics or key performance indicators should be implemented to provide real value. In general, management systems need to be very specific in their orientation to the industry as the different ISO norms for industry sectors also show.

The role of certifications as a success factor for organizational performance is ambiguous in the relevant literature. However, positive aspects have been pointed out and there are current publications that show a positive relationship, hereby confirming the importance of certifications of management systems.

The next chapter will touch current topics of interest within the large field of management systems. Some remarks on the topic of integration shall be given as well as on the topic of risk management. The last paragraph will focus especially on some current discussions within the field.

3.4 Current topics of interest and discussion of evaluation efforts of management systems in the context of sustainability

This chapter discusses some selected topics of interest in the face of the current literature, focusing hereby on integration, risk management and a general note on the limitations of this paper and on current academic discussions.

3.4.1 Connection between business processes and management systems using the sustainable balanced scorecard

Quality management systems can be designed to integrate a number of sub-systems, whereby approaches like the TQM or the EFQM serve as general frameworks to provide the philosophy while other tools like the balanced scorecard provide a more practical and detailed set of applications within the general management systems. As a result, these systems can become more and more integrated and tailored to the organization.

The question hereby is, what should be integrated and why. This was clearly shown in the chapters 3.3.3 and 3.3.4 of this paper, where the need to adjust the measure employed in the system should reflect the relevant sector or business model of the organization in question. This integration of relevant metrics and aspects to consider for management is however not static. It should incorporate relevant current factors that are of strategic importance to the organization. One such current factor of relevance is the dimension of sustainability. Corporate sustainability calls for a consideration of environmental and social aspects to be included in the organization's objectives, hereby expanding the view from a strictly financial side. Therefore, an integration of the sustainability aspect specifically within the concept of the balanced scorecard or generally in management systems is suggested in the literature (Hansen & Schaltegger, 2012; Asif et al., 2011).

The concept of sustainability is not new but there is a lack of knowledge within many organizations in relation to implementation issues and the aspect of output measurement. However, by integrating the aspect of sustainability within the balanced scorecard approach and recognizing sustainability as a fifth pillar, organizations can combine financial and nonfinancial issues and build a thorough and comprehensive performance management system (Kalender & Vayvay, 2016). This is called sustainable balanced scorecard (SBSC). To use companies in the aerospace sector as an example, by targeting sustainability and by providing sufficient reports about this subject, these companies can enhance their reputation, brand value and culture (Kuo et al., 2016). This may lead to the acquisition of new customers, the possibility to differentiate the company from competition or to manage risks from sustainability aspects that may confront the organization negatively. However, the relationship of sustainability aspects and current corporate strategies has not been investigated in detail and the application of balanced scorecard containing elements of sustainability is complex to understand which call for further scientific exploration (Kalender & Vayvay, 2016).

Incorporating new aspects of relevance to corporate activities into the balanced scorecard, as has been shown in the case of sustainability and discussed above, may clearly enhance management systems and hereby provide opportunities for further growth as well as to limit risks. However, the balanced scorecard is only a tool within a larger framework and need to be considered from a broader perspective. As such, the balanced scorecard is being criticized for being too narrow and must be contextualized within a larger framework that is comprised of strategy development and strategy execution. The factor of executing the strategy is hereby an especially relevant concept, which is often underappreciated in the literature but emphasized in the book "Strategy Execution" from Kaplan, Norton (2008), the original proponents of the balanced scorecard (Ansari, 2010).

Kaplan, Norton (2008) propose an architecture for a comprehensive and also an integrated management system that is capable to explicitly link strategy formulation and planning with the operational execution. Hereby, six major stages shall be included that are shown below that can link strategy with operations:

- Strategy development with recourse to mission, vision and values as well as strategic analysis with corresponding strategy formulation,
- Strategy planning with the use of tools like balanced scorecards or strategy maps or other themes,

- After formulating the high-level plans, an alignment of the organization with the strategy should be pursued by linking the plans to the organizational units, employing formal communication processes and by matching strategic objectives with employee's personal objectives,
- After the alignment of organizational units and employees with strategy, operations should be planned, using a variety of tools like quality and process management, dynamic budgeting etc.,
- While the plans are being executed, a close monitoring process should be applied to be used subsequently for learning in relation to the problems, barriers or challenges observed,
- Managers shall use the operational data obtained internally and combine them with new data from the external environment and competition for testing and adapting the strategy. This leads to a further loop within the integrated system of strategy planning and operational execution.

This process, proposed by Kaplan, Norton (2008) can be described as of a very general variety, where the specifics to the industry as well as the relevant outside forces need to be recognized and operationalized by management. This clearly shows that management systems are in a constant need to adapt and integrate aspects relevant to achieve effectiveness and efficiency within organizations. This was also the result of chapter 3.2.1 where this integrative approach of the balanced scorecard with the strategic map and the execution premium was highlighted.

3.4.2   Management systems and risk management principles toward a sustainable risk management

Within the last years, the way how companies manage risk has been changed from a more traditional approach to an approach called enterprise risk management (see chapter 2). This has largely been motivated by problems in relation to flaws of existing traditional methods that became obvious during the last financial crisis (Kirkpatrick, 2009). While traditional methods of mitigating risk are largely characterized by a more isolated approach, enterprise risk management systems are built to be more inclusive and integrated. Through the combination of traditional methods of managing risk with risk governance, better risk management seems possible. Hereby, risk governance includes the leadership on the direction of the entire risk management system. This risk governance is achieved by defining and implementing respective structures, by assigning responsibilities and authority as well as by establishing rules and procedures necessary for decision making (Lundquist, 2015).

There are frameworks for enterprise risk management that are discussed in the scientific theory and also applied practically. These include the two most important concepts, the COSO ERM and the ISO 31000 (see chapter 2.1.1). Both approaches do not provide a single all-encompassing solution to any organization's risk management practices. The frameworks are on the contrary characterized by a strong need of adaptation to the individual circumstances of the company or organization where it should be applied (Hunziker, 2018).

What makes enterprise risk management systems of relevance to the discussion in this paper is that other management systems can be included into an enterprise risk management system. This is especially relevant in relation to the ISO 31000 norm that explicitly calls for an integration of other systems. Hereby, the existing borders between other areas like work safety, quality management or other important areas may vanish, and these fields can optimally be included and integrated within an enterprise management system that targets the entire organization (Romeike, 2018).

However, as risk is not necessarily considered as negative when viewed as deviation form expectations but can include positive surprises, risk management should deal with these changes as well (Romeike, 2018). Therefore, taking calculated risks may provide value to organizations. Such risk-taking behavior is inherent in the adhocratic culture mentioned in chapter 3.2 that is characterized by its flexibility and its positive relationship with the implementation and success of TQM (Gimenez-Espin et al., 2012).

Risk management is an important topic in management systems, since ISO based managemend systems require a risk-based approach. Incorporating this risk management into an enterprise-wide risk management, such as ERM, can be a helpful solution to deal with risks and with opportunities identified in the context of a management system on the right level within the organization: at the (top-) management level. In the context of sustainability scientists suggest the use of a sustainable risk management process (SRM) (Aziz et al., 2016) which is an extension the existing enterprise risk management considering more risks in the sustainability scope.

3.4.3   Current trends and discussions in the of evaluation efforts of management systems in the context of sustainability

This final paragraph is dealing with limitations inherent in the research part and is hereby trying to reflect in order to give some general remarks on potential areas that are worthy to be explored later in subsequent investigations. In addition, some current discussions and elements of interest to the topic shall be mentioned.

Given the sheer magnitude of the field of management and integrated management systems and the approach taken in this paper that was characterized by trying to give a general and very broad overview especially related to the success factors, it must be mentioned that there might still be relevant work to be considered that has the potential to give a more detailed view of the topic. As such, a more structured and comprehensive approach to the literature review especially related to the success factors can be considered.

In addition, there is a general uncertainty in relation to the significance from results obtained within empirical studies because of data availability. For example, in the work of Dincer et al. (2017), only a limited number of European airlines could be included in the study because data on other airlines was not available. Furthermore, these authors mention that data for non-financial variables could not be obtained, while being considered as of high relevance. They conclude that more data shall be used in further studies to increase the reliability of the results. This example also shows that some areas are especially difficult to investigate because of data availability. This may also be of relevance to the topic of sustainability where Kalender & Vayvay (2016) mentioned that organizations do face problems to operationalize and measure their corporate social activities well. In such an environment it may be especially difficult to researchers to obtain relevant data for further use in scientific studies related to sustainability.

Interestingly, as has been noted, there are differences and open questions with regard to the usefulness and the state of application of management systems across sectors. Hereby, it may be useful to investigate the reasons for these differences. It may seem worthwhile to a) evaluate success factors due to their general nature and b) to evaluate industry-specific aspects that may be used within a management system as a helping factor for management.

Related to the differences in sector, differences due to geography or economic development may be worth to be considered as well. As noted by Panuwatwanich & Ngyyen (2017), Vietnamese construction firms can be characterized by their poor performance which has led to an inefficient use of capital in these firms. When comparing these firms to firms in a country where the construction industry is considered to be more efficient and evaluated as having more proficiency, the factors to include within an integrated management system may also differ widely. It is therefore encouraged to always keep these specifics in mind when industries from diverse geographical locations are going to be compared.

As the differences in contributing factors of a variety of corporate cultures have been mentioned, it may be useful to further clarify which individual factors of a specific culture are of relevance for quality management. This may also vary due to differences in industry sectors that differ in their required skills and competencies of employees, market characteristics and other factors. A better understanding of these individual requirements is encouraged because "it is important that companies understand their organizational culture profiles in order to integrate the quality management principles and choose [the] most appropriate approach for strategy development and continuous improvement" (Lapina et al., 2015).

Measurement is being considered as fundamental to the workings of management systems and several remarks related to the need of measuring relevant metrics that are best suited to the relevant industry sector shall be used, for example within the balanced scorecard approach. Hereby, the alignment of these measures to the respective organizational goals is of fundamental importance. However, the paragraph on this topic contained some examples of individual metrics that are potentially applicable but no clear definition or guideline on the data has been made.

Currently, large quantities of data are available that may help companies to deploy techniques such as the Industrial Internet of Things where sensors collect data of the manufacturing process or other smart applications. Known under the term Big Data, a number of applications are meant to be possible and the use of this data and the respective analytical applications are predicted to be revolutionary for operations management as claimed by Bumblauskas et al. (2017) in their literature review on big data in relation to the topic of maintenance.

The application of Big Data technology is being driven especially by financial institutions that are at the front in using such applications for example to track client behavior in real time and to provide related services in order to increase performance and profitability. Another industry that is generating a huge amount of data is healthcare. In this segment big data technologies may provide an overwhelming realm of potential applications but is also suffering from related challenges (Tiwari et al., 2018).

This revolution driven by data availability and possibilities for data analysis is however not exclusively relevant for specific aspects of operations but is currently bringing profound changes to the way, companies manage their business, customers and business models. Big data is hereby recognized as a key future technology that has the potential to bring huge benefits to companies as well as to provide respective risks (Raguseo, 2018). This huge influence is therefore relevant to consider within the topic of management systems and integrated management systems and should be elaborated more in relation to the technological feasibilities as well as to the demands to leadership and employee capabilities.

Interestingly, the choice, which analytics, key performance indicators and methodologies in the field of big data to employ is related to the requirements of the organizations strategies and is meant to differ from organizations to organizations. The aspects of culture, environment and management are critical factors of influence (Tiwari at al., 2018). In this sense, big data shows similarities to the influential factors for the success of management systems.

Part II: Personal Contributions in the Field of Research

4 Analysis of sustainable business process performance in the context of knowledge managements, risk managements, and agility

The underlying question of this part of the study of the authors' thesis was to identify similar patterns in the context of sustainable business processes by considering various aspects of influence on performance. One of these influencing factors are defined targets within business units but also on a strategic level that influences the performance of people involved, business units, and the operation of management systems.

Another factor is the application of risk management as a central component in management systems. The research in risk management and practical approaches to evaluate risks and deduce measures can be a good example for the evaluation of performance aspects of management systems.

Management methodologies, such as agile principles, lean production, Kaizen and so on are other examples of solutions identified by scientists and practitioners to optimize business processes concerning effectiveness or efficiency. The influence of these attributes on sustainable business processes are aspects which must be taken into consideration during research in regard to the performance effects of management systems. The same is true for the influence of knowledge management and organizational learning. The manner in which companies deal with innovations is also reflected in their process performance, informed with the assistance of management systems.

4.1 Analysis of sustainability factors, organizational learning and knowledge management on the performance of firms

4.1.1   Main research objectives

In this study, the authors compared the business strategy approaches of 12 automotive- original equipment manufacturers and their respective business strategies using annual reports. It was hypothesized that there might be a relationship between performance and knowledge management. The authors assessed business strategies and the importance of knowledge management compared to the business performance by using two approaches. First, the authores used the topic of organizational learning measured through knowledge management initiatives and intellectual capital

© Springer Fachmedien Wiesbaden GmbH, part of Springer Nature 2019
J. Kopia, *Effective Implementation of Management Systems*, Sustainable Management,
Wertschöpfung und Effizienz, https://doi.org/10.1007/978-3-658-26509-0_5

measurements within the automotive branch to identify the importance of this topic within the analyzed branch. Second, the definition of quantitative targets (mostly financial oriented) and their closing reported figures in the annual reports were compared.

Organizational strategies are being already discussed for decades. Diverse theories were developed during this time, including widely accepted theories such as the resource-based view of a company, in which the resources in an organization have to fulfill certain requirements, such as being valuable and their percentages or being non-substitutable, and non-imitable in order to reach a competitive advantage (Makadok, 2001; Hoopes et al., 2003). In addition to that capability specific for a company (Amit & Schoemaker, 1993) as a certain type of resource was added, which enhances the productivity of a firm and was important for the success of the company (Teece, 1997; Sirmon, 2003). Basic theories of concepts of competitive advantage were described by Michael Porter either using the low-cost strategy (cost-leadership or operational effectiveness strategy) or the differentiation strategy (through innovation). Both strategies require capabilities in form of people and skills, developed methods, technology, patents, etc. Both require skills and knowledge (Prahalad & Hamel, 1990; Cordes-Berszinn, 2013). The concept of dynamic capabilities was suggested (Teece, 2010) and the focus of resources was also put on intangible goods, such as knowledge, skills, and the ability to use internal and external competencies to adapt to the changing environment. Organizational knowledge and change management gain in importance in a globally operated world where customers have more choices than ever before. This increased transparency makes it possible to choose between many different suppliers. New business strategies are being developed to identify new ways to keep a competitive advantage. In this context the way an organization deals with knowledge becomes important. Especially the rapid development of technologies forces industries to evaluate such technologies to be innovative and to adjust supply chain, products, and services (Kimizm, 2005). The European Union and it's EUROPE 2020 initiative places emphasize on this topic as well. Neither is knowledge clearly defined in scientific literature nor the way to measure it. Scientists suggests different models such as the use of the IC-concept (Bontis & Nikitopoulos, 2001), the house of quality method, benchmarking method, the EFQM-model (European Framework of Quality Management), the EVA-method, the balanced scorecard method similar to measuring performance (see Chapter 2.2). The basic principle of IC is to measuring intangible assets in the capital market and was confirmed (but also citified) by scientists already in the 1990s (Argyris & Schön, 1996). Since there are more

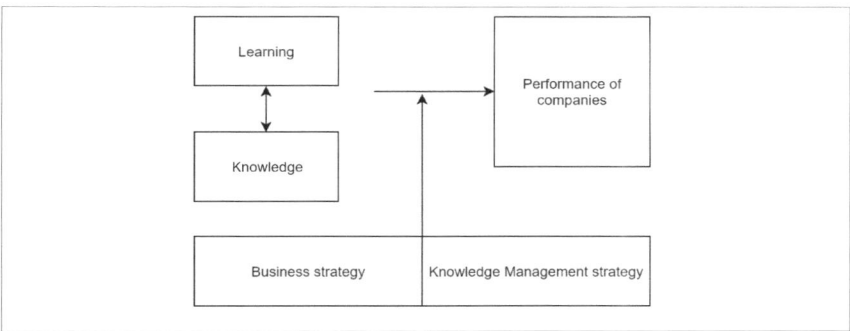

Figure 38 The connection between organizational learning, knowledge management, and intellectual capital, and how this influences performance

(Source: Own, based on Vera, D. and Crossan, M. (2001), Organizational learning, knowledge management, and IC: an integrative conceptual model, Organizational Learning and Knowledge Management. New Dir-ections 4th international conference, pp. 616-634)

than sixty methods to calculate IC (Ramanauskaitė & Rudžionienė, 2013) it generally is rarely used for reporting of knowledge within companies. There is also the controversy about how IC is connected to organizational performance (Bontis, 2001; Nedelcu et al., 2014). Kimizm (2005) understood knowledge management in the context of organizational learning and the elements of creation, sharing, and applying knowledge. Organizational learning, as introduced in chapter 1.3.1, popularized by scientists already in the 1990s (Kimizm, 2005), is connected to the ability to use knowledge and change the performance of a company (see figure 38). Especially the BSC-dimension "learning and growth" is primarily focused on learning, knowledge, skills, and motivation, aspects of the topic will be covered in this study.

The objectives of this study are as follows:

- Identifying whether the theoretically developed connection between organizational learning and knowledge management on sustainable business processes is practiced in organizations.
- To show that the effect of knowledge management and organizational learning is reflected as intellectual capital.

4.1.2   Research methodology and database

The automotive industry requires innovation in order to strive in a competitive landscape and was therefore selected as a viable industry for this study. Within this industry. Because worldwide competition takes place, technical progress is very important (Ove et al., 2013). This is particularly true for the automotive OEMs (Original Equipment Manufacturers) and its suppliers. Knowledge plays a key role in the automotive industry, and there are some existing knowledge management-frameworks that support knowledge management within this industry (see chapter 1.3). Williander (2006) analyzed the learning challenges in the automotive industry showing inherent inertia. Aggeri (2008) and Omar et al. (2011) investigated the approaches to the hybridization topic of the automotive industry. The results show that all companies use a double loop learning technique for the environmental analyses to react appropriately to changing market condition. The authors showed that Toyota has the most successful approach. Rover created a business unit called "Rover Learning Business" for the double loop learning process utilizing a tight connection and close relationship to universities and other knowledge exchange networks. Learning is often connected to HR-strategies. Phutrakhul, P. (2014) analyzed five Asian automotive organizations (Mitsubishi, Honda, Nissan, Toyota, Suzuki) and discovered 40 different HR-strategies. According to the author, the HR strategy is mainly responsible for the success in strategic knowledge acquisition, skills, and learning. The result shows that a strategic human resource practice ("Harvard model") is the best for long-lasting success (in contrast to a traditional HR-strategy – as the "Michigan model").

This research focusses on different types of qualitative and quantitative indicators of strategies within the automotive industry to discovery how organizations achieve certain goals within a defined timeframe. While in the first part, qualitative data is used, the second potion utilizes, a quantitative comparison strategy. The input data is based on annual reports and other published papers by the organizations, starting from the publicized qualitative information on strategic goals within the last 5-8 years. Similarities and differences are analyzed based on clusters and contrasted against any goal about the issue of organizational learning, HR-strategies, knowledge management, or IC. The quantitative data was extracted with a focus on sales strategies, related targets, and other parameters. The data was being normed by year.

The following hypotheses were tested:

- H1: The business top-level strategies within the automotive sector shows a high degree of similarities.
- H2: Values such as IC, organizational learning, and knowledge management are values which are used in the strategies of organizations in the automotive industry. Nevertheless, their effort regarding this varies.
- H3: Despite the fact the organizational learning and knowledge management influences performance these topics are not reflected by the top-level strategies of the organizations.
- H4: The automotive branch defines defensive strategic targets which are not adjusted regularly. The defined targets themselves are limiting the performance of the company.

4.1.3 Results of the research of the effects on business strategies and the influence of knowledge management and the importance of sustainable business processes

Most businesses in the automotive field publish their strategies in official reports, such as annual reports. In order to qualitatively analyse the business strategies of the automotive branch, information of annual reports is compared. Focus is set on the high-level targets (and the specific question of the existence of any knowledge management or organizational learning topic) which are usually reported to the stakeholder of the organization in these reports. Table 15 shows the strategies of twelve different OEMs.

Most strategies focus on profit growth but also on attracting employee. This is a sign that organizations are facing challenges to win highly skilled individuals. The quality of specific goals is another often cited element of the strategies. There is a lot of similarities in the strategies analyzed (Kompalla & Kopia, 2016). Some manufacturers like Ford, Honda, and Toyota are highlighting their responsibilities for the environment and social engagement. Looking at hypothesis one, the statement can be confirmed. Nevertheless, in addition to similar qualitative targets, the defined outcomes of the manufacturers vary. For instance, Mercedes intends to achieve a sales leadership, Audi on the other hand, focusses a continuous growth (based on the Sustainability Reports of the organizations between 2007 and 2016).

The fact that the attractiveness of the businesses for employees is stated in several ways by the organizations shows the importance of attracting new employees with the required skills. Expressions, such as "globally attractive employer" which is mentioned in the sustainability reports are highlighting this aspect. In addition to that, organizations publish knowledge management targets in their sustainability reports which confirms hypothesis two. Typical indicators are a number of training days for employees per year (this value varies considerably

Table 15 Business targets of automotive enterprises

Brand		Skoda	Mercedes	Volkswagen	BMW	General Motors	Audi
TOP-strategic targets		Profitability and financial strength	Capital & cost discipline; Sustainable profitability	Group return on sales before tax > 8 %	Profitability	Drive core efficiencies	Leading financial force
		Sales growth	Sales leadership	Unit sales of > 10 Mio. by 2018	Growth	Grow our brands	Continuous growth
		Top employer with global talent pool	Flexible footprint and productivity improvement	Leading employer	Shaping the future	Lead in technology and innovation	Globally attractive employer
		Strategic spearhead focused on price/value, practicability and space	Technology leadership	Leader in customer satisfaction and quality	Access to technologies and Customers	Earn customers for life	Global image leader
Knowledge & organizational learning targets		Supporting Volkswagen Group targets (1.3 training days per year / employee)	Supporting universities, research institutions, & multi-disciplinary science projects around the world. Daimler Corporate Academy (DCA): Intensive training of employee (4.1 training hours per year/ employee)	Volkswagen Group target for KM: Strengthen dual vocational education and training internationally. Introduce personnel development in leadership and management to same standards worldwide.	Strategic HR planning will ensure that next year again BMW can identify the competencies they need to pursue the corporate strategy and recruit personnel accordingly (3.9 training days per year/employee)	Talent pipeline & invest in growth-stage companies that can help to commercialize promising new technologies; Own research and development labs, evaluating projects as startups	Employee as success factors. Audi idea program for employees. 1500 training courses / year; company owned training center; Knowledge exchange & partnering with 31 scientific institutions worldwide. Talent management

Brand		Toyota Europe	Toyota group	Suzuki Motors	Ford	Honda Motor Co. Ltd	Nissan Motor Corp.
TOP-strategic targets		Customer Delight	Stable base of business	Development of Human Resources → motivate employees	Great Products, a full family of vehicles with best-in-class quality, fuel efficiency, safety and smart design;	Investor relations	Brand power
		Environmental Leadership	Contribute to communities / Contribute to the future of mobility	Globalization: Strengthening of Global Management	Strong Business, balanced portfolio of products & global presence	Major social responsibility initiatives	Cost leadership and Sales Power
		Good Corporate citizen	Sustainable growth	Stable Management. Diversif. source of profit	Better World, sustainability strategy	Environment	Enhancing quality
		Self reliance with focus on locally produced products	Exceed customer expectations	Top priority on quality and customer focused	One Team, One plan, one Goal	Philanthropy and Safety	Zero emission leadership & Business Expansion
Knowledge & organizational learning targets		Personnel and Labor Toyota Way (Challenge, Genchi Genbutsu, Teamwork, Kaizen, Respect)	See Toyota Europe	In-House Training (On the Job Training (OJT)), Voluntary Skill Development (4.3 training days per employee / year)	Collaborate with industry and cross-industry organizations to develop common solutions in a non-competitive environment developing a global, leading-edge HR technology platform for entire salaried work force	Managing human resources through thorough practice of the Three Principles based on Fundamental Belief, Respect for the Individual	Corporate culture of learning. Organization that grows through constant learning, supporting employees' personal growth through proactive HR development; empowerring employees to reach their full potential (2.5 training days per employee / year)

(Source: own elaboration based on the results of own research)

between one day and 4.1 days between organizations, being comparable to other industries, ATD research report 2014). The general topic of sustainability is important for all firms analyzed in this study. All companies defined goals to support sustainable business processes. It seems clear that this kind of processes is an important aspect which requires the skill and the experience of the employees and the right organizational culture (see figure 16) in order to gain the required level of knowledge and proficiency. Knowledge management and organizational learning is not highlighted in the top-level strategies of the surveyed organizations which confirms hypothesis three. Resource-based targets and financial values are still the dominant factor in any top-level strategy and defined targets. Nevertheless, specific reports on a lower level focus on the subject of knowledge management and organizational learning.

Like the qualitative targets, the OEMs also publish quantitative values. These values will be utilized to assess the question behind hypothesis four and five. The summary can be seen in table 16 which illustrations the sales targets and general values in a comparison between various OEMs. The presented companies have different time-intervals for their strategies which are announced in their long-term strategic goals. The timespan can range from 5 to 11 years. The financial reports assessed here are from the years 2007 and 2015. The values are normalized regarding their actual values and their planned values using the following definitions:

AAI = Increase of the actual average sales rate per year given within a certain time span

This value compares the sales performance within a certain timeline.

PAI = Planned average sales increase in a certain timespan.

TAR = Target achievement rate – within a certain timespan.

This is the value of the sales rate based on the fiscal year (originated in the strategic plan) and divided by the planned value of the sales rate. 100 percent means a complete achievement of the planned value (goal).

PI = Planned total sales increase within the given strategy timespan.

The planned sales value is divided by the initial sales value (starting from the beginning of the first strategic publication).

Looking at hypothesis four it can be stated that business strategies of the analyzed automotive businesses segments tend to be conservative. Table 16 shows that six out of eight manufacturers (75%) reached their target before the intended year. This is an achievement rate of more than 100%. Three of these six OEMs have surpassed this value by more than 20 percent. Reaching a positive goal within the given target range can be a satisfying outcome for the stakeholders, which might be one reason why this conservative approach of planning was chosen.

Table 16 Comparison of the quantitative sales targets within the automotive industry

	Merce-des Benz	Honda Motor Co. Ltd.	Volks-wagen group	Nissan Motors	Audi	Skoda	BMW	Toyota group	Ford
Actual aver-age sales in-crease (AAI)	13,90%	9,22%	6,27%	6,0%	5,90%	5,66%	4,73%	3,71%	5,54%
Planned av-erage sales increase (PAI)	8,45%	11,63%	5,60%	5%	3,15%	7,93%	3,71%	3,50%	No tar-get
Target achievement (TA)	124,73%	71,67%	99,30%	130,34%	120,67%	68,80%	102,50%	101,00%	No tar-get
Planned sales in-crease (PI)	50,00%	93,55%	61,55%	30,34%	32,16%	70,65%	20,00%	18,79%	No tar-get
Target	1,5 Mio	6 Mio.	10 Mio.	4,8 Mio.	1,5 Mio.	1,5 Mio.	1,8 Mio.	10 Mio.	No tar-get
Timespan	5 years	6 years	11 years	5 years	9 years	7 years	5 years	5 years	5 years

(Source: Annual financial reports of Mercedes Benz, Honda Motor Co. Ltd., Volkswagen group, Nissan Motors, Audi, Skoda, BMW, Toyota group, Ford (2007-2015); Strategic targets: http://www.evo-bus.ch/Projects/c2c/channel/documents/1931896_Daimler_UBS_Paris_DJSchmidt_Handout.pdf (page 25), accessed 19.01.2016; http://www.bmwgroup.com/annualreport2008/nav/index.html? http://www.bmwgroup.com/annualreport2007/strategie_number_one/strategiegebaeude.html, ac-cessed 10.01.2016; http://factsanddetails.com/japan/cat23/sub184/item928.html, accessed 01.01. 2016; http://www.carmagazine.co.uk/car-news/industry-news/nissan/nissan-announces-its-power-88-five-year-plan/, accessed 10.12.2015)

Examining the reports, it is also important to notice that the OEMs did not reset targets even though they had accomplished their goals much earlier (e.g. in the case of Nissan, Mercedes, Audi). This is also true for Volkswagen, which achieved its set goal in 2014 instead of 2018 (Volkswagen, 2015). Three out of eight OEMs did not limit their strategic targets this way. They exceeded their sales target by values of 20-30% but did not redefine new targets after reaching their initial goals. The hypothesis that strategic targets limit the performance of the business can, therefore, not be confirmed.

Targets which are too ambitious are harder to reach. For the empiric analysis, the planned average sales increase value is important. Honda has the highest PAI value with 11.63 percent per year (the other organizations have a value between 3.7 and 9.2 percent). Despite this fact, that the PAI and the sales performance were very good, Honda (Honda, 2016a) did not attain its defined target (only reaching 4.3 million instead of 6 million cars per year). This is an example of a sales plan where an exaggerated target lead to a negative business performance related to problems with quality[2]. Volkswagen, on the other hand, established very ambitious goals. This might be one reason for the diesel affair as a sign that too many different objectives or too much focuse on a goal can result in problems in other areas

Companies which do not have specific qualitative and quantitative strategies show better performance results if they define quantitative or qualitative targets. As an example, Ford did not set specific goals in their strategy (Ford Strategy, 2016). Ford ranked only at place seven (out of nine organizations within the compared strategies). Another example is Honda, with its ambitious targets on the strategic perspective site, which do not create specific business strategies on the operational level and therefore might be problematic regarding overall performance (Honda, 2016b). This is the proof of the second part of hypothesis five.

Generally, it can be said that strategy settings, and the definition of targets are varied within the analyzed OEMs. In addition to that, the extended timespan of the targets also results in less transparency since, within that timespan, may different things might happen. For example, almost all OEMs had a decrease in sales during the financial crisis in 2009 but still reached their targets (measured in 2012 – the end of the time span of the planned target etc.).

It can be concluded that targets outlined in business strategies within the automotive branch focusing on traditional values (such as financial values, growth rate etc.) which are oriented toward stakeholders which emphasize these financial value. Nevertheless, the importance of the attractiveness for new employees, special reports and information for aspects in the context of work situation of employees and possible training efforts, shows the importance of necessary skills becomes a vital component of the strategy. The subjects' knowledge and organizational learning are recognized within the OEMs even though it is not visible in the top strategies of the companies but rather in lower level information and reports (such as knowledge management strategies, corporate social responsibility reports, quality reports etc.).

Most companies define their targets more defensive than aggressive, resulting in a high level of goal achievement (75%). Based on this research, it can be stated that strategic targets do not limit business performance. Most companies which have reached their target earlier and did not defined new targets, increased the performance up to

---

[2]   http://www.fool.com/investing/general/2015/04/15/how-honda-motor-co-pulled-off-its-2014-turnaround.aspx, accessed 01.12.2017

the previously defined milestone of the strategic target. This analysis also found indications that a too optimistic target might impact future goals negatively.

Publicly announced targets can enhance the ability to achieve goals within organizations. They should, therefore, be realistic with a variety of objectives to prevent that people focus too much one specific goal, forgetting other important aspects. It was also discovered that companies that lag specific qualitative or quantitative targets tend to underperform compared to companies with specific targets.

The following limitations must be stated: this research only compare a small number of organizations. The aspects of knowledge management, organizational learning, and intellectual capital could not be integrated as deeply as necessary to identify a relationship or influences between strategies, knowledge management and performance. This research also focused on efficiency rather than effectiveness which is also an important part of performance. Further research is necessary in all areas to gain a better understanding of this research subject.

4.2 Research of the importance of knowledge management on firm's performance demonstrated on the automotive industry

4.2.1 Objectives of the study regarding the importance and connection between intellectual capital and business process performance

Based on the findings and limitations of the study of chapter 4.1, another research approach was used to investigate the research topic from a different perspective. Therefore, the objective of this study is to:

- Identify a correlation between knowledge management and organizational learning and intellectual capital.
- Finding correlations between the success and the business process performance of organizations and their intellectual capital values.

The resource-based view and the concept of competitive advantage was developed by scientists in the 1980s (Penrose, 1959; Mwailu & Mercer, 1983; Rumelt, 1984) and extended with the importance of intangible goods and dynamic capabilities (Teece et. al., 1997, 2010). Creating a unique value for the customer which is hard to imitate is vital for organizations today – innovation is a key element of business models (Teece,

2006). The market value of a firm is defined by scientists, such as Johnson (1999) etc., as market value measured mainly based on traditional financial values (see chapter 1.3.3). New concepts take IC as one way to measure knowledge and to use it for the development of a better understanding of its nature (Papula & Volna, 2011; Seleim & Khalil, 2011; Pinto, 2013). Papula & Volna (2011) developed a framework for knowledge management evolution using IC (see Papula & Volna, p. 499).

In addition to that the topic organizational learning is related to knowledge and knowledge management (see chapter 4.1). It was popularized 1990 by Senge (1990) and highlighted by scientific literature over the last decade as a requirement for organizations to be successful (Hatchuel et al., 2005; Kazanjian & Drazin, 2012).

The question whether knowledge management, IC, or organizational learning will influence the performance of a business, was not yet answered clearly by scientific research. Nevertheless studies by scientists, such as Appuhami (2007), Cohen and Kaimenakis (2007), Al-Twaijry (2009), Ting & Lean (2009) etc. identify influence factors on performance.

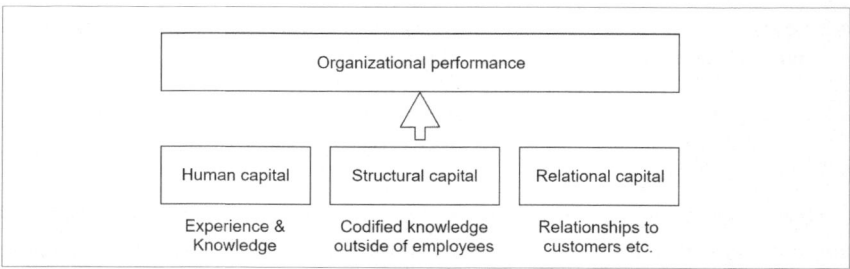

Figure 39 Organizational performance measured using intellectual capital

(Source: Own representation based on Sumedrea, S. (2012) Managementul organizatiei, Editura ASE, Bucuresti, pp.273-277)

Measuring knowledge aspects within organizations is not an easy task and not clearly defined. Diverse methods were suggested in scientific and practical literature since the 1950s. Sveiby (2010) found 35 measurement methods (2014) categorized them into four groups (see chapter 1.3.3). One of such method is the Value Added Intellectual Coefficient (VAIC). The other of this thesis identified a correlation between IC and the sales growth rate in the automotive industry in their research by using the VAIC-method (Kompalla et al., 2016d).

VAIC was suggested by Public (2008) and measures the effectiveness of intangible resources. This calculation is based on the Value-added method using three distinct values: the human capital, the structural capital, and the capital employed (see figure 39).

4.2.2   Quantitative research using a mathematical model

The author of this thesis used the result of the study of chapter 4.1 to study the subject in more depth. He uses a quantitative comparison of the VAIC values based on a correlation analysis within the automotive business.

Despite some critique about the subjectivity of the values (which are only taken from the balanced sheets of the organizations) used within the VAIC-calculation, the methods makes

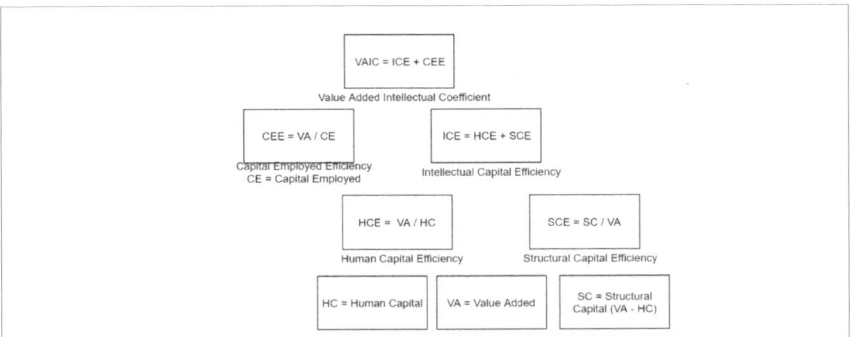

Figure 40 The calculation of intellectual capital

(Source: own interpretation based on Ståhle Pirjo, Ståhle Sten, Aho Samuli, (2011) ,Value added intellectual coefficient (VAIC), a critical analysis, Journal of intellectual capital, Vol. 12 Issue: 4, pp.531-551)

it easy to compare companies based on this value. The advantage of this method is that it allows an international comparison using large sample sizes. Lazzolino & Laise (2013) suggested that VAIC are an innovation indicator the efficiency of the intellectual capital. Other scientists also highlighted the benefits of these method for measuring IC (Ting & Lean, 2009; Zeghal & Malloul, 2010; Clarke et al., 2011; Guo et al. 2012).

The author of this PhD-thesis used the calculation presented in figure 40 to calculate the VAIC which is based on Ståhle (2011).

Method and database

As started in the study of chapter 4.1, this research also compares annual reports and financial reports of 6 globally operating automotive organizations within the years 2008 and 2014. By applying a linear regression analysis and descriptive analytics the VAIC was analyzed and interpreted to answer the hypotheses which are describes as follows.

This chapter describes the identification of possible correlation between the intellectual capital and performance aspects of organizations. The performance will be measured using financial values (sales growth rate, operating margin). IC is calculated using the VAIC method evaluating the single component of the used values and comparing them with other branches. The VAIC is also analyzed regarding a possible correlation to the operating margin and the annual sales growth rate.

Hypotheses:

1. In the automotive business the most dominant value in the context of IC is the Human Capital Efficiency (HCE).
2. The VAIC values are not higher but lower than in other non-machinery branches.
3. The financial values (Operating margin) and the VAIC-value correlate with each other.
4. The financial values (Sales growth rate) and the VAIC-value correlate with each other.

4.2.3 Research results of the quantitative analysis of intellectual capital and the influence on performance

Quantitative Analysis using single VAIC value components

In this chapter the first step of the analysis is summarized. It will compare the average VAIC value of the automotive industry with other branches. The data was taken from a database selected for global automotive groups and single automotive OEMs located in Europe and Japan.

VAIC components

Based on the formula of the last chapter, the VAIC was calculated and aggregated in

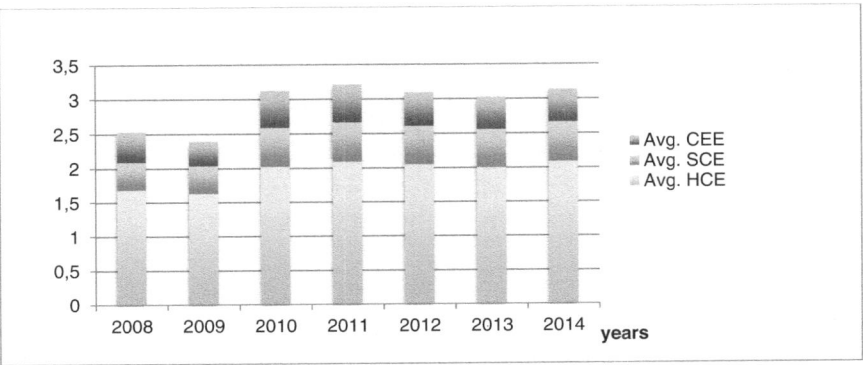

Figure 41 Components of Value Added Intellectual Coefficient value within research database according to financial year

(Source: own elaboration based on the results of own research)

figure 41. The aggregation of each component is based on an average value of the analyzed companies. It can be seen that the VAIC component Human Capital efficiency is by far the biggest with 66% (compared to SCE with 18%, and CEE with 16%). This finding was also confirmed by other scientists (Svanadze & Kowalewska, 2015) using the WIG

20 companies of Poland which are the largest companies on the Warsaw Stock Exchange without an industry focus. This shows that bigger industries seem to have similarities regarding the VAIC components and confirms hypothesis one.

The authors of this studies calculated the VAIC and compared the differentiation within years (table 17). It can be seen that the VAIC varies between each organization and year but is generally seen constant with the exception of Nissan which values vary within a range of 25%. Interestingly it can be seen that the years of the financial crisis in 2008/2009 is visible in the data showing a decrease of VAIC in 2009.

Table 17 Average VAIC according to financial year between 2008 and 2014 within of selected organizations

VAIC values						
Year	Volkswagen-gen group	Skoda Group	Daimler Group	Audi Group	BMW AG	Nissan
2008	2,96	3,73	2,32	3,33	3,74	0,74
2009	2,32	3,05	1,73	2,85	3,97	2,65
2010	2,72	3,70	2,96	3,37	4,55	3,45
2011	2,68	3,83	3,07	3,56	4,79	3,42
2012	2,50	3,62	2,93	3,53	4,60	3,41
2013	2,57	3,50	3,09	3,28	4,26	3,45
2014	2,63	4,08	3,12	3,24	4,21	3,62
Average per brand	2,63	3,64	2,75	3,31	4,30	2,96
Total average	**3,27**					

(Source: own elaboration based on the results of own research)

The average VAIC in total is 3,27 which is higher than industry standard calculated by other scientists (e.g. Nedelcu et. al., 2014). Contrasting this value against the already cited WIG 20, it is significantly lower. Looking at industries which focus on employed capital (e.g. the banking industry) – see table 18, which also have a higher VAIC value, seems to show that knowledge and all its context does not count as much in the automotive field as in other

Table 18 Value Added Intellectual Coefficient values of different branches and regions

Branch	Average VAIC value
Automotive branch (paper research database 2008 - 2014)	3,32
Banking sector Kuwait (1997 - 2006)	5,12
„WIG 20" Poland (2010-2013)	4,27
Automotive branch Romania (2000-2013)	1,34

(Source: own elaboration and data from Abdulsalam, F., Al-Qaheri, H., Al-Khayya, R. (2011), The intellectual capital Performance of Kuwaiti Banks: An Application of VAIC™ Model, Scientific Research, Business, 3, pp. 88-96; 556.   Salome Svanadze, Magdalena Kowalewska, (2015), The measurement of intellectual capital by VAIC method – example of WIG20, Online Journal of Applied Knowledge Management, A Publication of the International Institute for Applied Knowledge Management Volume 3, Issue 2, 2015;Nedelcu, A.C., Banacu, C.S., Frasineanu, C., (2014), The Impact of intellectual capital on automotive firms's performance – case study, Proceedings of the 8th international Management conference, Management Challenges for sustainable development, Nov. 6th -7th, (2014), Bucharest, Romania)

industries. Nevertheless, there is a slight increase in the VAIC values over time in the analyzed automotive companies which could indicate that VAIC related topics (such as knowledge knowledge management, organizational learning, capabilities for innovation etc.) driven topics becomes more important. This confirms hypothesis 2.

Analysis of correlation between the VAIC value and other KPIs

In the background of performance reporting, there is no central KPI which all organizations use. In its annual report of 2007 BMW focusses on ROCE (Return on capital employed) while Daimler uses Value-added. Nissan uses classical values, such as operating margin and market share. All of them report the sales growth rate and the operating margin, which is the reason why the authors took these values to identify a correlation between VAIC and performance.

The correlation between Operating Margin and VAIC is as follows:

The coefficient of determination (R2) is defined as the proportion of which the independent variable explains the dependent variable's variation. The authors used R2 to analyze the correlation suggested in their hypotheses.

Table 19 Correlation of operating margin and the Value Added Intellectual Coefficient

Correlation of VAIC and Operating margin	
Average R^2	55,57%
Average R	74,55%

(Source own elaboration based on the results of own research)

Hypothesis 3 is confirmed because there is a strong correlation between the operating margin

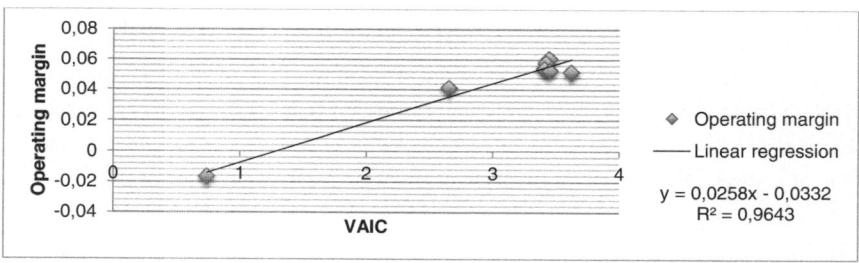

Figure 42: Correlation of Value Added Intellectual Coefficient and operating margin – example of Nissan

(Source: Own evaluation based on annual reports)

and the VAIC since 55.57% of the variance of the operating margin can be explained with the VAIC value. This average value is different comparing each automotive manufacturer alone. Figure 42 shows Nissans as an example with the highest values for correlation with an R2 of 0.96. The correlation between Sales Growth Rate and VAIC is shown in figure 42.

Similar to the above calculated values, the correlation between the VAIC and the Sales Growth Rate were calculated. Authors, such as Nedelcu et al (2014) identified a significant difference of correlations between these two values. The author of this thesis identified an average correlation of 53% in their study of six global operating automotive (see table 20).

Table 20 Correlation of the Value Added Intellectual Coefficient and sales growth rate

Correlation of VAIC and sales growth rate	
Average R^2	53,29%
Average R	73,00%

(Source: own elaboration based on the results of own research)

Taking one example with a high correlation (e.g. Daimler), it can be seen that R2 has a high value of 0.92 (see figure 43).

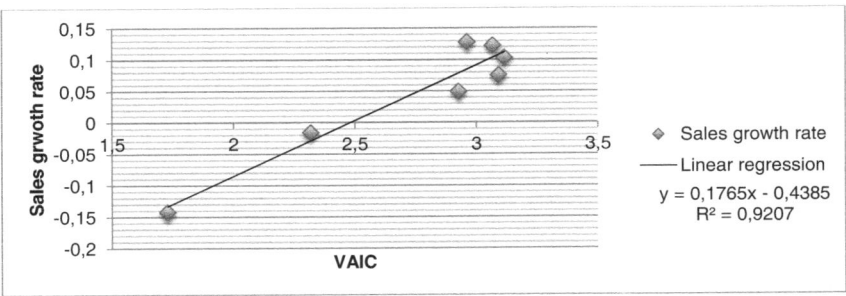

Figure 43 Value Added Intellectual Coefficient value and sales growth rate – a correlation using the example of Daimler

(Source: Own evaluation based on annual reports)

The findings confirm hypotheses 3 and 4.

The research analyzed annual reports of large automotive manufacturers regarding a correlation between their performance and their intellectual capital. For IC calculation the VAIC method was used which offers the benefit of the available information necessary for the calculation but also the weakness of the subjective nature of some of the used values. It is important to differentiate between available values from different levels of an enterprise and compare it to a similar value and scope of another enterprise.

This study found a high dominating VAIC component of HCE with 66%. Regarding the VAIC value itself, it was found that the automotive branch has low values compared as in other industries which are not so dependent on tangible assets, such as machinery. The average VAIC value of the automotive industry increased by 25% within 2008 and 2014 which might be an indicator that intangible assets become a more important topic here as well. This would be a logical assumption considering the pressure of innovation toward high technology driven elements in the automotive field.

Using linear regression models high correlations were found between the average VAIC values of the automotive firms and the performance indicators sales growth rate and operating margin which could indicate that the focus on IC might lead to better performance. It can be concluded that the VAIC is an important component for measuring knowledge and knowledge management which reflects that this topic influences the output of an organization and therefore its performance. The evaluation of the effects can be measured using intellectual capital methods.

There were some limitations to this study. First of all, there was a limited amount of organizations. Using a larger sample size is suggested for future research. The identified correlation must also be investigated more intensively since correlation is not causation. Future research also should perform multi-regression analyses in order to identify the relationship between the VAIC components and each of the business key performance indicators.

4.3 Study of the connection between business process performance evaluation and enterprise risk management

4.3.1 Objectives of the study of enterprise risk management measurement methodologies

As discussed in chapter 2.1.1 risk management is important for today's businesses. It includes various levels from the operational perspective and risks during certain processes up to risk on the top level, mostly called enterprise risks which have to do with strategic goals and the survival of the business. The author of this thesis (Kopia et al.,

2017a and 2017b) performed two types of research about this topic applying the following objectives:

1. Identifying a connection between enterprise risk management and business performance.
2. Suggesting a method for measuring enterprise risk management using a multidimensional approach based on existing frameworks.
3. Applying the developed measurement approach to a specific organization in the form of a case study to evaluate its usage.

Risks for organizations becomes even more complex in today's environment since more topics must be dealt with, such as social issues, knowledge issues, operational issues etc. (Global Corporate & Specialty SE, 2016). The management of risks is an important day-to-day activity for organizations to prevent losses because of risks that could not be reduced, avoided, outsourced or mitigated. Historically risk management was seen as a separate function operated by a risk officer (RO) or a chief risk officer (CRO). But isolated risk management did not lead to the success as it was expected. ERM on the other hand is an integrative approach of risk management ideally performed in every process of the organization which not only involves financial risk management required by regulations but also includes an in-depth risk awareness approach in many different areas.

Organizations today also face the challenge having to report regarding the topics sustainability and social or environmental issues forced by the EU Directive 2014/95/EU (see chapter 0). This increases risk awareness in other areas as it has been traditionally done (Liangrong, 2013; Kaye, 2014). Therefore, sustainability should be integrated into risk approaches and practices as a newly emerging area in the field of enterprise risk management. Integrating sustainability within the risk management process is also called sustainability risk management (SRM). Sustainability is a complex issue with long-term effects and therefore generally a challenging topic. Considering risks in that context can be very useful (Smith, 2003).

ERM is a strategic topic and involves strategic decisions. Therefore, ERM influences the outcome of these decisions which can be positive or negative. Nevertheless, it can be said, that ERM influences the performance of an organization in this way.

These two types of research attempt to find an answer to some of the discussed topics in the scientific literature: How does ERM influence the performance of a company, and how can this influence be measured. The authors developed a framework based on literature research and by testing their hypothesis using a case study.

Risk management and its definition was the topic of chapter two.

4.3.2　Applied research methodologies

For this research, a meta-analysis of recently published scientific papers from between 2010 and 2016 was used to identify common findings within the existing literature. The analysis of these papers was based on a qualitative comparison of the content and the generated results of the scientists. Common themes were identified, summarized and used for the second part of this study.

The second part of this study is the practical verification of the recommended framework. This research is based on a case study approach using the developed framework to practically test it within an organization. The company, where the case study took place (ABC), is a large, globally operating manufacturer. ABC operates in five countries and deals with logistical processes in its everyday business. ABC has an established risk management process and sees risk management as an integral part of its business despite that there is no established standardized ERM in all areas of the business in place. The authors conducted a test of his framework using a factual example via a case-study approach by interviewing employees working in different departments within that organization.

4.3.3　Research results of the current status of enterprise risk management measurement methodologies and the suggestion of an assessment framework

The author of this PhD-thesis uses a meta-analysis of recent scientific studies in the field of enterprise risk management for the development of a theory. The following section describes the process and the result of a meta-analysis by Kopia et al. (2017a) who analyzed studies with the research question stated in the last section. This authors focused on studies on the subject of risk management and ERM between the years 2010 and 2016. Based on their findings, the authors then formulated a generic approach to a holistic framework for assessing ERM.

Besides the studies already mentioned, Appendix B: Summary of the ERM-studies shows an overview of the results of identified papers in that topic. Generally, it can be said that the literature research confirms the findings of other authors (such as Kraus & Lehner, 2012): no real consensus can be identified in the scientific research. The results will be detailed in the following sections.

No clear correlation could be identified

The authors analyzed 18 studies within the given years. 16 of them could not find evidence that there is a connection between ERM and the performance of a company. Two studies, on the other hand, found a connection, namely that there is a connection between financial values, such as cash flow volatility, ROA, ROE, Book Value, Turnover, and Tobin's Q value and ERM. They also identified influences of ERM on management consensus, better decision making, and communication about risk as well as corporate governance.

The problem is that the studies are not comparable with each other. Particularly performance is interpreted differently, although mostly financially oriented. Despite some indicators of ERM influence on companies' performances, the analysis of the authors on this topic did not find a clear correlation.

No qualitative approaches exist

The studies in this analysis utilize quantitative methods to evaluate the connection between business process performance and enterprise risk management. Values were taken from annual reports using public databases etc. that mostly contain financial figures. This suggests that it is not easy to obtain sufficient data of other areas than of the financial perspective. This makes it difficult to compare results because the effect of ERM might be more drastic in non-financial values. These non financial information might involve a qualitative assessment of the research design which is time-consuming and also subjective in nature.

No connection to relevant topics, such as SRM

Since most indicators chosen in the literature-studies were finance based, there is only limited information from areas such as sustainability, corporate social responsibility etc. and measuring aspects like damage potential and prevention, quality risks, employee-related aspects, knowledge effects etc. These values might be important for recognizing and influencing the f ERM on an organization (Gates et al., 2012). One study included six non-financial values in its research but didn't go deep enough to create valuable results. Including non-financial aspects in the assessment, such as ethical, political, environmental or social effects, would create a more beneficial image of the influence f ERM has on organizational processes and outputs.

No standardized assessment processes

There is neither a common definition of ERM nor a defined way of implementation, monitoring or measuring it. To assess ERM, a maturity level-based approach can be taken. Some studies assess ERM using Standard & Poor's risk management Quality Scale (S&P risk management quality scale, Sithipolvanichgul, 2016) but this method has its focus on the insurance industry. Other studies assess maturity by asking the question whether a risk management officer and a risk board exists (requirements based on the COSO framework as stated above). In one study there is a comparison between traditional risk management capabilities and the firm's value.

Kopia et al. (2017a) suggest using the COSO ERM framework for assessing ERM since it is widely accepted and includes many distinct aspects despite being subjective due to its self-assessment philosophy. A different approach could be an external audit with the goal to reach SOX-compliance (McNally, 2013). Nevertheless, it must be stated that the existence of a risk management officer or an audit committee should not be the only criteria to assess the maturity of ERM. A deeper understanding of ERM and the effects on operational and strategic processes is necessary. Effects on performance cannot be measured in financial perspectives alone. Other sources of risks which include aspects of sustainability, social responsibility etc. that measure quantitative and qualitative are also necessary must be included as well (see figure 44).

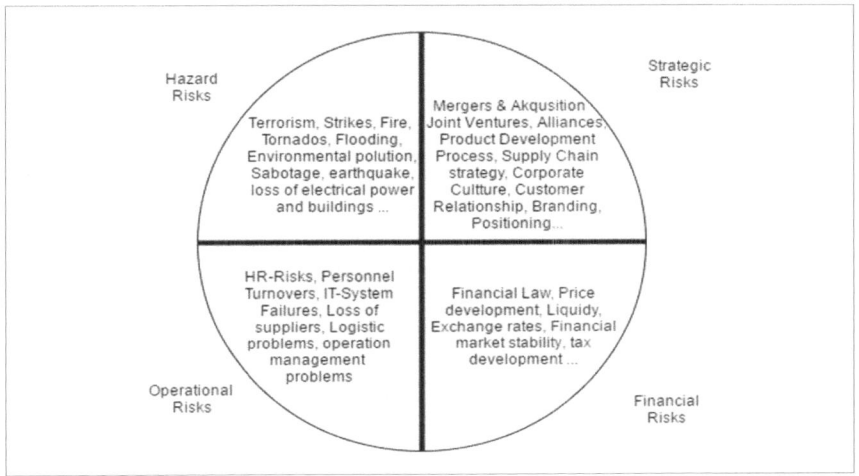

Figure 44 The sources of risks in the enterprise risk management context
(Source: own elaboration, based on Elkins, D., (2006), Managing Enterprise Risks in Global Automatic Manufacturing Operations, presentation at the University of Virginia, January 23, 2006)

To go through the cyclic risk management process (see figure 44) all process steps must be developed and improved over time. COSO and ISO 31000 focuses on the improvement aspect of ERM. Possible ways to measure the status of ERM can be maturity level measurements (e.g. RIMS, The Risk and Insurance Management Society, 2016). The RIMS framework uses seven aspects in which most key drivers and KPIs used to assess ERM do not have any financial aspect. The internal view based on maturity levels might have an influence on the output of organizations. This may possibly be of a diverse nature starting from financial figures but also regarding other aspects as stated above. Quantitative and qualitative approaches are necessary to understand influencing factors of ERM. Starting from risk identification, were threats have many different sources. The causes of risks can be seen in figure 44.

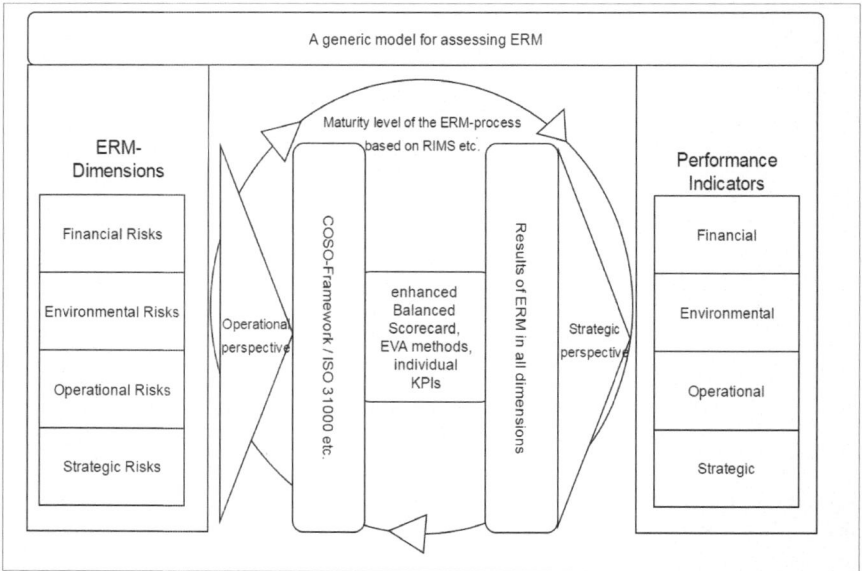

Figure 45 "Sustainable enterprise risk management" - A generic model for enterprise risk management evaluation

(Source: own development)

Identification as the first step in a risk management cycle is a complex topic by itself.

Risks, for the organization, can be positive and negative which also increases the complexity of the possible (counter) measures that can be implemented. The risk evaluation and response steps must include a brought spectrum of issues in order to reach a clear decision on how to deal with each individual risk/opportunity. This decision-making process should not be purely based on financial estimations but other values as well. The "risk-return tradeoff" must be calculated based on a number of different variables, enabling top management to make informed decisions. Utilizing ERM, risk awareness is possible. For this reason, ERM creates value for a company and, over time, improves the situation of an organization since top management is able to base strategic decisions on factual results obtained through the risk management process. The term performance is mostly seen under financial aspects (this "problem" is emphasized in many parts of this thesis) which is one reason most studies in this context use financial values. Nevertheless, the presented research of Kopia et al. (2017a and 2017b) highlighted, that other aspects should also be included as well. Performance can be interpreted as success seen from the perspective of all stakeholder which involve employees, the government, laws, regulations, the environment, social, and any cultural aspects as well. Especially if different industries are studied in this context, the reasoning becomes clearer. For instance, for a social enterprise, the performance of the organization is not financial success but its created social value and reputation. Performance regarding risk management is the ability and capability to efficiently and effectively manage risks which also mean to base decisions on the risk status and risk appetite of the individual organization (Frigo, 2011). Measuring ERM should be based on all sources in figure 45. Since organizations differ from each other, the risk management process should be individually created which also includs the assessment of risks and the monitoring and measurement of its success. Based on multiple dimensions KPIs should be established and collected using a BSC-approach. This way, existing BSC-methodologies within the company might be used and extended applying a risk perspective. Risk values from the operational level must be aggregated to the upper management using the KPIs from the BSC.

Kopia et al. (2017a and 2017b) suggested the following sustainable ERM model to assess ERM (see figure 45). It serves as a basis for further studies on this topic, in order to measure ERM within organizations and to analyze possible outcomes.

The following aspects of the generic model can be highlighted:

- A clear risk identification process should be established.
- Risk awareness is necessary in all areas of the company.
- The elaboration of risks should follow a standardized methodology.
- The response to risk (including the communication and reporting) should follow a standardized methodology.
- Predefined KPIs should be used to measure the risk status as well as the process quality of the risk management.
- Risks should be reported from the operational level upward to the strategic level of the company by aggregating the data.
- A continuous improvement should include the evaluation of the risk maturity levels and possible effects on the outcome in multiple aspects.

Results of the verification of an enterprise risk management evaluation model

It can be demonstrated that studies between 2010 and 2016 mostly try to discovery the financial effects of ERM but ignoring other performance perspectives. Diverse weaknesses in the existing studies were stated. The most important aspects include the lag of a separate framework that assesses ERM from all relevant perspectives. Even though generic frameworks such as COSO and ISO 31000 offer a good starting point, they use top-down approaches which leave many things open to be interpreted by practitioners. ERM is a very complex topic and will most likely affect the organization in many several aspects which might not be computable into financial values. The effects might also take a while to be noticeable, since the maturity of the risk assessment process increases over the years. Best practice for the organization will additionally include an individual risk identification process using all relevant sources of risk, individualized risk evaluation and response processes, and a customized approach to monitor the risks and so improve the risk management process through measurement initiatives. Measurement should be including all relevant phase and not only in the financial perspective. KPIs assess all facets required for a necessary overview has to be defined, similar to the BSC-approach. The output should be measured using non-financial values. The authors developed a generic approach which includes the risk assessment feature and the iterating cycle of evaluations, monitoring, measuring of risks, the risk management process using maturity models, EVA-models, and/or the BSC-method. The model can be the basis for further studies in that field which also should include detailed studies, including long-term studies, in each area.

Risk management within ABC - environmental aspects

ABC operates a business which deals with expensive machinery and equipment including some strictly regulated chemicals. An ISO based management system (ISO 14001) is in place that emphasizes a risk-based approach. The identification of environmental hazards is one part of the risk identification process of ABC. Being compliant to regulations also includes the awareness of certain risks which is being accomplished by establishing an internal team (the E-team) directly reporting to the relevant environmental risk committee (there are several risk committees for each department). The E-team is responsible for the following risk related responsibilities:

- Deriving rules from existing laws in the context of environmental protection
- Performing regular audits about the compliance of these rules

- Develop best practices by working closely with the environmental manager
- Collection of data and KPIs including reporting these to the management board (over the risk committee)

An environmental policy was developed by the E-Team serving as a mandatory document for all employees. It includes a checklist used for orientation of the team to evaluate whether there are any requirements in regard to their work and is it also used as the lead document for the ISO 14001 management system. The management system and related risk processes work hand in hand. The risk management approach was recommended by the E-team and consists of the following steps:

1. Identifying risks based on existing methods.
2. Mathematically calculating the respective impact of the risk. Environmental risks are considering to always create financial outcomes; therefore, the impact is stated in financial values. This step also involves stating the likelihood of a risk occurrence.
3. Maintenance of a prioritized list of risks.
4. Regularly communicating about the risks to relevant stakeholders including top management.
5. Development of risk mitigation measures.
6. Defining and measuring the risk management process.

The likelihood and impact of the risks result on entries in a risk. All risks with high (and selected medium) values have to include a countermeasure stated on the risk list.

Decisions on the countermeasures are usually made by upper management since it involves mostly budgetary decisions. Some risks are acceptable, some threats result in residual risks which are regularly monitored and re-evaluated. To assess the risk management process for the environmental risk management process by itself, the following KPIs are used:

Table 21 Key performance indicators used at the company in their environmental risk management process

Generic environmental KPIs	Emission rate (diverse substances) or a certain time period. Every increase over a certain threshold creates an incident which need to be treated.
Resource based KPIs	Usage of certain resources in percent

| Financial KPIs | Expenditures and fines. |
| Risk management maturity | Efficiency of risk assessment within a given time |

(Source: own elaboration based on the results of own research)

Risk management practices at ABC in other areas

There are similar processes in place for the sales department which report risks about potential losses of sales and markets due to influence factors like customer feedback, competition, political and economic situation, etc.

The role of the risk committee is the collection of single reports from all areas and to prepare a risk overview for upper management. A template as seen in table 22 is used for this purpose.

Table 22 Header of the reporting template to the general risk committee

General goal	KPIs	Last period	This period	Estimated future development	Measures

(Source: ABC from the case study)

ABC uses different KPIs on its risk report. Some of them are derived using qualitative, some of them using quantitative methods. The risk committee assesses the KPIs on a yearly basis and suggests improvements in the assessment method or period. The risk committee also defines the risk tolerance levels and the general risk appetite in workshops with risk owners and the upper management (Board members). These values are communicated internally as well as externally to define thresholds for early warning systems. Risks must include a strategic component, which is communicated through the top management's involvement at ABCs risk board. The board communicates risk-related topics such as risk tolerance levels, risk and quality goals, risk thresholds and the general risk culture to the employees. Different training and awareness measures are in place which include risk assessment factors in more detail for each department and region.

Looking from an ERM perspective discussed in the meta-analytic research, differ-ent ERM topics are implemented at ABC. This includes the use of the multi-dimensional approach in many different areas of the organization as well as aggregated reporting in the upper level of the management hierarchy of the organization. The overall risk governance structure also highlights the risk approach throughout the entire company. Risks are aggregated in each department over the department risk committee and summarized at the general risk committee. Decisions are made at board and executive level of the company. Risks is collected and pre-evaluating on different levels and be-fore they are included into the risk register at the general risk committee which presents the top risks to the board. There are also strategic risks which are collected at the general risk register and included into the risk matrix which is normalized to be suitable for all risk categories. This normalization process involves a risk translation matrix (seen in table 23). With the risk translation matrix, risks from various sources are evaluated and compared. For example, a risk in the legal area on level two is con-sidered a low risk, but high, if the source would be a financial risk.

Table 23 The translation matrix of risk classes

Category / risk level	Social	Technical	Political	Environmental	Financial	Operational	Infrastructural	Legal
Level 1	Low	Low	Low	Low	Low	Low	Low	Low
Level 2	Low	Medium	Low	Medium	Medium	Medium	Medium	Low
Level 3	Medium	Medium	Medium	Medium	Medium	Medium	Medium	Medium
Level 4	Medium	High	High	High	High	Medium	Medium	High
Level 5	High	High	High	High	High	High	High	High

(Source: ABC from the case study)

The last step in the risk management process is the reporting of the risks in an ag-gregated form resulting in a general risk register (also called enterprise risk catalog). This register contains all open and residual risks. A corresponding matrix (figure 46) gives an overview for the board that addresses risks according to clusters and nomen-clature. E.g. does the E stands for environmental risks. Number 099 is an environmental risk with a high likelihood of occurrence and impact. The abbreviations in the brackets show the mitigation strategy, in this case, the risk is transferred. All risks within the red and yellow categories must have a mitigations strategy.

The authors developed a risk management framework consisting of components which assist in implementing the framework, execute it, and measure it (to improve the process). Risk management is an ongoing process involving the following steps: definition of objectives with low frequency, risk identification, risk evaluation, risk reporting and communication and risk

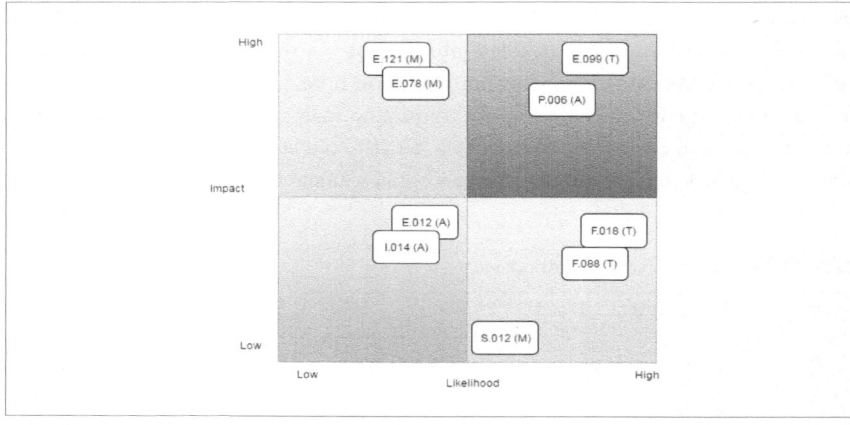

Figure 46 Risk overview on enterprise level (excerpt)
(Source: ABC from the case study)

monitoring and improvement with a high frequency. Each of the risk management processes commonly uses specific methods (Anderson, 2005; Gates et.al., 2012):

- Risk identification: This step uses special quantitative or qualitative methods to identify risks using approaches such as scenario analysis, sensitivity analysis, interviews, workshops etc.)
- Operational and related risks involve risks which occur within the next twelve months.
- Strategic risks and financial risks can be assessed for up to 5 years.
- A risk matrix can be depicted by using the two dimensions likelihood of occurrence and their level of impact. Each risk can be entered into that matrix to identify the severity of each risk).

- An appropriate risk response involves defining measures to reduce, avoid, mitigate, or outsource risks.
- A regularity executed or ad-hoc reporting including the relevant communication, training etc.
- A consistent monitoring of risk and the maintenance of an up-to-date risk register. The risk management process should also be consistently improved.

Since a successful risk management has positive effects on many aspects of the businesses, including process performance, it should be feasible to measure its strategic importance. The main purpose of the developed framework for ERM assessments is the following requirement:

- Risks has to be identified utilizing different sources relevant to the organization (see appendix G).

This requirement is met at ABC. All department have included risk management in their day-to-day business in addition to appointing a responsible person (risk owner) for risk management. The bigger departments also have a risk committee collecting possible threats and device measures for the globally operating business. Within the departments, risks are already assessed using multiple dimensions. A constant exchange with the risk management committee ensures that the method and values are useful and up-to-date.

- Risk evaluation and monitoring, as well as the measurement, is a cyclic process.

ABC's risk management approach is based on an ISO 31000 methodology which in itself demands a cyclic approach. Continues improvement is a vulnerable area at ABC, nevertheless, the company started to assess the development levels of the risk assessment by collecting maturity KPIs. These KPIs involved items like the response time to critical risks in individual areas, cost and saving of risks, risk prevention response, etc. At ABC, the response time to critical risks decreased within two years which shows a progress in risk management maturity. Several risks on the operational level, which consisted of error in a production facility, did not affect the performance but decreased the defect rate (which could be interpreted as a performance increase).

ABC does not use BSC in their risk management methodology but the individualized KPIs are collected in a comparable manner. Risk is evaluated on the operational level and aggregated upwards to the upper management. The results are reported to the management level in a clustered and prioritized view to make strategic decisions. The ERM adoption of ABC is considered as success since the ERM initiatives saved an estimated 10 million Euros by ABC management. This cost-savings can be interpreted as a performance benefit.

The above-presented case-study demonstrates the results of the research of Kopia et al. (2017b) and their developed ERM framework. In the case of ABC, the company is using an ERM which is adapted to the individuality of the organization. Compairing the requirements of the developed ERM framework and the implemented ERM most of the aspects of the frameworks are already in place. ERM is assessed based on many variables including aspects of sustainability and similar factors also including political perspectives, economic and social dimensions etc. The results can be concluded as follows:

1. An individual developed ERM framework was established at ABC with a dedicated reporting system in all relevant aspects which also include quantitative and qualitative values. This is a requirement of the ERM framework developed by the authors.
2. The implemented management systems of the company (ISO 14001) is integrated into the risk management process highlighting the risk-based method of management systems and the required continuous improvement process.
3. Company-specific KPIs were developed to assess the risks as well as the risk management itself.
4. KPIs are linked to the strategic goals and assessed on the top level of the organization generating strategic decisions and possible countermeasures.
5. The general risk committee prepares a report derived from different department committees showing the current risk status of the entire organization from various perspectives (financial values, quality values, security values, compliance values, production values etc.).

The case study demonstrated that ABC successfully uses an ERM with several aspects of the ERM framework developed by the authors. The ERM framework is a useful approach to assist in ERM implementation projects, to assess the maturity level of ERM, and to measure the output of the ERM initiatives.

4.4 Research on the effects of agile principles from business processes point of view

4.4.1   Objectives of the analysis of agile principles and business processes within the automotive and IT-industry

The objectives of this study are:

- Identifying differences and similarities between performance aspects of traditional manufacturing processes and agile processes
- Comparing lean logistics with agile logistics
- Constrasting lean production processes and agile production processes
- Identifying characteristics of agile principles for organizations in the highly adaptive sector and in the traditional long-term planning sector.

Kompalla & Kopia (2016) published a research about the relationship of agile principles and the effect of it on business strategies. The goal was to identify differences and similarities between long-term and flexible agile planning methods. Using a benchmarking method and a literature research the topic is elaborated within this research with the question whether the adoption of more flexible agile principles could be beneficial for the automotive business.

As stated in chapter "1.1   Performance evaluation - main target of organization", the scientific discussion about strategy is diverse and many different theories were created over time (Hacioglu et al., 2017). The planning of business strategies was mostly concentrated on fixed term planning after the Second World War. Due to generally stable markets during that times there was not much need for change for organizations. In addition to slower changing markets the competition was much smaller, especially from the international perspective. This changed with the technological development and the increased pressure through globalization. This change was different per branch but generally all industries are facing a shrinking stability regarding stable markets. The need for innovations grows, the need to enterprises to invest in knowledge and new business models increases (see chapter 1.3.3). The term VUCA (Volatile, Uncertain, Complex, Ambiguous) describes the raising competition which results in a constant and increasing change especially compared to the 1970s and 1980s (Highsmith, 2001).

Business strategies are becoming more customer focused today. This trend can be seen in the automotive branch as well. The options available for a customer when choosing a car increased over time. The automotive business changed their strategies toward a customer Centrix perspective within the last 30 years (Kompalla et al., 2016b). Changes in the business strategies of automotive firms are slow. The author of this PhD-thesis compared the strategies of automotive manufacturers and found out that these manufacturers focus on traditional- and stakeholder-based targets (e.g. sales growths, operating margin, ROI, customer satisfaction etc.) (Kompalla et al., 2015). Quantifiable goals are mainly defined for periods between 5-7 (sometimes 9) years and they are not often adjusted (see research of the author of this thesis presented in chapter 4). This is why agile principles become important (see chapter 1.2.3) – they offer the flexibility to react more quickly to market needs. Agile principles have their roots in technology driven development projects, especially in software development (Cervone, 2011).

Agile principles in software development started at the late 1990s and developed into different methodologies, e.g. the scrum methodology (Maximini, 2015). The core idea is to develop products based on small incremental steps instead of the entire product over a longer period of time. A frequent feedback from the customer is mandatory in agile projects since the amount of alpha- or beta-products which are developed in each incremental step (sometimes called "sprints") have to be checked against the requirements. This way a constant change is easily handled within agile projects (in contrast to traditional development projects with fixed milestones and long-term planning).

The shift toward customer centric strategies lead to adaption within the product development within the automotive industry in their value creating processes (Mintzberg, 1994; Howard, Miemczyk & Graves, 2006). This is especially important in these processes which are in need of the capability of quick changes for the specific customer demand, as the production of the cars itself as well as in the logistical processes. Figure 12 demonstrated the difference between classic strategies and agile strategies concerning sources for strategic decisions. The latter empowers employees and other stakeholders to give feedback, to recognize patterns etc. instead of only collecting data. Changes are demanded in agile strategies and not feared.

4.4.2   Research methodology to identify the effects of agile principles

The research methodology used by the author of this thesis for this study is a literature analysis for existing studies in the field of agility and lean principles and methodologies and contrasting it to traditional plan-based strategies. The following steps are used:

1. Identification of basic differences and similarities of lean and agile principles within the sector of study and the effects on business process performance
2. Identification of the differences and similarities of agile and lean strategies and their effect on business processes.
3. Comparison of the agile manifesto and the use within traditional plan-based process management
4. Comparison of agile principles, agile strategies at and traditional plan-based strategies

4.4.3 Results and conclusion of the effects of agility on sustainable business processes

The author identifies applications of existing agile strtegies and methods applied by companies operating in the VUCA-environment (Kompallae al, 2016a) (the IT-sector is used in this case) and compares them to plan-based approaches (used by the automotive industry). Related lean principles and the Toyota production system (TPS) within the supply chain were discussed in chapter 1.2.3. Customer demand and market transparency and strong competition are just some reasons for the increased need of agility but the general technological develop, changing laws and regulations, and the constant need for innovation are also challenging. Today business strategies are more to create value for the customer then to just fulfill some needs (Teece, 2010). Agility enables business competence Pandey et al. (2009) in many different areas of the organization. Lean production and agile principles are similar approaches with different goals. Lean focusses on efficiency while agile focusses on the capability to adapt to change. In addition to the outlines in previous chapters table 24 shows a comparison of lean principles and agile principles in logistics and manufacturing. Both principles are often used together and mixed as a "leagile" approach (Vinodh et al., 2009). Hybrid strategies using lean and agile principles within the supply chain is an approach which assists in identifying the best decoupling point (Rachel & Towill, 1999).

Table 24 Lean and Agile goals within production and logistics

Factors	Lean logistics / manufacturing	Agile logistics / manufacturing
Objectivity	Efficiency	Flexible to meet demands
Methodology	Remove all waste	Satisfy customers
Constraint	Customer service	Cost
Rate of change	Long-term and stable	As fast as necessary according to the customers requirements
Performance measurement	Productivity, utilization	Lead times, service level
Type of work	Uniform, standardized	Variable, adaptive
Way of control	Formal planning cycles	Less structured by empowered staff

(Source: own elaboration based on Waters, D. (2003), Logistics- An Introduction to Supply Chain Management, ISBN 0–333–96369–5)

The principle of decoupling point (see figure 13) which is the optimal point of agile and lean principles in the way that the organization needs to react flexible. The research of this PhD-candidate compared agile approaches with plan-based approaches of traditional industries. Markets which can be defined as VUCA describe the situation in global competition (Kompalla & Kopia, 2016). With the perspectives of the four dimensions of VUCA this research focused on the comparison of business strategies of organizations which use agile principles (mainly organizations which use software development as one of their core processes in the IT branch and the new economy) to those of the automotive industry. Traditionally planned organizations especially in the manufacturing business develop tangible goods which cannot be changed as flexible as intangible goods or services (such as software products) from one day to the other. Raw material has to be available, machinery must fit the new circumstances, production- and delivery methods have to be adapted – the complex process needs more time. The term slow moving cash cow was suggested by Martin (2015). The change on all these areas also create much larger risks than in the organizations of the new economy since these changes might also involve investments in production adaptions of high costs. Because of that, companies like that operate in markets which are not as VUCA as other markets are. Internal processes and the organizational culture also is different (Reeves, 2015) since the business strategies are stable over a longer period of time. The automotive industry operates with automobile lifecycles of several years. Within these years the business models of those manufacturer is mostly stable. Business plans and targets are defined for up to 5-7 years in the annual reports (see chapter 4.4.1) which fits to the average planning horizon. A new product line based on an adaption of the "old" version of the car is usually developed within that time span. Completely new cars take more years to be developed. Chances to the production plan might affect the production strongly and might increase the production cost because of the increase in complexity, logistics, changes of quality, and changes in the supply and so on.

Despite the nature of these two worlds – the highly agile operating companies of the new economy and the slower operating companies in more traditional and often manufacturing markets – both can learn from each other. Mostly the traditional plan-based approach should adapt some basic principles since the market demands flexibility and efficiency (often meaning cost-efficiency from the customer perspective) at the same time. Higher flexibility also allows a better response to upcoming risks, e.g. the raising prices of oil, natural disasters etc.). Implementing trial and error approaches through rapid prototyping, frequent customer involvement in the development process and alike can be beneficial for the automotive business to react more quickly to sudden incidents as changing market conditions. Inventions such as the Toyota Production System, TQM, and similar approaches (see chapter 1.2.1) were suggested by practitioners of traditional industries, showing that there is a need for an organizational culture within the automotive field which is open to change and efficiency.

Most car manufacturer today already use some agile principles and also lean production, TQM, etc., which also put the focus on involvement and motivation of employees but the overall strategy is still very traditional. In fact, agility can also be seen as a predecessor of agility (Victor et al., 1998). For car manufacturers both methodologies can be interesting for the supply chain as well as for their business strategies.

The reality looks different though. Examples, such as Volkswagen, show that their decision-making process for business strategies is still centralistic and top-down (Wall Street Journal, 2016) which is not optimal from the perspective of employees in the sense creating successful new ideas and innovations (employee empowerment). Table 25 show the result of the detailed comparison between agile aspects based on the original agile manifesto, typical

Table 25 Comparison of agile principles, agile strategies and traditional plan-based strategies

Cluster	Agile aspects according to agile manifesto	Characteristic of business strategy	Agile principle applied?
Example of Application	Software development, Agile production or agile logistics	Automotive industry	
1.Cluster: Flexibility	Flexibility regarding varying circumstances regardless of development and production stage	Frozen zones and long lasting business strategies with targets, that do not get changed often	No
	Close connection and interaction between people who decide and people that execute	Business strategy is defined mostly centrally by highest level of management	No
	Focus on the functional product and incremental value add weekly	Defined stages with Planning, Definition, Communication and Operation	No
2. Cluster: Information	Working as closely together as possible (locally)	Decentralized working places	No
	Constant but small value-add steps	Periodic long-term changes	No
	Pull, Order-triggered development/production, regular delivery of "usable" units	Developments based on customer analysis and predictions. Mostly One time activity of strategy formulation	Partially
3. Cluster: Team	Teams are organizing and structuring their processes by themselves	Mostly centralistic top-level decisions with high degree of rotation on management level	Partially
	Permanent search for improvement	Periodic improvement/adaptions. Only in exceptional situations the strategy is "revamped"	Partially
	Trustworthiness and motivation for individuals	Mostly dependence on top-management strategy but execution with individuals	Partially
4. Cluster: Value-Add	Lean procedure	Focus on 4 -5 key targets which contain aspects of efficiency and lean approaches	Yes
	Functional product is the main focus	Operating margin, increasing sales with high qualitative standards are the main focus.	Partially
	Quality and Design regularly emphasized	High standard of quality is a main target	Yes

(Source: own elaboration based on the findings)

characteristics of business strategies in general, and agile principles used in the automotive business strategy development. It can be summarized that the business strategy of the automotive branch does not uses the benefits of agile principles.

Table 25 was extended by the author of this thesis comparing agile principles with the business strategies of Alibaba and a traditional automotive manufacturer (see appendix D) (Kompalla et al., 2016a). Alibaba is a representative company operating in a VUCA environment (Tan et al., 2009). It is known for its flexibility and agile characteristics which is also applied at the strategic level. The frequently changing customer expectations from the Business-to-Business market needs to be fulfilled. Without a corresponding agile, flexible and lean strategy, this task would fail. This way the company made strong changes from a Business-to-Business portal to a Cloud-Service-Provider (Coresight Research, 2016). The principles of trial and error are applied using separate projects to initiate and test new ideas. Employees are invited to create new solutions and improvements in their day-to-day business. The most successful projects are chosen to be elaborated more intensively eventually creating an entire new business model for the company. The focus is on future customer demand and on multiple strategies which can be beneficial to survive in the competitive landscape. The finding that companies implementing more than one strategy (of Porters originally suggested strategies of cost leadership, differentiation, and focus) was also discovered by other scientists (Studeny, 2015). The regular planning cycles are short term and focus on a permanent co-creation process which is executed as follows:

- The identification of future customer needs through knowing and monitoring the signals from the market
- Getting feedback from key customers and early adopters after the development of a draft, alpha-product, or prototype
- Creating products quickly with decisions which only involve the lower and middle management, not the top management
- Testing and continuously improving the product

An open communication and innovative culture which enables all employees to bring in ideas and suggestions is mandatory. This also involves the flexibility to change job positions within the company to gain experience in different areas (Reeves, 2015).

The new economy grew quickly within the last decade. Their focus is the fact that they are capable of quick innovations and flexibility regarding their products which are demanded by their customers. Experimentation is important in order to identify possibilities to solve the problems of their customers and used by large organizations in that field (e.g. Apple, Facebook, Amazon etc.). Most internet-based companies are organized to enable agile methodologies as well as efficient processes (lean) – they found their decoupling point. Organizations of the new economy usually operate an open communication in their organizational culture. This culture has to appreciate changes and must be accepted by every employee (Martin, 2015).

The planning and operation of businesses is different in organization which use agile approaches compared to those which use traditional plan-based approaches. Business strategies and organizational cultures therefore also show differences. Since today's market is VUCA which also affect more traditional markets, it is important for all industries to adapt certain aspects of agile methodologies, lean thinking and alike. The automotive industry is traditionally a predictive and very slow industry with long lifecycles. But the quickly changing customer demands, sudden changing market conditions as oil- and gas-prices, new competitors with new ideas and technologies (e.g. self-driving cars developed by the hi-tech industry) and other worldwide operating competition makes it necessary to develop a culture of innovation which is ready to execute quick changes. Concepts, such as TQM, lean manufacturing, Kaizen etc. were suggested by traditional industries, such as the automotive field and their highly cost intensive (and therefore value creating) supply chain process. Most manufacturers use these principles for years already within their production processes showing that there is a need to a change in the traditional ways within the manufacturing industry. The also influences processes outside the production. Coming back to the evaluation of management systems, based on the presented researches, it can be seen that different approaches to production and generic methodologies to improve the efficiency and effectiveness of business processes are an influence factors for performance. Nevertheless, this research showed that these principles do not affect the business processes as strongly and did not yet reach the strategic level of an organization in regards to the definition of business strategies, the development of innovational products, or product lifecycles.

5 Research on the influence of integrated management systems on business process performance

This chapter summarizes the research of the PhD-candidate in the field of integrated management systems. The objectives of the research is to address factors influencing integrated management systems in regard to business process performance. It includes success factors for management systems as an indicator of effective or efficient use of integrated management systems and involved processes. These success factors involve common strategies to improve integration of management systems. These strategies involve the high-level structure aspects of leadership styles and organizational cultures, which are more favorable for a useful implementation and operation of management systems, the use of knowledge management and organizational learning and the possibility to measure the efficiency or effectiveness.

5.1 Assessing the high-level structure of an integrated management system

5.1.1 Objectives for the analysis of integrated management systems with a high-level structure

The following objectives are focused on in this research:

- Identifying best practice approaches for the integration of management system implementations.
- Identifying success factors with the biggest influence on management system implementation including the differences between implementation phases and operational phases.

In this study the PhD-candidate analyzed the ways organizations implement and execute management systems based on ISO. The research deals with the question of what best-practices exist to establish or operate more than one management system.

In the context of ISO-based management systems, for instance ISO 9001, ISO 14001, ISO 27001, OHSAS 18001, ISO/TS 16949 (see chapter 5.3.3), ISO 50001 etc. it can be seen that there is a growing number of companies receiving certification on the

© Springer Fachmedien Wiesbaden GmbH, part of Springer Nature 2019
J. Kopia, *Effective Implementation of Management Systems*, Sustainable Management, Wertschöpfung und Effizienz, https://doi.org/10.1007/978-3-658-26509-0_6

basis of these standards (see appendix C). ISO stated that there are over 1.5 million ISO 9001 and ISO 14001 certifications worldwide (ISO, 2015b). This growing trend is mainly driven by the Asia-Pacific area (see chapter 5.3.4). Many large companies operate more than one management system. This raises the question of whether there are any benefits, problems, synergies, and best-practices regarding the operation and integration of management systems. Integrated management systems (IMS) are one possibility to operate multiple management systems. An IMS is one management system that operates different sub-management systems by using the synergies between the requirements of each as much as possible. ISO developed a so-called high-level structure (HLS or Annex SL) which enables a better integration of their management system standards (ISO HLS, 2015). The HLS (see chapter 3.1.2) replaced an older ISO guideline ("Guide 83") to integrate the 31 management system standards of ISO more easily.

Despite several approaches in the past for an easier integration (such as UNE 66177, PAS 99 etc.) there is almost no collective agreement in the ways of integration. This is the case neither in practice nor in scientific research, despite a consensus that integration is beneficial (see chapter 3.2). The study of Kopia et al. (2016) will, therefore, examine this topic regarding its success factors based on a survey of 32 companies from different industries.

There are some general topics that are similar in all management systems, specifically ISO based management systems. These topics include standard definitions and the scope of the management systems, responsibilities of management, and the PDCA-cycle (also known as Deming-Cycle), a cyclic approach of the phase planning, executing, checking, acting, which also include the improvement aspects. ISO does not require a fix PDCA-method but is a process which enables constant improvement.

5.1.2   Applied Research Methodology

The author of this thesis used two research methods to answer the hypotheses:

1. Quantitative study:
   Based on a survey of 32 organizations (all the organizations operate more than one management system) of diverse industries and sizes in the German market, empirical data is collected and quantitative assessed.

2. Qualitative analysis:
   Using an exploratory case study approach, answers to some of the hypotheses are identified for which the quantitative analysis did not clearly bring a result.

   For the case study, two companies of the sample size were selected, and semi-structured interviews took place involving different people from the organizations working in different functional levels.

The following hypotheses are formulated on the basis of the research:

1. Companies operating more as one management system incorporate them into an integrated management system and assimilate each system one after the other.
2. Considering success factors, the commitment of the management and the availability of resources have the biggest influence.
3. Success factors change over time: during the implementation, they are different than later during the operation of the IMS.
4. The main problems with the implementation of an IMS are of political nature and a matter of communication.

5.1.3   Results of the empirical research of the analysis of integrated management systems with high-level structure

Integration of management systems is not a new topic and has been discussed in the scientific literature for years. Authors, such as Slater (1991) already assessed that topic presenting some benefits from integration. New research from Jorgensen et al. (2006) highlighted advantages as well. Generally, research shows benefits of integration (Beechner &

Table 26 Usage of integrated management systems as a result of the survey

Approaches for the integration of management system standards	Frequency	Percentage	Cumulative Percentage
Yes, we are using an integrated management system	97	52,7	52,7
Yes, we are trying to integrate the management systems into an integrated management system	48	26,1	78,8
No, we are operating our management systems independently	39	21,2	100,0
Total	184	100,0	

(Source: Own representation based on Katniak (2012), A Survey Analysis of integrated management systems in the UK, Sheffield Hallam University)

Koch, 1997; Ahsen & Funck, 2001; Zutshi & Sohal, 2005; Karapetrovic, 2008; Bernardo et al., 2009; Rebelo 2014a, 2014b, and 2015 etc.). Zeng et al. (2011) and Raišienė (2012) further elaborated on the synergies of equal requirements of management systems. These interoperability's is generally favored in scientific research. An example of a categorization of motivations for an IMS was suggested by Rajkovic & Aleksic (2009). Several reasons for integration exist and most companies integrate their management systems into an IMS (see table 26).

Besides the general agreement on benefits of integration, there is no common though on the way how to best integrate management systems and no long-term studies (Min, 2015). Questions, such as the dependency of the size of the organization, the nature of the industry etc. are not answered, despite there are some suggestions coming from certification bodies with the

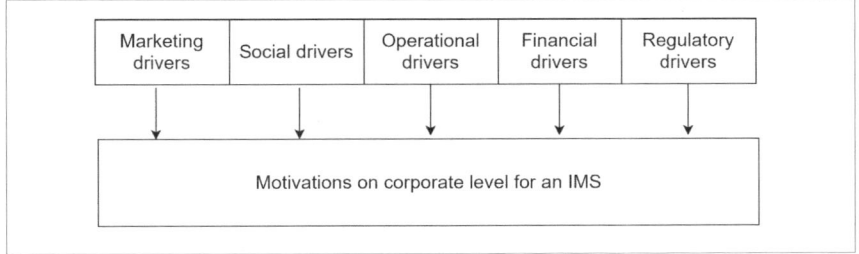

Figure 47 Motivations for the establishment of an integrated management system
(Source: Own representation based on Rajkovic, D., & Aleksic, M. (2009), Corporate motives on implementation of integrated management system (IMS), International Journal for Quality Research, 3(3))

PAS 99 (BSI, 2015) and scientific research (Mohammad et al., 2013; Oliveira, 2013;
Rössler & Schlieter, 2015; Samy et al, 2015; Bernardo et al., 2016). Another discussion
is the depth of integration of each management system. This level of integration was
also matter of research of scientists in the past (Bernardo et al, 2015).

Based on the literature analysis of the authors of this thesis the following basic
requirements were identified using the research of the scientists stated above (Kopia
et al., 2016):

- The commitment of the management, especially the top-management is necessary
  (see analysis of leadership aspects in chapter 5.2).
- The integration of management systems into an IMS requires experience with management systems
- The implementation of an IMS should use a step-by-step approach rather than a
  big-bang approach even though a simultaneous integration is possible (see figure
  48).
- The implementation of an IMS requires an established project management process
- An IMS should be driven internally instead of forced from the outside
- The measurement of the level of maturity of an IMS should be evaluated which
  includes the continuous improvement process using a methodology which fits to
  the company.
- There must be a strategic alignment with the strategic goals and the management
  systems since strategic goals are used to define processes and operational strategies which also includes management systems.

Case studies

The findings of the case studies are presented in this section. Company A is large company having more than 25.000 employees. Company B employees under 1000 employees (but more than 500). Both organizations operate an IMS. The results of each part of the case study research is summarized in Appendix A: Results of the research in management system's implementation.

The results of the case studies make clear that it is important to have management support and a motivated project team during the implementation phase. Difficult aspects are the identification of the synergies of the management systems besides some generic aspects required by the HLS. The project phase deals with commitment of people, research regarding

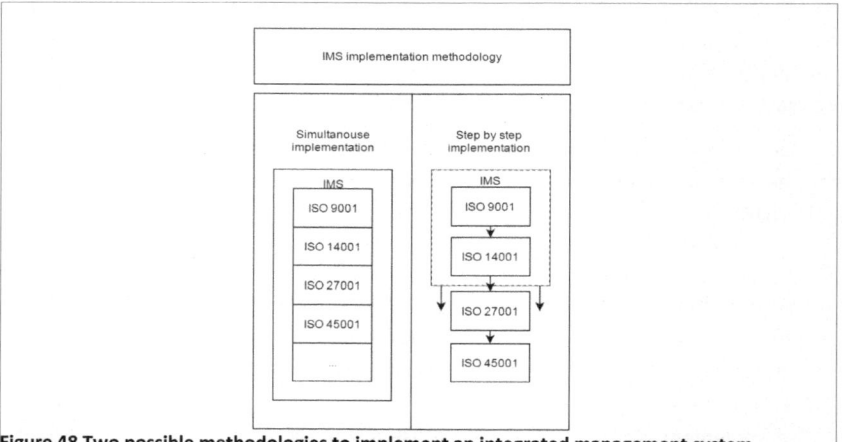

Figure 48 Two possible methodologies to implement an integrated management system
(Source: own elaboration based on the results of own research)

synergies, establishing of rules, regulations, the creation of documents, and help of external consultants. Success factors of this phase are related to project success – holding deadlines and budgets, creating processes and content, completing a first-time certification etc. A running IMS after the implementation is not a project anymore. In this phase other success factors are important, especially the operation of a constantly improvement cycle mainly done by the "normal employee" of the process and not the project team members. New requirements of ISO have to be integrated and measures on the basis of risk identification have to be defined. One similarity is the commitment of the management which is also important in the operation of the management system(s) (Kopia, 2016) especially in the management review processes and the initiation of changes. Despite some differences in both companies, the organizational culture was mentioned to be important for management system integration. A functional structure with a classic management style resulted in problems regarding the communication within the examples.

Both hypotheses (3 and 4) could be confirmed.

Empirical analysis

The results of the empirical analysis are illustrated in this section. Question one was concerned with the number of management systems per company showing that 80% of the company used 3 or more management systems (see figure 49)

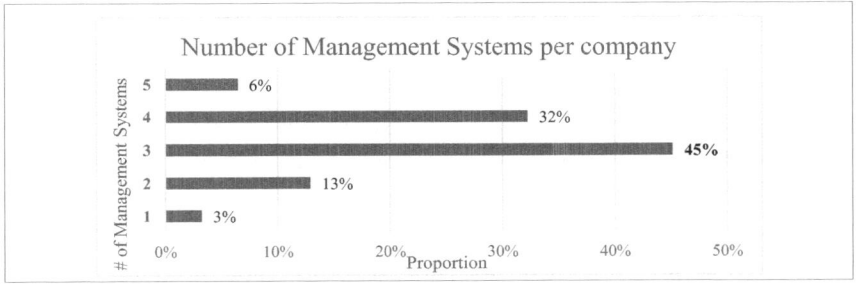

Figure 49 Number of management systems per company in the study
(Source: Own elaboration on the basis of the survey answers)

Most companies were familiar with the integration on the basis of the HLS (at the time of the study this topic was new). Almost ¾ of the companies of the selected samples operate an IMS on the basis of their own interpretation (figure 51). Most of the organizations also fully integrate their management systems into an IMS (figure 52) using the step-by-step approach (82% of the companies).

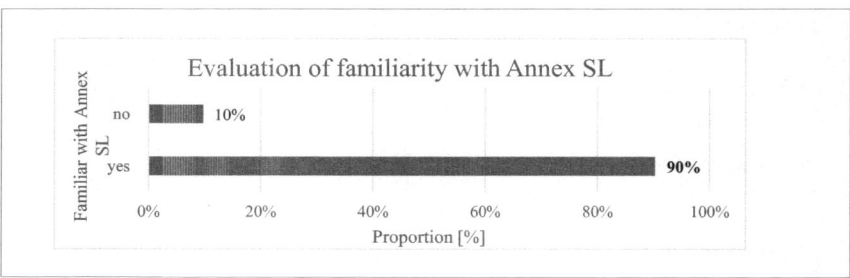

Figure 50 There is a high familiarity with the high-level structure
(Source: Own representation)

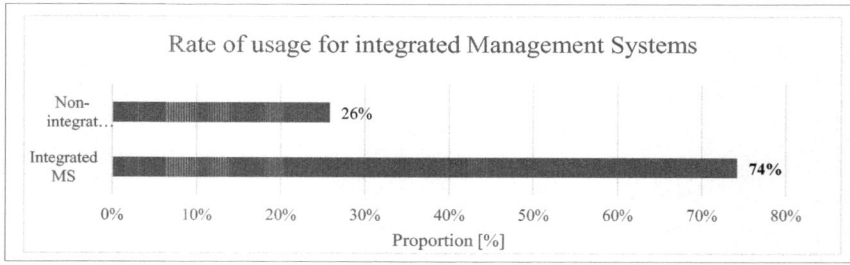

Figure 51 Level of usage of some kind of integration
(Source: Own elaboration based on the results of own research)

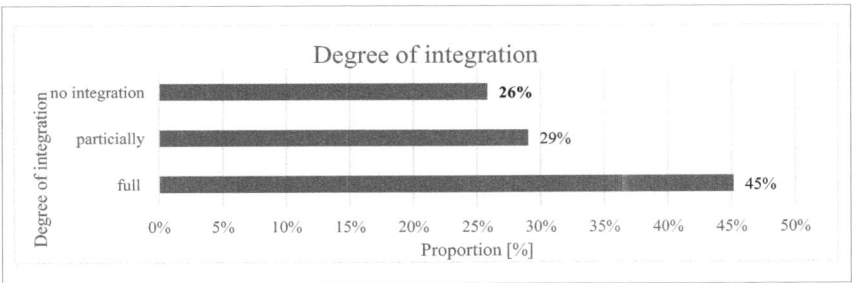

Figure 52 The degree of integration within the management systems
(Source: Own elaboration based on the results of own research)

The reasons why the organizations integrate their management systems confirm the findings of other researchers highlighting the synergies of resource usage, processes etc. Nevertheless 13% of the companies mention that an IMS increases the complexity of the management system process in that regard that it slows down decisions (see figure 53). Resource availability and the help of external parties during the implementation phase was stated as most important regarding the success of the implementation of an IMS (see figure 54).

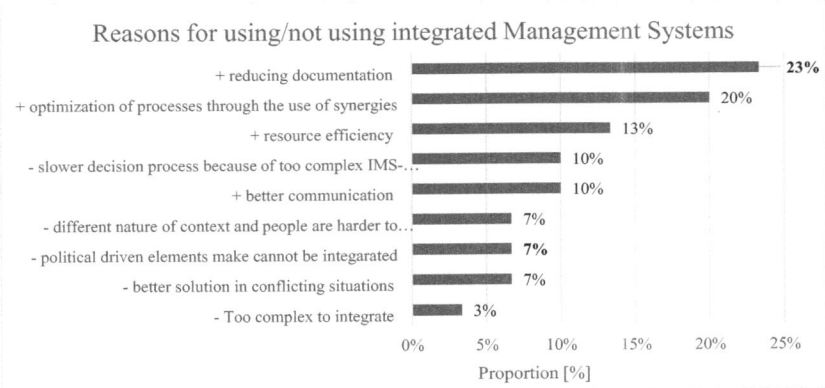

Figure 53 Drivers and problems of an integrated management system
(Source: Own elaboration based on the results of own research)

The research of Kopia the author of this thesis confirmed the findings of other studies Kopia et al. (2016): most companies integrate their management systems stating the benefits of synergies in processes, documentation, and resource usage. Hypothesis 1 is confirmed.

Some negative aspects were discovered regarding the increase bureaucracy and slow decisions when using an IMS since many different stakeholders of all aspects of the diverse management systems have to be managed. Despite generic approaches, such as the quality thought (as in Kaizen or TQM), some management systems are much closer to a specific topic or requirements by laws and regulations. This way different organizational areas with different cultural backgrounds have to find common agreements on certain elements required by the IMS. This mixture of requirements and the balance when managing it might be problematic in an IMS.

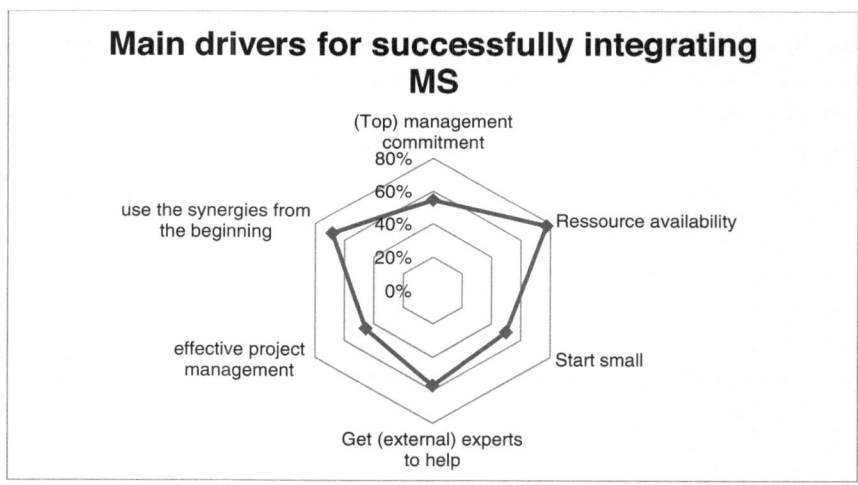

Figure 54 Success factors for implementing an integrated management system
(Source: Own elaboration based on the results of own research)

Hypothesis 2 can only be partially confirmed. The availability of resources is a very important topic. But the use of the synergies between the management systems were rated as very important as well. Considering the fact that most organizations use a step-by-step implementation process, this seems logical. The effort it took to establish one management system should be used to integrate the next management system. Top management support was considered to be important but not at most.

This research confirmed other researches in that field (Kopia et al., 2016). There is a high degree of integration of management systems into an IMS in organizations of all industries, especially if more than two management systems are established. The HLS helps to make the integration easier by defining common elements which have to be defined for all ISO-based management systems. In addition to the generic HLS most organizations use the help of external experts to implement an IMS because of the best-practices experts bring with them. Regarding the implementation most companies use a step-by-step approach and integrate one management system at a time in order to prevent problems concerning different requirements (e.g. quality, information security, environment etc.) and organizational cultures (e.g. different departments and different globally existing locations). Despite a lot of existing research about the benefits of integration and some research regarding the success factors there is not much research on how to approach the integration itself practically. It is suggested that Annex SL / HLS should give more practical advice on how to implement an IMS. The use of the HLS might affect the performance of a management system and should be considered in the evaluation of an integrated management system.

Future studies should increase the size of the samples and analyze the IMS implementation in more detail in order to make precise suggestions of how to approach an IMS implementation project.

5.2 Study on leadership styles within integrated management systems

5.2.1 Objectives of the study of leadership styles and integrated management system

The last chapter showed that there are success factors for the implementation of management systems, such as the HLS. This research analyzed the aspect of management commitment and leadership as another important requirement of the success of management system and IMS implementation projects. The author conducted an exploratory study at 15 German companies which possess an ISO management standard certificate. The objectives of this study is:

- Identifying effects of leadership styles on integrated management systems.
- Identifying outcomes in related business processes and therefore in the performance of business processes.

5.2.2   Research methodology and hypotheses

The PhD-candidate (Kopia, 2016) used a survey study based on semi-structured interviews and evaluated 15 organizations in the German market which have an ISO 27001:2013 certification. ISO 27001 is one of the first ISO management systems which uses the HLS. Different employees working in different levels were asked in this research.

The following three hypotheses were the basis for this research:

1. The HLS is most beneficial for organizations concerning the integration of multiple management systems.
2. A very important factor of management system-introductions is the leadership style and management commitment.
3. The transformational leadership style is favorable in operating of an integrated management system.

5.2.3   Research results for the study of leadership styles and management systems

Leadership were already discussed in chapter 5.2 and 1.2.1 regarding the influence on companies' performance. Leadership itself is a very complex topic since it involves aspects of psychology which are not the matter of this thesis. Nevertheless, there are some common aspects in regard to different leadership styles and their influence on people (Judge & Piccolo, 2004). Often used categories of leadership styles are based on Bass et al. (1996) who suggested dimension of differentiation: Trust, Admiration, Loyalty, Respect, Goleman (1995) who invented the principles of emotional intelligence (IE), or Avery (2004) and his leadership styles

Table 27 Different leadership styles and their characteristics as result of the research

Leadership characteristic	Coercive	Directive	Affiliative	Democratic	Pacasetting	Coaching
Style	Demanding, immediate compliance	Motivating toward a vision	Harmony creation	Consensus looking	Setting of high goals	People development for future
Communication	Do what I say	Come with me	People first	What do you think?	Do as I do now	Try this
Aspects of EI	Self-Control	Self-Confidence	Relationship-Building, empathy	Collaboration	Conscientiousness	Developing others, empathy
Similarity to leadership styles by Avery / Bass	Classical, transactional	Transactional	Transformational	Organic, Laissez-Fair	Transactional	Visionary, transformational

(Source: own elaboration, based on Bass, B. M., Avolio, B. J., Atwater, L. E. (1996), The transformational and transactional leadership of men and women. Applied Psychology: an International Review 45: 5–34; Goleman, D. (1995), Emotional intelligence. New York: Bantam Books; Avery, G.C. (2004) Understanding Leadership: Explaining the Paradigms Gayle C. Avery Sage Publications Ltd (2004))

classical, transactional, visionary, and organic. In table 27 the author of this thesis (Kopia, 2016) identified common elements in these different categories of leadership styles. Other studies in the context of TQM highlighted the topic empowerment of employees through leadership tactics (Kennedy & Schleife, 2007; Njie et al., 2008; Thamizhmanii & Hasan, 2010; Daily et al., 2011) which is specifically important for TQM since the core idea is the openness and commitment for improvement in each employee. The fact the management systems are based on a

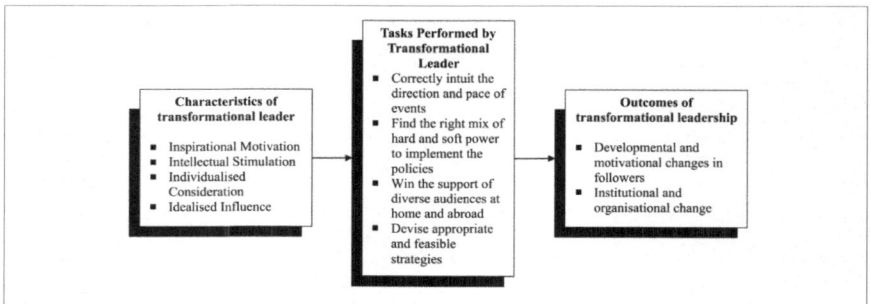

Figure 55 Characteristics of a transformational leadership style

(Source: McGuire David, Hutchings Kate, (2007) Portrait of a transformational leader: the legacy of Dr Martin Luther King Jr, Leadership & Organization DevelopmentJournal, Vol. 28 Iss: 2 p154-p166)

continuous improvement cycle (see chapter 3.2), leadership style which is open for improvements and changes and which motivated employees is more compatible (e.g. the transformational leadership style a seen in figure 55) (Seo et al. 2012; Alharbi, 2012).

High level structure and integration

Similar to the results presented in chapter 0, most organizations have more than one management system (2/3) and already are familiar with the HLS (see figure 56). Most of the companies integrate their management systems into an IMS (66%) even though at the time of this study not all management systems were based on the HLS. Most companies highlighted the benefits of integration (14 out of the 15 companies). Most interestingly – and in contrast to the findings of the research of the last chapter) – the top-down approach of the HLS without giving detailed suggestions of how to integrate was mentioned as benefit since it opens the possibility of interpretation and flexibility. Hypothesis one can be confirmed.

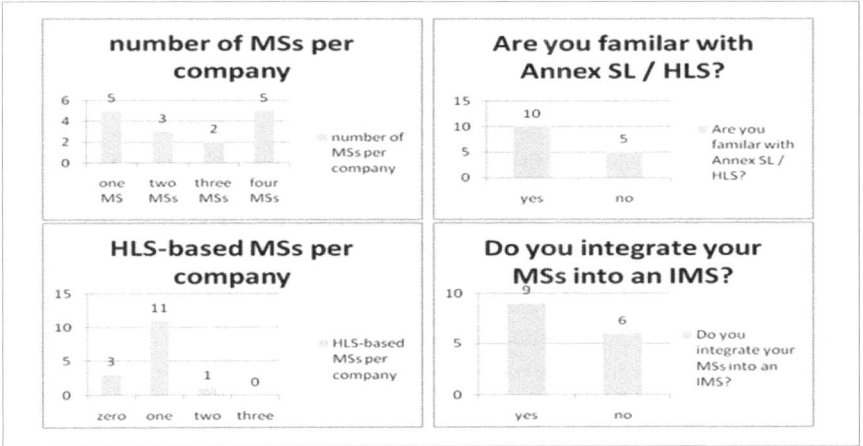

Figure 56 Research results concerning integration of management systems
(own elaboration based on the results of own research)

Leadership

Regarding hypothesis 2 the following result was found: The influence of the top management was rated highly (see figure 57).

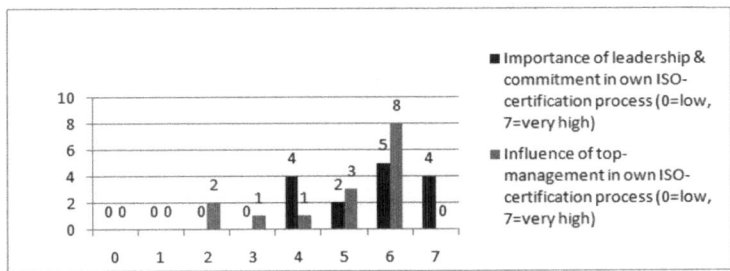

Figure 57 Research results of questions related to top management and leadership influence
(own elaboration based on the results of own research)

Hypothesis 2 can be answered positively.

The favorable leadership characteristics can be seen in figure 58. It can generally be said that the following characteristics are favorable in the context of management system standard's implementation: Affiliative leadership, Leadership with a high commitment, Leadership which motivates the employees. The aspects of leadership and commitment highlighted by the HSL and the use of a transformational style can be clearly confirmed in this study (hypothesis 3).

Even though there are differences in the suggested leadership characteristics and style by scientists (Harms et al., 2010), a leadership style with the ability to easily enable change and create a motivational atmosphere among employees is beneficial for management system's implementation. This involves being affiliative, empathic and able to create trust which can be

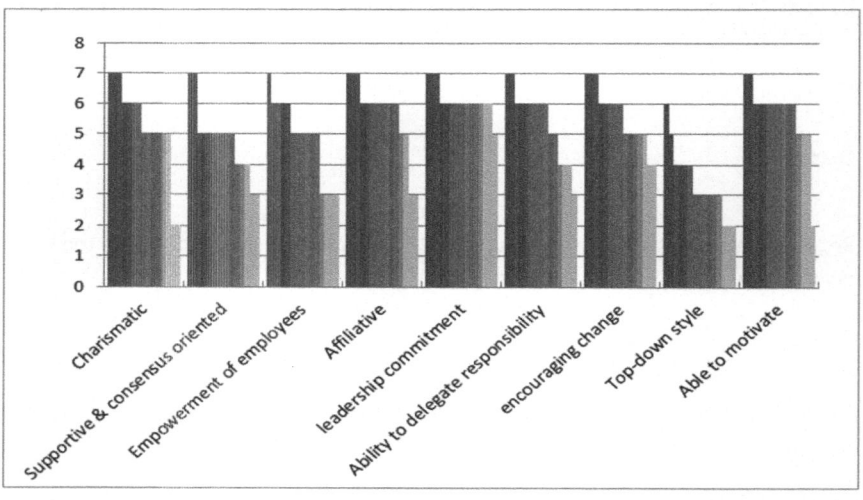

Figure 58 Favorable leadership characteristics in management system implementations
(Source: own elaboration based on the results of own research)

found in most leadership style models, especially Bass's suggested transformational and Goleman's suggested affiliative leadership style. In contrast to that the transactional leadership style and a top-down-approach was rated with the lowest grade (mean of 3.4), showing that this style of leadership is not favorable in the context of management systems.

The authors of this thesis (Kopia, 2016) developed a model of similar leadership styles and tested their characteristics in the context of management system's integration, especially also integrated management systems. In addition to that the benefits of the HLS were analyzed in the same context. As in the last chapter, it could be shown that the HLS offers benefits when management systems are integrated. Most organizations integrate their different management systems into an IMS which offer benefits in form of different synergies. The second aspect considered the leadership style which were suggested by different scientists over the last 20 years. Transformational and transactional leadership styles were compared with aspects of emotional intelligence and discussed in the survey in the context of the used management systems. It could be shown that a leadership style which appreciates change and a culture of open communication and motivation is more likely to create successful implementations of management

Table 28 Research results for questions about leadership characteristics

Leadership characteristic	Mean	Standard Deviation	Variance (Standard deviation)	EI category based on Goleman	Typical for transformational, transactional, or servant style
Charismatic	5.30	1.53	2.35	Several	transformational
Supportive & consensus	4.8	1.15	1.31	Affiliative	Transformational / Servant
Empowerment of employees	4.86	1.30	1.70	Several	Transformational / servant
Affiliative	5.67	1.24	1.52	Affiliative	Transformational / servant
Leadership & commitment	6.13	0.52	0.27	Several	Transformational / Transactional
Ability to delegate responsibility	5.4	1.18	1.40	Several	All (doing it differently)
Encouraging change	5.6	0.99	0.97	Several	Transformational / servant
Top-down style	3.4	1.12	1.26	Coercive	Transactional
Able to motivate	5.67	1.18	1.38	Several	Transformational / Transactional

(Source: own elaboration based on the results of own research)

systems. This concerns the transformational leadership style with visionary and affiliative characteristics. The leadership style is another aspect to consider during a management system implementation and operation. Leadership styles effect the performance of a management system and related business processes.

This study was limited in regards to the amount of companies which were involved into the study. Further research is necessary to understand the different characteristics in more detail and in a broader context regarding different industries or markets.

5.3 Quantitative assessment of integrated management systems and the relationship to process improvements through knowledge management

5.3.1 Objectives of the research

The objectives of this study are as follows:

1. Identifying industry-specific adaptions of management systems.
2. Identifying relationships between management systems certifications and process productivity.
3. Identifying elements of management systems within the business targets and operational processes.
4. Finding a correlation between knowledge management and organizational learning and management system usage.

Management systems are widely established to enhance businesses in various areas (e.g. Quality, Environment, Energy, Information Security etc.). The author of this thesis did an exploratory research of question whether there is a connection between management system standards and the business strategy within the automotive industry.

The automotive industry is one of the industries which use management systems often. As the Toyota Production System some of the best practices which resulted in public standards were originated in the automotive business or its surrounding industries. In fact, the automotive business contributes to the popularity of ISO based systems, such as ISO 9001 (or the adapted version 16949) and ISO 14001. Business strategies on the other hand are necessary to define targets and set guidelines to realize the business processes in that way the organization produces value. For this research the definitions of the VDA (German Association of the Automotive Industry) are being used. The focus is on OEMs. Strategy is a widely discussed topic which goes on for many years. Different strategic approaches were identified by scholars and practitioners over time (Lüftenegger, 2014). New theories of strategy focus on guidelines for strategy, as the Mintzbergs suggestions of the 5Ps (1994) and Porters generic approaches of differentiation, cost leadership, cost focus, and cost differentiation (1980). The focus on competitive forces (Porter's five forces, 1979) and resource based planning became less important since it mainly is concerned with external factors. Concepts based on capabilities were developed (Johnson & Scholes, 2009) (see chapter 1.1) which put their emphases on internal aspects, such as capabilities of the organization and the employees, knowledge, organizational learning, innovation etc. The internal perspective is concerned with efficiency and effectiveness of processes which is a core aspect of management system standards, such as ISO management systems, TQM etc.

5.3.2   Research Methodology

In order to get results on all objectives, multiple studies were performed using the following research methodologies:

1. For the identification of industry-specific adaptions of management systems, a qualitative and quantitative analysis was performed. The author of this thesis analyzed quantitative data based on existing databases by comparing the number of management system certificates typical for the automotive business.
   Then available data with performance indicators (e.g. number of produced vehicles) is compared with the development of the introduction of typical management systems within the automotive industry. In order to prevent a misleading correlation of mature markets, the sample size of this analyses includes only geographic region which has a growing trend (Asia-Pacific).

2. For the identification of the connection of management systems with the business targets the type and the introduction year of the management systems is compared to the published business targets (table 31). In order to identify any connection this analysis was done using two deductions:

    a. If the specific strategic target were defined within the published strategy (e.g. quality leadership), the introduction of a management system (whose goal is to increase quality) within a reasonable range of time is assumed (e.g. TQM, ISO 9001, or the automotive specific quality management system ISO 16949 etc.) and the correlation was positively rated.

    b. If the introduction of a management system (e.g. environmental management) was done before an outlined target and emphasized as a new strategic targets later (e.g. reducing environmental pollution), the connection was positively rated.

3. A correlation analysis was performed, in order to find a correlation between knowledge management and organizational learning and management system usage. This was done using the calculated value for intellectual capital as a measurement for the intellectual capability (by using knowledge management methodologies) and the year of the introduction of management systems.

The study is based on the following hypotheses:

1. There is a correlation between the use of (integrated) management systems and the operational goals of business processes outlined by the business strategies of the companies.

2. Considering the content of outlines targets within the business strategies of the organizations and their use of management systems there are overlapping topics. This shows that there is a linkage between strategies and organizational processes reflected by management systems.

3. There is correlation between management system usage and the VAIC-value (which represents organizational learning and knowledge management).

5.3.3   Overview of characteristics of integrated management systems within the automotive industry

Management systems are widely adopted worldwide. They offer guidelines, best-practices, evaluation criteria, and standardized processes for organizations to become better in the management of a certain field. The number of ISO certified organizations grew within the last two decades. Table 29 illustrates the number of certificates of the different management standards based on ISO. It can be seen that the standard for the automotive industry (ISO/TS 16949 – see below) is high with almost 60.000 certifications in 2014. Considering that this certification only exists in the automotive field when the other standards can be applied to all industries (except ISO 13485), the importance of certifications within the automotive industry becomes clear.

Table 29 Comparison of number of international standard certificates in the market between 2013 and 2014

International Stan-dard	Number of certificates 2013	Number of certificates 2014	Increment in per-cent
ISO 9001	1.126.460	1.138.155	1
ISO 140001	301.622	324.148	7
ISO 50001	4.826	6.778	40
ISO 27001	22.349	23.972	7
ISO 22000	26.847	30.500	14
ISO/TS 16949	53.723	57.950	8
ISO 13485	25.655	57.950	8
ISO 22301	-	1.757	
Total	1.561.482	1.609.294	3

(Source: own representation based on ISO annual report, (2015b), http://www.iso.org/iso/annual _report_2015.pdf, accessed 08/08/2016)

Management systems are used widely within the automotive branch (see table 30). Many ISO-based management systems exist within the automotive industry and re-lated businesses as the metal-industry and other suppliers. For these certificates as ISO 9001 and ISO/TS16494 (Franceschini & Cecconi, 2006) are important.

Most of the manufacturing companies in the automotive business implemented a management system, such as ISO 9001 / ISO/TS 16494, ISO 14001, or more generic principles, such as Kaizen, EFQM, the Malcom Baldrige Criteria for Performance Excel-lence, and TQM (Katarzyna, 2015). ISO/TS 16494 became a mandatory standard in the automotive sector and grew 8% in 2014 mostly because of the certification efforts of Chinese manufacturers. Many OEMs demand this certificate from their suppliers. ISO/TS 16494 focusses on the decrease of the defect rate within the supply chain. The standard is based on ISO 9001 which was extended of automotive specific aspects by the IATF (International Automotive Task Force) (Brückner, 2009).

ISO/TS 16949 standard was the third largest standards within the automotive in-dustry compared to number of certifications in 2014 (Katarzyna, 2015) (see table 30). Franceschini et al. (2011) found that 77 percent of the ISO/TS 16949 certificates are related to the top 10 automotive OEMs. ISO/TS 16949 has similar advantages than ISO

9001 (Ostadi et al., 2010). The following benefits were mentioned in scientific literature (Sroufe & Curkovic, 2008; Bevilacqua et al., 2011; Mohamad et al., 2010): impact
on the quality image, reduction of the defect rate and a higher product quality, a consolidated market position, better plant performance etc.

Katarzyna (2015) investigated the polish automotive industry and found that 60
percent of the organization in the sample size of the survey implemented an ISO 9001
management system, 41 percent implemented ISO 14001, and 27 percent implemented an ISO TS 16949 management system. The following systems follow: OHSAS
18001 with 15 percent, Kaizen with 10 percent, TQM with 7 percent, ISO 27001 with 3
percent.

5.3.4   Results of the research of quantitative assessment of management systems
         and the relationship to process improvements through knowledge manage-
         ment

Appendix C and figure 59 illustrate that the number of management system certifications typical for the automotive industries is mostly lead by the Asian-Pacific area
in 2016 (with a similar trend the year before that). This is especially true for the ISO
16949 certificate as the quality management certificate for the automotive business.
The reason is that a significant part of the production moved to these areas. The correlation between the number of certificates and the number of production of cars confirms the hypothesis of the growing number of certificates and the growing productivity in that region. The correlation is the result of the importance of this specific management system and the influence of that on the automotive business as requirement
of the implementation of the system into the business processes.

Table 30: Number of vehicle production per country in 2016 compared to new certificates in 2016 (top 3 are highlighted)

#	Country	Cars	Commercial cars	Total	Change	# of ISO 16949 2016
11	Thailand	805,033	1,139,384	1,944,417	1.8%	1.574
10	Brazil	1,778,464	377,892	2,156,356	-11.2%	1.200
9	Canada	802,057	1,568,214	2,370,271	3.8%	521
8	Spain	2,354,117	531,805	2,885,922	5.6%	965
7	Mexico	1,993,168	1,604,294	3,597,462	0.9%	1.575
6	South Korea	3,859,991	368,518	4,228,509	-7.2%	5.352
5	India	3,677,605	811,360	4,488,965	7.9%	5.289
4	Germany	5,746,808	315,754	6,062,562	0.5%	3.460
3	Japan	7,873,886	1,330,704	9,204,590	-0.8%	1.506
2	USA	3,934,357	8,263,780	12,198,137	0.8%	4.293
1	China	24,420,744	3,698,050	28,118,794	14.5%	28.830

(Source: Own elaboration based on the International Organization of Motor Vehicle Manufacturers, http://www.oica.net/, accessed 03.02.2018 and data of Appendix C)

Generally, it can be stated that the productivity correlates with the introduction of management systems and confirms hypothesis one. Implementing management systems such as ISO 9001, ISO/TS 16949 and alike create benefits for the company within the production processes.

In order to assess hypotheses two and three the business strategies of the automotive manufacturer BMW and Daimler which are operating in the premium segment, and General

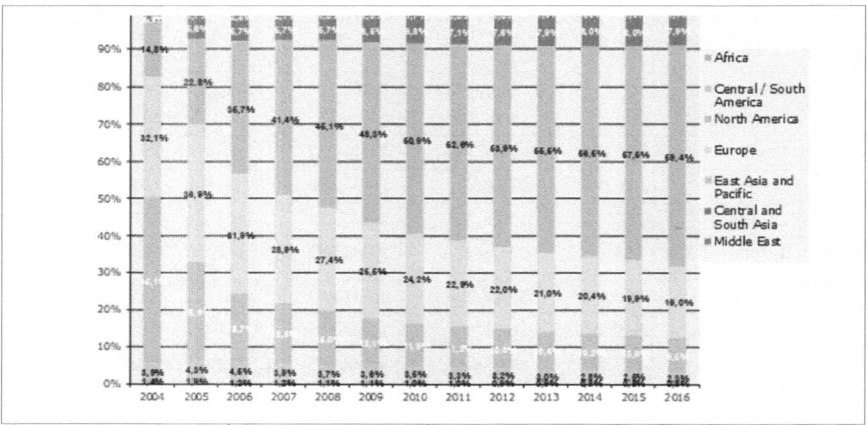

Figure 59 Comparison of the regional share of ISO 16494 certificates 2004-2016
(Source: see Appendix C)

Motors, Toyota, and Volkswagen (VW) which focus on high volumes and the mass market are used as input for the comparison. The first aspect of the research is strategy
initiation. BMW and Volkswagen called their business strategy "Mach18" and "Number
One" in 2008 and 2007. Through a competitor analysis specific targets were identified
at Volkswagen with the goal to become number one in several categories (especially
competing against the rival Toyota). The VW group owns a number of brands and the
strategy had to be customized for each sub organization. Similar to VW BMW announced the corporate strategy „Number One". Specific targets were defined for the
next 4 years and future targets for 2010.

In 2011 Daimler announced its strategy „Mercedes-Benz 2020". Due to the decreased sales rate within the years before, the strategy focused on growth and leadership in technology.

Toyota's report announced strategic targets, such as sustainable growth and the
focus on sales within the European market. Specific to Toyota there is a strong focus
on customizing and adapting strategies to the specific regions more than to its brands
especially compared to its potential rival Volkswagen.

The strategy of General Motors was focused on sales after the bankruptcy in 2011.
The core priorities were defined as earning customers for life, grow the brand, become
the lead in technology and innovation, drive core efficiencies and create a culture to
win.

Most of the presented strategies were defined for longer than the average timespan for strategic targets of 5 years. It can be seen that the strategies of the presented OEMs are similar not just regarding their defined timespan of the target but also because of the content (e.g. sales and growth, customer focus, efficiency etc.). The strategies show the focus of the automotive

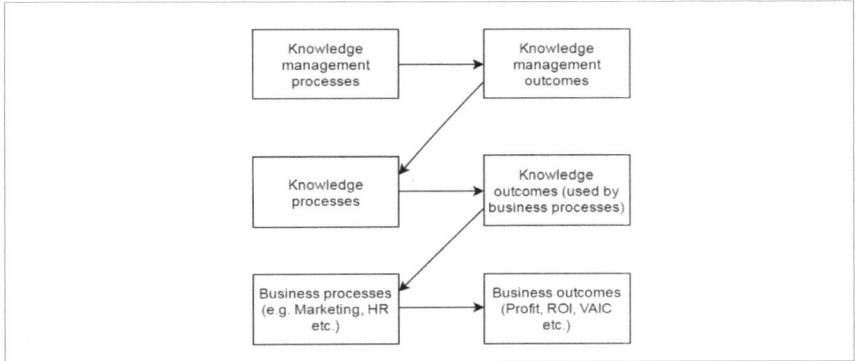

Figure 60 The influence of knowledge management on the performance of businesses
(Source: Own based on Dalkir, K. (2005). Knowledge Management in Theory and Practice. Burlington; Oxford: Elsevier/Butterworth Heinemann.)

manufacturers toward the internal and external perspective. VW's Mach18 strategy emphases employee satisfaction but also sales growth and customer satisfaction. Toyota on the other hand defines targets for sustainability in the sustainability report (Toyota, 2015b). Targets as technology leadership can be found at the strategies of Mercedes, BMW, and GM.

The PhD-candidate of this thesis identified the connection between knowledge management processes and the business outcomes as suggested by McEllroy (2003) – see figure 60 (Kompalla et al., 2017) which is used in this research to identify correlations. The author of this study assessed the topic based on a literature research and a correlation analysis using the following concept (see figure 61):

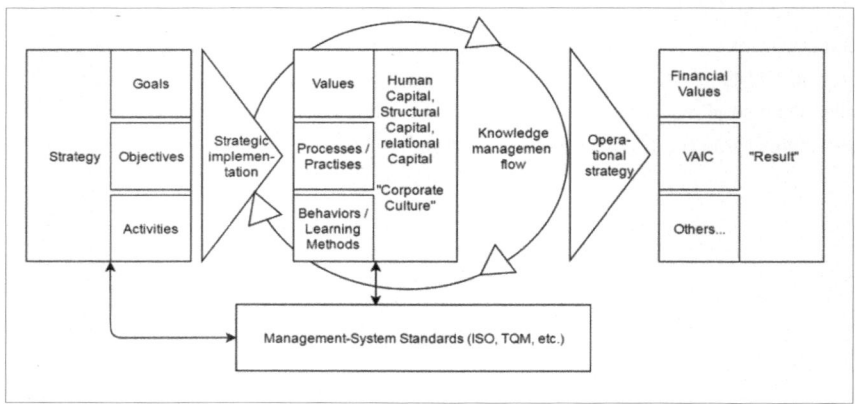

Figure 61 Framework to assess the influence of KM on the result of the company
(Source: own elaboration based on the results of own research)

The results show that similar management systems were introduced at the studied companies mainly in the area of quality and environmental management (ISO 9001, ISO 14001 in the 1990s and between 200-2005 resp., ISO 50001 after 2010). Organizational targets mostly include employee attractiveness, quality focus, and growth in profitability etc. Quality in the strategies of the manufacturers is an issue in the strategic goals defined in 2006 and 2007. The respective management systems were introduced in the late 1990s, therefore, it is not easy to identify any connection in this regard. But in the area of environmental aspects including energy, the targets were defined closer to the introduction of respective management systems. For example, Daimler's strategy (2011) to be the "leader in green technology" can be one result of the introduction of the ISO 14001 management system the years before. The targets of the leader in zero emission was announced by Nissan.

Management systems and business strategies announced by the manufacturers have common goals. In order to analysis the data in the context of hypothesis two, table 31 shows that the main goals of respective management systems fit to high-level targets of business strategies published in reports of the manufacturers. It can be seen that there is a high overlapping content which confirms hypothesis two.

Table 31 Comparison of strategic targets and the introduction of management systems in the automotive business

Brand	Release Year of MMS	Strategy anounce	Content of business strategy	
VW "Mach18"	ISO 9001: 2005	2007	• Leading employer • Leader in customer satisfaction and quality • Growth (sales > 10 Mio.)	• Profitability (21 % Return on capital employed) • *Since 2008 (Mach 18+): Ecological leader*
BMW "One"	ISO 9001: 2005 (BMW M) ISO 14001: 1998 (BMW US)	2007	• Shaping the future: Sustainability & efficient dynamics • Access to technologies and customers	• Growth • Profitability
Daimler "2020"	ISO 9001: 1998 ISO 14001: 2004 ISO 50001: 2013	2007	• Flexible footprint and productivity improvement • Technology leadership • Sales leadership	• Capital & cost discipline; Sustainable profitability • *Since 2011: Leading in green technology and safety*
Audi "Route 15"	ISO 9001: 1996 ISO 14001: 2001	2006	• Globally attractive employer • Customer enthusiasm an global Image leader in emotion and quality	• Continuous growth • Leading financial force
Honda	ISO 9001: 2005 - 2015 ISO 14001: 2001 - 2010	2010	• Major social responsibility initiatives • Philanthropy and Safety	• Environment • Focus on investor relations
Skoda	Not available	2011	• Top employer with global talent pool • Strategic spearhead focused on price/value, practicability and space	• Sales growth • Profitability and financial strength
Nissan "Power 88"	ISO 14001: 2011 ISO 50001: 2012 (US)	2011	• Brand power • Enhancing quality	• Zero emission leadership & Business Expansion • Cost leadership and Sales Power
Toyota "Global vision"	ISO 9001: 1998 ISO 14001: 1998 (Kentucky plant)	2011	• Contribute to communities / Contribute to mobility future • Exceed customer expectations	• Sustainable growth • Stable base of business

(Source: own elaboration based on the results of own research)

For hypothesis three a correlation analysis was done comparing the VAIC-value of one manufacturer (chosen because of the availability of data) with the implementation dates of the management system standards. The VAIC represents the knowledge component of the suggested model (figure 61). The analysis shows that there are four phases within 20 years in which the automotive businesses introduced management systems (see figure 62).

There is a positive correlation between the introduction of a management system and the VAIC-value ranging between 0,47 and 0,65 within the years 1997 and 2014. What can also be seen is that external effects (such as the financial crisis) have a more dramatic effect on the VAIC-values than internal driven changes (such as the introduction of a management system).

Table 32 Overlapping topics of management systems and business strategies

Manage-ment System	MMS Criteria	MMS Criteria as part of business strategy?
ISO 9001	Customer orientation & Quality Steering Plans	Yes: "Leader in customer satisfaction and quality"
	Traceability	Yes: "Profitability"; "Capital & cost discipline"
ISO 14001	Environmental declaration EMAS	Yes (since 2011): "Environment"; "Ecological leader"
	Emergency preparedness	Yes: "Sustainability"; "Sustainable growth"
ISO 50001	Energy efficiency	Yes (since 2011): ""Efficient dynamics"
	Energy Saving	Yes (since 2011): "Zero emission leadership"
Overlapping criteria of ISO 9001, 14001 and 50001	Targets	Yes: Qualitative & quantitative business strategy targets
	Organizational Context, Resources and Politics	Yes: "Leading employer"; "Contribute to communities"
	Training / Communication	No
	Performance Evaluation / Surveillance and Measuring	Yes: Periodical tracking of quantitative targets
	Internal Audit	No
	Leadership and Management Review	Yes: "Leading financial force", "Leadership"
	Processing	Yes: "Exceed customer expectations"

(Source: own elaboration based on the results of own research)

Hypothesis three can be confirmed. Nevertheless, the identified correlation is only vague and needs to be analyzed in more detail in future research using a different or a more detailed research methodology.

Several similarities were discovered in the strategic targets of the big automotive OEMs. Most targets focusing long-term growth strategies with fixed value-based goals measured with financial indicators. Nevertheless, despite this external perspective the companies also state some targets from the internal perspective. This involves aspects of sustainability, employee satisfaction, and process efficiency etc. – some of them reflected by management systems. Despite that, the connection between published targets a management systems is minimal.

Management systems are widely adopted in the automotive business and improve the business performance of the organizations. Especially management systems which increase the

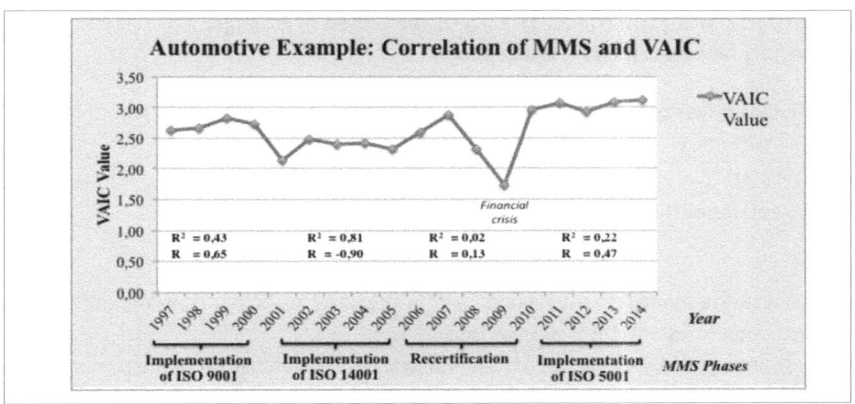

Figure 62 Correlation analysis of management systems and the Value Added Intellectual Coefficient-value
(Source: own elaboration based on the results of own research)

quality of the products (e.g. ISO 9001, ISO/TS 16949) are the most used management systems in the automotive industry highlighting that management systems support the defined business strategies from the internal perspective.

5.4 Analyses of current trends of use and evaluation of management system performance within the service sector

5.4.1   Objectives of the analysis of management system performance within the service sector

The objectives of this study is to:

- Analyze the management systems within the service sector regarding differences and similarities and their success rate.
- Identifying used approaches of implementation and evaluation of the performance of the management systems.

In order to identify key performance indicators for the evaluation of management systems, this study identifies approaches in a particular industry. This study focusses on the research of the author of this thesis who investigated the higher education system in Germany regarding their quality management systems. For the research the service industry was selected with a focus on private universities because these universities quickly developed and evolved since the 1990s. The research uses two scientific approaches. The first is literature study on current developments of quality management systems within the private university field including the realized methodologies, measurement methods, and existing evaluations. The second approach is theory development through deduction based on a survey in which a category system for quality assurance characteristics is suggested. The analysis of Council's statements of the involved universities used the method described by Mayring (2015). Based on deductive analysis criteria are elaborated, with which the texts are skimmed and the results are deducted.

5.4.2   Research methodology for the analysis

As in every market a raising competition results in pressure. This becomes also true for private universities since the market share increased dramatically in the recent years. To distinguish themselves from each other, the offered quality of the education is a primary indicator. The research of the author of this thesis therefor presents quality management initiatives within the private university field in Germany by comparing the integration of the management systems and the documentation and evaluation (Golowko et al., 2017). Until present there is no standard quality management system in the educational field. But in order to increase the transparency in the market, standardized ratings are useful. This also involves the evaluation step. Especially a qualified evaluation demonstrates the real willingness to manage and improve the quality by making it transparent who evaluates and with what results.

The quality of education can be assessed on the basis of the approach developed by Lisiecka (2000) and Godzwon (2006). Applying this approach quality can be assessed with external and internal activities using self-assessment at first and later make comparison to other organizations and institution in that branch. The indicators presented in table 33 can be used as basis (see table 33).

Table 33 Indicators for quality in education used in this study

Curriculum	Curriculum - structure of the curriculum (program/goals, tasks, focus on development of functional tasks, focus on students' activities, and integration of programs within and between areas) - courses and programs - key competencies that students develop in the given school.
Achievements	Achievements (evaluated by external, independent agencies) – quality achievement compared with the set goals.
Learning and teaching	Learning and teaching - teachers' work - students' work and experience - meeting the needs of the students - monitoring and evaluating the work of students and teachers.
Students' support	Students' support - students' personal, social and spiritual growth - progress and achievement monitoring - support in all aspects of learning, progress, students' and teachers' personal development.
School ethos	School ethos - school policy - school atmosphere and relations - specific goals of each individual school - orientation towards students', teachers' and parents' satisfaction.
Resources	Resources - school resources - teachers, professional associates, the principal; their education, teacher's teamwork, cooperation; being open to innovation - material resources and premises - efficient human and material resources.
Management, leadership and quality assurance	Management, leadership and quality assurance - approaches to leadership and management.

(Source: Own, based on Golowko Nina, Kopia Jan, Geldmacher Wiebke, Förster-Pastor Ulrike S., (2017), Quality management and assurance at german private universities - a comparative study, Calitatea: Acces la Success, Bucharest, vol. 18, no. 157, pg. 85-94, 2017, ISSN 1582-2559)

Contrasting the suggested KPIs against the eight components of TQM (see chapter 3.2.1), similarities can be seen. It can be deduced that there are similarities between typical organizations and educational institutions since they all have similar processes within their value chain. A quality management system for the educational market therefore should be similar to those of the normal market.

The basis for the research approach was the accreditation procedure of the German Council of Science and Humanities which certifies private educational institutions in Germany.

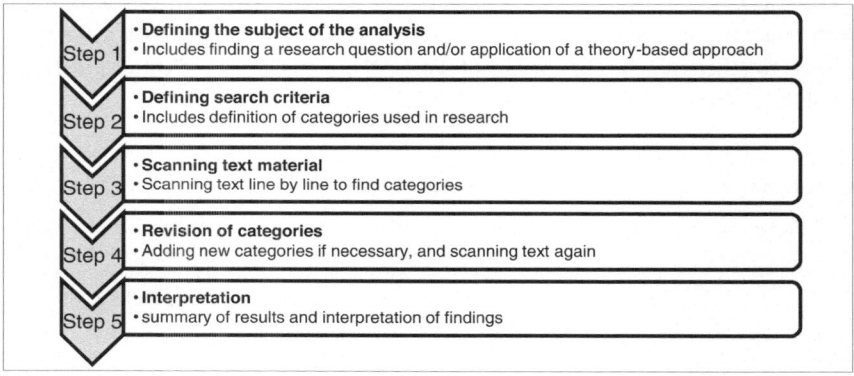

Figure 63 Research methodology of the study of management systems in the service sector
(Source: own illustration based on Mayring, P. (2015), Qualitative Inhaltsanalyse, Grundlagen und Techniken, 12th ed., Beltz, Weinheim, Basel)

The goal is to assure the quality regarding the scientific consistency. This research was done in 2016. Up to October 2016 there were 142 statements written regarding the accreditation of private institutions. During the accreditation several quality related issues are being assessed. This material serves as source for this research. The selections were chosen on the basis of efficiency and representativeness, so that 27 samples were selected for the final study (19% of the existing samples). The research samples are scanned for the answer to questions regarding quality and quality management systems (see below). The information is extracted using qualitative approaches by Maring (2015). The research methodology is illustrated in figure 63.

Step 1:

The research questions are:

- What are quality management systems which private universities in Germany use?
- How is the quality reported, published and evaluated?
- How is the quality management process?

Step 2:

The assessment methods for quality in private universities is done using procedures within the institutions by themselves. This is mainly done using a self-assessment and additionally by using an external auditor to gain the accreditation.

Step 3 and 4:

The extraction of information from the report was done using a qualitative content analysis. With the help of the software QCAmap which assists in sorting and analyzing texts systematically (Mayring, 2014).

Step 5:

The fifths step was the comparison of the analysis with standard quality management systems. As a result, a theory was deducted.

5.4.3   Results and discussion

Institutionalization:

The main question of this category is the responsibility which is taking for the quality management system. The diversity of this question can be seen in figure 64. A designated quality manager is only available at two universities. One university within the sample selection established a quality department. The other results show that the quality topic is prioritized differently. Quality management is generally more centered in the administrational parts of the universities and topic of managers.

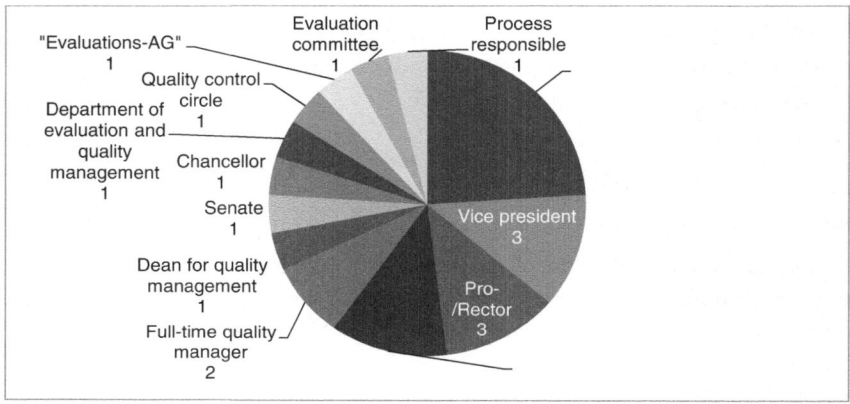

Figure 64 Responsibilities for quality management in private universities
(Source: own elaboration based on the results of own research)

Evaluation: Who evaluates whom about what?

The central question in the evaluation is who is assessing the quality management system

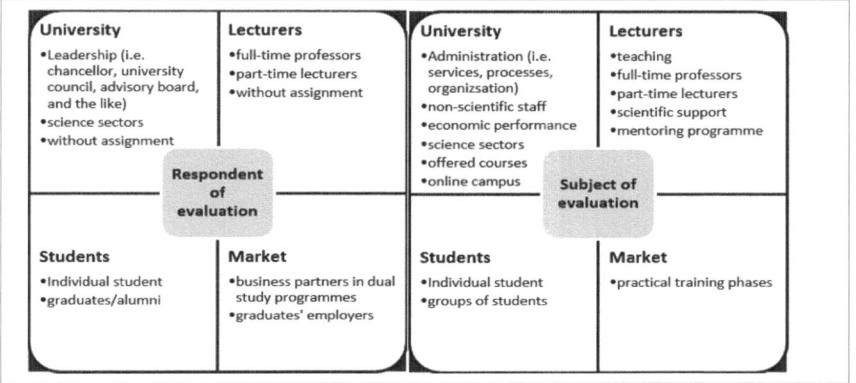

Figure 65 The respondents and the subject of the evaluation
(Source: own elaboration based on the results of own research)

and what basis is used. The answers illustrated in figure 65 show a diverse image because of the number of different stakeholders and their perspectives within the evaluation (see figure 80). The proportion of the answers are visible in figure 66.

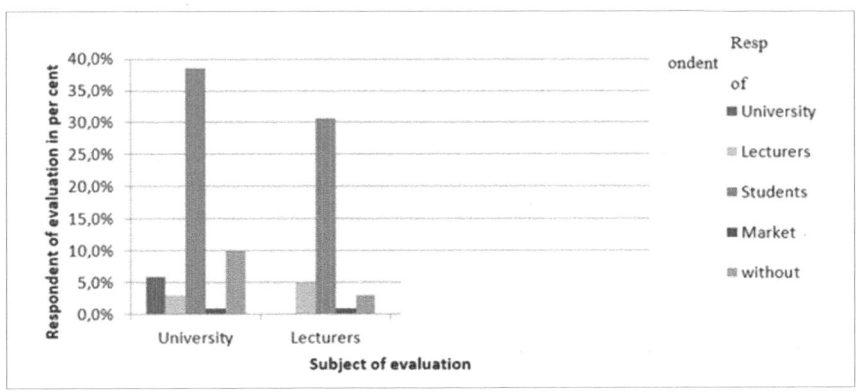

Figure 66 Proportion of the question who is evaluating whom
(Source: own elaboration based on the results of own research)

The following dimensions are criteria for evaluations which are answered by students:

- Administrational processes
- Quality of the services
- General organizational topics
- Quality topics regarding the staff
- Availability of study programs, offered scientific sectors, modules and concepts
- General academic conditions

Lecturers are asked about administrational services, available courses, services, processes etc.

The results of this topic of the research raises concerns about the overall quality of the evaluations. Most interestingly the non-teaching or non-academic employees are not involved in the evaluations which is a big difference to other branches where there is no distinction of the way who is being asked within a quality assessment. Another concern is the fact that no professor is evaluated after the person is selected as professor. Any problems or improvements of certain aspects concerning individual professors are ignored. The same is true for students and their performance except the grades. Also, the evaluations do not include the opinions of graduates or other external companies. Some other problems relating to the evaluation are the time of the survey (Schulz et al., 2006) and the measurability of the criteria (Aleca & Mihai, 2016).

Table 34 The content of evaluation of the management systems

Criteria	Content
Individual	Satisfaction, Workload, learning effort, Problems with courses, Individual problems, Target achievements
Study conditions	Study situation, Quality of service, Processes, Range of courses
Teaching	Learning success, Quality of teaching, Improvement of curriculum
Career	Professional career, Professional development, Studies' contribution to prof. development, Professional success

(Source: own elaboration based on the results of own research)

There is also the problem that the following processes are almost not existing:

- Generating of final reports including meetings after the evaluation
- Performing random inspections of the quality management systems
- Involving the evaluation of professors and students. Especially the monitoring of students and student groups does not happen in German universities.

Table 34 illustrated the criteria and the corresponding content of the evaluation.

Transparency of results

Universities in the sample size report mostly internally only to the board. There is also the problem that not all stakeholders are involved, information about the results are not transparent enough.

Consequences:
Which measures do the universities draw from the evaluation results?

The problem of the transparency was stated above and can be problematic regarding the question of drawn consequences. The measures announced by the universities in the samples are mainly invole improvement of study (13), improvement of services (9), training programmes for lecturers (9), separation from lecturer (6), and a bonus system (5). Many different countermeasures are the result of evaluations which can be seen positively. Nevertheless, the reactions doesn't seem to be systematic or following a best-practice approach. This is a matter for improvement.

External quality assurance:

Most universities have accredited programs (80%) which means that they were evaluated externally in order to reach that goal. Besides this "forced" accreditation there is only

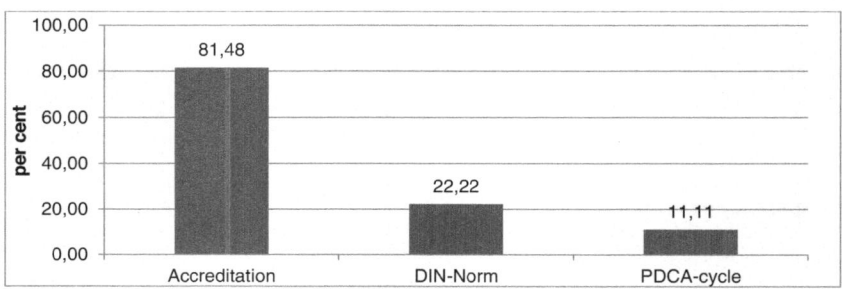

Figure 67 Quality management models used by the organizations assessed in this study
(Source: own elaboration based on the results of own research)

a few universities which follow widely adopted quality management standards as ISO 9001. Only one university in the sample selection is certified on the basis of ISO 9001 though six generally follow the ISO 9001 approach. Three universities follow the Deming-cycle.

No university applied standards such as TQM, EFQM etc. The accreditation of the German Accreditation Council's regulations is most important. This is also true for public universities but 27% of them claim to follow a TQM- or EFQM-approach (Schmid, 2014).

The diversity of the quality approaches within the educational institutions makes it difficult for customers to compare the different offers on the market. It is necessary that a sustainable quality management system is developed which makes this comparison easier.

Discussions

Educational institutions, such as university, have quality assurance models in place in order to evaluate and improve their performance regarding quality. Quality is a selection criterion for customers, therefore it can be very important to survive in the competitive landscape. Private universities developed a strong focus on specific customer expectations in order to fit within a niche which cannot be served by other institutions, such as state-owned universities. This is why private universities increased regarding their market share.

This study analyzed the quality management systems in the service sector showing that there is an increasing awareness of the quality topic within that specific branch. Nevertheless, there is no concurrent quality management within the selected institutions but rather a heterogeneity of different approaches. These approaches are not only including different internal quality management processes but also differences in the evaluation which are based on a self-assessment approach on the one hand and on an external accreditation process by the German Council of Science and Humanities on the other. In order to be accredited private universities have to have a quality management system but the Bologna process didn't define exact recommendations about that. This is the reason of the diversity in quality management approaches within the selected samples. It is necessary to develop a best practice approach for quality assessment and evaluation within that branch in order to create a better comparability. This further enhances the chances of universities to grow – not only nationally but also internationally. Since there are widely adopted and accepted quality management systems available (ISO standards, TQM, EFQM etc.) it might be useful to adapt these standards that they fit into the educational market. This requires that universities identify all their stakeholder's expectations, designate quality managers with special responsibilities, measure quality regularly which includes all relevant sources (especially students, professors, external companies, non-academic staff etc.), publish and communicate the results through reports openly, performing measures on the basis of the finding and improve the quality management system constantly.

6 Research and development of a measurement model for the effects of management systems on sustainable business processes considering risk management and balanced score card

This chapter focusses on the development of measurement models that were developed as a result of studies within the PhD-research program. It begins with the presentation of studies that include important reasons for this research. The first chapter highlights the knowledge gaps and problems in the implementation and use of integrated management systems based on the authors work experience in consulting and the auditing of management systems. It also analyses the current requirements of the EU regarding sustainability in reporting and the necessity to measure and report business process performance with more than only financial values. In the last part, the author develops an evaluation model for integrated management systems and verifies it for practical use.

6.1 A quantitative analysis of management system audit results to identify knowledge gaps of management system performance evaluation

6.1.1 Objectives of the analysis

This study has the following objectives:

- Identifying which aspects of ISO international standards create most non-conformities in management systems during audits (internal as well as external).
- Discovery success factors for management system certifications and reasons for non-conformities based on different perspectives. A special focus is placed on aspects of performance evaluation, continuous improvement, and risk management.

An important part of management systems is the certification by a third-party auditing company. With a third-party (also called external) audit, the presence and successful operation of a management system or an integrated management system is officially confirmed. The requirements for an auditing company to perform audits is regulated by standards issued by an accreditation body of the country. For ISO standards there are two ISO standards applicable to perform audits: ISO/IEC 17021 and ISO 19011. Both standards define the requirements for auditing management systems for different purposes. ISO/IEC 17021 defines the requirements for performing an external audit for auditing companies. ISO 19011 serves as a guideline for performing audits in a more general matter and can also be used by non-auditing companies to assess their own management system using internal audits or in supplier audits. It answers question about the evaluation process of competence for individual matters.

Auditing companies themselves must be officially authorized by the accreditation body before they are able to perform external audits. After confirmation, auditors working for the auditing companies are able to evaluate the management system of other companies using an external audit process which requires the auditors to check every aspect of the management system at the locations of the company. This is done based on guidelines for the required length and scope of the audit which usually follows a 3-year re-certificate cycle. There are smaller verification audits in the years between these 3-year cycles. In each audit, auditors identify conformities and non-conformities in accordance with the requirements of the management system. There are major non-conformities and minor non-conformities. Major non-conformities result in an unsuccessful external audit. Minor non-conformities might result in stipulations that requirements have to improve until the next audit.

External audits performed by auditors follow a similar approach which is regulated in the previous documents. Therefore, it is possible to compare the results of ISO-based management systems audits with each other. This is especially true after the introduction of the high-level structure stated in chapter 3.1.2 and chapter 5.1 which mandates that the requirements of each management system are based on this generic structure. In table 12 the basic arrangement of the high-level structure is visible. Despite the differences in content of each management system standard, each management systems follows a cycling approach of continues improvement (e.g. based on the Plan-Do-Check-Act-cycle) including common requirements. The requirements used in this research can be summarized as follows:

- A risk-based approach is required for management systems. This risk-based approach has the purpose to identify risks and define measures in a concise and continues way.
- Commitment and involvement of the management. Management systems based on ISO are aimed to improve the organization and the related business processes regarding the nature of the management system. This requires the involvement of

the management by defining goals and the acquisition of the essential resources (including human resources and the training). It also involves concise planning, evaluation, and improvement.

- An evaluation and improvement process. It is important to assess the management system on a regular basis through a recurring evaluation based on measurement methods such as key performance indicators. To reach the goals defined by the management, the use of the management system must be improved, which should involve linking the defined strategical goals set by the management.

Looking at the high-level structure these stated items involve the following chapters 5: leadership, 8: operating, 9: performance evaluation, 10: improvements. Chapter 5 involves the commitment of the leadership and goal setting which also is reflected in the risk strategy of the organization. Chapter 8 involves the actual operation of the management system and related business processes. Within this phase, the management system can "produce its value" and improve the aspects which were defined and planned before. To evaluate and measure these values, chapter 9 requires the performance evaluation. An improvement process discussed in chapter 10 entails a close link to the responsibility and decision making of the management which closes the cyclic approach of the management system.

Based on existing external audits executed in organizations through the years 2015 and 2018, the above- detailed aspects are being analyzed.

6.1.2   Research method

This research uses an empirical analysis based on the results of external audits and audit findings. The database consists of audit reports and information gathered during external audits and publicly available management reports of 25 organizations. All information was analyzed and the necessary data for the analysis was extracted.

The organizations examined operate in diverse industries: 12 organizations are in the medical sector, 8 in the service industry, and 4 in the energy sector. The organizations are of varied sizes, ranging from small business with 8 employees to large organizations with over 1.500 employees. The external audits took place between 2015 and 2018. The audits employed international standards ISO 9001 and ISO 27001, as well as combination audits using ISO 14001 by an audit team in which the PhD-candidate and other auditors were involved.

The audit results included interviewing different employees during the audits.

The results were empirically tested using the calculation of the standard deviation, variance value, and mean value.

The standard deviation is calculated as follows:

$$s = \sqrt{\frac{1}{N-1} \sum_{i=1}^{N} (x_i - \overline{x})^2},$$

X(i) equals one sample value
x̄ equals the mean of the sample
N equals the sample size

The following hypotheses were tested:

1. There are more non-conformities in areas of the high-level structure chapters 5, 8, 9, and 10.
2. There are more non-conformities in separated management systems than in integrated management systems in the high-level structure chapters 5, 8, 9 and 10.
3. The older the management system is the fewer non-conformities can be found.
4. Evaluations of management systems typically do not include a link to the strategic level.
5. The evaluation of management systems is frequently done using KPIs. There are more non-conformities if these KPIs have no connection to sustainability or strategic elements of the organization.
6. The strategic linkage of the management system can be seen between the linkage of the risk management approach of the management system to the enterprise (and strategic) risk management of the company.

6.1.3   Results and implications of the research results of the evaluation of management system audit results

The result of this analysis can be seen in figure 68 in which the number of non-conformities is being presented organized by chapters of the high-level structure of

ISO based management system standards. Because of the database used, it can be concluded that there are more

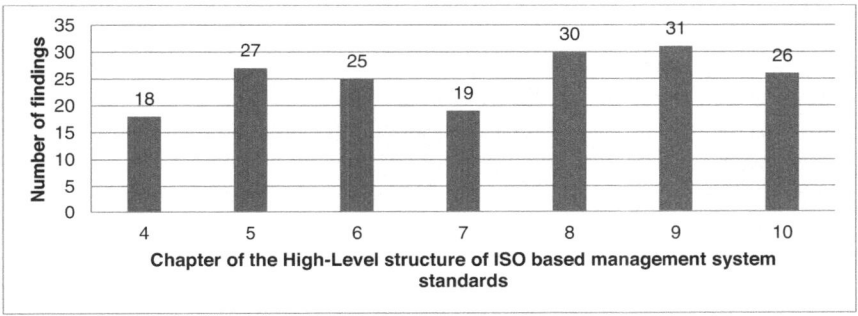

Figure 68 Number of non-conformities in external management system audits in 25 organizations
(Source: own elaboration based on the results of own research)

non-conformities in chapter 5, 8, and 9 than in the other areas of the chapter structure. Table 35 shows that the mean is 25. Based on this result and despite a relatively low standard deviation

Table 35 Standard deviation, mean, and variance of the research results of the number of non-conformities

Mathematical expression	Value
Sample Standard Deviation, s	5.014
Variance (Sample Standard), s^2	25.142
Population Standard Deviation, σ	4.6423
Variance (Population Standard), σ^2	21.551
Mean (Average):	25.143

(Source: own elaboration based on the results of own research)

of 5.01 the result show that audit findings in the chapters 5, 8, 9, and 10 falls above the mean, compared to the other chapters. Chapter 6 of the HLS must also be mentioned as the information discussed in this chapter require a concise risk management approach within the management system. This confirms hypothesis 1.

14 of the 25 organizations used an integrated management system. Despite the higher volume of companies using an IMS, the total number of non-compliant audit results were higher in organizations without an IMS (see figure 69). Table 36 shows that the mean is approximately 11 for organizations using an IMS and 14 for organizations that have separate management systems or only one. The standard deviation is also smaller within organizations using an IMS compared to the standard deviation of companies who do not use an IMS. This could be interpreted as follows: the development and operation of an IMS take more time and effort. Most organizations that have an IMS have many years of experience in running a management system and are therefore able to solve problems of this matter more easily. They seem to be more efficient, eventually generating a better performance in the context of the specific management systems they are using. This study shows that these companies tend to have a

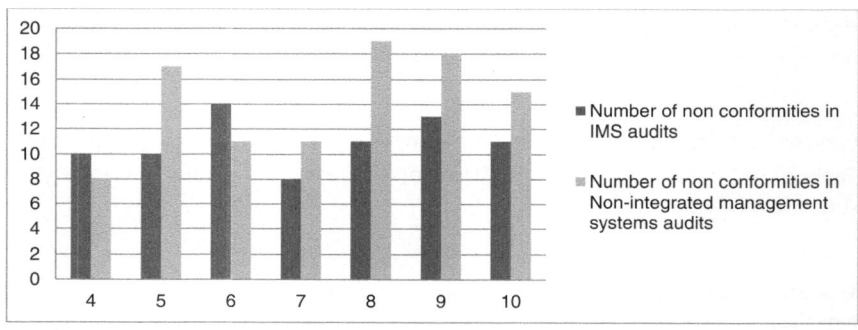

Figure 69 Number of non-conformities in external management system audits in 25 organizations (Source: own elaboration based on the results of own research)

lower number of non-conformities in audits and fewer problems in general and seen within the context of chapters 5, 8, 9, and 10 specifically (standard deviation is 2.0 with a variance of 4 compared to the standard deviation of 4.2 with the variance of 17.5 in the other organizations which operate no IMS). Concerning the risk-based approach of chapter 6 of the HLS, it is noticeable that the number of non-conformities in this matter seems to be independent from the integration status of the management system.

With these results, hypothesis two can be confirmed.

Table 36 Standard deviation, mean, and variance of the research results of the number of non-conformities compared to integration aspects

IMS organizations	
Mathematical expression	Value
Sample Standard Deviation, s	2
Variance (Sample Standard), s^2	4
Population Standard Deviation, σ	1.853
Variance (Population Standard), $σ^2$	3.429
Mean (Average):	11
Non IMS organizations	
Mathematical expression	Value
Sample Standard Deviation, s	4.180
Variance (Sample Standard), s^2	17.476
Population Standard Deviation, σ	3.870
Variance (Population Standard), $σ^2$	14.980
Mean (Average):	14.143

(Source: own elaboration based on the results of own research)

A similar conclusion can be drawn by examining the age of the management systems that were audited between the years 2015 and2018. Figure 70 shows that there are additional

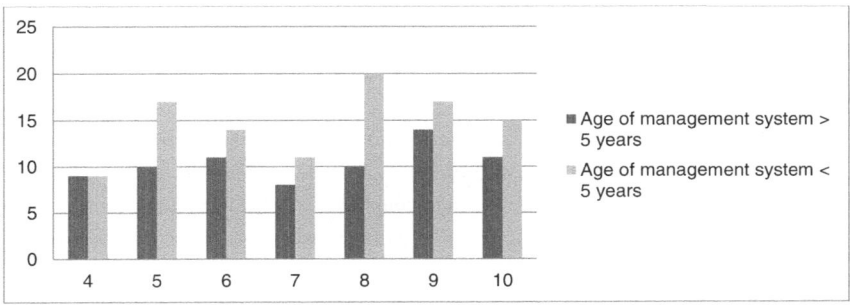

Figure 70 Age of management system > 5 years and < 5 years
(Source: own elaboration based on the results of own research)

audit findings in companies with management systems newer than five years. This confirms the last finding, stating that the level of experience with a management system has a significant impact on the success rate of the management system. With a standard deviation of 1.9 and an average of 10, older management systems are more stable and tend to perform better regarding the number of audit findings (see table 37). This confirms hypothesis 3.

Table 37 Standard deviation, mean, and variance of the research results comparing the number of audit results and the age of the management system

Mathematical expression	value
> 5 years	
Sample Standard Deviation, s	1.902
Variance (Sample Standard), s^2	3.619
Population Standard Deviation, σ	1.761
Variance (Population Standard), $σ^2$	3.102
Mean (Average):	10.429
< 5 years	
Sample Standard Deviation, s	3.773
Variance (Sample Standard), s^2	14.238
Population Standard Deviation, σ	3.493
Variance (Population Standard), $σ^2$	12.204
Mean (Average):	14.714

(Source: own elaboration based on the results of own research)

This part of the study analyzes the findings of audit results in comparison to the number of KPIs used that have a connection to common sustainability topics and strategic relevance. A connection to sustainability topics or strategic relevancy used in this analysis was understood as follows:

- The KPI does not only measure one aspect specific to the management system (e.g. the failure rate of a machine, the amount of security incidents within a certain scope etc.), but more basic aspects involving facets regarding the business in general(e.g. raised efficiency or quality of a process, better test results for employee training, improvement of environmental pollution etc.)
- The KPI is used or is a part of a "bigger" reporting system which is used in a higher level of the hierarchy in an organization (management reports, decision-making sessions, strategic meetings, enterprise risk management processes, balanced scorecard etc.).
- The KPI involves elements of sustainability reporting required by the EU (see chapter 6.2) or similar reporting which requires to report in multiple dimensions

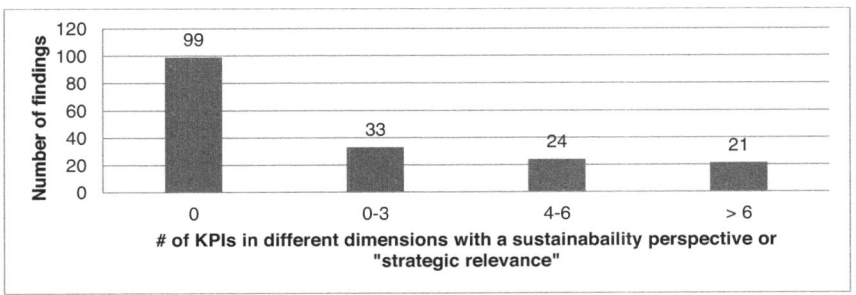

Figure 71 Number of KPIs in different dimensions with strategic relevance
(Source: own elaboration based on the results of own research)

Figure 71 shows that most of the audit findings were identified within the audits at companies that are using KPI's without a strategic relevance. This variance of 1374 (with a standard deviation of 37) can be interpreted as an important aspect. One reason might be that KPIs which have a greater impact on the general business and business processes performance provide a higher awareness to the management level. This awareness, in turn, will automatically create the willingness to solve problems or improve related aspects.

Table 38 Standard deviation and variance of the strategic relevance of performance indicators compared to audit findings

Mathematical expression	value
Sample Standard Deviation, s	37.0709
Variance (Sample Standard), s^2	1374.25

(Source: own elaboration based on the results of private research)

It must be stated that the number of organizations using KPIs with a strategic relevance is very low in the sample size. Figure 72 shows that only 11 of the 25 companies use KPIs with strategic relevance which equals 44%. On the other site, it can be shown that there are fewer

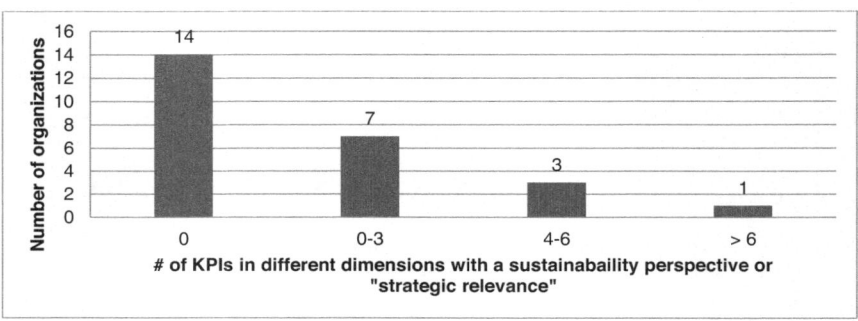

Figure 72 Number of organizations which use KPIs with "strategic relevance"
(Source: own elaboration based on the results of own research)

audit findings at the 11 companies that use strategical KPIs (see figure 73). This confirms the hypothesis number five.

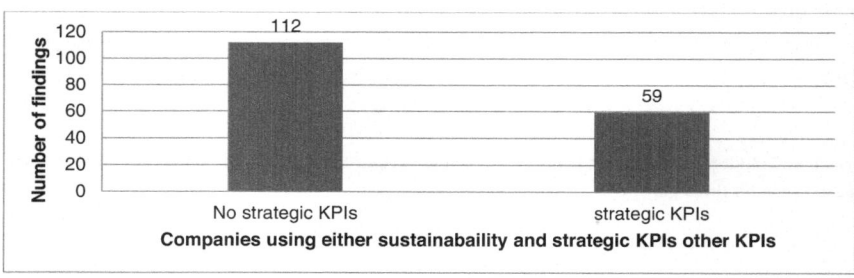

Figure 73 Number of audit findings comparing companies using strategic performance indicators or not
(Source: own elaboration based on the results of own research)

To analyze the strategic linkage one step further, the audit reports and interviews
showed that there are common similarities regarding the evaluation of the maturity of
management systems (see figure 74). The reason might be that there is neither clear
definition of maturity of management systems nor measurement methods even
though the international standards require to evaluate the management on a regular
basis. Most organizations evaluate their management system based on the KPIs already discussed.

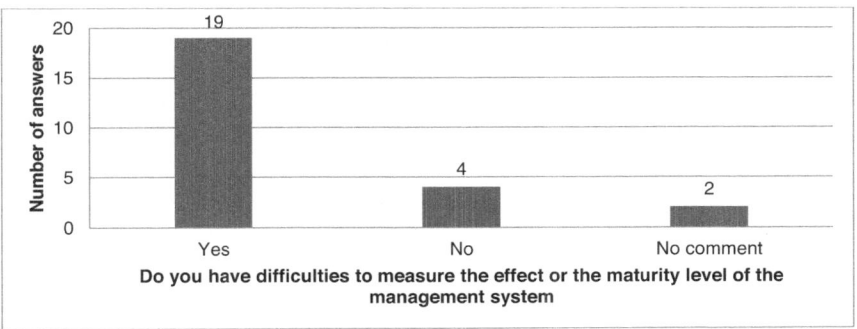

Figure 74 Difficulties to measure the effect or the maturity level of the management system
(Source: own elaboration based on the results of own research)

Figure 75 shows that there is no clear connection between revenue of the companies and the audit findings (of the 25 companies there is an average distribution of turnover between the selected values of 28%, 35% and 37%). The correlation between non-conformities and turnover has no statistical relevance.

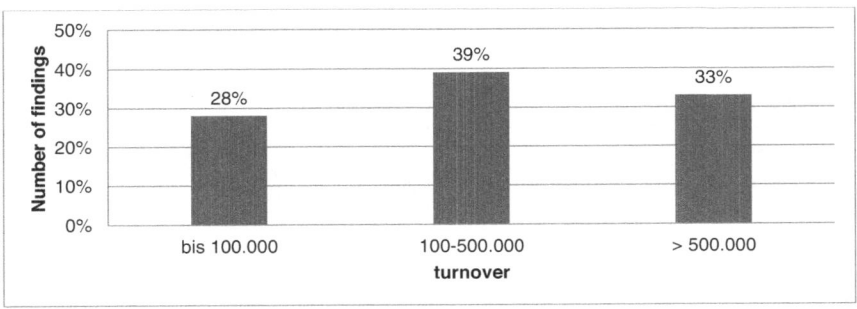

Figure 75 Number of audit findings in comparison to turn over
(Source: own elaboration based on the results of own research)

To research hypothesis 6, figure 76 indicates that there appears to be a trend to not integrate the required risk-based approach of management systems into the over-all risk management of the company. Neither are these systems implemented as an organization-wide risk

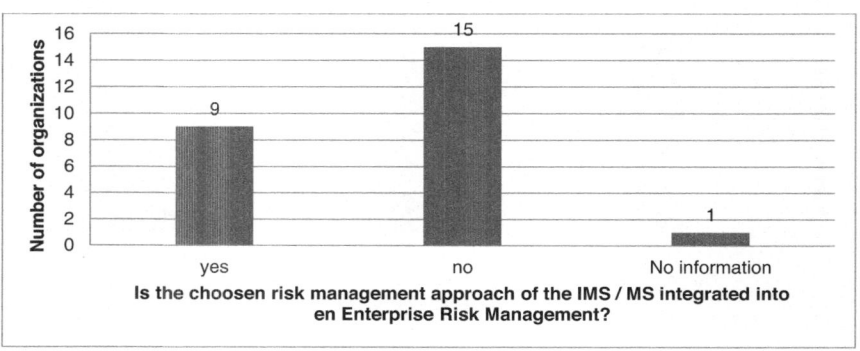

Figure 76 The integration status of the risk management approach of the management system in regards to enterprise risk management
(Source: own elaboration based on the results of own research)

management or ERM approach nor are is risk management linked to it. This confirms hypothesis 6.

Figure 77 presents the aspect of audit findings compared to the integration of risk management into a company-wide ERM. It can be concluded that there are additional non-conformities if no integrated risk management approach is used.

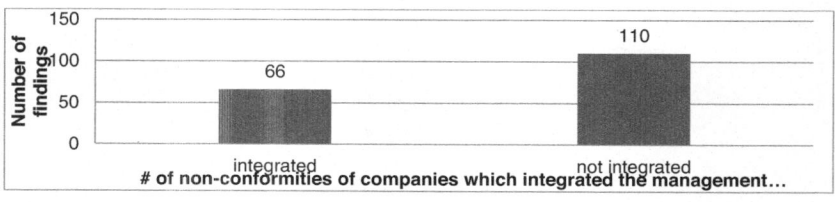

Figure 77 # of non-conformities of companies that integrated the risk management of the management system into the organizational-wide risk management
(Source: own elaboration based on the results of own research)

In conclusion, it can be stated that all hypotheses could be answered positively. Within the samples of organizations used in this research, there was a higher tendency of non-conformities found in external audits in some areas of HLS-chapters more than in others. In this case the chapters 5, 8, 9, and 10, which represent aspects of leadership and management involvement, the operation of the management system and related business processes, the performance evaluation of the management system, and the continuous improvement had more non-conformities. The other chapters 1-4 as well as 6 and 7 showed to be less problematic in management system audits.

The risk management aspect of HLS discussed in chapter 6 is the next issue that often generates non-conformities and might indicate the necessity for the use of a standardized risk management process. This is also highlighted by the research in hypothesis 6 which shows that the integration of risk management in the management system into the organization-wide risk management process (as far as one exists within the company) is beneficial to companies. Companies using an ERM have experience on how to aggregate risks from various levels and use it strategically. A more strategic evaluation of the performance of the management system also seems to be beneficial (hypothesis 4 and 5). The reason might be that the transparency of results and improvements of organizational processes on the upper level of the organization enhances the chance that there are fewer non-conformities within external audits. One could interpret this as the linkage of management systems to upper-level decision making processes. This could be beneficial for the goals of the management systems and also for performance of related business processes. Older management systems and those that are integrated into an IMS show fewer non-conformities which also highlight the importance of gained knowledge and experience.

To summarize the findings the following can be said:

- Within management systems, the role of leadership is an important aspect because upper management defines the goals and strategies of the management system, it's role, responsibilities, and determining its scope. Upper management is also indirectly linked to the evaluations and improvements of the management systems (including the necessary reporting) and has therefore a very important function.
- There is a necessity to link the management system to strategical elements of the organization to increase the performance of sustainable business processes. This can be done by using several features including an integrated risk management approach as well as integrated evaluation methodology using KPIs which are observable to the upper management.

There are some limitations to that study. Foremost the low number of samples used for this study most be mentioned. An additional weakness is that there is no differentiation between different industries and the management standards used. Further studies should analyze these topics using a larger sample size and a take a more detailed look into the distinct characteristics of the industries and the management system standards utilized. It is also important to find out more about the applied approach to risk management and evaluation to identify common problems and strength of the different methods.

In the following chapters, a model to evaluate the performance of a management system is developed as a proposal to solve one of the above summarized results.

6.2 Analysis of the implication of the new EU directive for disclosing non-financial information and sustainability reporting

6.2.1   Objectives of the investigation of sustainability reporting within the EU

The objectives of this study are to:

- Analyze the implications of the EU directive for companies of varied sizes.
- Highlight the content of the directive and deriving requirements for non-financial reporting as an important aspect of the recommended model developed in this PhD-thesis.

Organizations usually publish annual reports and management reports that state different angles of the financial status of the company. Recently, companies also start to publish reports about different aspects outside of financial values, such as corporate social responsibility (CSR), sustainability etc. Unlike financial reports and KPIs, these reports do not follow a standardized format or KPI usage. The EU Parliament developed this directive 2014/695/EU with the goal to also publish non-financial information. From the first day of January 2017, all Public Interest Entities (PIE) with 500 or more employees have to fulfill this directive by also reporting about social, environmental, human rights, anti-corruption, and employee matters. This requirement to publish non-financial information is the first approach of this kind within the EU (2014/95/EU 2014) and will also influence companies with less than 500 employees, such as Small- and Medium Entities (SME). Before the new EU directive, there was no legal requirement to publish non-financial information (Szabó, 2015). The EU started the accounts modernizations directive 2003/51/EC (2003/51/EC 2003) in which aspect beyond the scope of financial information was mentioned. The EU was focusing on environmental information and employee matters. These requirements were put into place by EU member states, including Germany (Lanfermann, 2015). Szabó (2015) also identified

several other approaches for non-financial reporting within the EU, either on a volun-
tary or a mandatory basis. But these approaches were only valid for some individual
EU countries or limited to state-owned organizations. Some of the examples are:

- Mandatory greenhouse gas emission reporting in the UK.
- Mandatory Corporate Sustainablity reporting for all French limited companies
  which must list over 60 non-financial items (Institut RSE 2012)

There are three reasons the EU should harmonize the different approaches of reporting within the EU (Szabó, 2015): The EU Commission assumes that investors have
a wider interest in the information of companies than only financial aspects. In addition, optional reports regarding other dimensions of organizations would result in the
publication of only positive matters and there would be no need to publish negative
aspects as well. A harmonized approach would force all companies to publish data regardless of being positive or negative. The third reason is the comparability of non-
financial information which is only possible if the KPIs have similar definitions and are
available.

6.2.2   Research method

This research uses two steps:

1. Analysis of the consequences of the EU directive on sustainability reporting.
   The author of this thesis analyzed the history of the publication of non-financial
   information and the new EU directive regarding KPIs
2. Comparative study of existing sustainability reports and analysis of the requirements for sustainability reporting of big and medium-sized companies

This study uses the EU directive 2014/95/EU 2014 and the sustainability reports of
big organizations as a database.

6.2.3   Results and conclusion of the analysis of implication of the new EU directive
for disclosing non-financial information and sustainability reporting

Based on the defined scope of companies which have over 500 employees, it is estimated that 6.000 organizations within the EU must develop such a report (European Comission, 2018). Nevertheless, enterprises consist of various parts, divisions and subsidiaries like suppliers. It is estimated that the number of organizations that must prepare CSR reports is larger than 6.000 (Howitt 2014).

Each of the following topics has to be addressed in the report or excluded from it with a detailed explanation of the reasons for the exclusion (2014/95/EU 2014):

1. Information about environmental matters including current and foreseeable impacts on environmental issues like health and safety, greenhouse gas emissions, water and air pollution etc.
2. Information about social and employee matters, such as gender equality, labor rights, working conditions, health, and safety etc.
3. Information about human rights
4. Information about anti-corruption
5. Information about bribery matters

The last three include detailed information about human rights abuses, the availability of instruments in place to fight corruption and bribery etc.

In more detail, the following information has to be presented by the organizations (2014/95/EU 2014) – see table 39:

Table 39 Information necessary for sustainability reporting required by the EU directive 2014/95/EU 2014

• A brief description of the company business model
• A description of the policies pursued by the company in relation to those matters, including due diligence processes implemented;
• The outcome of those policies
• The principal risks related to those matters linked to the company's operations including, where relevant and proportionate, its business relationships, products or services which are likely to cause adverse impacts in those areas, and how these risks are managed
• Non-financial key performance indicators (KPIs).

(Source: own representation based on the Directive (2014)/95/EU of the European Parliament and the Council of 22 October (2014) amending directive 2013/34/EU as regards disclosure of non-financial and diversity information by certain large undertakings and groups (2014))

It is also important that reports are compared with the same financial year and not advertised much later and after the corresponding balance sheet of that year. This correspondence might create benefits by identifying connections between financial and non-financial values (Szabó, 2015) which is an important aspect of many different areas discussed in this thesis.

On the one hand, the requirements offer strict reporting, but a flexibility in disclosing only some information on the other. The directive does not define a specific reporting format and KPIs, but only recommends general elements if they cover the mandatory topics in accordance with the 2014/95/EU 2014 requirements.

An essential element that was modified, is the role of statutory auditors, whose responsibility it is to ensure that the requirements of the directives are met. They do not review any non-financial KPIs since these values are more qualitative than quantitative. The review or certification process itself is not defined by the EU but is the responsibility of the member states.

There are many different non-financial KPIs, and the EU directive does not express any specific KPI requirements. KPIs are different depending on the region, the nature of the business etc. Nevertheless, there are some generic KPIs that can be used by a wide range of organizations. Table 40 shows some example KPIs.

In contrast to general KPIs useful for reporting, there are industry-specific KPIs. In table 41 below, KPIs for the food industry are given. This specific example by DANONE shows that not all aspects of the EU directive are described. It misses the human right actions. In 2014

Table 40 Examples of generic performance indicators used in non-financial reports

Type of indicator	Content and Examples
General Performance Indicators for Environment	• Primary energy consumption • Share of renewable energies compared to total energy consumption • Material consumption and recycling quota • Water used and air bound emissions • Environmental costs
General Performance Indicators for Social and employee concerns	• Percentage of employees satisfied with their work • Number of nonfatal injuries and illnesses • Women as percentage of employees • Women in top-management • Number of hours volunteered by employees

Type of indicator	Content and Examples
	• Significant collaborations with corporate partners, nonprofits, and NGOs
General Performance Indicators for Respect for human rights	• Percentage of staff with access to staff forum, grievance procedure or other support • Number of human rights policy assessments among workers • Number and breakdown of code violations (e.g., unrespectful treatment, discrimination, collective bargaining, employee relations, employee privacy, right to organize, working hours) • Percentage of staff that experienced harassment, discrimination, etc. as expressed in employee surveyor channeled through external party (e.g. unions)
General Performance Indicators for Anti-corruption and bribery matters	• Number of complaints received • Nature of the received complaints (based on an established and applied rating) • Number of disciplinary actions for corruption and bribery

(Source: own elaboration based on BMW Sustainable Value report 2014 (2015), http://www.bmw-group.com/d/0_0_www_bmwgroup_com/investor_relations/corpo-rate_events/_pdf/2013/Charts_Dr_Reithofer_BPK_2013_d.pdf,accessed"_d.pdf,   accessed 20.10.(2015); Danone (2014) Sustainable report, Strategy and performance, Bringing health through food to as many people as possible, (2015) http://www.danone.com/uploads/tx_bidanonepublica-tions/Danone_Sustainability_Report_
2014_light.pdf, accessed 07.04.2015).

there was no need to report any value of that kind in the EU member states (with the above-mentioned exceptions of France and the UK). DANONES report for 2017 will have to include this aspect as well.

The EU directive only requires organization up to a certain size to report non-financial values. What would be the impact for small and medium-sized enterprises? Except a possible requirement to report information as a supplier for a bigger organization, there is no visible impact (the directive even state that SMEs should not be forced to do any reporting). Nevertheless, it might make sense for SMEs to also evaluate non-financial information and contrast them with financial values. Examples can be the cost of energy as a percentage of total turnover, the accident rate of employees, the number of awareness training for employees concerning anti-corruption, law, information security, health, and safety etc. The directive indicates that EU member states should not inhibit the disclosure of information of other groups as well. It might happen that EU member states require certain information from SMEs as well.

Table 41 Specific performance indicators of sustainable reports

Type of indicator	Content and Examples
Industry specific Performance Indicators for Environment	• Total water withdrawn from the surrounding area • Water consumption in the production processes • Final discharge of Chemical Oxygen Demand (COD) • Net COD ratios (kg/metric ton of products) • Total quantity of waste generated • Total quantity of waste eliminated
Industry specific Performance Indicators for Social and employee concerns	• Total managers Female/Male of which directors and executives • Average age Female/Male • Total workforce of which international staff • Total workforce of which local staff
Industry specific Performance Indicators for Anti-corruption and bribery matters	• Number of subsidies included in the mid-yearly reporting on internal fraud

(Source: own elaboration based on Danone (2014) Sustainable report, Strategy and performance, Bringing health through food to as many people as possible, (2015) http://www.danone.com/ uploads/tx_bidanonepublications/Danone_Sustainability_Report_2014_light.pdf, accessed 07.04. 2015)

In a study of German companies, 80 % of the companies stated that sustainable development was a relevant topic (Hahn & Scheermesser, 2006). Hahn & Scheermesser also categorized companies into the categories of sustainability leaders, environmentalists, and traditionalists which differentiate themselves by their effort of the report regarding CSR and environmental issues. Environmentalists are mostly larger organizations which use standardized management systems as EFQM, ISO 14001, ISO 9001, EMAS etc. which makes reporting easier. Traditionalists are mostly SMEs. Publicly listed companies, such as the DAX 30, already have experience in CSR-reporting. Most of the companies (see above example of BMW) publish reports with all aspects already included for several years. Smaller companies are not so experienced. According to Mazars (2015) only 33% of the TecDAX and 42% of the SDAX report CSR topics.

The EU directive 2014/95/EU forces companies to report in regard to sustainability and corporate sustainability issues. Before this directive was put in place, there was no mandatory report within the EU. For larger organizations and publicly listed PIEs reporting non-financial information is mandatory. Since these large organizations already reported such information in regular intervals, the directive does not have much impact. Nevertheless, there will be a harmonization effect on more transparency because the directive requires to report information from all specified topics. Smaller companies, that are currently required to report, must find ways to identify the right KPIs and reporting format. This also includes SMEs which are not forced to report by the EU directive, but potentially because of regulations by single-member states. SMEs also will most likely have to report their CSR and sustainability KPIs toward a larger organization which with they have a business relationship (such as a supplier).

There is an allegation that the EU directive does not stress reporting as much as it should, expressly in regard to the still open issues about certification or auditing processes. Nevertheless, it is not an easy task to find the right balance between strict requirements and enough flexibility for organizations of all industries and countries to be able to comply. For management systems and the measurement of effectiveness and efficiency, the availability of data in the form of reports and KPIs are a benefit.

6.3 Developing a model to evaluate the performance of integrated management systems in the context of sustainable business processes and risk management

6.3.1   Objectives of the research

The diverse management system standards (standards based on different initiatives as ISO, or more generic standards such as TQM, EFQM, and Kaizen etc.) are used globally and industry-wide. In this thesis, the author presented different views on performance evaluations as well as an examination of scientific literature which demonstrate that there is still no consensus about the question whether and under what circumstances a management system standard is beneficial for an organization. The reasons, as discussed in chapter 1, might be that performance itself is a very nonspecific term and not clearly defined in the organizational context. But, performance is a central element, and it is evident that the MSS have an influence on an organization. Performance, therefore, must to be measured. As discussed earlier, the measurement of performance is as diverse as the field of MSS. This thesis contains research on several aspects which highlight the necessity and opportunity to evaluate integrated management system performance. The objectives of this chapter is:

- Development of a holistic model to evaluate the performance of integrated management systems based on the Execution Premium, Strategic Map and the PDCA-cycle of management systems

- Testing of the model in the context of sustainable business processes and risk management

6.3.2   Applied research methodology

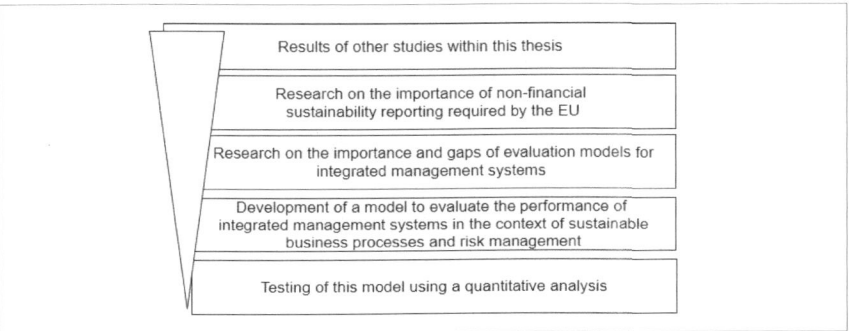

Results of other studies within this thesis

Research on the importance of non-financial sustainability reporting required by the EU

Research on the importance and gaps of evaluation models for integrated management systems

Development of a model to evaluate the performance of integrated management systems in the context of sustainable business processes and risk management

Testing of this model using a quantitative analysis

Figure 78 Research method of chapter 6
(Source: own elaboration based on the results of own research)

This study uses theory development, based on the theories and research elaborated within this PhD-thesis. It also uses a quantitative assessment of the developed theoretical model to test its underlying theory and practical use. Chapter 6 of this thesis mainly involved the most urgent reasons why this research was performed. This includes the knowledge gaps and problems in the implementation and use of integrated management systems based on the authors working experience. This experience was gained in consulting projects and auditing of management systems. The requirements of the EU regarding sustainability reporting and the necessity to measure and report performance business process performance with more than only financial values is another aspect highlighted in this part of the thesis. Based on these findings, the authors developed a model to evaluate the performance of integrated management systems and verified it for practical use.

The methodology can be seen in figure 78.

6.3.3   Theory development applied to evaluate the performance of integrated management systems

There are common principles of performance measurement (Source: own interpretation based on the results of own research):

- Performance evaluation is the basis for improvement. Without the evaluation of "something", there is no way to improve systematically.
- Performance measurement can be done using different methods and different indicators.
- Performance indicators can include financial values (historically this is the most predominantly used way to assess performance), including other values with various properties in an organizational context, such as:
  - o process performance,
  - o measurements of quality, time
  - o efficiency, effectiveness, efficacy
  - o stakeholder or more specific customer or employee satisfaction,
  - o employee involvement and motivation,
  - o knowledge and knowledge management,
  - o organizational culture,
  - o leadership aspects,
  - o use of technology,
  - o number or value of tangible or intangible assets,
  - o agility and possibility to change,
  - o operative or strategic ability to manage crisis,
  - o risks,
  - o competition,
  - o internationalization,
  - o social and environmental aspects (e.g. Trible Bottom Line) and so on.
- Performance measurement is important for the success of a company because it rates its value in the market and serves as an internal indicator for continuous improvement.
- Performance is driven within the company and not from the outside. Even though the outside world triggers internal reactions and therefore has an influence on performance, everything which influences performance measurement elements actively is within the company (e.g. number of patents, willing to do good work as an employee, the defect rate of machinery etc.). Financial performance is indirectly defined and sets internally: e.g. the sales rate of a product is a result of market reactions. But these are based on performance aspects such as product quality, meeting of customer demands, correct research and development, fitness or correctness of the 5 P's product, place, price, promotion, (and people) (McCarthy, 1960) etc.).

- Performance is influenced by many different variables and therefore measured in different dimensions (see point 2).

The difficulty of the value of performance measurement methods and models is the precise identification of the linkage between the input and the outcome (Dowell et al., 2000; Litten, 2005). What input influences the outcome is the most important question. In that regard, organizations want to influence and increase, and therefore change, performance. Changing performance requires to know the input parameters. Depending on the chosen performance aspects, one way to identify linkages is by using a diagnostic model. Some examples for diagnostic models are as follows:

- Burke & Litwin (2008) suggested a causal model for organizational performance and change (see figure 79). It shows the interconnection between internal and external factors which influence the performance of an organization measurable as individual and organizational performance.

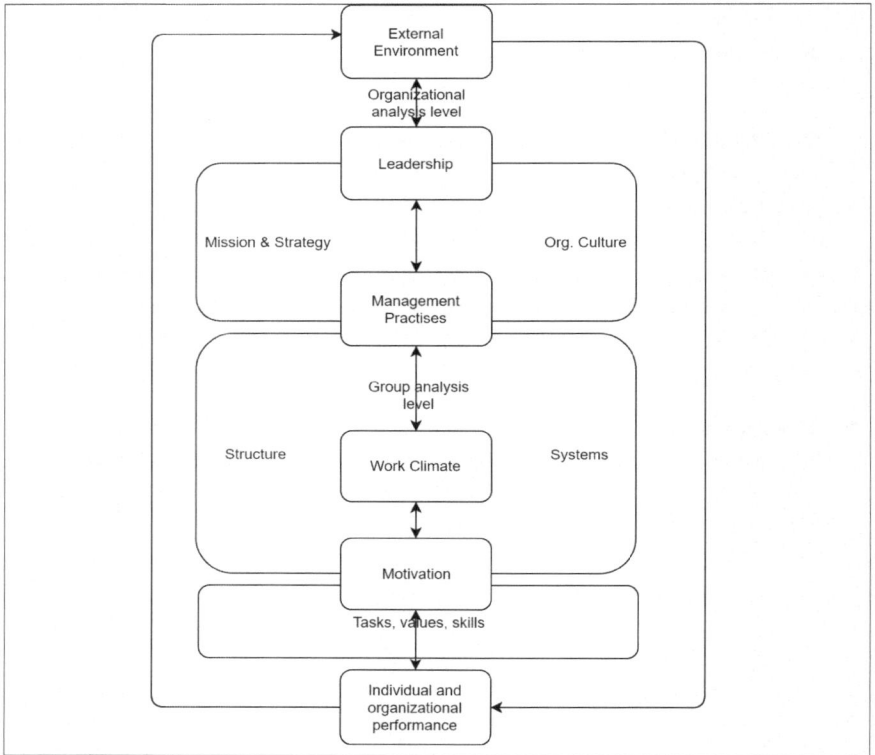

Figure 79 Model for organizational performance and change
(Source: own representation based on Burke W. Warner, Litwin George H., (1992) , A Causal Model of Organizational Performance & Change, published in Journal of Management in 1992, Vol.18, No. 3, 523-545)

- Another model was suggested by Nadler et al. (1997) (see figure 80). It is called the congruence model and shows the flow of inputs to outputs and the interconnections.

The authors suggest that it is necessary to understand the systems of the organization and how its elements are tied together. These elements consist of internal and external sources, strategies, its outputs, and the transformation aspects in which people and equipment transform input to output.

There are other approaches to analyze and understand the complexity of the way organizations transform inputs to outputs (e.g. Weisbord Six-Box Model (Weisbord, 1978), 7-S-Framework (Peters et al, 1980), Force Field Analysis (1947), Four Quadrants-Method of Bolman and Deal (1984) etc.).

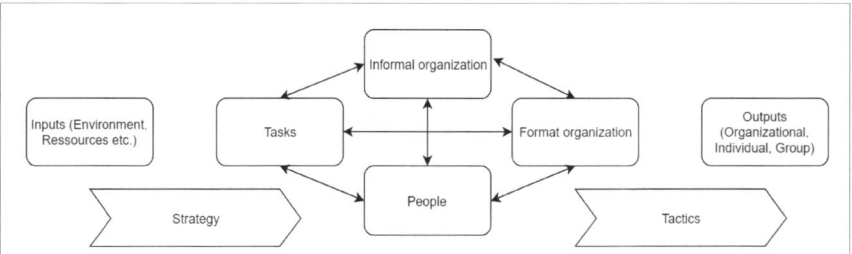

Figure 80 A diagnostical model which describes the connection of Inputs and Outputs
(Source: Own representation, based on Nadler, D.A. Champions of Change: How CEOs and TheirCompanies Are Mastering the Skills of Radical Change.San Francisco: Jossey-Bass, 1997)

Diagnostical models demonstrate the complexity of organizational processes and measurement. It is important to assess the organization based on several aspects–some of them are also included in miscellaneous diagnostically models:

- environmental aspects and laws,
- the purpose and mission of the company,
- its strategy,
- the use of technology, systems, and related tasks,
- people motivation and culture,
- leadership style,
- learning and skills, and
- communication.

Contrasting these aspects against management systems, the result shows that there are overlapping areas (see table 42). As it can be seen in table 42, there are many general aspects of management systems, which are also a topic in the mentioned diagnostical models.

- Management systems are applied within the organization.
- Management systems require a continuous improvement and therefore a way of measuring its performance.
- Management system work within the organization and are closely tied to organizational processes (e.g. ranging from efficiency and effectiveness as well as defect rates of manufacturing processes to change- and risk management).
- Different management systems and management system standards can be integrated into IMS. This IMS consists of many different elements and aspects which have to be measured.
- Management systems should fit the organizational strategy (e.g. ISO requires a strategic fit by the requirements of the strategic goal and policy setting).

Table 42 Topics of diagnostical models used in management systems

Element	ISO MSS standards	EFQM	TQM	ERM
Environment and social responsibility	X	X		
Strategy	X	X	X	X
Structure	X	X	X	X
Technology	X	X	X	X
Change and risk management	X	X	X	X
Cultural (motivation, climate etc.)	X	X	X	
Leadership	X	X	X	
Learning, skills	X	X	X	

(Source: own interpretation based on the results of own research)

Based on the above-mentioned points, the following can be assumed. The measurement model, method or system for a management system must fulfill the following requirements:

1. Capability to use different measurement methods supporting different dimensions.
2. Openness to integrate different indicators.
3. Capability to integrate the measurement system used within the organization.
4. Possibility to aggregate data to see and understand the results on a higher level.

5. Option to generate results for the organizational strategy as well as for continuous improvement.

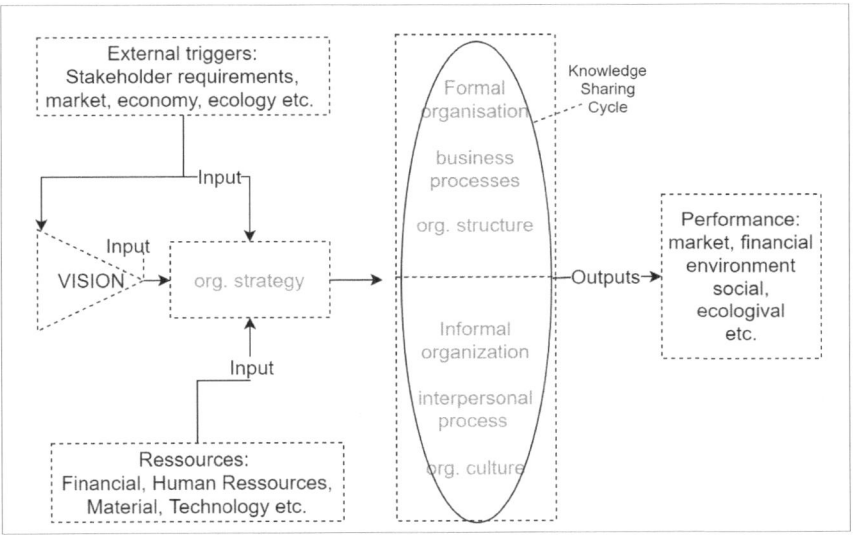

Figure 81 Diagnostical model for aspects of performance measurement; green showing the aspects related to management systems

(Source: Own elaboration, based on Kompalla Andreas , Kopia Jan, Foerster Ulrike, Geldmacher Wiebke, (2017), Analysis of correlations between coprporate strategy and operational strategy considering management system standards, Ecoforum, Volume 6, Issue 3 (2017), ISSN: 2344-2174)

Highlighting the aspects that have to do with management systems (see table 42) shows that most of the elements within the organization are related to management systems and therefore must be assessed in performance measurements. This might be the reason, why ISO explains that their standards for management systems „help organizations improving their performance [...]" (ISO, 2017b). Nevertheless, a clear linkage between ISO standards, TQM and performance, and an aswer to which one to use is better, or to use both, has not been found so far (Sun, 2000; Magd & Curry, 2003; Sampaio et al., 2009; Martinez-Costa et al., 2009; Tyler, 2017). Especially the influence of TQM on ISO 9001 and vice versa was studied in regards to their external and internal drivers, success factors, and order of implementation (Lee et al., 1999; Sampaio et al., 2009; Prado-Roman et al., 2014). This suggests that there are many similarities. Whether management systems have a positive, negative or any influence at all, is still a matter of discussion for ISO as well as for TQM (Hoque & Alam, 2003; Kaynak 2003; Chong & Rundus, 2004; Sholihin & Ayu, 2009; Sampaio et al., 2009; Martı́nez-Costa et al., 2009; Daily, 2011; Tari et al, 2012; Ming-Hsien Khan, 2014; Karim, 2015;).

Regarding the integration of management systems, there are signs that integration is beneficial for organizations (Katniak, 2012; Kopia, 2016). This is not true for IMS in general, concerning organizational performance where the scientific consensus is unclear, and similarly for the analysis of only one management system (Griffith & Bhutto, 2008).

Figure 81 shows that the output is the measured performance. These outputs are influenced by the inputs and the transformation processes. This is in accordance to the above mentioned diagnostical models by using elements from the knowledge sharing cycle. A very important resource in this regard, is the ability to innovate or, using a more general term the use of organizational competences (Prahalad & Hamel, 1990; Kompalla et al., 2016c). According to Teece et al. (1997), these capabilities are important assets for companies to be able to adapt to the changing environment. The concept of dynamic capabilities was also discussed by other authors (Cordes-Berszinn et al., 2013) as a major factor in the competitive landscape which comes in the form of knowledge and knowledge processes.

Performance measurement today is still mostly financialy oriented measuring performance using indicators such as market share, different kinds of turnover rates, the cash value and cash flow of an organization, net or gross profit, diverse Return Rates (ROI / ROE), Earnings before taxes etc. (Richard et al., 2009). It is accepted by scientists that performance itself is a multi-dimensional subject involving not only financial aspects but also others, such as operational matters, as well, (Martin, 2016, Caldarola, 2016). Operational indicators include measurement of efficiency, product costs, customer satisfaction, the quality of the design, delivery time, cycle time, market share and similar aspects (Terziovski et al., 1997; Naveh & Marcus, 2005).

Considering table 42 and the overlapping topics in management systems, some of these indicators might be useful to measure the performance of a management system as well. Most ISO based management systems require an organization to assess the maturity of the management system by defining key performance indicators and measuring them to continuously improve the system over the years.

Performance measurement initiatives and values can result from different areas of the organization (see figure 82), from the operational field as stated above and from the strategical level.

Operational aspects of performance measurement also include the area of knowledge and learning which was standard by diverse scientists, such as Sveiby (1997), Stewart (1997, 2014), Bontis et al. (2001), Pulic (2008) etc. These experts emphasize the value of intangible assets measured using (see also chapter 0):

- Intellectual capital (IC) methods and the Value Added Intellectual Coefficient (VAIC),
- Calculated Intangible Value (CIV),
- Intangible Driven Earning (IDE),
- the Skandia Navigator,
- Activity Based Costing,
- business process Reengineering,
- Zero Based Budgeting,
- IC Rating etc.

Besides intellectual capital, there are environmental aspects, health and safety regulations, and the important subject of corporate social responsibility (CSR) and sustainable development. For some organizations, it is a necessity to report their performance in in a regular manner, e.g. to identifying their position within the Global Reporting Initiative (GRI) – a standardized measurement report for sustainability and the Triple Bottom Line.

It is obvious that an organization must identify its core values, based on its vision, in order to assess performance on an individual level (Yin & Schmeidler, 2009). A chosen management system (or more than one) must fit into these values in order to be useful. It should be incorporated into the strategy and the derived procedural elements including the corporate culture. By doing this, performance is easily defined as it is connected to the values of the organization. Strategy and use of management systems, therefore, have some dependencies.

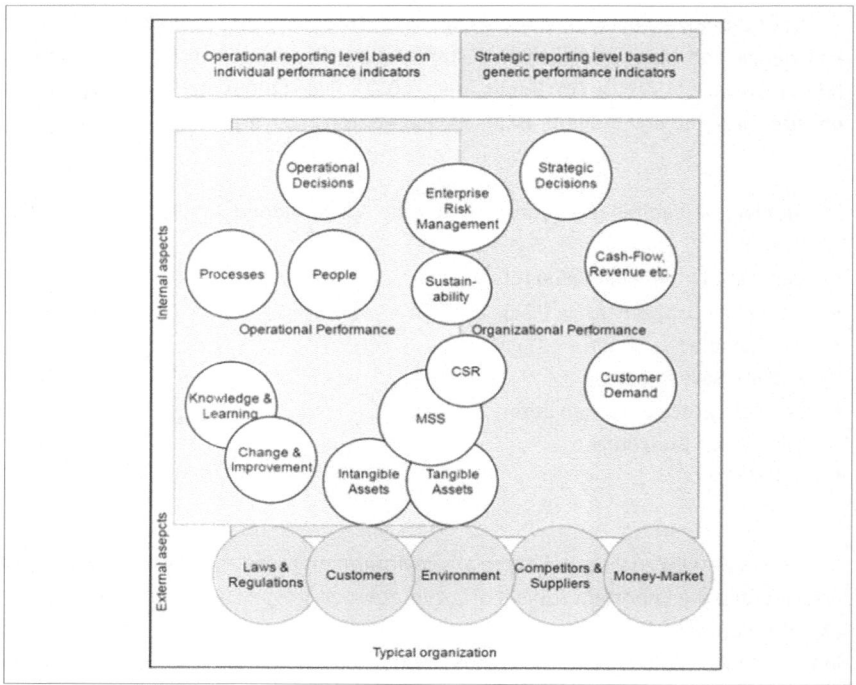

Figure 82 Performance aspects of the operational and organizational area
(Source: Own elaboration based on the results of own research)
Figure 82 also identifies sources of indicators, which might be useful for performance measurement.
One framework is enterprise risk management (ERM), which is used by some organizations to manage
their strategic risks concisely (e.g. by implementing the COSO-framework – see chapter 2.1).

6.3.4   Proposal of a holistic model to evaluate the performance of integrated management systems in the context of sustainable business processes and risk management

Risk management is one important aspect of many management systems and therefore an ideal element to assess the level of maturity of the implementation of the management system given the developed maturity models in that context. ERM brings another useful benefit to the organization: through ERM risks are assessed on various levels, starting from the bottom to the top, risks are identified and aggregated to an upper level to make strategic decisions. This important strategic is useful for the assessment of management systems as well. Most elements of management systems are executed on the operational level, but the assessment and strategic impact should be visible on the strategic level (Quazi, 2001; Schylander & Martinuzzi, 2007). There are frameworks which assess different aspects in that regard. The author of this thesis (Kopia et al., 2017c) suggested a framework to assess risks, using financial and not financial values with a holistic measurement approach. A useful method is the Scorecard Method, e.g. by implementing the BSC proposed by Kaplan and Norton (1992) and partially based on Drucker's Management by Objectives (MBO) (1954), which addresses operational and strategical elements at the same time (Tarí, 2012). BSC addresses the problem to assess multiple dimensions by presenting the following perspectives:

- Financial perspective – "shareholder view"
- Internal business perspective – "process excellence view"
- Innovation, knowledge, and learning perspective – "Value creation and innovation view"
- Customer perspective – "Customers view?"

The BSC can also be extended with any other measurement perspective (e.g. the sustainably balanced scorecard - SBSC – see below). BSC has an additional benefit: it can be strategically linked to create a strategic management system. This is called "Strategic Map" and connects the strategy with the performance measurement aspects. It was originally suggested by Kaplan & Norton (2004). The goal of strategic maps is the creation of synergies within the organization and its business units. Chapter 3.2.1 shows that the research in this area supports these findings. In addition to a strategic map, there is another important link which was suggested by Kaplan & Norton as well. The "Execution Premium" implements a cyclic approach which guides the strategic alignment time-wise using six stages (and enabled the organization to apply operational excellence as a basis to align the operational processes with the strategic goals (Asif et al., 2010)):

1. Development of the strategy with 3 inputs: internal context, external context, existing strategy.

2. Planning the strategy. This step involved the actual development of the BSC (individually for each organization) and the Strategy Map.
3. Alignment of the organization with its strategies.
4. Planning of the necessary operations. This also includes a financial perspective.
5. Monitoring of the results including the learning and knowledge perspective.
6. Continuous improvement by testing of the results. If results are not positive or in conflict with the set strategy, allignment of the outcomes by adapting the operational procedures, returning to step 1, or 4 respectively.

This cyclic approach has similarities with the cycling approach of most management systems require (mainly based on Deming's PDCA-cycle Plan, Do, Check, Act). Overlapping both approaches results in a systematic methodology to operate management systems, link them

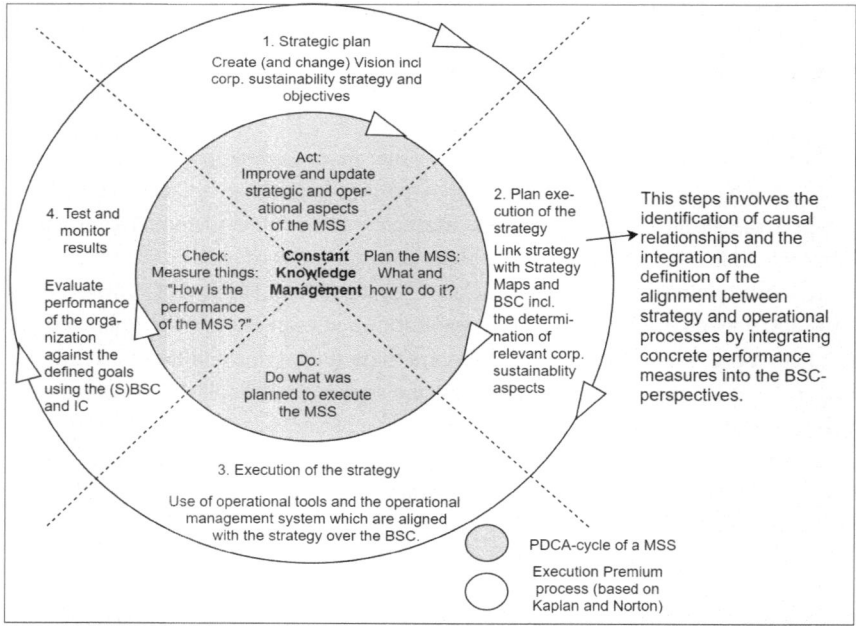

Figure 83 Suggested models of the alignment of the Execution Premium, Strategic Map and the Plan-Do-Check-Act-cycle of management systems
(Source: own development)

to strategy and incorporate measurement elements (see figure 83). Continuing through the process of figure 83 involves strategic thinking and therefore strategic involvement, a necessity for the efficient and effective usage of management systems. Regardless of the nature of the management system (e.g. Quality as in ISO 9001, TQM, EFQM, Energy as in ISO 50001, Information Security as in ISO 27001), the core value of the company should be an element of the goals of the management system. These goals should be included in the first two steps of the execution premium-process and also focus on continuous improvement of the effective and efficient use of knowledge management.

The requirements in the planning step come from different stakeholders and need to be transformed into concrete measures. Most management systems require a risk-based approach to define and rate measures resulting in a list of measurements based on organizational risks and opportunities. The doing-phase is like the execution-phase in the BSC-process. Most important is the use of an effective knowledge management (which is true for all process steps). The strength of organizational learning and knowledge management for the success of management systems was highlighted in this thesis. The checking-process can be accomplished in the monitoring-phase, the act-phase is comparable to step 6 in the suggested Execution Premium using KPIs that also include knowledge management aspects (e.g. the IC measured via VAIC). The continuous improvement element is the central element in all management systems (step 5 and 6).

Different authors confirm the strategic use of BSC in the context of management systems or Enterprise Risk Management (Chen et al., 2006; Woods, 2007; Schmutte, 2007; Acharyya, 2008; Nagumo & Donlon, 2009). According to the authors, the BSC method can be categorized in either an intervening or in a moderating category (Kaynak, 2003, Chong & Runduns, 2004). The growing trend is a validation of the alignment between the strategy of the organization with the operational parts should be linked in the context of the measurement efforts. One such linkage can be done using BSC together with strategy maps and the Execution Premium. Another example for this is the proposed sustainability balanced scorecard (SBSC) (Figge et al. 2002; Wagner 2007). It extends the BSC with a sustainability dimension. In scientific research approaches to integrate sustainability into the BSC using different methodologies were developed:

- The sustainability indicators must be integrated into the fourth dimensions of the BSC (Epstein & Wisner, 2001; Monteiro et al. 2003), or

- The sustainability aspects should be developed separately, and linked afterward through a "sustainability scorecard", or
- Keep sustainability as a separate, non-market element in the present form of the scorecard (Figge et al., 2002; Hubbard et al, 2009; Länsiluoto & Järvenpää, 2010) which makes it easier to integrate this dimensions into existing BSC since there is no adaption needed for the existing scorecard and strategic map.

Adding another dimension can be complex since, as it was stated above, the importance is within the linkage of the elements. This results in a cause-and-effect-relationship like the diagnostical models of performance measurement (see above). The problem is that there are competing indicators in such a complex system. Having performance in mind, indicators of different sustainability aspects compete against other goals and indicators which might result in an unusable SBSC. This might occur if the generated performance measurement values are not weighted usefully. It is important to choose the right indicators with the right weighting factors in the linked structure between the different dimensions. Hubbard et al. (2009) suggested to use a step-by-step approach which can be summarized as follows:

- Decide about the general relationship between profit-making, sustainability and its multiple objectives. The sustainability aspect is the value system.
- Define the corporate sustainability strategy.
- The corporate sustainability strategy and the value system result in a generic SBSC architecture (some examples are suggested below).
- Use the BSC-process Strategy Mapping to manifest the correct strategic setting.
- Define performance indicators.

Several different models and SBSC architectures were suggested (Brignall, 2002; van Marrewijk, 2004; Raisch et al., 2009; Hubbard et al., 2009; Hansen & Schaltegger, 2012):

- Strong hierarchical models of the SBSC link indicators toward a financial perspective.
- The semi-hierarchical approach of the SBSC defines the financial perspective as a competing dimension, not a resulting dimension

- Systematic-driven SBSC uses a network method to make it possible to link every element with each other as within a network structure
- Combining the SBSC with the sustainable performance index (OSPI) in order to use a compromise between a complex reporting system and a useful managerial tool

To assess the maturity of an integrated management system based on the suggested model, the author of this thesis defines the following formula:

$$\text{Maturity} \quad \frac{\#\ of\ operational\ KPIs}{\#\ of\ strategic\ KPIs} * \frac{Trend\ of\ all\ operational\ KPIs\ in\ \%}{Trend\ of\ all\ strategic\ KPIs\ in\ \%} =$$

Notes and requirements:

→ In integrated management systems, all KPIs have to be included in the calculation

→ The management systems should at least contain 5 KPIs for the operational and 3 for the strategic level (which can also include aggregated KPIs for reporting to upper management). The goal should be to have as many strategical as operational KPIs.

→ A trend analysis of the development of the KPIs should include the values of at least 3 years and is calculated as follows (n=number of KPIs):

$$\frac{1}{n} * \sum_{i}^{n} Target\ reached\ per\ KPI_i\ in\ percent$$

It is the average value in percent of all KPIs.

The maturity of an integrated management system measured this way includes the relationship of operational and strategical KPIs, as well as the performance development of the management systems over a period using a trend analysis based on the mathematical calculation. Within this thesis, it is assumed that the goal of an integrated management system is to reach a high maturity because it results in a mature integrated management system. This positively effects the strategic decision-making process by constantly measuring the progress using KPIs (generated using the balanced scorecard method and dashboards on different levels).

6.4 Verification of a developed model to evaluate the performance of integrated management systems in the context of sustainable business processes and risk management

6.4.1   Quantitative assessment of the holistic model

This chapter describes a verification of the developed model on real examples using a quantitative analysis based on survey data. The following hypotheses were defined as basis:

Hypotheses

Based on the presented findings in chapter 6.3, the following hypotheses are suggested:

1. Organizations, which operate two or more MSS, use an integrated management system.
2. Organizations, which use balanced scorecard as performance measurement, integrate their management system measurement into their BSC.
3. The maturity level of a management system increases over time.
4. Organizations use the BSC method as a strategic tool, not only as a tool to measure performance.
5. If BSC is in use: Strategic Map and Execution Premium is used. In regards to this hypothesis the following question is answered: is there any existing link between the PDCA-cycle of management systems, the strategic map or Execution Premium as suggested by the author (figure 83)?
6. The maturity level of the management systems corresponds with the success rate of the management system (figure 84).

260 medium and large-sized organizations from the German, Austrian, and Swiss market in the energy-, production-, and service-industry were selected and asked for their readiness to provide answers to survey questions when the initial question was answered positively (The initial question was: Do you use the BSC?). 60 organizations returned an answer. 41 of those 60 positively answered the initial question with "yes". These 41 organizations were assessed by using semi-structured (mostly online- and telephone) interviews with middle management employees conducted between 2015 and 2018. The questions consisted of open and closed questions, related to the hypotheses.

An empirical analysis was also added to this questionnaire based on inquiries (see appendix E). They were answered by 27 organizations. The interview questions can be seen in appendix E.

6.4.2   Effects of using the suggested measurement model

Management systems are used extensively and are mostly integrated. Most organizations use some kind of management system. Over half of all organizations in the survey use more than one system, and almost half of the organization integrate them into one management system.

- 35 (85%) of organizations use management systems based on ISO. One organization additionally uses a TQM-approach in its production units to increase quality but not following a specific framework or TQM-methodology. 6 organizations have defined their own standards for quality which are ISO-oriented.
- 26 out of 35 organizations use 2 or more management systems:
    - 27 of them are certified based on ISO 9001,
    - 15 based on OHSAS 18001
    - 11 based on ISO 14001
    - 4 based on ISO 50001
    - 8 based on ISO 27001.
- 21 organizations fully integrate their management systems in one IMS (Kopia et al, 2017c) (= 51%). 14 operate them separately or partially integrate some aspects.

This confirms Hypothesis 1.

BSC is a recognized and used instrument in many organizations and utilized by 68% of the companies in the survey. The usage is widely accepted and adopted by organizations as a performance measurement instrument. The main results are as follows (see appendix F and table 43 for the corresponding data):

- 41 of 60 organizations which were originally selected use BSC as performance management system (which represent 68%).
- No specific trend could be found regarding the industry or the size of the company in the context of the BSC-usage. 10 organizations are operating in the energy industry, 17 in the service industry and 14 in the production industry.
- 35 organization use Strategy Mapping as a tool to link the operational with the strategic level. This represents 85% of organizations and indicates that organizations understand the importance of strategic linkage. However, only 13 organizations use the Execution Premium Model originally suggested by Kaplan & Norton. This is only one-third of the organizations. The survey did not go deep enough to

identify reasons. Nevertheless, 7 organizations stated that they do not use the Execution Premium Model but their individual iterative approach that links strategy to operations. Considering this aspect, this pertains to20 of 41 organizations (almost 50%).

▪ The importance of corporate sustainability was answered positively by 56% of the organizations (23). Only 13 use SBSC in this context.

The interview results can be seen in appendix F.

The answers to these questions confirm hypothesis 2, 3, and 4.

Table 43 Correlation matrix of the variables of the questionnaire

Dimensions	Correlation (R / R²) against MPD	Mean	Standard Deviation	Variance	P-Value
R2 BU	0,612 / 0,374	7,214	1,499	2,248	0,0005
R3 IMS	0,180 / 0,032	5,929	2,371	5,624	0,360
R4 IBSC	0,624 / 0,388	7,214	1,423	2,026	0,0003
R5 YIMS	0,577 / 0,332	6,464	1,551	2,406	0,001
R6 YBSC	0,270 / 0,073	6,392	1,594	2,543	0,164
R7 FM	0,331 / 0,110	7,686	1,257	1,582	0,085
R1 MPD	1,000	7,679	1,248	1,556	

(Source: own elaboration based on the results of own research)

It can be observed that most organizations in this study used Strategy Mapping as one part of their BSC-approach. They emphasized the alignment factor of the operational to the strategic level based on this instrument. Organizations also use diverse KPI on various levels to get an insight view into distinct aspects of the organization. This also includes elements of

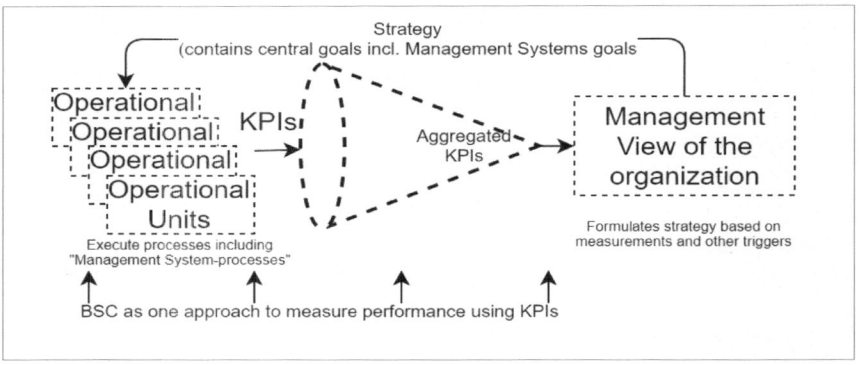

**Figure 84 Decision process based on key performance indicatorsand the balanced scorecard includ-
ing the management system perspective**

(Source: own elaboration based on the results of own research)

management systems in some companies since management systems "live" within the
day-to-day processes (Hypothesis 4). 32% of organizations use the Execution Premium
approach which further demonstrates that the linkage between strategy and the operational level is recognized as a crucial factor (Hypothesis 5). The interviewees confirmed that they use several indicators as KPIs on the operational level, which is then
aggregated into a compounded number of KPIs for the upper management. This approach is a confirmation that the suggested model in this research displayed in figure
85 shows a useful approach to measure the performance of management systems and
to use the results for a continuous improvement process. Figure 84 shows an excerpt
of the model developed in the last chapter (see figure 83) highlighting the evaluation
aspect. The fact the most companies see a positive correlation between management
systems and performance can be interpreted as a result of the increased transparency
possible by using the BSC approach, and therefore the stronger involvement of the
upper management. Without a clear way to measure the efficiency and effectiveness
of the management system, this result would not be possible.

    Financial performance is still the most dominating factor for the companies in this
study. Sustainability aspects seem to also be of growing importance and most likely,
because it is required by law or generally a topic with high necessity.

    For the empirical part, the results show a different picture. In the correlation
analysis, the highest correlation was found in the variables IBSC and BU (against the
performance indicator: the MPD-variable). The variable IBSC shows the integration of

a management system into the BSC of the organization and demonstrates that a prominent level of integration indeed seems to lead to better performance. This cannot be clearly confirmed by the qualitative part of this study in which 39% organizations seem to integrate their management system measurement into the BSC. This does not confirm hypothesis 2, which suggested that most of the companies using BSC also use elements of management systems. Nevertheless, the fact that there is a correlation and that 39% of the organizations use such an integrative approach these result can also be interpreted positively in the context of hypothesis 2.

Hypothesis 6 can be answered by calculating the maturity level based on the formula in the last chapter. This results in the following table (44).

Table 44 Maturity level of the organizations assessed in the research

Maturity level	Organizations
High	0
Medium	9
Low	14
Very low	2

(Source: own elaboration based on the results of own research)

Hypothesis 6 cannot be confirmed. Most organizations in the survey state that their management systems perform very well. Calculating the maturity level of the systems show a mostly low maturity level. In the research of chapter 6.3 (the primary database of the calculation of the maturity level) it was shown that most organization do not use many strategic KPIs which is the reason why most management systems in an organization do not perform as well, despite the good values of operational KPIs reported by employees (this seems to be a subjective impression of the involved stakeholders). If the use of strategical KPIs would have been robust, the maturity might have better values.

The BSC is used as a strategic planning instrument rather than a measurement tool, a confirmation in the qualitative part as well as the quantitative analysis. This confirms hypothesis 4. Considering the correlation, a strategical use of the BSC also correlates to a higher performance of a company.

A significant correlation was also identified in the question regarding the duration of the existence of the management system and the development of performance. Hypothesis 3 is therefore confirmed: The longer the management system (or the integrated management system) is in use, the better the performance of the organization.

This seems logical considering the gained experience and therefore better use and a decreased financial investment into the management system over time.

The more frequent KPIs are evaluated, the better the performances result. It seems reasonable that more frequent attention and quicker reaction to any event because of actual measures result in better output. This will probably be only true up to a certain frequency. Almost no correlation was found between the performance of the organization and the level of integration of the management system.

To summarize this part, the following can be said: In this study, the author developed an integrated model to link operational performance elements to the strategic level using the BSC-approach, Strategy Map, and the Execution Premium and connect it with the PDCA-Cycle of management systems. A formula to calculate the maturity level including the generic performance of management systems, was also proposed. In a qualitative and quantitative analysis, the stated hypotheses were tested, which described a model based on questions. To develop a framework, past development and current trends in the field of performance measurement are summarized. The scientific literature does not clearly answer the question of how management systems can be measured and how the use of management systems influence performance. One reason was identified as the problematic, the definition of performance. It was establish, that BSC is a widely discussed approach to measure performance within organizations but it is also an accepted method used by practitioners. The advantage of the BSC is the multi-dimensional approach of measurements, which is necessary to evaluate all relevant aspects of the organizations at all applicable levels. This also includes elements of management systems. Through the strategic linkage of the BSC from the operational to the strategic level, using Strategy Map and Execution Premium, the visibility for the top management level is increased, resulting in strategic consequences which again are quantifiable on the operational level.

The proposed model was tested in the survey and came to the conclusion that there are companies which already use elements of the Execution Premium together with management system-implementations linking operational units and strategic aspects using the BSC and strategic maps. Most companies also see the benefits of the BSC usage and the increased transparency on various levels. Even though financial values are still dominate over other indicators, performance is increasingly measured using the Triple Bottom Line and other values in regards of sustainability on the one side (in fact organizations in this study use the SBSC) and the operational level on the other. A positive correlation was also identified between SBSC or BSC used as a strategic instrument and in contrast to using the performance of BSC only as "tool".

Even though the verification of the model was not fully possible because the model itself is not yet implemented, it can be said, that the suggested model is a valid method to evaluate the performance of management systems within companies because the verification confirmed the main goals of the model using the following points:

1. It is strongly connected to the strategic goal settings process.
2. It is strongly connected to the development of operational processes through the strategy.
3. It can be used to measure values from all relevant aspects including methods and KPIs used in enterprise risk management evaluations, Six Sigma-projects, TQM-approaches etc.
4. It can report measures aggregated for the top management.
5. The maturity level can be evaluated.

The following limitations must be stated: due to the complexity of the topic and the extend of the methodology, only a small sample size was used in this study. The selection of organizations also did not differentiate between sizes, industry, or regions. The model itself was not used by any organizations since it was developed most recently within this thesis. Future research should go into further detail about the following aspects:

- Results by analyzing organizations which used the suggested model for several years.
- Differences between size, industry, and geographic region in regard to the study questions.
- A richer understanding of the method that creates connections between the processes linking strategy with operational levels and the role of management systems.
- A more exact definition of KPIs for management systems which are used in the context of BSC.
- The effects of this integrated approach using a longitudinalstudy

Final conclusions

The goal of this thesis was to suggest a model to evaluate the performance of integrated management systems within the context of sustainable business processes and risk management. The author based his thesis on different research methodologies. The first methodology involved a literature research of relevant fields. By identifying the current state of knowledge and existing research gaps the author deduced problems, existing approaches and solutions. The writer of this thesis further conducted personal scientific studies to elaborate on important aspects for this thesis that also takes advantage of knowledge and insights gained in years of practical experience. The author is intensely involved in the implementation, development, and evaluation of integrated management systems with different companies and also very interested to improve knowledge for practical use and for the scientific community. With this thesis, the author intends to solve an important aspect of his day-to-day work, namely, the evaluation of the effects and the maturity of integrated management systems used by organizations and their business processes worldwide.

A special focus was set on sustainability since this area is of great importance. Sustainability requires organizations to define, evaluate and reach different goals than in the past. This implies that an organization has to set more than traditional targets, such as increasing the stock value, the turnover, or other financial values. The financial value was historically seen as the most important aspect of organizations to reach and report, and many scientific studies are grounded in this idea. This is one reason why many research approaches to understanding the topic of management systems, their integration into each other, and their effects on business processes performance are financially oriented. The lag of studies for the evaluation of the performance of integrated management system shows that there is not enough research in the area of overall performance, and specifically business processes. Sustainability brings new insights into this domain. A sustainable business process is not only a process, which generates a financial value based on an input, but it also generates outputs in various other aspects. Some of these aspects are parts of the sustainability thought, e.g. better outputs regarding the environmental and social perspective. In addition, other elements necessary to perform well might include other aspects. For example, the creation of knowledge, knowledge sharing, transfer of knowledge t, organizational culture, its image toward society and its responsibility within (this also includes corporate social responsibility). Organizational culture is reflected by leadership style, a topic which also won increasing attention over time. Different types of leadership styles are required

© Springer Fachmedien Wiesbaden GmbH, part of Springer Nature 2019
J. Kopia, *Effective Implementation of Management Systems*, Sustainable Management, Wertschöpfung und Effizienz, https://doi.org/10.1007/978-3-658-26509-0

for different phases in an organization and their influence on employees' well-being and mental attitudes. This includes defined targets and the way the businesses, including management systems, are operated and the level of performance reached.

There are various perspectives regarding the meaning of performance depending on the stakeholder and aspects to be considered when the performance of an integrated management system is being evaluated. Performance evaluation on management systems is necessary. Every system requires a constant improvement process to increase in maturity over time. To reach this initial goal, this thesis used the methodology stated next.

Part one of this paper employed a literature researches to study the current scientific data in the field of performance evaluations of management systems and business processes as well as risk management.

Chapter 1 covers the literature review in the field of performance in the context of organizations and business processes. The results show that inputs are transformed to outputs using a triangle of three elements: processes, structure and behavior. Each element being a separate area to consider and to understand the connection and ways to evaluate. Effective and efficient processes, structure, and behavior are affected by diverse factors, such as the political situation, technological development and so on. Adopted management methodologies are also influencingd factors and include management systems and approaches, such as total quality management (TQM), Supply-Chain-Management (SCM), Just-in-Time (JIT)-production, and alike. The scientific research in this field revealed that the evaluation of performance requires the measurement in different dimensions. The balanced scorecard approach, including extensions o and other multi-dimensional assessment methodologies and frameworks are examples of what was highlighted in this chapter. Despite the general understanding that organizations exist to maximize profit, evaluating performance in the context of management systems is more about evaluating multiple dimensions on various levels.

After the study related to processes, the next analysis assesses parts of the structure. Based on the findings, the author concluded that there is a shift from structure to behavior within evaluation concepts of organizations and an increasing importance of leadership styles in the context of performance measurement in scientific research in the last decades. From "Fordism" in the 1930s to "Toyotism" in the 1950s, the invention of other management styles based on JIDOKA, Kaizen, 5S, agility and the corresponding continues improvement methods. TQM, Six Sigma, balanced scorecards etc. shifted the way performance of management systems and sustainable business processes are reached, supported and evaluated.

Business process management is another new concept to optimize process efficiency aiming to collect as much data as beneficial to ensure efficiency and making the quick automation of processes and the rapid prototyping of products possible. Agile methodologies contrast with traditional methodologies and seem to result in better performance because they embrace a rapid change in products, services, and processes. They also enable constantly adapting strategies. The possibility to change as quickly as necessary is a fundamental requirement of today's businesses and therefore an important aspect within an evaluation process of a management system to measure performance.

The "lived" philosophy and culture is the focus of another study in this thesis. Based on research, it can be said, that organizational culture influences the performance of the organization. This includes the way the organization deals with knowledge. Knowledge creation, transfer, sharing, and preservation is required in a knowledge-driven world where patents and ideas sometimes have more value than existing products and services. Every organization must develop an organizational culture fitting to the market needs, which is reflected by their leaders and management style. The result of this third study showed that the performance of an organization is influenced by these topics. The research also summarized established measurement methods to evaluate knowledge within an organization using intellectual capital. The results of the study show that, despite being intensively discussed in the scientific community, the measurement of knowledge and knowledge management is neither researched well nor solved in practice.

In chapter 2, aspects of risk management were studied as an essential part of an organization in order to be prepared for seen and unseen events. Besides traditional risk management, based on basic risk management principles and methods (e.g. involving the approaches of risk identification, risk measurement, risk monitoring, risk mitigation etc.), an enterprise risk management philosophy emphasis the awareness that risks are of different origins throughout the organization, having different impact with the need for a central governance structure to assess them. Risks within enterprise risk management can be of strategic, operational and of financial relevance. Management, therefore, assesses them on multiple levels and aspects using a risk governance methodology, which requires the organizations to integrate an enterprise-wide, concise management system. Within this risk management system, there is also a requirement to report risk and risk status from all levels as well as evaluate the risk management methodology itself by using an internal control system. Existing and well-established risk management frameworks, such as COSO or ISO 31000 serve as an example of models to assess multiple aspects of an organization affecting strategical and operational outcomes. This research also discovered that there is not enough scientific consensus about the effects of an enterprise risk management on the performance of firms. This makes this topic like the lag of consensus discussion in the field, pertaining to the effects of management systems. In the second research of this chapter, the author ascertained that existing approaches of the evaluation of the effects of enterprise risk management yield to the use of the balanced scorecard. Scientific research also includes aspects of sustainability within this measurement approach by using an integrated balanced scorecard in which sustainability aspects are considered together with the traditional dimensions. The balanced scorecard requires key performance indicators of various sources. In this context, scientific research states the importance of Big Data technologies to generate KPIs of valuable results.

To understand what success and failure of management systems means, the authors studied the relationship between sustainable business processes and integrated management systems by focusing on success factors of management systems in chapter 3. The origins of management systems are highlighted including widespread systems, such as TQM, the European Foundation for Quality Management (EFQM), and ISO international management system standards. Similarities between these systems and the general trend of the integration of management systems are emphasized. Most companies use integration to create synergies between management systems. In this chapter, the PhD-candidate of the studies summarizes the most important aspects of management systems based on literature research, which involved the following:

- leadership commitment and goal setting,
- definition of goals by the management,
- involvement of requirements of interested parties,
- evaluation of the performance,
- constant improvement processes.

A second study identified success factors of integrated management systems. The focus of this research was to outline the necessity of the strategic linkage of the management system with a strategic level in order to influence top-level decision processes. Benefits of the high-level structure of ISO international standards, which enables the jointly use of multiple management systems due to the underlying similar structure of requirements, were also uncovered. Using HLS allows management systems to profit from synergies generated through similar processes and documents, especially applying the risk-based approach, monitoring, evaluation, and continuous improvement processes.

In the third literature review, the author identified leadership aspects that are favorable in regard to management systems. The role of organizational culture as an influencing factor for the success of management systems and efficiency and effectiveness of business processes is also evaluated. Different organizational cultures are compared, showing that the corporate cultures of adhocracy and clan seem to benefit management systems. This is in compatriot to other types of cultures derived from scientific research like the market culture and the hierarchy culture. The role of the employ within a management system is also considered important in the context since employees are directly involved in the operation of the processes and are greatly influenced by the organizational culture and leadership styles. The result of this study showed that the connection between behavioral aspects of employees, leadership styles, and the organizational culture influence performance in an organization. Since management systems are integrated into many different processes from the operational to the strategic level of an organization, it is necessary to include this perspective in an evaluation approach of performance.

To understand differences between industries and geographical regions, a literature review assessing industrial segments and geography showed that there are industry-specific management systems. Since management systems have similar requirements, these management systems have common elements, a necessary evaluation being one of them. Industry-specific key performance indicators are used. It was also the result of the studies in this chapter that there are companies that integrate their performance indicators into an organizatio wide measurement and controlling system. This makes it clear that organizations already look for ways to solve one of the problems this thesis tries to assess.

The last research portion centers on the aspects to use controlling systems to understand the importance of the linkage between the measurement of a management system and the strategic level of an organization. Based on literature research, the study concluded that the incorporation of new aspects into a strategic instrument, like the balanced scorecard, may enhance management systems and thereby provide opportunities for further growth of the organization. The strategic linkage of management systems with strategic levels, similar as it is suggested by the research in the field of enterprise risk management detailed in the last chapter, showed beneficial outcomes.

Part two of this thesis is the personal contribution of the author of this thesis to the field of study. It contains empirical researches which extend the findings of other researches stated in part 1 to deduct an evaluation model.

In chapter 4, the author analyzed the linkage between intellectual capital and the firm's performance in order to show the importance of knowledge management on the effect of performance. According to scientists, knowledge and learning is connected with a firm's performance, which involves the outlined business strategy of the company containing defined targets. Then the study targets defined by organizations of the automotive sector and their outcomes over a certain period of time is compared. The author researched them applying qualitative comparison on the one side and a quantitative approach based on normalized values of the sales targets on the other. The objective of the research was to identify possible connections between defined targets, their nature and reported organizational performance. It was found, that defined targets included mainly financial values, but with an increasing trend to report aspects of sustainability (most likely due to existing regulatory requirements). Of special importance in the targets in the sample size was the common focus on the attractiveness of the organization for new employees showing that skilled people are a rarity and of value. This indirectly proves the importance of knowledge, skilled people and their experience in today's businesses, knowledge as a success factor for organizations. Another confirmation of the importance of knowledge and its influence on a firm's performance could be observed in lower level reports. They included topics in the area of knowledge management, organizational learning, corporate social responsibility, and organizational culture. This was confirmed in another study by the author in which the value of intangible assets, measured in the form of intellectual capital, was compared with performance development over time. In this study, the connection between intellectual capital as a way expressed by organizations to deal with knowledge aspects and the performance of a company was analyzed quantitatively. Using a correlation analysis, it can be shown that in large and robust growing industries (automotive) the value of intellectual capital increased between 2008 and 2014. Also, it was shown, that a higher sales growth correlated to higher values in intellectual capital which might indicate a relationship between these values and must be further evaluated.

Using a meta-analysis, the second study assessed the topic of the evaluation of business process performance and its connection to enterprise risk management. Recent studies affirmed the in part one suggested influencing factor of enterprise risk management on the performance of an organization. The author demonstrated that there is no clear correlation between the performance of an organization and the use of enterprise risk management that is mostly based on financial evaluations only. The findings in this thesis highlighted the importance of the assessment of the performance of management systems using multiple dimensions several times.. Another outcome of this research was the fact that there is no standardized assessment approach, which confirms the problem that there is no valid model or methodology to assess management systems including systems for risk management. To improve this situation, the author suggested a generic approach to enterprise risk management-assessment to improve future measurement efforts in this area which:

- Uses operational inputs including sustainability dimensions (financial risks, environmental risks, operational risks, and strategic risks),
- Uses different performance indicators as output,
- Uses a regular risk status reporting based on an extended balanced scorecard and specific KPIs typical for the industry.
- Assesses the maturity level of the risk management process regularly to constantly improve it.

The suggested model was evaluated using a case study approach. It can be concluded that the suggested model can be practically used for an enterprise risk management assessment.

Another important topic in this thesis is the value of intangible assets for the performance of organizations. To identify a connection between intellectual capital expressing measurement efforts of organizations to rate knowledge and other intangible assets, the author conducted a quantitative study using a correlation analysis. It could be shown that the values of intellectual capital increased between 2008 and 2014 within the selected automotive industry business. Higher sales growth correlated to higher values for intellectual capital, which indicates a connection. The author must state, that this correlation warrants further evaluation to identify scientific verification of this matter.

The conclusion of the last part of chapter four revealed that modern management approaches, such as agile principles and lean manufacturing in the production industry are beneficial for the efficiency and effectiveness of organizations. This highlights the importance of a quick adaptation in a rapidly changing marketplace and the importance of these operational principles and tactics as influencing factors for performance.

Chapter 5 focusses the research in the field of integrated management systems and the influence on the performance of business processes. With this empirical research, the author answered the question what success factors exist for the implementation and operation of an integrated management system. Due to the nature of a project during an implementation of the management system, which usually involves a special project team, a strict budget, a time limit etc. the success factors of management systems implementation are different then the factors during the operation. In this study, the author confirmed the results of other studies detailed in part one which stated that leadership commitment is very important for the success of a management system implementation. This study also confirmed that a transformational and affiliative leadership style is favorable over other styles during the operational state of an integrated management system. Another confirmation could be drawn regarding the fact that the high-level structure of ISO international management system standards is positively rated concerning the integration of management systems by giving guidance on the use of common elements. These elements include the success factor of leadership commitment, a risk-based approach, and a continuous improvement process with requirements regarding the assessment and evaluation of the management system. Regarding the effect of knowledge management, a correlation between the introduction of a management system and the value of intellectual capital in the automotive business between 1997 and 2014 was revealed, showing the importance of intangible assets for organizations and the importance to assess this in evaluation methods regarding performance measurement. A study in the service sector showed that sector-specific management systems need of a concise method to assess performance and outcome of the management system within this industry.

In chapter 6 the PhD-student further identified knowledge gaps and problems in the evaluation of integrated management systems. This was accomplished by taking the results of the studies stated in the last chapters, adding additional personal research results and then formulating possible solutions to the discovered problems. The author is personally involved in a number of management systems audits and is therefore in the possession of valuable data which can be used to further elaborate on this topic. The results of the quantitative analysis showed that there are more non-conformities in certain areas of the requirements of management systems than in others. These areas are related to the topics discussed in this thesis:

- leadership and management commitment,
- the operation of the management system,
- the performance evaluation and

- the continued improvement process.

This confirms the other findings of the researches performed in this thesis. The author hypothesis is that these topics are linked to common problems similar to all organizations. The results of the study confirm the following findings:

- The commitment of management and leadership style influences the success and the performance of an integrated management system.
- The performance evaluation of the management system is problematic for most organizations. This involves also the selection of the correct key performance indicators, which are usually not linked to upper-level goals or to the sustainability targets of the organization.
- Organizations that use performance indicators that are linked to a strategic level, have fewer audit findings in their management systems.
- If companies integrate the risk management of their management system into a organization-wide risk management methodology, they have fewer audit findings.

To understand the upcoming requirements of the EU regarding sustainability and its effect on management systems, the author analyzed the content of the EU directive 2014/695/EU. The result showed that the consequences for medium- and large-sized businesses within the EU makes it necessary to create detailed reports about sustainability on a regular basis. These reports also require the definition and evaluation of key performance indicators in that field, allowing customers and other stakeholders to see the performance of an organization not only from the financial perspective but also in other pertinent areas. These indicators should include topics about environmental aspects, social and employee concerns, respect and human rights, anti-corruption and bribery matters, and aspects that are of importance to the evaluation of the performance of management systems in the context of business process performance.

In summary, the research contained in this PhD-thesis demonstrate the following elaborated points:

- Performance evaluation of management systems is a problematic topic for practitioners as well as for scientist mainly due to a lag of a concise understanding of the definition of performance and a missing methodology.

- Performance of organizations is often stated as a financial performance only. Assessing performance on other levels is necessary which means that the evaluating of performance requires other values and assessment approaches. Some of the important topics to include in the evaluation is operational excellence, which includes process efficiency and effectiveness and also involve all processes of a company.
- Different method and models exist to assess performance in multiple dimensions. One such model is the balanced scorecard. The balanced scorecard was extended to also include different purposes, e.g. sustainability and risk management perspectives to assess performance on even more aspects as in the original suggestion.
- The performance of management system integration and operation, including successful certification, involve most importantly four aspects: management commitment, certain leadership styles, a compliant and useful method of evaluation of the management system and a continues improvement process.

Considering these findings, the authors developed a model for the evaluation of the performance of integrated management systems in the context of sustainable business processes and risk management in the last chapter of this thesis. It includes the use of the balanced scorecard together with a strategic mapping process and the execution premium based on Kaplan & Norton (2008). Strategic mapping and the execution premium is required to set the basis for operational excellence. This allows the possibility to provide for a consistent strategy where there is a linkage of information from the top level of a company to the bottom and vice versa using valuable performance indicators. It is an integrated model, which links operational performance elements to the strategic level using the balanced scorecard-approach and by applying the process of strategy mapping, and the execution premium and connecting it with the plan-do-check-act-cycle of integrated management systems. It encourages the use of knowledge management and organizational learning since it was determined that effective management of knowledge enables innovations important to survive in today's competition. Knowledge management is connected with organizational learning reflected by leadership styles and their definition of the organizational culture influencing employee behavior. Focusing the values of these intangible assets, including the capability of innovation, emphases process excellence in which the evaluation of the status is important to assess the maturity level and to improve. These are core principle of management systems. Different management systems developed over time (TQM, EFQM, Kaizen, Six Sigma, lean, and agile, ISO based management systems etc.) emphasize these aspects in a different variety showing that they assist in improving business performance. Viewed from the risk management perspective, bigger organizations use enterprise risk management to assess all risks of the organization to derive strategic decisions. Risk management is a basic requirement in management systems and therefore a part of the process.

The model developed by the author suggests evaluating performance based on indicators of diverse dimensions. Sustainability aspects affects the society and are forced by regulations and certain management systems itself. They must also be included in an evaluation model. Besides indicators coming from sustainability, operational and strategic processes efficiency and effectiveness is a mandatory perspective, which needs to be assessed, as well as aspects, that are of importance to a specific subject of the management system and to the industry-specific targets of the company. Hence, there are not the same indicators for all organizations but commonalities with specific purposes. The models also included the measurement of the maturity levels, including the generic performance of integrated management systems.

The last step was the verification of the suggested model using a quantitative analysis based on a survey and interviews. In this manner the author evaluated and compared approaches and methodologies like the suggested evaluation model. The results showed that the suggested model is a valid method to evaluate the performance of management systems in companies especially because of the following points:

1. The model connects integrated management system evaluations with strategic goal settings since it can be used to report results of evaluations aggregated to the top management
2. The model is connected to the development of operational business processes on the basis of the defined strategy of the organization.
3. The model can be used to measure values from all relevant dimensions including the methods and KPIs used sustainability and in enterprise risk management evaluations.
4. The model suggests known and well-established methods.

It can be concluded that the proposed model solves some of the problems discovered by other authors and scientists, during the day-to-day work and scientific research of the author of the PhD-thesis. Using different research approaches in the research project, a holistic measurement framework to assess performance evaluations of integrated management systems was deduced and empirically tested. This thesis identified the strategic relevance of integrated management systems and their evaluation since management systems connect a wide variety of topics from the operational to the strategic level.

This framework serves as a starting point for further research in this field. Further elaborations should be based on a broader spectrum of firms in different industries, geographic locations, and sizes. A longitudinal perspective would also give important insights into the usefulness of long-term use of that model. It is also necessary to develop a better understanding of each of the suggested steps of the framework and its dependencies. Within the continuous improvement cycle, it would be interesting to identify commonalities and differences between company sizes and culture, aspects of sustainability, leadership styles and types of management systems in use. In addition to that, more specific key performance indicators focusing business processes should be evaluated depending on the industry and the type of management system to serve as more concrete recommendations for scientists and practitioners.

Bibliography

A. Mondal, S.K. Ghosh (2012), *Intellectual capital and financial performance of Indian banks*, Journal of intellectual capital, 13 (4) (2012), pp. 515-530

Aba, E. K. Badar, M. A., Hayden, M. A. (2016), *Impact of ISO 9001 certification on firms financial operating performance*, International Journal of Quality & Reliability Management, 33 (1), pp. 78-89.

Abdulsalam, F., Al-Qaheri, H., Al-Khayya, R. (2011), The intellectual capital Performance of Kuwaiti Banks: *An Application of VAIC™ Model*, Scientific Research, iBusiness, 3, pp. 88-96

Acharyya, Madhu (2008) In Measuring the Benefits of Enterprise risk management in Insurance: *An Integration of Economic Value Added and Balanced Score Card Approaches*, Working paper for the Society of Actuaries

Adedeji Babatunji Samuel , Mohammad Mizanur Rahman , Idris Khairuddin , Mohammad Jamal Uddin , Md Saidur Rahaman (2017), *A synthesised literature review on organisational culture and corporate performance*, Journal of Advanced Research in Social and Behavioural Sciences 7, Issue 1 (2017) 83-95 83 Journal of Advanced Research in Social and Behavioural Sciences Journal homepage: www.akademiabaru.com/arsbs.html ISSN: 2462-1951

Aggeri, F. (2008), *Managing learning in the automotive industry* – the race for hybridisation 16th International Conference 2008. Ecole des Mines de Paris, Chalmers University of Tech./VINNOVA

Agota Giedrė Raišienė (2012), *Advantages and limitations of integrated management system: the theoretical viewpoint*, ISSN 2029-7564 (online) SOCIALINÈS TECHNOLOGIJOS SOCIAL TECHNOLOGIES (2011), 1(1), p. 25–36

Agustina Linda, Baroroh Niswah (2016), The Relationship Between Enterprise risk management (ERM) And Firm Value Mediated Through The Financial Performance, Review of Integrative Business & Economics Research Vol 5, No. 1, pp. 128-138

Ahmed A.S. Seleim, Omar E.M. Khalil (2011) *Understanding the knowledge management-intellectual capital relationship: a two-way analysis*, Journal of intellectual capital, Vol. 12 Issue: 4, pp.586-614,

Ahsen von, A., Funck, D. (2001), *integrated management systems — Opportunities and Risks for Corporate Environmental Protection*, Corporate Environmental Strategy, Vol 8 No. 2, pp. 165-176.

Albrecht, P., Maurer, R. (2005), *Investment- und Risikomanagement. 2nd edition*, Stuttgart: Schäffer Poeschel.

Aleca, O. E., Mihai, F. (2016), Best Practices in Academic Management. Study Programs Classification Model. Amfiteatru Economic, 18(42), 462-473

Alharbi Mohammad, Yusoff Prof. Dr. Rushami Zien, (2012), *Leadership styles and their relationship with quality management practices in public hospitals in Saudi Arabia*, International Journal of Economics and Management Sciences, Vol. 1, No. 10, 2012, pp. 59-67

Al-Mashari, M., & Zairi, M. (2001). *The effective application of SAP R/3: A proposed model of best practice. Logistics Information Management*, 13, 156–166.

Al-Twaijry, A. (2009). *Intangible assets and future growth: evidence from Japan*. Asian Review of Accounting, 17(1): 23–39.

Almeida, J., Domingues, P. & Sampaio, P. (2014), *Different perspectives on management system integration*. Total Quality Management & Business Excellence, 25, 338–351.

D'Amato, A., Henderson, S. & Florence, S. (2009). *Corporate social responsibility and sustainable business. A guide to leadership tasks and functions*, Center for Creative Leadership, Greensboro, North Carolina.

Ambe, I. M., Badenhorst-Weiss, J. A. (2010), *Strategic supply chain framework for the automotive Industry*. African Journal of Business Management Vol. 4(10), pp. 2110-2120, 18 th August, 2010

Ambler, S. W. (2011), *Examining the agile Manifesto*. Retrieved December 8, 2015, from http://www.ambysoft.com/essays/agileManifesto.html, accessed 02.03.2017

© Springer Fachmedien Wiesbaden GmbH, part of Springer Nature 2019
J. Kopia, *Effective Implementation of Management Systems*, Sustainable Management, Wertschöpfung und Effizienz, https://doi.org/10.1007/978-3-658-26509-0

Amir, Faiza. (2011), *Significance of Lean, Agile and Leagile Decoupling Point in Supply Chain Management*. Journal of Economics and Behavioral Studies. Database for Advances in Information Systems, Vol. 30, No. 2, 66-81.

Amit R., Schoemaker P. J. H., (1993), *Strategic Assets and Organizational Rent*, Strategic Management Journal, Vol. 14, No. 1.

Amrit Tiwana, (1999), *The Knowledge Management Toolkit*, Prentice Hall PTR First Edition December 06, 1999 ISBN: 0-13-012853-8

Amy Van Looy, Manu De Backer & Geert Poels (2011), *Defining business process maturity*. A journey towards excellence, Total Quality Management & Business Excellence, 22:11, 1119-1137

Anderson, Dan. R. (2005), Corporate Survival: *The Critical Importance of Sustainability risk management*, Universe, Lincoln

Andraski, J.C. (1994), *Foundations for a Successful Continuous Replenishment Programme*, International Journal of Logistics Management, Vol 5, No. 1, pp 1-8

Anderson Dan R, (2005), Corporate Survival: *The Critical Importance of Sustainability risk management*, IUniverse, Lincoln

Ansari, S. (2010), Reviewed Work(s), *The Execution Premium: Linking Strategy to Operations for Competitive Advantage* by ROBERT S. KAPLAN and DAVID P. NORTON, The Accounting Review, 85 (4), pp. 1475-1477.

Appuhami R. (2007*), The Impact of Intellectual Capital on Investor's Capital Gain on Shares: An Empirical Investigation in Thai Banking*, Finance and Insurance Sector, (2007), Department of Accounting, University of Sri Jayewardenepura, Sri Lanka

Arabella Volkov (2012), Value Added Intellectual Co-efficient (VAIC TM), *A Selective Thematic-Bibliography*, Journal of New Business Ideas & Trends, (2012), 10(1), pp. 14-24.

Arena, M., Arnaboldi, M., Azzone, G. (2010), *The organizational dynamics of Enterprise risk management*, Accounting, Organizations and Society, 35, pp. 659-675.

Arenas, F. (2012) - Organizational Knowledge and Organizational Performance*: A Dynamic Relationship, Proceedings of the 9th International Conference on intellectual capital*, Knowledge Management & Organisational Learning, Bogotá, Colombia, Academic Publishing International Limited, pp.6-16.

Argyris, C. and Schön, D.A. (1996), *Organizational learning II, Theory, Method and Practice*, Addison-Wesley Publishing Company, US.

Asif, M., Searcy, C., Zutshi, A., Ahmad, N. (2011), *An integrated management systems approach to corporate sustainability*, European Business Review, 23 (4), pp. 353-367.

Asif, M., Fischer, O.A.M., Bruijn, E.J., Pagell, M. (2010) Integration of management systems: *A methodology for operational excellence and strategic flexibility*. Oper. Manag. Res. (2010), 3, 146–160

Assiri, A., Zairi, M. and Eid, R. (2006), *How to profit from the balanced scorecard*. Industrial Management & Data Systems, 106(7), pp.937-952.

Auer, K., Miller, R. (2002), *Extreme Programming Applied*. Addison-Wesley

Avery, G.C. (2004) *Understanding Leadership: Explaining the Paradigms* Gayle C. Avery Sage Publications Ltd (2004)

Aziz, N.A.A., Manab, N.A. and Othman, S.N. (2016), *Sustainability Risk Management (SRM): An Extension of Enterprise Risk Management (ERM) Concept*, International Journal of Management and Sustainability, Vol. 5 No. 1, pp. 1-10.

Baird K, Hu KJ, Reeve R (2011*). The relationships between organizational culture, total quality management practices and operational performance*. International Journal of Operations & Production Management, 31(7): 789-814

Ballantyne, Ryan, (2013), *An Empirical Investigation into the Association between Enterprise risk management and Firm Financial Performance*, Lawrence Technological University

Banker, R. D., Chang, H., Pizzini, M. J. (2004), The balanced scorecard: *Judgmental Effects of Performance Measures Linked to Strategy Author(s)*, The Accounting Review, 79 (1), pp. 1-23.

Barafort, B., Mesquida, A.L., Mas, A. (2017), *Integrating risk management in IT settings from ISO standards and management systems perspectives*, Computer Standards & Interfaces, 54, pp. 176-185.

Barrese, James, Stephen G. Fier, David M. Pooser, and Paul L. Walker (2015), *Enterprise risk management Sophistication and Firm Risk, World Risk and Insurance Economics Congress*, Munich, Germany

Bass, B. M., Avolio, B. J., Atwater, L. E. (1996), *The transformational and transactional leadership of men and women*. Applied Psychology: an International Review 45: 5–34. doi:10.1111/j.1464-0597.1996.tb00847.x

Baxter, Ryan J. and Bedard, Jean C. and Hoitash, Rani and Yezegel, Ari, (2013), *Enterprise risk management Program Quality: Determinants, Value Relevance, and the Financial Crisis,* Contemporary Accounting Research, Forthcoming. SSRN: http://dx.doi.org/10.2139/ssrn.1684807

Baykitz Tekin (2014), *An assessment of knowledge management maturity among the public institutions in turkey*, M.S., Department of Information Systems, the graduate school of informatics institute of middle east technical university

Bea, F. B., Haas, J. (2016), *Strategisches Management. 8th edition,* München Konstanz: UVK.

Beasley, M., Branson, B., Pagach, D. (2015), *An analysis of the maturity and strategic impact of investments in ERM,* J. Account. Public Policy, 34, pp. 219-243.

Beasley, Mark S., Chen, Al, Nunez, Karen, Wright, Lorraine, (2006), *WORKING Hand IN Hand: balanced scorecards AND Enterprise risk management*, Strategic Finance, Vol. 87 Issue 9, p49

Beck, K. et al. (2001), *Principles behind the agile Manifesto*. Agile Alliance. http://agilemanifesto.org/. Retrieved 1 January (2016).

Beck, K., Cockburn, A., Jeffries, R., and Highsmith, J. Agile Manifesto. http://www.agilemanifesto.org . (2001), 12-4-2002.

Becker, J., & Kahn, D. (2011), The Process in Focus. In J. Becker, M. Kugeler, & M. Rosemann (Eds.), Process Management – *A Guide for the Design of business processes* (2nd ed.) (pp. 1-12), Berlin, Germany: Springer. http://dx.doi.org/10.1007/978-3-540-24798-2_1

Beechner, A.B. and Koch, J.E. (1997), *Integrating ISO 9001 and ISO 14001*, Quality Progress, Vol. 30 No. 2, pp. 33-36

Benedict, T. et al (2013), BPM CBOK Version 3.0: *Guide to the business process Management Common Body Of Knowledge*. CreateSpace Independent Publishing Platform

Bernardo Merce, Castán Farrero José M, Casadesús Martí, (2016), *The impact of management systems integration through the value chain*, 1st International conference on Quality of Life June (2016) Center for Quality, Faculty of Engineering, University of Kragujevac

Bernardo Merce, Alexandra Simon, Juan José Tari, José F.Molina-Azoríncm (2015), *Benefits of management systems integration: a literature review*, Journal of Cleaner Production Volume 94, 1 May (2015), Pages 260-267

Bernardo, M., Casadesus, M., Karapetrovic, S., Heras, I. (2009), *How integrated are environmental, quality and other standardized management systems?* An empirical study, Journal of Cleaner Production, Vol 17 No. 8, pp. 742-750.

Bernardo Merce, José Castán Farrero, Martí Casadesús, (2016*), THE IMPACT OF MANAGEMENT SYSTEMS INTEGRATION THROUGH THE VALUE CHAIN,* 1 st International conference on Quality of Life June(2016) Center for Quality, Faculty of Engineering, University of Kragujevac 1 st International conference on Quality of Life June (2016) 179

Berta Email Whitney,Lisa Cranley,James W. Dearing,Elizabeth J. Dogherty,Janet E. Squires, Carole A. Estabrooks (2015), *Why (we think) facilitation works: insights from organizational learning theory*, Implementation Science201510:141, https://doi.org/10.1186/s13012-015-0323-0

Bessire, D. (2000), French tableau de bord versus American balanced scorecard: *misery and glory, of metaphors*. In Proceedings of the Sixth Interdisciplinary Perspectives on Accounting, Conference, Manchester: The University of Manchester/UMIST, vol. 3, chapter 3.14

Beugelsdijk, S., Koen, C.I., & Nooderhaven, N.G. (2006), *Organizational culture and relationship skills*. Organization Studies, 27(6), 833-854. http://dx.doi.org/10.1177/0170840606064099

Bevilacqua, M., Ciarapica, F.E., Giacchetta, G. and B. Marchetti (2011), *Overview on the application of ISO/TS 16949:2009, in a worldwide leader company in the production of stainless steel tubes for automotive exhaust systems*, International Journal of Productivity and Quality Management 7(4), 410–439.

Bierbusse, P. and Siesfeld, T. (1997), *Measures that matter*, Journal of Strategic Performance Measurement, Vol. 1, No. 2, pp. 6–11

Boisot, M.H., (1998) Knowledge Assets: *Securing Competitive Advantage in the Information Economy*, New York: Oxford University Press, (1998).

Bontis, N., (2001), Assessing knowledge assets: *a review of the models used to measure intellectual capital*, International Journal of Management Reviews, 3 (1) (2001), pp. 41-60

Bontis, N., (2001), Assessing knowledge assets: *a review of the models used to measure intellectual capital*. International Journal of Management Research, 3(1), pp.41-60.

Bontis, N., and Nikitopoulos, D. (2001),*Thought leadership on intellectual capital*, Journal of intellectual capital, 12(3), 183–191.

Boyles, J.E., Cairns, G., de Grosbois, J., Jackson, A., Kosilov, A., Pasztory, Z., Yanev, Y. and Mazour, T. (2009), *Assessment of organization's knowledge management maturity*, International Journal of Nuclear Knowledge Management", Vol. 3,No. 2, PP 170-182

Braam, G.J.M., (2012), *balanced scorecard's Interpretative Variability and Organizational Change*. In Quah, C.H. and Dar, O.L. (Eds.), Business Dynamics in the 21st Century, pp.99-112. InTech: Rijeka

Bright, K., Cooper, C. L. (1993), *organizational culture and the Management of Quality: TOWARDS A NEW FRAMEWORK*, Journal of Managerial Psychology, 8 (6), pp. 21-27.

Brignall, S., (2002), *The unbalanced scorecard: a social and environmental critique*, in Neely, A., Walters, R. Austin (Eds), Performance Measurement and Management: Research and Action. Cranfield, UK: Cranfield School of Management

Bromiley, P., McShane, M., Nair, A., Rustambekov, E. (2015), *Enterprise risk management: Review, Critique, and Research Directions, Long Range Planning*, 48, pp. 265-276.

Brooking, A. (1998), intellectual capital: *Core Asset for the Third Millennium Enterprise*. London: International Thomson Business Press.

Brückner, Claudia, (2009),*Qualitätsmanagement für die Automobilindustrie*,Grundlagen, Normen, Methoden, Symposium Publishing GmbH, ISBN-13: 978-3939707202

Brünger Christian, (2009), Erfolgreiches Risikomanagement mit COSO ERM: *Empfehlungen für die Gestaltung und Umsetzung in der Praxis Gebundene Ausgabe – 28*. August (2009), ISBN-13: 978-3503114399

Buble, M., Dulčić, Ž., Pavić, I. (2001), *Methodological approach to organizational performance improvement process*. Management: Journal of Contemporary Management Issues, 6(1-2), 1-15. Retrieved from http://hrcak.srce.hr/184567" HYPERLINK "http://hrcak.srce.hr/184567

Buch, K. Rivers, D. (2001), TQM: *the role of leadership and culture*, Leadership & Organization Development Journal, 22 (8), pp. 365-371.

Buchmüller Melanie, Thorsten Eidmüller, Andreas Mussmann, Jan Kopia, (2018), *THE STATUS OF MODULAR SOURCING COMPARED TO OTHER PROCUREMENT STRATEGIES*, Ecoforum, Volume 7, Issue 1 (2018), ISSN: 2344-2174

Budzier, Alexander and Flyvbjerg, Bent, *Why Do Projects Fail?* (2015), Bent Flyvbjerg and Alexander Budzier, *Why Do Projects Fail?*, Project Magazine, Summer.. Available at SSRN: https://ssrn.com/abstract=2722475

Bukowitz, W. and Williams, R. (2000), The Knowledge Management Fieldbook, London: Prentice Hall

Bumblauskas, D., Gemmill, D., Igou, A., Anzengruber, J. (2017), Smart Maintenance Decision Support Systems (SMDSS) based on corporate big data analytics, Expert Systems With Applications, 90, pp. 303-317.

Bassam Hussein, Lebanon Ayman Dayek, (2014), *business process Reengineering (BPR) Key Success Factors*, International Journal of Applied Management Sciences and Engineering, 1(1), 58-66, January-June (2014)

Burke W. Warner, Litwin George H., (2008) , *A Causal Model of Organizational Performance & Change*, published in Journal of Management in 1992, Vol.18, No. 3, 523-545

Bußian Aykut, Singer Klaus, Kopia Jan, (2016), Geldmacher Wiebke, *Perspectives on big data and business intelligence technologies in the context of audit tasks*, BASIQ INTERNATIONAL CONFERENCE, BASIQ2016, 6/2/2016

Caldarola Richard, A.L., (2016), *Linking the balanced scorecard to Organizational Shareholders' Expectations*. American Journal of Economics and Business Administration, 8(1), pp.14-22.

Callahan, C., Soileau, J. (2017), *Does Enterprise risk management enhance operating performance?*, Advances in Accounting, 37, pp. 122-139.

Cameron Kim S. (Autor), Quinn Robert E. (Autor), (2005), Diagnosing and Changing organizational culture: *Based on the Competing Values Framework 3* , ISBN-13: 978-0470650264, Jossey-Bass

Campbell J. ,*On the Nature of Organizational Effectiveness*. In: Goodman P, Pennings J, editors. New Perspectives on Organizational Effectiveness. San Francisco: Jossey-Bass, (1977), pp. 13–55.

Cao, L., Mohan, K., Xu, P., Ramesh, B., (2009), *A framework for adapting agile development methodologies*. European Journal of Information Systems 18, 332–343

Capelo, C. and Ferreira Dias, J., (2009), *A system dynamics-based simulation experiment for testing mental model and performance effects of using the balanced scorecard*. System Dynamics Review, 25(1), pp.1-34.

Carlile, P., E. Rebentisch, (2003), Into the black box: *The knowledge transformation cycle*. Management Sci. 49 1180–1195

Cervone, H. F. (2011), *Understanding agile project management methods using Scrum*. OCLC Systems & Services: International digital library perspectives, 27(1), 18-22.http://dx.doi.org/10.1108/10650751111106528

Characteristics of Organizational Environments and Perceived Environmental Uncertainty, Robert B. Duncan, Administrative Science Quarterly, Vol. 17, No. 3 (Sep., 1972), pp. 313-327, Published by: Sage Publications, Inc. on behalf of the Johnson Graduate School of Management, Cornell University, DOI: 10.2307/2392145

Charnes, A., Cooper, W.W and Rhodes, E. (1978) *Measuring the efficiency of DMUs,* European Journal of Operational Research, 2, p. 429-444

Chattopadhyay, S.P. (2007), *Management education reform in a knowledge management Environment*, Journal of American Academy of Business, Vol. 11, No. 1, pp. 168-172.

Chen, Y.S., Beasley, M. and Nunez, K., (2006), Working Hand in Hand: *balanced scorecard and Enterprise risk management*. Strategic Finance, March, pp.49-55.

Chi, D.J. and Hsu-Feng, H., (2011*), Is the balanced scorecard really helpful for improving performance?* Evidence from software companies in China and Taiwan. African Journal of Business Management, 5(1), pp.224-239.

Chiapello, E., & Lebas, M. (1996), The Tableau de Bord, *a French Approach to Management Information, Communication presented at the19th Annual Meeting of the European Accounting*, Association, Bergen (Norway), 2-4th May.

Child, J. (1977), Organizations: *A guide to problems and practice*. New York: Harper & Row

Chong, V.K. and Rundus, M.J., (2004), *Market Competition and Organizational Performance, Total Quality Management*. The British Accounting Review, 36, pp.155-172.

Choo, C. W., & Bontis, N. (Eds.), (2002), *The Strategic Management of intellectual capital and Organizational Knowledge*. New York: Oxford University Press, Inc.

Choo, C.W. (1998) The Knowing Organization*: How Organizations Use Information to Construct Meaning, Create Knowledge, and Make Decisions*. New York: Oxford University Press

Christopher, M. (2005), *Logistics and supply chain management: Creating value-added networks*.Harlow, England: Prentice Hall

Clarke, M., Seng, D. and Whiting, R.H., (2011), *Intellectual capital and firm performance in Australia*, Journal of intellectual capital, Vol. 12, Issue 4, pp. 505-530

Cockburn, A., (2007), Agile Software Development: *The Cooperative Game*. AddisonWesley.

Cockburn, Alistair & Highsmith, Jim. (2001), Agile software development: *The people factor*. Computer. 34. 131 - 133. 10.1109/2.963450.

Coetzee R., van der Merwe & L. van Dyk, (2016), Lean implementation strategies: *how are the Toyota way principles addressed?* South African Journal of Industrial Engineering November (2016) Vol 27(3) Special Edition, pp 79-91

Cohen, S., Rousell, J. (2005), Strategic Supply Chain Management: *The Five Disciplines for Top Performance.* New York: McGraw-Hill.

Cohen Sandra, Kaimenakis Nikolaos, (2007), *Intellectual capital and corporate performance in knowledge-intensive SMEs,* The Learning Organization, Vol. 14 Issue: 3, pp.241-262, https://doi.org/10.1108/09696470710739417

Cordes-Berszinn, Philip (2013), *Dynamic Capabilities: How Organisational Structures Affect Knowledge Processes,* Palgrave Macmillan, Retrieved 16 September (2014).

Crosby, P. B. (1979), *Quality is free: the art of making quality certain.* New York: McGraw-Hill Companies.

Curbera F., Doganata Y., Martens A., Mukhi N.K., Slominski A. (2008) Business Provenance – *A Technology to Increase Traceability of End-to-End Operations.* In: Meersman R., Tari Z. (eds) On the Move to Meaningful Internet Systems: OTM (2008), OTM (2008), Lecture Notes in Computer Science, vol 5331. Springer, Berlin, Heidelberg

Curwen P.J. (1976) Utility Maximisation. In: *The Theory of the Firm.* Palgrave Macmillan, London, https://doi.org/10.1007/978-1-349-15645-0_19

Cyert, Richard, March, James G. (1992), *A Behavioral Theory of the Firm (2 ed.),* Wiley-Blackwell. ISBN 0-631-17451-6.

Daft, R. L. (2004), *Organization theory and design.* Mason, Ohio: Thompson.

Daily, B., Bishop, J., & Steiner, R. (2011) *The Mediating Role Of EMS Teamwork As It Pertains To HR Factors And Perceived Environmental Performance.* Journal of Applied Business Research (JABR)

Dalkir, K. (2005). Knowledge Management in Theory and Practice, Oxford: Elsevier-Butterworth Heinemann.

Dalkir, K. (2011), *Knowledge Management in Theory and Practice, 2nd Ed.,* Cambridge, MA: Massachusetts Institute of Technology

Daniel Katz, Robert L. Kahn,(1967),*The Social Psychology of Organizations,* American Journal of Sociology 72, no. 6, (1967), 677. https://doi.org/10.1086/224406

Danone (2014) Sustainable report, Strategy and performance, *Bringing health through food to as many people as possible,* (2015) http://www.danone.com/uploads/tx_bidanonepublications/Danone_Sustainability_Report_2014_light.pdf, accessed 07.04.2015

Davenport, T. H. (1993), *Process Innovation - Reengineering Work through Information Technology.* USA, Harvard Business School Press

David G. Sirmon, Michael A. Hitt, (2003),*Managing Resources: Linking Unique Resources, Management, and Wealth Creation in Family Firms,* Entrepreneurship Theory and Practice, Vol. 27, No. 4, pp. 339-358

De Geuser, F., Mooraj, S. and Oyon, D., (2009), *Does the balanced scorecard Add Value?* Empirical Evidence on its Effect on Performance. European Accounting Review, 18(1), pp.93-122.

de Hilal, A. V., U. Wetzel and V. Ferreira (2009), Organizational culture and performance: *a Brazilian case.* Management Research News, Vol. 32, No: 2, 99-119.

Deal T. E. and Kennedy, A. A. (1982) Corporate Cultures: *The Rites and Rituals of Corporate Life, Harmondsworth,* Penguin Books, (1982), reissue Perseus Books, (2000)

Dees, J. G., & Anderson, B. B. (2006), Framing a theory of social entrepreneurship: *Building on two schools of practice and thought.* In R. Mosher-Williams (Ed.), Research on Social Entrepreneurship: Understanding and Contributing to an Emerging Field. ARNOVA Occasional Paper Series, 1(3), 39-66

Deming, W. (1986), *Out of the crisis.* Cambridge, Mass.: Massachusetts Institute of Technology, Center for Advanced Engineering Study.

Denison, D. R. (1990), *Corporate Culture and Organizational Effectiveness.* New York: John Wiley & Sons.

DeToro, I., & McCabe, T. (1997), *How to Stay Flexible and Elude Fads.* Quality Progress, 30(3), 55-60.

Digalwar, Abhijeet & Sangwan, Kuldip Singh. (2011), *An overview of existing performance measurement frameworks in the context of world class manufacturing performance measurement*. Int. J. of Services and Operations Management. 9. 60 - 82. 10.1504/IJSOM.2011.040322

Dioguardi G. (2010) The Production Pole: *From Fordism to Toyotism*. In: Network Enterprises. Innovation, Technology, and Knowledge Management. Springer, New York, NY

Dolatabadi Rezaee, H. et al. (2010), *Studying the impact of organizational culture on successful implementation of knowledge management system in organizations*. Paper presented at the Sixth International Conference on Information and Communications Technology Management. Tehran. February (2010)

Domingues, P., Sampaio, P., Arezes, P. M. (2016), integrated management systems assessment: *a maturity model proposal*, Journal of Cleaner Production, 124, pp. 164-174.

Dowell, G., Hart, S. and Yeung, B., (2000), *Do corporate global environmental standards create or destroy market value?*. Management Science, 46(8), pp.1059–1074.

Drucker, P. (2001), *the next society: a survey of the near future*, The Economist, Vol. 3, No. 1, pp. 2-20.

Drucker, P.F., (1954), *The practice of management*, Harper & Row: New York.

Dumas M, La Rosa M, Mendling J, Reijers HA., (2013*), Fundamentals of business process management*. Berlin: Springer, (2013)

Dumas, M., La Rosa, M., Mendling, J., & Reijers, H.A. (2013), *Fundamentals of business process Management*. Berlin, Germany: Springer. http://dx.doi.org/10.1007/978-3-642-33143-5"978-3-642-33143-5 Fagan, M.H. (2006),

Dybå, T., Dingsøyr, T., (2008), Empirical studies of agile software development: *a systematic review*. Information and Software Technology 50, 833–859.

Edgar H. Schein, (2010), *organizational culture and Leadership* (The Jossey-Bass Business and Management Series (US)), ISBN-13: 978-0470190609, Jossey-Bass

Edvinsson, L. & Malone, M. S. (1997),*Intellectual, Capital:Realizing Your Company's True Value By Finding Its Hidden*, Brainpower, New York: Harper Business

EFQM Excellence Model, AKYAY UYGUR, SEVGI SÜMERLI, *International Review of Management and Business Research*, (2013), Vol. 2 Issue.4, ISSN: 2306-9007 , pp. 980-993

Elkins, D., (2006), *Managing Enterprise Risks in Global Automatic Manufacturing Operations*, presentation at the University of Virginia, January 23, (2006)

Elzinga, D.J., Horak, T., Bruner, C. (1995), Business process management: *survey and methodology*, IEE Transactions on Engineering Management, Vol. 24 No. 2, pp. 119-128

Epstein, M. J,. & Manzoni, J. F. (1997), *The balanced scorecard and tableau de bord: translating, strategy into action*. Management Accounting (US) 79, 2, 28-36

Epstein, M.J. and Wisner, P.S., (2001), *Using a balanced scorecard to Implement Sustainability*. Environmental Quality Management, 11(2), pp.1-10.

Evans, M.M.; Dalkir, K. and Bidian, C. (2014). *A Holistic View of the Knowledge Life Cycle: The Knowledge Management Cycle (KMC) Model,* The Electronic Journal of Knowledge Management, 12(2): 85–97.

F. Leymann and D. Roller, *Production Workflow: Concepts and Techniques*, Prentice-Hall, Upper Saddle River, NJ, USA, (1999).

Feigenbaum, A. (1983*) Total quality control*. New York.

Figge, F., Hahn, T., Schaltegger, S. and Wagner, M., (2002), *The Sustainability balanced scorecard - Linking Sustainability Management to Business Strategy*. Business Strategy and the Environment, 11(5), pp.269–284.

Forsyth, Donelson R. (2006) *Group Dynamics 4e [International Student Edition]*. Belmont CA.: Thomson Wadsworth Publishing.

Franceschini F., Galetto M., Maisano D. and L. Mastrogiacomo (2011), *ISO/TS 16949: Analysis of the Diffusion and Current Trends*, Journal of Engineering Manufacture 225(5):735–745.

Franceschini, M. Galetto and P. Cecconi,(2006), *A worldwide analysis of ISO 9000 standard diffusion Considerations and future, development*, An International Journal Vol. 13, No. 4, 2006 pp. 523-541

Fraser, J.R.S., Simkins, B.J. (2016), *The challenges of and solutions for implementing enterprise risk management,* 59, pp. 689-698.

Fraser, P., Moultrie, J., & Gregory, M. (2002), *The use of maturity models / grids as a tool in assessing product development capability.* In IEEE International Engineering Management Conference pp. 244-249, Cambridge: IEEE

Frigo, Mark L, Anderson, Richard J. (2011), *What Is Strategic risk management?,* Strategic Finance - Montvale- 92, No. 10, pp. 21-22

Gardner, R. (2004), *The process focused organization,* Quality Press, Milwaukee, WI.

Gates, S., Nicolas, J.-L.Walker, P., (2012), Enterprise risk management: *A process for enhanced management and improved performance,* Management Accounting Quarterly, 13 (3), pp.28-38

Geldmacher Wiebke, Just Vanessa, Kopia Jan, Aykut Bussian, (2016*), Requirements towards sustainable future urban mobility in germany,*BASIQ INTERNATIONAL CONFERENCE, BASIQ 2016, 6/2/2016, Konstanz,Germania, published in CONFERENCE PROCEEDINGS , pg. 50-59, ISSN 2457-483X

Gemeinsamkeiten und Unterschiede von Lean Management und agilen Methoden Ayelt Komus Waldemar Kamlowski Working Paper des BPM-Labors Hochschule Koblenz, 6.5.2014, Lean Management und agile Methoden, BPM Labor, Hochschule Koblenz, Prof. Dr. Komus

Gianpaolo Iazzolino, Domenico Laise, (2013), *Value added intellectual coefficient (VAIC): A methodological and critical review,* Journal of Intellectual Capital, Vol. 14 Issue: 4, pp.547-563, https://doi.org/10.1108/JIC-12-2012-0107

Gimenez-Espin, J. A., Jimenez-Jimenez, D., Martínez-Costa, M. (2012), *Organizational culture for total quality management,* Total Quality Management & Business Excellence, pp. 1-15.

Golafzani, M. K., & Chirani, E. (2016). *Organizational Culture and the Financial Performance of Manufacturing Firms.* International Journal of Advanced Biotechnology and Research, 7(3), 1701-1711.

Godfrey M. Kinyua, Dr. Stephen M.A. Muathe, Dr. James M. Kilika (PhD), (2015), *Effect of Knowledge Conversion and Knowledge Application on Performance of Commercial Banks in Kenya,* International Journal of Education and Research Vol. 3 No. 10 October (2015)

Godzwon, Z. (2006), *Quality systems in university education – chosen examples, Proceedings of the Scientific Conference Quality of Education in the society of knowledge,* UMCS'(2006), Lublin, 79-86

Goldratt, E. (1990) *Theory Of Constraints,* North River Press, Inc.

Goleman, D. (1995), *Emotional intelligence.* New York: Bantam Books.

GOLOWKO Nina, KOPIA Jan, GELDMACHER Wiebke, FÖRSTER-PASTOR Ulrike S., (2017*), Quality management and assurance at german private universities - a comparative study,* Calitatea: Acces la Success, Bucharest, vol. 18, no. 157, pg. 85-94, 2017, ISSN 1582-2559

Gordon, L.A., Loeb, M.P., Tseng, C-Y. (2009), *Enterprise risk management and firm performance: A contingency perspective,* J. Account. Public Policy, 28, pp. 301-327.

Grau, Corinna & Moormann, Jürgen. (2014). *Investigating the Relationship between Process Management and Organizational Culture: Literature Review and Research Agenda.* Management and Organizational Studies. 1. 1-17. 10.5430/mos.v1n2p.

Griffin (1997), *Business Today.* Management Journal: Random House Incorporation

Griffith, A. and Bhutto, K., (2008), *Improving environmental performance through integrated management systems (IMS) in the UK.* Management of Environmental Quality: An International Journal, 19(5), pp. 565-578.

Groover, Mikell G., Automation, Production Systems, and Computer integrated Manufacturing (2000), Prentice Hall (1614), ASIN: B01K0PQVMK

Guo, W.C. , Shiah-Hou, S.R. and Chien, W.R. (2012), *A study on intellectual capital and firm performance in biotech companies,* Applied Economics Letter, Vol. 19 No. 16, pp. 1603-1608

Habidin et al., (2012), A Proposed Strategic balanced scorecard Model: *Strategic Control System and Organizational Performance in Malaysian Automotive Industry.* IOSR Journal of Business and Management, 1(6), pp.39-44.

Dincer, Hacioglu, Ümit, Hasan, Alayoğlu, Nihat (Eds.), (2017), *Global business strategies in Crisis, Strategic Thinking and Development,*Springer International Publishing, ISBN 978-3-319-44590-8

Hahn, T., Scheermesser M. (2006), Institute for Futures Studies and Technology Assessment (IZT), *Approaches to Corporate Sustainability among German Companies*, Berlin, John Wiley & Sons, Ltd., Corporate Social Responsibility and Environmental Management page 150-165.

Hammer M. (2007*), The 7 deadly sins of Performance Measurement and how to avoid them*, Sloan Management Rewiew, Vol. 48 No. , pp. 19-28

Hammer Michael , ChampyJames, (1995), Business Reengineering. *Die Radikalkur für das Unternehmen*. 5. Auflage. Campus-Verlag, Frankfurt/ New York 1995, ISBN 3-593-35017-3

Hammer Michael, (1990), *Reengineering Work: Don't Automate, Obliterate*, Hardvard Business Review, July, (1990)

Hammer Michael, Champy James, (1993), *Reengineering the Corporation: A Manifesto for Business Revolution*, Harper Business, new edition (2006), ISBN-13: 978-0060559533

Hansen, E.G., Schaltegger, S. (2012), Pursuing Sustainability with the balanced scorecard: *Between Shareholder Value and Multiple Goal Optimisation*, Centre for Sustainability Management, Leuphana Universität Lüneburg.

Harmon, P. (2014), business process Change, Third Edition: *A business process Management Guide for Managers and Process Professionals*. Burlington: Morgan Kaufmann.

Harmon, P., Wolf, C. (2014): The State of business process Management (2014), http://www.bptrends.com/bpt/wp-content/uploads/BPTrends-Stateof-BPM-Survey-Report.pdf, accessed 12.11.2017

Harms, Peter D., Credé Marcus (2010), *Emotional Intelligence and Transformational and Transactional Leadership: A Meta-Analysis*, Journal of Leadership & Organizational Studies 17:1, pp. 5–17

Hatchuel, A., Le Masson, P. and Weil, B. (2005), The Development of Science-Based Products: *Managing by Design Spaces*, Creativity & Innovation Management Journal, 14 (4), pp. 345-354.

Hawawini, G., Subramanian, V., Verdin, P., (2003*), Is performance driven by industry or firm specific factors? A new look at the evidence*, Strategic management journal 24.1, pp 1-16

Hayes, Will, Lapham, Mary Ann, Miller, Suzanne, Wrubel, Eileen, Capell, Peter (2016), *Scaling Agile Methods for Department of Defense Programs*. Software Engineering Institute. CMU/SEI-2016-TN-005.

Heckl D, Moormann J. Process performance management. In: Rosemann M, vom Brocke J, editors. *Handbook on business process management* 2. Berlin: Springer, (2010), pp. 115–135.

HEINEMANN Bastian, CEAUSU Ioana , BUCHMUELLER Melanie,KOPIA Jan, (2017), *Quality management system certification and the continuous improvement process by the example of a training company in germany*, Quality-Access to Success , vol. 18, no. 156, pg. 97-101, (2017), ISSN 1582-2559

Henry Mintzberg: *Mintzberg on Management*. Inside Our Strange World Of Organizations (1989), New York and London: Free Press/Collier Macmillan

Highsmith, J. (2001), *History: The agile Manifesto*. agilemanifesto.org, accessed 04.04.2016

Hillson, David. (2010), *Exploiting Future Uncertainty: Creating Value from Risk*. Farnham, Surrey, GBR: Ashgate Publishing Group

Hoffman James, Hoelscher Mark L., Sherif Karma (2005), Social Capital, *Knowledge Management and Sustained Superior Performance*, Journal of Knowledge Management, Vol. 9, No. 3, pp.170-182

Hofstede, G., B. Neuijen, D. D. Ohayv and G. Sanders (1990), Measuring organizational cultures: A Qualitative and

Homburg, C., Artz, M., & Wieseke, J. (2012), Marketing performance measurement systems: *does comprehensiveness really improve performance?* Journal of Marketing, 76(3), 56-77

Hoopes, D.G., Madsen, T.L.,, Walker, G. (2003*),Guest Editors' Introduction to the Special Issue: Why is There a Resource-Based View? Toward a Theory of Competitive Heterogeneity*, Strategic Management Journal, 24, pp. 889–902.

Hoque, Z. and Alam, M. (2003), Total Quality Management and the balanced scorecard Approach: *A Critical Analysis of Their Potential Relationships and Direction for Research*, Critical Perspectives on Accounting, 14, pp. 553-566.

Hossaini, S., & M. Najmi, (2004), *Excellence model EFQM from idea to practice*. Saramad paublication, Seventh edition (In Persian).

Howard, M., Miemczyk, J., & Graves, A. (2006), *Automotive supplier parks: An imperative for build-to-order?* Journal of Purchasing and Supply Management, 12, 91-104

Howitt R, (2014), *The time is now for company non-financial reporting*, Euractiv.com.

Hoyt Robert E., Moore Dudley L., Liebenberg Andre P., (2006), *The Value of Enterprise risk management: Evidence from the U.S. Insurance Industry*, University of Georgia, http://www.autocar.co.uk/car-news/industry/vw-10m-sales-2015, accessed 05.12.2015

Hubbard, G., (2009), Measuring Organizational Performance: *Beyond the Triple Bottom Line*. Business Strategy and the Environment, 18(3), pp.177-191.

Hunziker, S. (2018), *Ganzheitliches Chancen- und Risikomanagement*. Wiesbaden: Springer.

Hunziker, S., Meissner, J. O. (2017), *Risikomanagement in 19 Schritten*. Wiesbaden: Springer Gabler.

Hys Katarzyna, (2015*), Tools and methods used by the Polish leading automotive companies in quality management system*. Results of empirical research

Ishikawa, K. (1985) *What is total quality control?* The Japanese way, Prentice-Hall, New Jersey

Iversen, J., Nielsen, P. A. and Norbjerg, J. (1999), *Situated assessment of problems in software development.*

Jacobs, R., Mannion, R., Davies, H. W. T., Harrison, S. T., Konteh, F., Walshe, K (2013), *The relationship between organizational culture and performance in acute hospitals.* – Social Science & Medicine, 2013, Vol. 76, pp. 115-125. DOI:10.1016/j.socscimed.2012.10.014

James S. House, F. Thomas Juster, Robert L. Kahn, Howard Schuman, and Eleanor Singer, (2004), *A Telescope on Society*, Survey Research and Social Science at the University of Michigan and Beyond, ISBN 978-0-472-06848-7, DOI: 10.3998/mpub.11842

Janićijević Nebojša , Management, Vol. 15, (2010), 2, pp. 85-106 N. Janićijević: *Business processes in organizational diagnosis,*

Javidi, H. (2006), *Familiarity with organizational excellence based on EFQM model*. World top quality, No. 8, (In Persian).

Jerome McCarthy: Basic Marketing: *A managerial approach.* (1960).

Jeston, J., Nelis, J. (2013), *Business process management: practical guidelines to successful implementations*, Third edition. Burlington: Routledge.

Johnson, G. , Scholes, K. , Whittington, R., *Fundamentals of strategy*, Pearson Education, (2009)

Johnson, G., Whittington, R., and Scholes, K., (2012), *Fundamentals of Strategy*. Harlow: Pearson Education, (2012):134.

Johnson, H.A., W. (1999),*An integrative taxonomy of intellectual capital: Measuring the stock and flow of intellectual capital components in the Firm*, International Journal Technology Management, Vol.18, Nov. 5/6/78, pp. 562-575

Jones, G. R. & Hill, C. L. (2009), *Strategic Management: An integrated Approach*. Houghton Mifflin: Boston, USA

Jorgensen, T.H, Remmen, A., Mellado, M. *integrated management systems – three different levels of integration*. Journal of Cleaner Production. (2006), Vol.14 (8), p.713-722.

Juan Ignacio Martín, Castilla, Óscar Rodríguez, Ruiz, (2008) *EFQM model: knowledge governance and competitive advantage*, Journal of intellectual capital, Vol. 9 Issue: 1, pp.133-156, https://doi.org/10.1108/14691930810845858

Judge, T.A. and Piccolo, R.F. (2004) Transformational & transactional leadership*: A meta-analytic test oftheir relative validity*. Journal of Applied Psychology, 89(5), 755-768

K.K. Kuriakose, Baldev Raj, S.A.V. Satya Murty, P. Swaminathan, (2010), *Knowledge Management Maturity Models* – A Morphological Analysis, Journal of Knowledge Management Practice, Vol. 11, No. 3, September (2010)

Kalender, Z. T., Vayvay, Ö. (2016), *The fifth pillar of the balanced scorecard: sustainability*. Procedia - Social and Behavioral Sciences, 235, pp. 76 – 83.

Kaplan, (2012), *Internal control systems*, http://kfknowledgebank.kaplan co.uk/KFKB/Wiki%20Pages/Internal%20control%20systems.aspx, accessed 10.07.2016

Kaplan, R. S., Norton, D. P. (1992), *The balanced scorecard – Measures That Drive Performance*, in: Harvard Business Review, January/February, Vol. 70, pp. 71-79

Kaplan, R. S., Norton, D. P. (2000), *Having Trouble with your strategy?* Then Map it., Harvard Business Review, 78 (5), pp. 3-11.

Kaplan, R. S., Norton, D. P. (2008), *The Execution Premium: Linking Strategy to Operations for Competitive Advantage*, Boston: Harvard Business Press.

Kaplan, R., and Norton, D.P. (2004), Strategy Maps: *Converting Intangible Assets into Tangible,* Outcomes. Boston: Harvard Business School Press

Kaplan, R.S. and Norton, D.P., (1992), The balanced scorecard--*Measures That Drive Performance.* Harvard Business Review, 70(1), pp.71-79.

Kaplan, R.S. and Norton, D.P., (2008), *The Execution Premium: linking strategy to operations for competitive advantage.* Harvard Business School Press: Boston.

Karapetrovic, S. (2008), *Integrative augmentation of standardized systems.* Int. J. Qual. Res., Vol 2, pp 15–22.

Karim, A., (2015), *ISO Certification and Financial Performance: A Review.* The Journal of Global Business Management, 11(2), pp.32-38.

Katniak (2012), *A Survey Analysis of integrated management systems in the UK*, Sheffield Hallam University

Kaur and Sengupta, Kaur, R. and Sengupta, J. (2013). *Software processmodels and analysis on failure of software development projects*, preprintarXiv:1306.1068

Kaye, Leon (2014), *Why Sustainability is Integral to Enterprise risk management*, http://www.triplepundit.com/2014/10/sustainability-integral-enterprise-risk-management‗10.02.2016

Kaynak, H., (2003*), The Relationship between Total Quality Management Practices and their Effects on Firm Performance.* Journal of Operations Management, 21(4), pp.405-435.

Kennedy A.F., Schleife L., (2007) *Team performances measurement: A system to balance innovation and empowerment with control*, Advances in Management 16 pp. 261-285.

Kettinger, W. J., Guha, S. and Teng, J. (1995), *The process reengineering life cycle methodology*: a case study in Grover, V. and Kettinger, W.J. (Eds), business process Change: Reengineering Concepts,Methods and Technologies, Idea Group Publishing, London

Kılıç, Merve. (2015). *The Effect of Board Diversity on the Performance of Banks: Evidence from Turkey.* International Journal of Business and Management. 10. Forthcoming. 10.5539/ijbm.v10n9p182.

Kim Christopher S., Spahlinger David A., Billi John E., (2009), *Creating Value in Health Care: The Case for Lean Thinking*, JCOM December (2009) Vol. 16, No. 12, pp. 557-562

Kimiz Dalkir (Autor), Marco Beaulieu, (2017), *Knowledge Management in Theory and Practice*, 22. Dezember (2017), Mit Pr, ISBN-13: 978-0262036870

Kimiz Dalkir, Jay Liebowitz, (2011), *Knowledge Management in Theory and Practice,* MIT Press, Hardcover: 504 pages, ISBN-10: 0262015080, ISBN-13: 978-0262015080

Kimizm, D. (2005*), KNOWLEDGE MANAGEMENT IN THEORY AND PRACTICE.* Elsevier Butterworth–Heinemann, ISBN: 0-7506-7864-X

Kirkpatrick, G. (2009), *The corporate governance lessons from the financial crisis.* OECD Journal: Financial Market Trends, Vol. 2009/1. retrieved http://www.oecd-ilibrary.org/finance-and-investment/the-corporate-governance-lessons-from-the-financial-crisis_fmt-v2009-art3-en, 23.01.2018.

Kleemann, B., Seitz, N., Wio, H.-J. (2007), *Das Führungskräftetraining für top+Qualität und Six Sigma bei Siemens Power Generation*, in: Töpfer, A. (eds), Six Sigma – Konzeption und Erfolgsbeispiele für praktizierte Null-Fehler-Qualität. 4th edition, Berlin Heidelberg New York: Springer, pp. 278-288.

Kochikar, V.P. (2000), *The Knowledge Management Maturity Model: A Staged* Framework for Leveraging Knowledge, KM World 2000, Santa Clara, CA.

Kock, N. (2005) *Business Process Improvement through E-Collaboration: Knowledge Sharing Through The Use Of Virtual Groups* Idea Group Publishing London. pp19-21

Kohlbacher M. (2010), The effect of process orientation: a literature review, business process Management Journal, Vol 16 No. 1, pp. 135-152

Kohlbacher, M., & Gruenwald, S. (2011), *Process orientation: conceptualization and measurement.* business process Management Journal, 17(2), 267-283. http://dx.doi.org/10.1108/1463715111 1122347

Kompalla A, Kopia J, Tigu G, (2015), *Characteristics of business strategies and management systems within automotive industry,* Ovidius University Annals, Series Economic Sciences, vol. 15, no. 2, (2015), pg. 267-274

Kompalla A, Kopia J, Tigu G,(2016a), *An application of agile principles on business strategies with-in it-based industries and automotive enterprises,* Zeitschrift für interdisziplinäre ökonomische Forschung, vol. 01, no. (2016), pg. 112-122, ISSN 2196-4688

Kompalla A., Kopia J., Tigu G., (2016b), *Limitations of business strategies and management systems within automotive industry, 10th International Technology,* Education and Development Conference, INTED2016, 3/7/2016, Valencia, Spania, published in INTED2016 Proceedings, pg. 3817-3827, ISSN 2340-1079

Kompalla Andreas , Jan KOPIA, Ulrike Foerster, Wiebke Geldmacher, (2017), *Analysis of correlations between coprporate strategy and operational strategy considering management system standards,* Ecoforum, Volume 6, Issue 3 (2017), ISSN: 2344-2174

Kompalla Andreas , Kopia Jan, (2016)c, *Evaluation of the agile manifesto within business strategies,* Journal of Economics and Public Finance, vol. 02, no. 02, pg. 227-239, 2016, ISSN 2377-1038

Kompalla Andreas, Kopia Jan, Tigu Gabriela, (2016)d, *Analysis of correlation between intellectual capital and traditional key performance indicators within the automotive industry,* International Business Information Management Conference, 27TH IBIMA, 5/4/2016, Milan, Spania, published in IBIMA Conference Proceedings, pg. 10-20, ISBN 978-0-9860419-6-9

Kondalkar, Kondalka (2009), *Organization Effectiveness and Change Management,* PHI Learning, 30. Januar (2009), ISBN-13: 978-8120337039

Kontio, J. (2007*), Business process re-engineering: a case study at Turku University of Applied Sciences,* Proceedings of European and Mediterranean Conference on Information Systems (2007) (EMCIS2007), 24- 26.

Kopia Jan, (2016), *Study on integration and leadership styles of management systems based on a high level structure,* ICMLG 2016 4th International Conference on Management Leadership and Governance St Petersburg Russia , ICMLG 2016, 4/14/2016, St Petersburg , Rep. Central Africa, published in ICMLG 2016 4th International Conference on Management Leadership and Governance St Petersburg , pg. 431-441

Kopia Jan, Just Vanessa, Geldmacher Wiebke , Bußian Aykut, (2017a), *Organization performance and enterprise risk management,* Ecoforum, vol. 6, no. 1, (2017), pg. 1-1, ISSN 2344-2174

Kopia Jan, JUST Vanessa, Wiebke GELDMACHER, Aykut BUßIAN, (2017b), *Meaning and usage of a conceptual enterprise risk management framework –a case study,* Ecoforum, Volume 6, Issue 2(11), 2017, ISSN: 2344-2174

Kopia Jan, Kompalla Andreas, Ceausu I, (2016), *Theory and practice of integrating management systems with high level structure, Quality – access to success,* vol. 17, no. 155, pg. 52-59, 2016, ISSN 1582-2559

Kopia Jan, Kompalla Andreas, Melanie Buchmüller, Bastian Heinemann, (2017c), *Performance Measurement of management system Standards Using the balanced scorecard,* Amfiteatru Economic, Amfiteatru Economic Journal", Vol. XIX, Special 11/2017, pp. 981-1002, Nov. 2017

Kotter, J. P., and J. L. Heskett, (1992) *Corporate Culture and Performance.* New York: The Free Press

Kraus Verena, Lehner Othmar M., (2012), *The nexus of enterprise risk management and value creation: a systematic literature, reviewacrn, Journal of Finance and Risk Perspectives,* Vol. 1, Issue 1, p. 91-163, Oct. 2012, ISSN 2305-7394

Kucukaltan, B., Irani, Z., Aktas, E. (2016), *A decision support model for identification and prioritization of key performance indicators in the logistics industry, Computers in Human Behavior,* 65, pp. 346-358.

Kueng P., (2000), *Process performance measurement system: a tool to support process-based organizations.* Total Qual Manag. (2000),11(1):67–85. doi: 10.1080/0954412007035

Kueng, P., Meier, A., & Wettstein T. (2001). *Performance measurement systems must be engineered.* Communications of the Association of Information Systems. 7(3)

Kumar, M., Basu, P., Avittathur, B. (2018), Pricing and sourcing strategies for competing retailers in supply chains under disruption risk, European Journal of Operational Research, 265, pp. 533-543.

Kung, P., Hagen, Claus., (2007), *The fruits of business process Management: an experience report from a Swiss bank.* business process Management Journal Vol. 13(4), pp. 477-487.

Kuo, T.C., Kremer, G.E.O., Phuong, N.T., Hsu, C.W. (2016), *Motivations and barriers for corporate social responsibility reporting: evidence from the airline industry*, Journal of Air Transport Management, 57, pp. 184-195.

Lagrosen, S., Lagrosen, Y. (2003), *Quality configurations:a contingency approach to quality management*, International Journal of Quality & Reliability Management, 20 (7), pp.759-773.

Lahajnar, S. i Rožanec, A. (2016). *The evaluation framework for business process management methodologies.* Management, 21 (1), 47-69. Preuzeto s https://hrcak.srce.hr/16135

Lahti, M., Shamsuzzoha, A. H. M., & Helo, P. (2009), *Developing a maturity model for Supply Chain Management.* International Journal of Logistics Systems, and Management, 5(6), 654-678.

Laisasikorn, Kittipat, Rompho, Nopadol, (2014), *A Study of the Relationship Between a Successful Enterprise Risk management system, a Performance Measurement System and the Financial Performance of Thai Listed Companies*, Journal of Applied Business & Economics, Vol. 16 Issue 2, p81

Lander, E., Liker, J. K , (2007), *The Toyota Production System and art: makinghighly customized and creative products the Toyota way*, International Journal of Production Research, University of Michigan, USA.

Lanfermann G. (2015), *EU-Richtlinie zur Angabe von nichtfinanziellen Informationen*, WPg 7/2015, page 323-326.

Länsiluoto, A. and Järvenpää, M., (2010), *Greening the balanced scorecard.* Business Horizons, 53(4), pp.385–395

Lapiņa, I., Caune, J., Gaile-Sarkane, E., Borkus, I. and Ozoliņš, M. (2015). *Development of Managers Competence Model in Dynamic Environment.* Proceedings of the 19th World Multi-Conference on Systemics, Cybernetics and Informatics (WMSCI 2015), Vol.2, 219-224.

Lay, G., Schat, H.-D., Jäger, A. (2009), Mit EFQM zu betrieblicher Exzellenz: *Verbreitung, Ausgestaltung und Effekte des Qualitätsmanagementmodells der European Foundation for Quality Management,* retrieved: https://www.econstor.eu/handle/10419/29348, 23.01.2018.

Lee R., Dale B. (1998), *Business process management: a review and evaluation*, business process Management Journal, Vol. 4 No. 3, pp. 214-225

Lee, G., Xia, W., (2010), *Toward agile: an integrated analysis of quantitative and qualitative field data on software development agility.* MIS Quarterly 34, 87–114

Lee, T.Y., Leung, H.K.N. and Chang, K.C.C., (1999), *Improving quality management on the basis of ISO 9000.* The TQM Magazine, 11(2), pp.88–94.

Liangrong Zu, (2013), *Sustainability risk management*, In: Idowu, S.O., Capaldi, N., Zu, L., Das Gupta, A. (Eds.), (2013), Encyclopedia of Corporate Social Responsibility, Springer-Verlag, Berlin

Liao, Shin-Wie, (2012), *Does ERM (Enterprise risk management) Help Firm's Performance in Times of Crisis?*, University of Amsterdam, Amsterdam Business School, Master in International Finance

Liker, J. and Franz, J. (2011), *The Toyota Way to continuous improvement.* McGraw Hill.

Lindfors, C. (2003*), Process orientation: An approach for organizations to function effectively.* Retrieved from http://cic.vtt.fi/lean/singapore/LindforsFinal.pdf

Lisana, (2014), *Review on the effectiveness of agile unified process in software development with vague system requirements*, ARPN Journal of Engineering and Applied Sciences,Asian Research Publishing Network (ARPN), VOL. 9, NO. 10, OCTOBER (2014) ISSN 1819-6608 All rights reserved. www.arpnjournals.com, pp. 1763-1768

Lisiecka, K. (2000), *About need of assurance and evaluation of quality of educational services*, Problems of Quality 2, 14-19

Litten, L., (2005), *Measuring and Reporting Institutional Sustainability*. Annual Forum of the Association for Institutional Research, 1 June (2005), San Diego: California.

Luca Magdalena, (2014), *Risk in Contemporary Economy* International Conference ISSN-L 2067-0532 ISSN online 2344-5386 XVth Edition, 2014, Galati, Romania, Dunarea de Jos ,University of Galati – Faculty of Economics and Business Administration

Lüftenegger, E. R. (2014), *Service-dominant business* design Eindhoven: Technische Universiteit Eindhoven DOI: 10.6100/IR774591

Lund, D.B. (2003), *Organizational culture and job satisfaction*, Journal of Business & Industrial Marketing, 18 (3), pp.219-236

Lundquist, S. A. (2015), *Why firms implement risk governance – Stepping beyond traditional risk management to enterprise risk management*, J. Account. Public Policy, 34, pp. 441-466.

Madsen, D.Ø. and Stenheim, T., (2015), *The balanced scorecard: A Review of Five Research Areas*. American Journal of Management, 15(2), pp.24-41.

Madsen, D.Ø., (2014), Interpretation and use of the balanced scorecard in Denmark: *Evidence from suppliers and users of the concept*. Danish Journal of Management & Business, 3/4, pp.13-25.

Magd, H. and Curry, A., (2003), ISO 9000 and TQM: *are they complementary or contradictory to each other?*, The TQM Magazine, 15(4), pp.244-256.

Makadok, R. (2001), *Toward a Synthesis of the Resource-Based View and Dynamic-Capability Views of Rent Creation*. Strategic Management Journal, 22, (5), pp. 387–401

Makhija, M. (2003), *Comparing the resource-based and market-based views of the firm: empirical evidence from Czech privatization*. Strategic Management Journal, Vol. 24, No. 5, Pp. 433- 451.

Mangalaraj, G., Mahapatra, R., Nerur, S., (2009), *Acceptance of software process innovations—the case of extreme programming*. European Journal of Information Systems 18, 344–354.

Manuel F. Suárez-Barraza, Juan Ramis-Pujol, Mariana Estrada-Robles, (2012) *Applying Gemba-Kaizen in a multinational food company: a process innovation framework*, International Journal of Quality and Service Sciences, Vol. 4 Issue: 1, pp.27-50, https://doi.org/10.1108/17566691211219715

Martin A, (2015), Leadership: *Talent management: Prepare a ready agile workforce*, International Journal of Pediatrics and Adolescent Medicine, 2(3-4), 112-116

Martin, A., (2016), *ISO 9001 Impact on Operational Performance*, 20th International Conference on ISO & TQM 20-ICIT. University of Buraimi: Oman, 26-28 September 2016. Buraimi: Oman.

Martinez-Costa, M., Choi, T.Y., Martinez, J.A. and Martinez-Lorente, A.R., (2009), ISO 9000/1994, ISO 9001/2000 and TQM: *The performance debate revisited*. Journal of Operations Management, 27(6), pp.495-511.

Mate, A., Trujillo, J., Mylopoulos, J. (2017), *Specification and derivation of key performance indicators for business analytics: A semantic approach*, Data & Knowledge Engineering, 108, pp. 30-49.

Matthews, J.R. (2011), *Assessing Organizational Effectiveness: The Role of Performance Measures, The Library Quarterly: Information, Community*, Policy, 81 (1), pp. 83-110.

Maximini, D. (2015), *The Scrum Culture: Introducing Agile Methods in Organizations*. Management for Professionals, Springer, (2015)

Mayring, P (2014), *Qualitative Content Analysis, Theoretical Foundation, Basic Procedures and Software Solutio,* Available at http://nbn-resolving.de/urn:nbn:de:0168-ssoar-395173" HYPERLINK "http://nbn-resolving.de/urn:nbn:de:0168-ssoar-395173, accessed 22.11.2016

Mayring, P. (2015), *Qualitative Inhaltsanalyse, Grundlagen und Techniken*, 12th ed., Beltz, Weinheim, Basel

Mazars, (2015), *How public companies are dealing with the upcoming CSR reporting requirements,* mazars.de, http://eng.mazars.de/Home/Our-expertise/Impulse/Content/CSR-Reporting, accessed 07.04.2015

McCormack, K. P., & Johnson, W. C. (2001), *Business process orientation – Gaining the e-business competitive advantage*. Florida: St. Lucie Press.

McElroy, M. (1999), *The Knowledge Life Cycle*, Presented at the ICM Conference on KM, Miami, FL

McGee, J., Thomas, H. and Wilson, D. (2010) Strategy: *Analysis and Practice*, McGraw-Hill, Maidenhead.

McGuire David , Kate Hutchings, (2007) *Portrait of a transformational leader: the legacy of Dr Martin Luther King Jr*, Leadership & Organization Development Journal, Vol. 28 Iss: 2 p154-p166

McInerney, Claire (2002), *Knowledge Management and the Dynamic Nature of Knowledge*. Journal of the American Society for Information Science and Technology. 53 (12), 1009–1018.

McKinsey (2016), *Taking control of organizational risk culture*, retrieved: https://www.mckinsey.com /~/media/mckinsey/dotcom/client_service/risk/working%20papers/16_taking_control_of_organizational_risk_culture.ashx"_taking_control_of_organizational_risk_culture.ashx, 12.02.2018.

McKinsey Quarterly November (2015), *Four fundamentals of workplace automation*, By Michael Chui, James Manyika, and Mehdi Miremadi

McNally, J. S. (2013). *The 2013 COSO framework & SOX compliance: One approach to an effective transition*. Strategic Finance, COSO.

McNair, C.J., Lynch, R.L., & Cross, K.L. (1990), *Do financial and non-financial measures have to, agree?* Management Accounting (US) 72, 5, 28-39

McShane, M. K., A. Nair, and E. Rustambekov (2011), *Does Enterprise risk management Increase Firm Value?*, Journal of Accounting, Auditing and Finance 26(4), pp.641-658.

Meissner, H.G. (1997), *Der Kulturschock in der Betriebswirtschaftslehre*, In: Engelhard, J. (ed.), Interkulturelles Management, Wiesbaden: Gabler, pp. 1-12.

Mewes Wolfgang, (1971), *Die kybernetische Managementlehre EKS* - 1 Einleitungsschrift, (1971), ISBN-13: 978-3922062004

Meyer, M. and Zack, M. (1996), *The Design and Implementation of Information Products*, Sloan Management Review, 37(3), 43–59

Meyerson D, Martin J. (1987), *Cultural change: an integration of three different views*. Journal of management Studies, Vol. 24, No. 6, pp. 623-647

Mike Kennerley, Andy Neely, (2002) *A framework of the factors affecting the evolution of performance measurement systems*, International Journal of Operations & Production Management, Vol. 22 Issue: 11, pp.1222-1245, https://doi.org/10.1108/01443570210450293

Mikes, A. (2009), *Risk management and calculative cultures*, Management Accounting Research, 20, pp. 18-40.

Milan Zeleny, (2005), *Human Systems Management: Integrating Knowledge, Management and Systems*, World Scientific Pub Co Inc (September 1, 2005), ISBN-10: 9810249136, ISBN-13: 978-9810249137

Min John Zaw, (2015), The Alignment of integrated management systems and Business Objectives: *A Case Study Approach Applied to Small and Medium Enterprises in Singapore*, School of business and tourism southern cross university Australia, Doctoral thesis

Mead, George Herbert (1934), *Mind, self, and society: From the standpoint of a social behaviorist*. Chicago, IL: The University of Chicago Press. doi: http://dx.doi.org/10.7208/chicago/9780 226516608.001.0001;

Ming-Hsien, L., Al-Refaie, A. and Ghnaimat, O., (2012), *Effects of ISO 9001 Certification and KAAE on Performance of Jordanian Firms*. Jordan Journal of Mechanical and Industrial Engineering. 6(1), pp. 45-53.

Mintzberg, H. (1979*), The Structuring of Organizations*. Englewood Cliffs, New Jersey: Prentice-Hall, Incorporated.

Mintzberg, H. (1994), *The Rise and Fall of Strategic Planning: Reconceiving Roles for Planning, Plans, Planners*. New York: The Free Press.

Mirjeta Domniku, (2014), *The most usual ways to increase efficiency and companies performance through employee engagement and treatment – case study: kosovo's companies*, volume 9, issue 2, research journal of economics, business and ict, ISSN 2045-3345

Mohamad, D., Deros. B.M, Wahab. D.A., Ismail. A. R. and Ling, (2010), *CASE STUDY OF ISO/TS16949 APPLICATION IN AUTOMOTIVE INDUSTRY*, National Conference in Mechanical Engineering Research and Postgraduate Studies, Faculty of Mechanical Engineering, UMP Pekan, Kuantan, Pahang, Malaysia, pp. 559-563

Monteiro, P.R., Castro, A.R. and Prochnik, V.(2003), A Mensuração Do Desempenho Ambiental No balanced scorecarde O Caso Da Shell. No VII Encontro Nacional sobre Gestão Empresarial e Meio Ambiente, FGV/USP, Outubro de 2003

Morin, E. (1977).*La Methode I: la Nature de la Nature*. Seuil.

Mohammad Musli, M.R. Osman, Rosnah M.Y.2 and N. Ismail (2013), *Strategies for Integrating Quality, Environmental, Safety and Health management systems*, Applied Mechanics and Materials Vol. 315, pp. 894-898

Mwailu & Mercer. (1983), Human Resource Scorecard: *A Road Map to balanced scorecard*. World Journal of Social, Sciences, 4(1), 70-79.

Nadler, D.A. Champions of Change: *How CEOs and TheirCompanies Are Mastering the Skills of Radical Change*.San Francisco: Jossey-Bass, 1997.

Nagumo Takehiko , Donlon Barnaby, (2006), *Integrating BSC and COSO ERM Frameworks*,Cost Management, July – August (2006)

Nagumo, T. and Donlon, B., (2009), *Integrating BSC and COSO ERM Frameworks*. Cost Management, July-August.

Najmi M., Fan I., Rigas J. (2005), *A framework to review performance measurement systems*, business process Management Journal, Vol 11 No. 2, pp. 109-122

Naveh, E. and Marcus, A.A., (2004), *When does the ISO 9000 quality assurance standard lead to performance improvement?* Assimilation and going beyond. IEEE Transactions of Engineering Management, 51(3), pp.352-363

Nedelcu, A.C., Banacu, C.S., Frasineanu, C., (2014), *The Impact of intellectual capital on automotive firms's performance – case study*, Proceedings of the 8th international Management conference, Management Challenges for sustainable development, Nov. 6th -7th, (2014), Bucharest, Romania

Neely A., Gregory M., Platts K. (2005), *Performance measurement system design*, International Journal of Operations and Production Management, Vol. 25 No. 12., pp. 1228-1263

Neely, A., Mills, J., Gregory, M., Richards, H., Platts, K. and Bourne, M. (1996) *Getting the measure of your business*. Manufacturing Engineering Group, University of Cambridge, Cambridge

Neely, A.D., Adams, C. and Kennerley, M. (2002) *The Performance Prism: The Scorecard for Measuring and Managing Business Success*, Prentice Hall / Financial Times: London

Newton Tim,(1995), *Managing' Stress, Emotion and Power at Work*, ISBN: 9780803986442, SAGE Publications Ltd

Niehaus, G. (2017), *Enterprise risk management and the risk management Process*, in: Pompella, M., Scordis, N.A. (eds), The Palgrave Handbook of Unconventional Risk Transfer. Basingstoke: Palgrave Macmillan.

Njie Litie, Thaddeus Teku Fon, Linus Awomodu, Gbolahan (2008) *Top management commitment and Empowerment of employees in TQM implementation*, Högskolan i Borås/Ingenjörshögskolan (IH), URI: http://hdl.handle.net/2320/3756" HYPERLINK "http://hdl.handle.net/2320/3756, access 1.10.2015

Noble, J.S. and Lahay, C.W. (1994) *Cycle time modeling for process improvement terms*, Proceeding, 3rd Industrial Engineering Research Conference, Atlanta, GA, pp.372–377

Nonaka, I and Takeuchi, H (1995), *The Knowledge creating company*, New York: Oxford University Press.

Nonaka, I. (1994), *A dynamic theory of organizational knowledge creation*, Organization Science, Vol. 5 No. 1, pp. 14-37

Nonaka, I., and Takeuchi, H. (1995), The knowledge-creating company: *how Japanese companies create the dynamics of innovation*. New York: Oxford University Press

Nordsieck, F. (1934), *Grundlagen der Organisationslehre* (2nd ed.), Stuttgart, Germany: Poeschel.

Norlida Abdul Manab and Zahiruddin Ghazali, (2013*), Does Enterprise risk management Create Value*, Journal of Advanced Management Science, Vol. 1, No. 4, pp. 358-362. doi: 10.12720/joams. 1.4.358-362

Nyssens, M. ed. (2006), *Social Enterprises in Europe: Between Market, Public Policies and Communities*. London: Routledge.

Ogbonna, E. and L. C. Harris (2000), *Leadership style, organizational culture and performance: empirical evidence from UK companies*. International Journal of Human Resource Management, 11(4), 766-788

Olaru, M., Stoleriu, G., Langă, C., Flood, I. (2011), *The Impact of the Implementation of ISO 9000 Quality management system on the Customer Satisfaction Evaluation Process by the Romanian SMEs*, Amfiteatru economic, Special Issue, Nr. 5, pp. 552-561.

Oliva, F.L. (2016), *A maturity model for enterprise risk management*, Int. J. Production Economics, 173, pp. 66-79.

Oliveira, J. A., Oliveira, O. J. & Nadae, J. (2010), *integrated management systems in industrial companies of the São Paulo state–Brazil*. Administrative Science Quarterly, 25(1), 129-141.

Oliveira, O. (2013), *Guidelines for the integration of certifiable management systems in industrial companies*. Journal of Cleaner Production, 57, 124–133

Olmstead, J. (2002), Creating the Functionally Competent Organization: *An Open Systems Approach*. Quorum Books.

Ostadi, B., Aghdasi, M. and R.B. Kazemzadeh (2010), *The impact of ISO/TS 16949 on automotive industries and created organizational capabilities from its implementation*, Journal of Industrial, Engineering and Management 3(3), 494–511

Osterloh, M., & Frost, J. (2006), *Prozessmanagement als Kernkompetenz – Wie Sie Business Reengineering strategisch nutzen können* (5th ed.), Wiesbaden, Germany: Gabler

Ove, B., Staffan, B. and Per-Olof, B. (2013) *The Strategic Importance of Supplier Relationships in the Automotive Industry*, International Journal of Engineering Business Management, Vol. 5, 17

Pandey, V. C., & Garg, S. (2009), *Analysis of interaction among the enablers of agility in supply chain*.J. Advances Manage. Res., 16(1), 99-114.

Panuwatwanich, K., Nguyen, T.T. (2017), Influence of total quality management on performance of Vietnames construction firms, Procedia Engineering, 182, pp. 548-555.

Papula Jan and Volna Jana, (2011), *intellectual capital as Value Adding Element in Knowledge Management*, Proceedings of the conference of the International School for Social and Business Studies, Celje, Slovenia

Parvaneh Saeidi, Saudah Sofian, Siti Zaleha Binti Abdul Rasid, (2014), *A Proposed Model of the Relationship between Enterprise risk management and Firm Performance*, IJIPM: International Journal of Information Processing and Management, Vol. 5, No. 2, pp. 70-80

Paulzen, O., and Perc, P.(2002), *A Maturity Model for Quality Improvement in Knowledge Management*, 13th Australian Conference on Information Systems, S. 243-253

Pee, L.G. and Kankanhalli, A. (2009), *A Model of Organizational Knowledge Management Maturity Based on People, Process and Technology*, Journal of Information & Knowledge Management Vol. 8, No. 2, PP 79-99.

Pee, L.G., Teah, H.Y., Kankanhalli, A. (2006), *Development of a General Knowledge Management Maturity Model*, Tenth Pacific Asia Conference on Information Systems, Kuala Lumpur, Malaysia

Penrose, E. T. (1959), *The Theory of the Growth of the Firm*. New York: John Wiley

Peral, J., Maté, A., Marco, M. (2017), *Application of Data Mining techniques to identify relevant key performance indicators, Computer Standards & Interfaces*, 50, pp. 55-64.

Peter F. Drucker (1985), *Innovation and Entrepreneurship: Practice and Principles*, New York: Harper & Row,

Peters, T. (1980), *The Planning Fetish. Manager's Journal*, Wall Street Journal.

Phichak Phutrakhul, (2014), *Human Resource Development Strategy in Automotive Industry (Eco-Car) for ASEAN Hub*, World Academy of Science, Engineering and Technology International Journal of Social, Behavioral, Educational, Economic, Business and Industrial Engineering Vol:8, No:10

Pinto M. (2013) *Knowledge management systems and intellectual capital Measurement in Portuguese Organizations: A Case Study*, In: Rocha Á., Correia A., Wilson T., Stroetmann K. (eds) Advances in Information Systems and Technologies. Advances in Intelligent Systems and Computing, vol 206. Springer, Berlin, Heidelberg

Pooser David M., Tobin Peter J. (2012), *ERM Determinants, Use, and Effects on the Firm*, American Risk and Insurance Association Annual Meeting, Minneapolis, MN, August 2012

Porter, M. E. (1985), *Competitive advantage.* Creating and sustaining superior performance. New York: Free Press

Porter, Michael E. (1979), *Competitive Strategy.* Free Press. ISBN 0-684-84148-7.

Porter, Michael E. (1985), *Competitive Advantage: Creating and Sustaining Superior Performance.* New York.: Simon and Schuster. Retrieved 9 September 2013.

Porter, Michael E. (2008) , *Competitive Advantage: Creating and Sustaining Superior Performance*, Simon and Schuster,

Prado-Roman, C., del Castillo Peces, C., Mercado-Idoeta, C. and del Castillo Peces, J.,(2014), *The effects of implementing ISO 9001 in the Spanish construction industry.* Cuadernos de Gestión, [e-journal, pp.1-23, DOI: 10.5295/cdg.140507cd.

Prahalad, C.K. and Hamel, G., (1990), *The core competence of the corporation.* Harvard Business Review, 68(3), pp. 79-91.

Paschek Daniel, Frank Rennung Adelin Trusculescu, AncaDraghici Procedia Computer ScienceVolume 100, (2016), Pages 1168-1175, open access, *Procedia Computer Science*, Corporate Development with Agile business process Modeling as a Key Success Factor, Author links open overlay,

Pugh, D. S., ed. (1990).*Organization Theory: Selected Readings.* Harmondsworth: Penguin.

Pulic A. (2008), *The Principles of intellectual capital Efficiency. A brief Description*, Croatian, intellectual capital Center, Zagreb

Quazi, H., (2001), *Sustainable development: integrating environmental issues into strategic planning,* Industrial Management & Data Systems, 101(2), pp.64-70.

Quinn, R. E. & Rohrbaugh, J. (1983), *A spatial model of effectiveness criteria: towards a competing values approach to organizational analysis.* Management Science, 29, 363-377

Quon Tony K., Zéghal Daniel , Maingot Michael, (2012), *Enterprise risk management and business performance during the financial and economic crisis, Problems and Perspectives in Management*, Volume 10, Issue 3, 2012, pp. 95-103

Rachel Mason-Jones, Denis R. Towill, (1999), *Using the Information Decoupling Point to Improve Supply Chain Performance*, The International Journal of Logistics Management, Vol. 10 Issue: 2, pp.13-26, https://doi.org/10.1108/09574099910805969

Raguseo, E. (2018), *Big data technologogies: An empirical investigation on their adoption, benefits and risks for companies*, International Journal of Informationan Management, 38, pp. 187-195.

Rahman, S. (2001), *A comparative study of TQM practice and organisational performance of SMEs with and without ISO 9000 certification*, International Journal of Quality & Reliability Management, 18 (1), pp.35-49.

Raisch, S., Birkinshaw, J., Probst, G. and Tushman, M., (2009), *Organizational Ambidexterity: Balancing Exploitation and Exploration for Sustained Performance.* Organization Science, 20(4), pp.685-695.

Rajkovic, D., & Aleksic, M. (2009), *Corporate motives on implementation of integrated management system (IMS),* International Journal for Quality Research, 3(3).

Ramanauskaitė Agnė, Rudžionienė Kristina, (2013), *intellectual capital valuation:, methods and their classification*, ISSN 1392-1258. EKONOMIKA 2013 Vol. 92(2),

Ramezan, M. (2011), *intellectual capital and Organizational Organic Structure in Knowledge Society: How Are these Concepts Related?.* International Journal of Information Management, 31(1), 88-95.

Ramirez, R., Melville N. & Lawler, E. (2012), *Information technology infrastructure, organizational process redesign, and business value: an empirical analysis.* Decision Support Systems, vol. 49, 417-429.

Rebelo Manuel Ferreira (2015) Systems 2015, 3(2), 45-59, doi:10.3390/systems3020045 *Integration of Standardized management systems: A Dilemma?* Manuel Ferreira Rebelo 1, Gilberto Santos 2,and Rui Silva 1

Rebelo, M. F., Santos, G., & Silva, R. (2014a), *A generic model for integration of Quality*, Environment and Safety management systems. The TQM Journal, 26, 143–159.

Rebelo1 Manuel Ferreira, Santos Gilberto, Silva Rui, (2014b), *A Methodology to Develop the Integration of the Environmental management system with Other Standardized management systems*, Computational Water, Energy, and Environmental Engineering, 2014, 3, 170-181 Published Online October 2014 in SciRes

Reeves, M., Ming, Z., Venjara, A. (2015), *The Self-Tuning Enterprise. (cover story)*, Harvard Business Review, 93, 6, pp. 76-83, Business Source Premier, 2015.

Reijers, H.A. (2006), *Implementing BPM systems: the role of process orientation*. business process Management Journal, Vol. 12 No. 4, pp. 389-409

Reitzel, William A. (1958), *Background to Decision Making*, Newport

Renault, B. Y., Agumba, J. N., Balogun, O.A. (2016), *Drivers for and obstacles to enterprise risk management in construction firms: a literature review,* Procedia Engineering, 164, pp. 402-408.

Richard et al., (2009), *Measuring Organizational Performance: Towards Methodological Best Practice.* Journal of Management, 35(3), pp. 718-804.

Richard T Mowday, Richard M Steers, Lyman W Porter,(1979), *The measurement of organizational commitment,* In Journal of Vocational Behavior, Volume 14, Issue 2, 1979, Pages 224-247, ISSN 0001-8791, https://doi.org/10.1016/0001-8791(79)90072-1

Rito-Silva, António & Martinho, David & Aguiar, Ademar & Flores, Nuno & Correia, Filipe & Ferreira, Hugo. (2009). *An Implementation Model for Agile Business Process Tools.*

Robbins, S. P, and Barnwell, Neil., (2002), *Organisation Theory: Concepts and Cases.* Prentice Hall, (2002).

Robins, S. (1999), *Organizational behavior management.* Translators: Parsaeian, A and Arabi, M. Tehran: Institute of Business Research Studies, p 967

Rodrigues Carl A., (2001), *Fayol's 14 principles of management then and now: a framework for managing todays organizations effectively,* Management Decisions, 39, 10, pp. 880-889

Röglinger Maximilian , Jens Pöppelbuß, Jörg Becker, (2012) *Maturity models in business process management,* Business Process Management Journal, Vol. 18 Issue: 2, pp.328346,https://doi.org /10.1108/14637151211225225

Rössler Richard, Schlieter Hannes, (2015), Towards Model-based Integration of management systems, 12th International Conference on Wirtschaftsinformatik, March 4-6 2015, Osnabrück, Germany

Romeike, F. (2018), *Risikomanagement.* Wiesbaden: Springer Gabler.

Rosemann, Michael & Brocke, Jan vom. (2010), *The Six Core Elements of business process Management.* Handbook on business process Management. 1. 107-122. 10.1007/978-3-642-00416-2_5.

Roslida Ramlee, Normah, Ahmad, (2015), *Panel Data Analysis on the Effect of Establishing the Enterprise risk management on Firms* Performance, Proceedings of 4th European Business Research Conference 9 - 10 April 2015, Imperial College, London

Rothlauf, J. (2014), *Total Quality Management in Theorie und Praxis: Zum ganzheitlichen Unternehmensverständnis,* 4th edition, Berlin: De Grypter.

Rumelt, Richard,(1984), *Towards a strategic theory of the firm,* in Lamb, R., (Ed.), CompetitiveStrategic Management, Prentice-Hall, 1984, Englewood Cliffs (NJ),

Rummler, G. A., Brache, A. P. (2013), *Improving performance. How to manage the white space on the organization chart,* Third edition. San Francisco: Jossey-Bass.

S. Jablonski and C. Bussler,(1996), *Workflow Management: Modeling Concepts, Architecture, and Implementation,* International Thomson Computer Press, London, UK, 1996.

Sajeva, Svetlana & Jucevicius, Robertas. (2018). *Determination of Essential Knowledge Management System Components and their Parameters.*

Sanchez, M.P.S. and Palacios, M.A´. (2008), *Knowledge-based manufacturing enterprises: evidence from a case study,* Journal of Manufacturing Technology Management, Vol. 19 No. 4, pp. 447-68.

Saeidi Parvaneh, Sofian Saudah, Rasid Siti Zaleha Binti Abdul, (2014), *A Proposed Model of the Relationship between Enterprise risk management and Firm Performance,* International Journal of Information Processing and Management (IJIPM) Volume 5, Number 2, pp. 70-80

Salome Svanadze, Magdalena Kowalewska, (2015), *The measurement of intellectual capital by VAIC method – example of WIG20*, Online Journal of Applied Knowledge Management, A Publication of the International Institute for Applied Knowledge Management Volume 3, Issue 2, 2015

Sammut-Bonnici, Tanya & Galea, David. (2015), *PEST analysis*. 10.1002/9781118785317.weom 120113

Sampaio. P., Saraiva, P. and Rodrigues, A.G., (2009), *ISO 9001 certification research: questions, answers and approaches*. International Journal of Quality & Reliability Management, 26(1), pp.38-58.

Samy, Gopalakrishnan Muthu, Samy, Chandramohan Palani, Ammasaiappan, Maheswari, (2015), *integrated management systems for better environmental performance and sustainable development - a review.source:* Environmental Engineering & Management Journal (EEMJ) . Vol. 14 Issue 5, p985-1000. 16p.

Schein, E.H. (1995), *Unternehmenskultur. Ein Handbuch für Führungskräfte*. Frankfurt a.M., Germany: Campus.

Schiuma, G. (2009), *The challenges of measuring business excellence in the 21st century*, Measuring Business Exellence, Vol. 13, No. 2, pp.1–3

Schlosske, A., Thieme, P. (2017*), Qualitätsmanagementsysteme*, in: Spath, D., Westkämper, E., Bullinger, H.-J., Warnecke, H.-H. (eds), Neue Entwicklungen in der Unternehmensorganisation. Berlin Heidelberg: Springer.

Schmid, A. (2014), *Stand des Qualitätsmanagements an Hochschulen - Ergebnisse einer Umfrage* , Available at http://www.th-wildau.de/fileadmin/dokumente/tqm/dokumente/Stand_QM_an_ Hochschulen__eine_Umfrage_2014.pdf".pdf , accessed 05.10.16

Smith Robert H., (2003), *Social Responsible Management of the Supply Chain,* Maryland, vol.3, no.2

Schmutte, A. M. (2007), *Six Sigma im Business Excellence Prozess – Wertorientierte Unternehmensführung mit balanced scorecard, EFQM und Six Sigma bei Siemens*, in: Töpfer, A. (eds), Six Sigma – Konzeption und Erfolgsbeispiele für praktizierte Null-Fehler-Qualität. 4th edition, Berlin Heidelberg New York: Springer, pp. 384-396.

Schmutte, A., 2007. *Six Sigma, Konzeption und Erfolgsbeispiele für praktizierte Null-Fehler-Qualität,* Herausgeber: Töpfer, Armin (Hrsg.).

Schulz, N., Greve, W., Koch, U., Koops, T., Wilmers, N. (2006), *Wie gut erfassen Fragebögen die Qualität der Lehre?* In: Krampen, G., Zayer, H.: Didaktik und Evaluation in der Psychologie, Hogrefe, Göttingen, 75-89

Schwaber, K., Beedle, M.(2001), *Agile Software Development with Scrum*. Prentice Hall, New Jersey,

Schwawel, C. and Billing, F. (2018), *Top 100 Management Tools, 6th edition*, Wiesbaden: Springer Gabler.

Schylander, E. and Martinuzzi, A., (2007), *ISO 14001 – Experiences, effects and future challenges: a national study in Austria*. Business Strategy and the Environment, 16(2), pp.133-147.

Sekerci Naciye, (2015), *Does Enterprise risk management Create Value for Firms?: Evidence from Nordic Countries*, published in "The Routledge Companion on Strategic risk management", Chapter 22, published by Routledge

Senge, P. (1990), *The fifth discipline: The art and practice of the learning organization*. New York: Doubleday/Currency.

Seo, M.-G., Taylor, S. M., Hill, S. M., Zhang, X., Tesluk, P. E., & Lorinkova, N. M. (2012), *The role of affect and leadership during organizational change*. Personnel Psychology, 46.

Seyyed Javadin, R. et al. (2012), *Knowledge management in small and entrepreneurial corporations*. Scientific-Research Journal of Entrepreneurship Development, 3 (11), pp 27-46

Shad, Lai (2015), *Conceptual Framework for Enterprise risk management performance measure through Economic Value Added*, Global Business & Management Research, Vol. 7 No. 2, p.1

Shah L, Etienne A, Siadat A, Vernadat F (2012) (Value, Risk)-*Based performance evaluation of manufacturing processes. In: INCOM proceedings of the 14th symposium on information control problems in manufacturing*, 23–25 May 2012. Bucharest, Romania, pp 1586–1591

Shima Nickmanesh, Mahmood zohoori, Andira Musriyama Musram, Akbar Akbari, (2013), *Enterprise risk management and Performance in Malaysia*, Interdisciplinary Journal of Contemporary Research in Business, Vol. 5, No. 1, pp. 670-707

Sholihin, M. and Ayu, C.L., (2009), *Total quality management, balanced scorecard and performance.* Jurnal Akuntansi & Auditing Indonesia, 13(1), pp.13–28.

Sidrova A., Isik O. (2010), *Business process research: a cross disciplinary review*, business process Management Journal, Vol 16 No. 4, pp. 566-597

Singer Klaus, Bußian Aykut and KOPIA Jan, (2016), *Implication of the new eu directive for disclosing non-financial information on sustainability, environment and social aspects*, 28th IBIMA Conference,IBIMA, 11/9/2016, Seville, Spania, published in Proceedings of the 28th IBIMA Conference, pg. 10-29, ISSN 2457-483X

Škrinjar R, Bosilj Vukšić V., Indihar Štemberger M. (2010), *Adoption of business process Orientation Practices: Slovenian and Croatian Survey*, Business Systems Research, Vol. 1 No. 1-2, pp. 5-20

Škrinjar, Rok & Vuksic, Vesna & Stemberger, Mojca. (2008). *The impact of business process orientation on financial and non-financial performance.* Business Process Management Journal. 14. 738-754. 10.1108/14637150810903084.

Slater, R.H. (1991), *integrated Process Management: A Quality Model.* Quality Progress., 1st Edition. Vol. 24. McGraw-Hill Professional

Smith, H., Fingar, P. (2003), *business process Management: The Third Wave.* Tampa: Meghan-Kiffer Press

Smith, M., & Bititci, U. S. (2016), *Interplay between performance measurement and management, employee engagement and performance.* International Journal of Operations and Production Management, 1-24

Smith, Robert H., (2003), *Social Responsible Management of the Supply Chain*, School of Business-University of Maryland, Resaerch@Smith, Spring 2003, vol.3, No.2

So, Y. and Durfee, E. (1998), *Designing organizations for computational agents.* In Carley, K., Pritula, M., and Gasser, L., editors, Simulating Organizations, pages 47–64.

Solomon Markos, (2010), *Employee Engagement: The Key to Improving Performance,* International Journal of Business and Management Vol. 5, No. 12, December 2010

Souza, R., & Voss, C. A. (2001), *Quality management: universal or context dependent? An empirical investigation across the manufacturing strategy spectrum*, Production and Operations Management, 10, 383-404.

Speckbacher, G., Bischof, J. and Pfeiffer, T., (2003), *A descriptive analysis of the implementation of balanced scorecards in German-speaking countries.* Management Accounting Research, 14(4), pp.361-388.

Springerplus. (2016), 5(1), 1797. *Published online 2016 Oct 18. doi*: 10.1186/s40064-016-3498-1, PMCID: PMC5069235, Business process performance measurement: a structured literature review of indicators, measures and metrics, Amy Van Looy, Aygun Shafagatova

Sroufe, R. and S. Curkovic (2008*), An examination of ISO 9000:2000 and supply chain quality assurance*, Journal of Operations Management 26(4), 503–520.

Ståhle Pirjo, Ståhle Sten, Aho Samuli, (2011) *,Value added intellectual coefficient (VAIC), a critical analysis*, Journal of intellectual capital, Vol. 12 Issue: 4, pp.531-551, https://doi.org/10.1108/1469193

Steers, Richard M., (1976), *Organizational Effectivness: A Behavirol view*, Santa Monica, CA. Goodyear

Stephen Gates, Jean-Louis Nicolas, Paul L. Walker., (2012), *Enterprise risk management: A process for enhanced management and improved performance,* Management Accounting Quarterly, 13 (3), pp.28-38

Stewart G. B, III, Stern, J. M., D. H. Chew, Jr. (1995), *The EVA® Financial System*, Journal of Applied Corporate Finance, 8(2), pp. 32-46.

Stewart , T. (1991) . *Intellectual capital: Your company's most valuable asset* . Fortune Magazine June : 44 – 60 .

Stewart, T. (1997).*intellectual capital: The New Wealth Of Organizations*, Nicholas Brealey Publishing, Business Digest, New York

Stewhart, W. A. (1931), *Economic Control of Quality of Manufactured Product*, ASQ Quality Press, New York

Studeny, M. (2015), *Comparative Analysis of Business Success in the Automotive Industry Using a Grounded Theory Approach.*

Suellen J. Hogan , Leonard V. Coote, (2014), *Organizational culture, innovation, and performance: A test of Schein's model*, Journal of Business Research 67 (2014) 1609–1621

Sullivan, E. (1986) *OPTIM: linking cost, time and quality*, Quality Progress, April, Vol. 19, pp.52–55.

Sumedrea, S. (2012) *Managementul organizatiei*, Editura ASE, Bucuresti, pp.273-277

Sun, H., (2000), *Total Quality Management. ISO 9000 certification and performance improvement.* International Journal of Quality & Reliability Management, 17(2), pp.168-179.

Svanadze, S., Kowalewska, M. (2015), *The measurement of intellectual capital by VAIC method example of WIG20*, Online Journal of Applied Knowledge Management, a Publication of the International Institute for Applied Knowledge Management, Vol. 3, Issue 2.

Sveiby K. E., (1997),*The Intangible Assets Monitor*, Journal of Human Resource Costing & Accounting, Vol. 2 Iss: 1, pp.73 - 97

Sveiby, K. E. (2010) *Methods for Measuring Intangible Assets.* Available: http://www.sveiby.com/files/pdf/intangiblemethods.pdf, accessed 05.10.2017

Szabó, D.G., Sørensen K.E. (2015), *New EU directive on the Disclosure of Non-Financial Information* (CSR), ECFR, page 307–340.

Tan Barney, Pan Shan L. , Lu Xianghua , Lihua Huang, (2009), *Leveraging Digital Business Ecosystems for Enterprise Agility: The Tri-Logic Development Strategy of Alibaba.com*, ICIS 2009 Proceedings, International Conference on Information Systems, (ICIS)

Tarí, J.J., Molina-Azorín, J.F., & Heras, I. (2012), *Benefits of the ISO 9001 and ISO 14001 standards: A literature review.* Journal of Industrial Engineering and Management, 5(2), 296-322, http://dx.doi.org/10.3926/jiem.488

Tatitcchi P., Tonelli F., Cagnazzo L. (2010*), Performance measurement and management: a literature review and research agenda*, Measuring business excellence, Vol. 14 No. 1, pp. 4-18

Taylor FW,(1896), *A Piece Rate System*. Econ Stud. 1896, 1(2), 89

Taylor, Frederick Winslow (1919*), The Principles of Scientific Management*, New York, NY, USA and London, UK: Harper & Brothers

Teece D. J. (2006*),Reflections on profiting from technological innovation*, Research Policy, 35(8)

Teece, D. J. (2010), *Business Models, Business Strategy and Innovation*. Long Range Planning, 43, 172-194.

Teece, D., Pisano, G. and Shuen, A., (1997), *Dynamic Capabilities and Strategic Management*, Strategic Management Journal, 18(7), pp.509-533

Teoh Ai Ping, Rajendran Muthuveloo (2015), *The Impact of Enterprise risk management on Firm Performance: Evidence from Malaysia, Asian Social Science*, Vol. 11, No. 22, pp. 149-159

Terziovski, M., Samson, D. (1999*), The link between total quality management practice and organisational performance*, International Journal of Quality & Reliability Management, 16 (3), pp.226-237.

Terziovski, M., Samson, D. and Dow, D., (1997), *The business value of quality management systems certification.* Evidence from Australia and New Zealand. Journal of Operations Management, 15(1), pp.1-18.

Thamizhmanii, S. Hasan, S. (2010), *A review on an employee empowerment in TQM practice*, Journal of Achievements in Materials and Manufacturing Engineering, Vol. 39, nr 2, pp. 204-210

Thanassoulis E., De Witte K., Johnes J., Johnes G., Karagiannis G., Portela C.S. (2016) *Applications of Data Envelopment Analysis in Education*. In: Zhu J. (eds) Data Envelopment Analysis. International Series in Operations Research & Management Science, vol 238. Springer, Boston, MA

Ting, I.W.K. and Lean, H.H. (2009). *Intellectual ca pital performance of fi nancial institutions in Malaysia*. Journal of Intellectual Capital, 10(4): 588–599.

Herbert A. Simon,(1959) , *Theories of Decision-Making in Economics and Behavioral Science.* The American Economic Review, Vol. 49, No. 3 (Jun., 1959), 253-283

Tiwari, S., Wee, H.M., Daryanto, Y. (2018*), Big data analytics in supply chain management between 2010 and 2016,* Computers & Industrial Engineering, 115, pp. 319-330.

Töpfer, A. (2007), *Six Sigma, balanced scorecard und EFQM-Modell im Wirkungsverbund,* in: Töpfer, A. (eds), Six Sigma – Konzeption und Erfolgsbeispiele für praktizierte Null-Fehler-Qualität. 4th edition, Berlin Heidelberg New York: Springer.

Rössler Richard, and Hannes Schlieter1,(2015),*Towards Model-based Integration of management systems,* 12th International Conference on Wirtschaftsinformatik, March 4-6 2015, Osnabrück, Germany

Y. SUGIMORI, K. KUSUNOKI, F. CHO & S. UCHIKAWA (1977),*Toyota production system and Kanban system Materialization of just-in-time and respect-for-human system,* International Journal of Production Research Vol. 15 , Iss. 6,1977

Trentin, S., McKeran, Ch. (2008), *Role of human factor in knowledge management.* Translated by Mohsenzade, A. Librarianship and Information. 10 (1)

Tseng, S.M. (2010), *The Correlation between organizational culture and Knowledge Conversion on Corporate Performance.* Journal of Knowledge Management, 14, 269-284.

Tubis, A., Werbińska-Wojciechowska, S., (2017), *balanced scorecard Use in Passenger Transport Companies Performing at Polish Market,* Procedia Engineering, 187, pp. 538-547.

Turi A, Mocan M, Ivascu L, Goncalves G, Maistor S, (2015), *From Fordism to Lean management: Main shifts in automotive industry evolution within the last century,* MakeLearn International Scientific Conference on Management of Knowledge and Learning, May (2015), pp 25-27

Tyler, F., (2017), *Exploring the Relationship of Supply Chain risk management to Quality Management.* In: Kounis, L.D., ed. 2017. Quality Control and Assurance - An Ancient Greek Term Re-Mastered. Rijeka: InTech. pp.135-154.

Urdang, L., & Flexner, S. B. (1968), *The random house dictionary of the English language: college edition.* New York: Random House

Uzun, D. (2007), Örgüt Kültürünün Bilgi Yönetimi Sürecine ve Örgütsel Performansa Etkisi: Beş Yıldızlı Otel İşletmelerinde Bir Uygulama, Doktora Tezi, Dokuz Eylül Üniversitesi, Sosyal Bilimler Enstitüsü, İzmir.

Van den Berg, Herman. (2002), *Models of intellectual capital valuation: a comparative evaluation, Conference: Knowledge Summit Doctoral Consortium 2002,* available at: www.researchgate.com, (accessed 20.12.2017)

van der Aalst W.M.P. (2004), *business process Management Demystified: A Tutorial on Models, Systems and Standards for Workflow Management.* In: Desel J., Reisig W., Rozenberg G. (eds) Lectures on Concurrency and Petri Nets. ACPN 2003. Lecture Notes in Computer Science, vol 3098. Springer, Berlin, Heidelberg

van der Aalst,Wil M. P. , (2013), *Hindawi Publishing Corporation ISRN Software Engineering Volume 2013,* Article ID 507984, 37 pages http://dx.doi.org/10.1155/2013/507984"507984 Review Article business process Management: A Comprehensive Survey

van Marrewijk, M., (2004), *A Value Based Approach to Organization Types: Towards a coherent set of stakeholder-oriented management tools.* Journal of Business Ethics, 55(2), pp.147–158.

Vera, D. and Crossan, M. (2001), *Organizational learning, knowledge management, and IC: an integrative conceptual model,* Organizational Learning and Knowledge Management. New Dir-ections 4th international conference, pp. 616-634, London, Ontario, Canada, Richard Ivery SoB

Victor, B., Boynton, A.C. (1998), *Invented Here: A Practical Guide to Transforming Work,* Harvard Business School Press, Cambridge, Mass.

Victoria Garibaldi de Hilal, Adriana, Ursula Wetzel, and Vicente Ferreira.(2009), *Organizational culture and performance: a Brazilian case.* Management Research News 32, no. 2 (2009), 99-119.

Vinodh, S., Sundararaj, G., Devadasan, S. R. (2009), *Total agile design system model via literature exploration.* Ind. Manage. Data Syst., 109(4), 570-588.

van der Aalst W. M. P. and K. M. van Hee,(2004), *Workflow Management: Models, Methods, and Systems*, MIT press, Cambridge, Mass, USA,

Wagner, M., (2007*), Integration of Environmental Management with Other Managerial Functions of the Firm: Empirical Effects on Drivers of Economic Performance.* Long Range Planning, 40(6), pp.611-628.

Wang, S., & Noe, R. A. (2010), *Knowledge sharing: A review and directions for future research.* Human Resource Management Review, 20(2), 115-131.

Wang, W. Y. and Chang, C. (2005), *intellectual capital and performance in causal models*, Journal of intellectual capital, Vol. 6, No. 2, pp. 222-236.

Waters, D. (2003), *Logistics- An Introduction to Supply Chain Management*, ISBN 0–333–96369–5

Waweru, Nelson and Kisaka, Eric Simiyu, (2011), *The Effect of Enterprise risk management Implementation on the Value of Companies Listed in the Nairobi Stock Exchange*, AAA 2012 Management Accounting Section (MAS) Meeting Paper

Weber, M. (1930), *The Protestant Ethic and the Spirit of Capitalism.* Translated by Talcott Parsons. New York, NY: Scribners.

Weber, M. (1978), *Economy and society: An outline of interpretive sociology.* Univ of California Press.

Wiig, K.M. (1993), *Knowledge Management Foundations*, Arlington, TX, USA: Schema Press

Wilkinson, G., Dale, B.G.(2002), *An examination of the ISO 9001:2000 standard and its influence on the integration of management systems.* Production Planning and Control. 2002, Vol. 13 (3), p.284-297

Williander, M. (2006),*On green innovation inertia - An insider researcher perspective on the automotive industry*, PhD

Wilson, L. (2009), *How to Implement Lean Manufacturing.* New York: McGraw-Hill Professional Publishing, 2009.

Wisutteewong, G., Rompho, N. (2015), *Linking balanced scorecard and COSO ERM in Thai Companies* Journal of Management Policy and Practice, 16 (2), pp. 127-134.

W.M. To, Peter K.C. Lee, Billy T.W. Yu, (2012), *Benefits of implementing management system standards: A case study of certified companies in the Pearl River Delta, China*, The TQM Journal, Vol. 24 Issue: 1, pp.17-28, https://doi.org/ HYPERLINK "https://doi.org/10.1108/17542731211191195

Womack, J., Jones, D.T. and Roos, D. (1990), *The machine that changed the world.* Rawson Associates..

Woods, M., (2007), *Linking risk management to strategic controls: a case study of Tesco plc.* International. International Journal of Risk Assessment and Management, 7(8), pp. 1074-1088

Yallwe, A., & Buscemi, A. (2014), *An Era of Intangible Assets.* Journal of Applied Financeand Banking, 17-26

Yeo, K.T., Ren, Y. (2009), *Risk management capability maturity model for complex product systems (CoPS) projects,* Systems Engineering, 12 (4), pp. 275-294.

Yildiz, E. (2014), *A Study on the Relationship between organizational culture and Organizational Performance and a Model Suggestion*, International Journal of Research in Business and Social Science, 3 (4), pp. 52-67.

Yin, H. and Schmeidler, P., (2009), *Why do standardized ISO 14001 environmental management systems lead to heterogeneous environmental outcomes?.* Business Strategy and the Environment, 18(7), pp.469-486.

Zafar Hina, Bahauddin Zakariya, Muhammad Haroon Hafeez, Mohd Noor Mohd Shariff, (2016), *Relationship between market orientation, organizational learning, organizational culture and organizational performance: mediating, impact of innovation*, South East Asia Journal of Contemporary Business, Economics and Law, Vol. 9, Issue 2 (Apr.) ISSN 2289-1560

Zairi M. (1997), *Business process management: a boundaryless approach to modern competitiveness,* business process Management Journal, Vol 3 No. 1, pp. 68-80

Zavareghi, R. (2008), *Perspective on strategies, tools and skills of personal knowledge management.* Paper presented at the First National Conference on Knowledge Management

Zeghal,D.&Malloul, A. (2010), *Analyzing value added as an indicator of intellectual capital and its consequences on company performance,* journal of intellectual capital, vol.11,No.1,pp. 39 -60

Zeng, S. X., Xie, X. M., Tam, C. M., & Shen, L. Y. (2011), *An empirical examination of benefits from implementing integrated management systems (IMS)*, Total Quality Management & Business Excellence, 22(2), pp. 173–186

Zhan, X., Chen, R. (2006), *Forecast-driven or customer order-driven? An empirical analysis of the Chinese automotive industry*. International Journal of Operations & Prod. Management, 26(6), 668-688

Zhu J. (2014) *Data Envelopment Analysis. In: Quantitative Models for Performance Evaluation and Benchmarking*. International Series in Operations Research & Management Science, vol 213. Springer, Cham

Živa Jurišević Brčić & Katarina Katja Mihelič (2015) *Knowledge sharing between different generations of employees: an example from Slovenia*, Economic ResearchEkonomska, Istraživanja, 28:1, 853-867, DOI: 10.1080/1331677X.2015.1092308

Zollondz, H.-D. (2011), *Grundlagen Qualitätsmanagement*, 3nd ed. Munich: Oldenbourg Verlag.

Zutshi, A., & Sohal, A. (2005*), integrated management system: the experiences of three Australian organisations*. Journal of Manufacturing Technology Management, 16, 211-32. http://dx.doi.org/10.1108/17410380510576840

***AIRMIC, Alarm, IRM: (2010), *A structured approach to Enterprise risk management (ERM) and the requirements of ISO 31000*, https://www.theirm.org/media/886062/ISO3100_doc.pdf, accessed 03.02.2018

***Annual financial reports of Mercedes Benz, Honda Motor Co. Ltd., Volkswagen group, Nissan Motors, Audi, Skoda, BMW, Toyota group, Ford (2007-2015); Strategic targets: http://www.evobus.ch/Projects/c2c/channel/documents/1931896_Daimler_UBS_Paris_DJSchmidt_Handout.pdf (page 25), accessed 19.01.2016; http://www.bmwgroup.com/annualreport 2008/nav/index.html?http://www.bmwgroup.com/annualreport2007/strategie_number_one/strategiegebaeude.html, accessed 10.01.2016; http://factsanddetails.com/japan/cat23/sub184/i tem928.html, accessed 01.01.2016; http://www.carmagazine.co.uk/car-news/industry-news/nissan/nissan-announces-its-power-88-five-year-plan/, accessed 10.12.2015

***Bain Company (2015) *Management tools and trends 2015*. http://www.bain.com/publications/articles/management-tools-and-trends-2015.aspx. Accessed Nov (2017)

***BMW Sustainable Value report 2014 (2015), http://www.bmwgroup.com/d/0_0_www_bmwgroup_com/investor_relations/corporate_events/_pdf/2013/Charts_Dr_Reithofer_BPK_2013_d.pdf,accessed"_d.pdf, accessed 20.10.(2015)

***BMW annual report 2007 (2007), http://www.bmwgroup.com/annualreport2007/strategie_number_one/strategiegebaeude.html"/strategie_number_one/strategiegebaeude.html, accessed 10.01.2016

***BSI, (2015), http://www.bsigroup.com/en-GB/pas-99-integrated-management, accessed 08/08/(2016)

***Committee of Sponsoring Organizations of the Treadway Commission (COSO) (Hrsg.), (1992), Internal Control – integrated Framework. AICPA, Jersey NY

***Committee of Sponsoring Organizations of the Treadway Commission (COSO) (Hrsg.), (2004), Enterprise risk management — integrated Framework Executive Summary September 2004

***Committee of Sponsoring Organizations of the Treadway Commission (COSO) (Hrsg.), (2009),http://www.coso.org/IC-integratedFramework-summary.htm, Internal Control— integrated Framework, Retrieved March 23, 2011

***Coresight Research, (2016), https://www.fungglobalretailtech.com/research/alibaba-group-strength-strength-overview-business-units-worlds-largest-e-commerce-company/, accessed 21.05. (2016)

***Daimler, (2011), https://www.daimler.com/Projects/c2c/channel/documents/2141471_daimler_mbc_day_20120329_01_zetsche_overview.pdf, accessed 01.11.2015

***Deutschland_012016.pdf?__blob=publicationFile , accessed 22.11.2016

***EU Directive (2003)/51/EC of the European Parliament and of the Council of 18 June (2003) amend-
ing directives 78/660/EEC 83/349/EEC and 86/635/EEC and 91/674/EEC and other financial institutions and insurance undertakings (2003).

***Directive (2013)/34/EU of the European Parliament and the Council of 26 June (2013) on the annual
financial statements, consolidated financial statements and related reports of certain types of undertakings, amending directive (2006)/43/EC of the European Parliament and of the Council and
repealing Council directives 78/660/EEC and 83/349/EEC (2013).

***Directive (2014)/95/EU of the European Parliament and the Council of 22 October (2014) amending
directive 2013/34/EU as regards disclosure of non-financial and diversity information by certain
large undertakings and groups (2014).

***EDUCBA, (2016), https://www.educba.com/the-8-crucial-tqm-elements/, accessed 08.07.(2016)

***EFQM (2010) EFQM—the official website. http://www.efqm.org. Accessed Nov (2016)

***EFQM (2017), *An Overview of the EFQM Excellence model*, retrieved: http://www.efqm.org/
sites/default/files/overview_efqm_2013_v2_new_logo.pdf, 22.01.2018.

***ENQA (2005), *Standards and Guidelines for Quality Assurance in the European Higher Education
Area* Available at http://www.unibo.it/qualityassuranceen/AttachmentHP/Standards%20and
%20Guidelines%20for%20QA%20in%20the%20European%20Higher%20Education%20Area.pdf,
accessed 26.10.2016

***Envelopment Analysis. Benchmarking: An International Journal 10(3), pp. 226–245.

***European Commission/EACEA/Eurydice (2014), *Modernisation of Higher Education in Europe: Ac-
cess, Retention and Employability. Eurydice* Report. Luxembourg: Publications Office of the European Union

*** European Commission/EACEA/Eurydice (2018), https://ec.europa.eu/info/business-economy-
euro/company-reporting-and-auditing/company-reporting/non-financial-reporting_en, accessed
03.02.2018

***Ford strategy, (2016), http://www.icmrindia.org/casestudies/catalogue/Business%20Strategy/
One%20Ford%20Strategy-Excerpts1.htm, accessed 12.01.2016

***Fraunhofer TEG (2005), *Studie Methoden im Innovationsprozess*, Stuttgart: Fraunhofer TEG.

***Global Corporate & Specialty SE, (2016), *Top10 Global Business Risks for 2016*, München, Germany

***Handbook of Organizational Creativity, Academic Press, (2012), Pages 547–568 Chapter 21 – Or-
ganizational Learning, Knowledge Management and Creativity, Robert K. Kazanjian, Robert Drazin,
https://doi.org/10.1016/B978-0-12-374714-3.00021-5

***Honda, (2016)a, http://www.fool.com/investing/general/2015/04/15/how-honda-motor-co-
pulled-off-its-2014-turnaround.aspx, accessed 08.01.2016

***Honda, (2016)b, http://www.reuters.com/article/us-honda-ceo-idUSBRE88K05120120921, ac-
cessed 03.12.2016

***Institut RSE Management (2012), Survey No. 7, The Grenelle II Act in France: *a milestone towards
integrated reporting.*

***Institute of risk management, (2006), About risk management, https://www.theirm.org/
about/risk-management/, 15.03.2016, London

***International Journal of Thesis Projects and Dissertations (IJTPD) Vol. 4, Issue 2, pp: (1-48), Month:
April - June (2016), Available at: www.researchpublish.com Page | 1 Research Publish Journals
Critical Success Factors of business process Reengineering, Case Study: IBM 1Oluwatosin Sorunke,
2Ameen Nasir

***ISO (2011), ISO/IEC 27005:(2011), https://www.iso.org/standard/56742.html, 23.01.2018.

***ISO HLS, (2015), http://www.iso.org/iso/home/standards/management-standards/mss-list.htm,
accessed 08/08/2016

***ISO annual report, (2015b), http://www.iso.org/iso/annual_report_2015.pdf, accessed
08/08/2016

***ISO (2017), *ISO 31000 revision moves towards a clearer and more concise text*, retrieved
https://www.iso.org/news/2017/02/Ref2165.html, 24.01.2018

***ISO, (2017b). *Management system standards.* Geneva: International Organization for Standardization. Available at: https://www.iso.org/management-system-standards.html.pdf , accessed 28 February 2017.

*** ISO, 2018, *ISO Survey of certifications to management system standards,* https://isotc.iso.org/livelink/livelink?func=ll&objId=18808772&objAction=browse&viewType=1, accessed 04.03.2018

***ISO 50001 *Energy management, retrieved,* https://www.iso.org/iso-50001-energy-management. html, *ISO 14000 family – Environmental management,* https://www.iso.org/iso-14001-environmental-management.html, *ISO/IEC 27000 family – Information security management systems,* https://www.iso.org/isoiec-27001-information-security.html, 22.01.2018.

***International Organization of Motor Vehicle Manufacturers, http://www.oica.net/, accessed 03.02.2018

***Japan Today (2015), *Japan's shinkansen best in world at safety, punctuality, tech, but not marketing, retrieved*: https://japantoday.com/category/features/kuchikomi/japans-shinkansen-best-in-world-at-safety-punctuality-tech-but-not-marketing, 11.02.2018.

****Learning, Innovation and Development,* (2009), Vol.2, No.1/2, pp.7 - 24

***Nissan strategy, http://www.carmagazine.co.uk/car-news/industry-news/nissan/nissan-announces-its-power-88-five-year-plan/"-five-year-plan/, accessed 10.01.2016

***Norm Din EN ISO 9001 (2000), *Qualitätsmanagementsysteme: Grundlagen und Begriffe,* München: Grin Verlag.

***One Small Step Can Change Your Life: The Kaizen Way, Workman Publishing (2014), ISBN-13: : 978-0761180326, Robert Maurer

***Open Knowledge Foundation (2016), Our mission [online, Available at https://okfn.org/about/ , accessed 19.10.16

***Organizational Diagnosis: A Workbook of Theory and Practice. Contributor, Marvin Ross Weisbord. Edition, 7, illustrated, reprint, annotated. Publisher, Addison-Wesley Publishing Company, 1978. Original from, the University of Michigan. Digitized, Aug 2, 2006. ISBN, 0201083574, 9780201083576

***PlanFabrik GmbH (2017), *Grafik Logistikkette.* Online: http://www.planfabrik.de/homepage/de/kompetenzen/supply-chain-management-a-logistik, accessed: 25.5.2017

***PwC (2017), *The top changes to the COSO ERM Framework you need to know now,* retrieved: http://pwc.blogs.com/resilience/2017/09/the-top-changes-to-the-coso-erm-framework-you-need-to-know-now.html"/the-top-changes-to-the-coso-erm-framework-you-need-to-know-now.html, 11.02.2018.

***Quantitative Study across Twenty Cases. Administrative Science Quarterly, 35, 286-316

***RIMS, *The Risk and Insurance Management Society,* 2016, https://www.rims.org/Pages/Default.aspx and https://www.logicmanager.com/pdf/rims_rmm_executive_summary.pdf, accessed 05.05.2016

***Senior Supervisors Group (2008) ,*Observations on risk management Practices during the recent Market Turbulence,* 6th March 2008, New York Federal Reserve Bank, USA.

***Steering Committee for the Review of Commonwealth/State Service Provision (1997), *Data Envelopment Analysis: A technique for measuring the efficiency of government service delivery,* AGPS, Canberra

****Sustainability reports of Skoda, Mercedes, Volkswagen, BMW, General Motors, Audi, Toyota Europe, Toyota group, Suzuki, Ford, Honda Motor Co. Ltd, Nissan Motor Corp.,* Annual reports and press releases (2007 – 2015)

***Systems & Services: *International digital library perspectives,* Vol. 27 Iss 1, pp. 18 – 22, Permanent link to this document: http://dx.doi.org/10.1108/10650751111106528"10650751111106528

***TCW (2011), *Konzepte und Lösungen von morgen,* [online Available at: http://www.tcw.de/static_pages/view/174%26usg , accessed 9.2.2016.

***The path and performance of a company leader: *A historical examination of the education and cognitive ability of Fortune 500 CEOs* Jonathan Wai a, Heiner Rindermann, Intelligence 53 (2015) 102–107, http://dx.doi.org/10.1016/j.intell.2015.10.001"2015.10.001

***Toyota, (2015)a, http://www.toyota.eu/sustainability/vision_strategy/Pages/default.aspx, accessed 5.11.2015

***Toyota, (2015)b, http://www.toyota.eu/sustainability/vision_strategy/vision_strategy/Pages/default.asp, accessed 24.10.2015

***TQM.com (2011), *Total Quality Management,* [online Available at: http://www.tqm.com/methoden/tqm, accessed 09th February 2011.

***Volkswagen, (2014), http://annualreport2014.volkswagenag.com/group-management-report/goals-and-strategies.html".volkswagenag.com/group-management-report/goals-and-strategies.html, accessed 28.10.2015

***Volkswagen, (2015), http://www.autocar.co.uk/car-news/industry/vw-10m-sales-2015"2015, accessed 05.12.2015

***Wall Street Journal (2016), http://www.pressreader.com/china/the-wall-street-journal-asia/20160224/282037621234300"282037621234300, Accessed 12.03.2016.

Appendix

Appendix A: Results of the research in management system's implementation

Part 1: Implementation – Starting points	
Company A	**Company B**
The introduction of ISO management systems was mainly driven externally by several stakeholders as a market sign. The first certification was ISO 9001 in 2002 directly followed by ISO 14001 in 2003.	Even though there was no law which requires an ISO-certification, company B implemented an ISO 14001 environmental management system in 2003 to deal with several legal restrictions. ISO 9001 followed 3 years later.
Both management systems were introduced simultaneously with the goal to develop an IMS. Some years later OHSAS 18001, ISO 50001, and ISO 27001 were added.	Both management systems were introduced after each other without any specific linkage at first. The IMS idea started after the company also certified its energy management system according to ISO 50001. They started their IMS with the implementation of the energy management system and integrated all management systems into an IMS. The newest management system which was introduced is ISO 27001.
Implementation – Best Practice	
Since two management system standards was implemented at the same time company A choose one project team consisting of two representatives, two coordinators for each area and a project manager which established a project management methodology for the implementation project. Synergies between the first two management systems were used as much as possible. ISO 9001 in version 2008 was structured to enhance its usability with ISO 14001 (in version 2004). Before that the integration was more difficult. Since no high-level structure existed during that time, the project team defined common requirements which were also driven by the business needs. They analyzed the business needs in workshops and mapped them with the requirements given by the standards.	Company B implemented both management systems separate from each other. Both topics were driven by different stakeholders - responsible employees were also geographically separated from each other. The structure of the implementation project was similar consisting of the representatives and employees from the technical areas. External consultants were hired to assist in that phase. The only thing which was shared between the two implementation projects was the document management system in which the teams defined a similar structure and common document templates for the policy documents. Initiated by the ISO 9001-team the document control was also defined for both areas.

© Springer Fachmedien Wiesbaden GmbH, part of Springer Nature 2019
J. Kopia, *Effective Implementation of Management Systems*, Sustainable Management, Wertschöpfung und Effizienz, https://doi.org/10.1007/978-3-658-26509-0

The basis of the integration was the PDCA-cycle which is similar for ISO 9001 and ISO 14001. Both standards also require some common documents and processes: - Document control - Training of employees - Control of non-conformance - Corrective and preventive action - Internal and external audits - Management reviews - Collecting of records - Top management commitment through policy definition	
On the basis of the similar processes the project team created a generic methodology for both systems where the representatives worked closely together. The goal was to use as much synergies as possible. The common elements were mapped with the continuous improvement process based on the PDCA-cycle of all systems. They defined one management board for both areas which met in regular intervals to both topics. Even though in this phase the implementation was in the project phase, the board meetings were already part of the later phases of a mature system. The team defined a reporting structure which assessed environmental and quality topics including all necessary measures which also included KPIs to get a clear idea of the status of both areas.	The reporting structure was not project based but was kept according to the functional organization which best fit to the topics environmental control and quality management - ISO 14001 mainly required control and monitoring, ISO 9001 required design and development of processes. The management was involved in the regular functional reporting structure.
The involvement of the management was strong at the beginning of the project. Resources were approved (2 new positions and time from other employees which was split between the IMS tasks and their normal work). Management reviews were done with both topics at the same time.	The management involvement was barely visible but resources were given in the form of a certain budget for external consultancy and work time for the management system tasks was approved. Remaining work in other areas was shifted to other people. Management reviews were separated in time as well as the concerning the people.
All Audits were integrated and included both topics as much as possible. Even though two auditors (in the third party audit) were involved the system was seen as an IMS.	All audits were separate from each other. The third party audit was done by two different auditing companies. The result was that the costs for both implementation projects including the external audits were high.

	The management suggested integrating both systems into an IMS for the next re-certification to use synergies more efficiently.
Later management systems as OHSAS 18001 were integrated into the IMS by using the following methodology: 1. Analyzing of the differences between the existing IMS and the new management system according to given requirements by performing workshops with trained people (incl. external specialists) – mainly a common element analysis and process maps 2. Acquiring the necessary resources (personnel incl. budget for training) 3. Implementing of only necessary elements forced by the standard and required by organizational rules and regulations. The goal was to not follow the standard step by step but to adapt those parts of the standards which were necessary to achieve the organizational goal (and satisfy the standard's requirements) 4. Integrate the new management standard into the PDCA-cycle by keeping all processes and structures of the IMS as stable as possible.	Company was not able to integrate both systems as expected. The main reasons were the different cultures of the involved people and the old and firm structures of the organization. It took 8 years to build an IMS when a new management system standard was introduced. New ISO management systems were the ISO 50001. Changing responsibilities and lesson learnt were the reason why company B now used the implementation of this standard to build an IMS. A consulting company guided company B for almost 2 years on a project based level which the consultancy lead. The most difficult part was to change the tasks and procedures (and people's minds) of the existing management systems into the new harmonized IMS. New roles were established to management this organizational change with an MSS (management system standard) task force. Together with the support of the management and the external consultants a generic set of processes and documents very similar to the later developed high-level structure by ISO were created. All representatives had to structure their management system according to this set of processes and documents – common elements were harmonized and generated together. The MSS task force which consists of different technical people including department heads of the areas was established and controlled the IMS. Harmonization was done in steps, starting from documentation and control-procedures, internal audit and management review, and preventive and corrective action. The first IMS was not practically usable ("too theoretical") though and had to be improved in diverse areas.

The introduction of the high-level structure did not change the IMS since most processes, procedures and documents were already integrated according the company's needs. Because of re-certification and during the continues improvement cycles company A will most likely have minor changes to some elements required by the standards.	The high-level structure did not yet have any effect on the IMS. Company B guessed that a re-certification on the basis of high level-based standard will most likely affect the IMS slightly. The newly required justification when a new MMS is introduced will be followed according to the defined process of the newly established IMS board.
Success factors of the implementation of the IMS: - The involvement of the (top) management - Enough trained personnel / resources with the organizational power (empowered) to change things - The corporate culture must fit in order to harmonize different and often very separate functional areas and responsible people with each other - Professional change- and project management - Discipline in the IMS-team	Success factors of the implementation of the IMS: - The involvement of the (top) management - Access to resources - An open organization culture willing to change - Develop generic and aggregated KPIs for IMS instead of using separated KPIs for the systems - Define clear implementation guidelines
The main obstacles were: - Many different requirements of all the standards (in the years 2002-2008), e.g. in the area of performance measurement in ISO 9001 and 14001 in earlier versions - The certification of an IMS was not an easy task since certification bodies usually only deal with their special topics. It is important to start early with the search for an auditor. - Missing knowledge of the ISO standards or the absence of specialists - Differences between stakeholder expectations	The main obstacles of the integration were: - Differences in document requirements of the standards, especially regarding a management system handbook and what documents needs to be public and which can be kept private - Different stakeholder's requirements are not easy to match (product and service quality as main goal versus fulfilling environmental or energy specific laws and regulations). - Low motivation level of employees and therefore limited communication between involved parties
Part 2: Generic statements and practices after years of operation of an IMS After several years of working with an IMS the following statements and lesson learnt were collected in the context of success factors of implementation and running of an IMS.	
Company A	Company B

- The project manager which was originally responsible for the IMS implementation project left the ISMS team too early. Even though the project was officially finished the ISMS organization was not fully established and able to work.	- If external consultants are hired for the IMS implementation it is important to have enough time for a knowledge transfer in order to efficiently operate the IMS
- The gap between the functional organization incl. its daily routines and the IMS-requirements should be defined within the implementation project and not during the maturity phase. Many things during the implementation were done quickly and because of time pressure. After the third party audit was over, company A still had an IMS in project conditions with which was not really practically used (even though certification bodies usually require a management system to be "active" for a while before certification)	- Define clear responsibilities especially when the project is finished.
	- The implementation project was driven by a complete restructuring of existing management systems and by many necessities which were theoretical defined but not practically used. It was almost impossible to use the first defined rules and regulations of the IMS after the project reached the last milestone. Involved people often switched back to older processes which worked for them before resulting in rework of some IMS guidelines.
- Continues improvement really starts when the IMS is running for several years not within the implementation phase.	- Get the acceptance of the employees in the project phase not later when all employees have to work with it.
- Several parts of an IMS are still separate depending on the technical area of the management system standards. Especially work instructions resulting from the standards requirements and required records. Due to its nature the IMS keeps these aspects as separate as necessary.	- Some parts of management systems are harder to integrate into the IMS. Especially product or service specific things in the product realization processes, the risk based approach required by newer standards, and planning processes are not easily harmonized.
- In the project phase the representatives worked 100% of their work time on the IMS, later they reduced that amount (substantially depending on the area). Nevertheless a running IMS needs resources which have time to do their work.	- It is necessary to constantly train and motivate people to work in the given set of rules and regulations required by the IMS

Table 2: Summary of IMS-integration of two case studies (Source: own elaboration based on the results of own research)

Appendix B: Summary of the ERM-studies

Title and authors	Year	Does ERM adds value? (yes, no, both)	Methodolo gy	Summary / results	Data used
ERM Determinants, Use, and Effects on the Firm, David M. Pooser, Peter J. Tobin	2012	no	Empirical	Firms with an ERM rating have a larger and greater operational diversification and lower levels of liquidity or free capital. No influence on ROA, premium growth, income growth, surplus growth was found.	ERM assessment: Standard and Poor's quality rating related variables Performance: Various variables as Size, Net Premiums Written Scaled by Policyholder, Surplus ratio, Policyholder Surplus Scaled by Net Admitted Assets ratio, Change in Net Income from Prior Year, Direct Premium, Standard Deviation of ROA, ROA, Portfolio Variance and other
risk management and Performance in Insurance Companies, Eikenhout	2015	no	Empirical	No significant evidence was found of a positive effects of ERM on performance (before and during the crisis years).	ERM assessment: Existance of Chief Risk Officer and Risk Commitee, Presence of an important Auditor firm, firm size Performance values: Data based on Annual reports: ROA, ROE, , Leverage
The Value of Enterprise risk management: Evidence from the U.S. Insurance Industry, Robert E. Hoyt, Dudley L. Moore, Jr. Chair of Insurance, Andre P. Liebenberg	2006	yes	Empirical	The use of ERM is positively related to firm size and institutional ownership, and negatively related to reinsurance use and leverage. A positive relation was found between firm value and the use of ERM.	ERM assessment: calculated based on firm size, institutional ownership, diversification, industry Financial value based on: Book Value, One-Year sales growths, Return on Asset, Tobin's Q etc.

Enterprise risk management Sophistication and Firm Risk, Barrese, James, Stephen G. Fier, David M. Pooser, and Paul L. Walker	2015	(yes)	Empirical	Sophisticated risk management practices are related to a higher variation in operating cash flows / greater cash flow volatility.	ERM assessment: answers to 25 risk management survey questions taken from RIM database, an international organization for risk management professionals Performance: ROA, Tobin's Q, Size, Liquidity, Sales Growth, Leverage, Dividend Status, Coefficient of Variation of Cash Flows
The Relationship Between Enterprise risk management (ERM) And Firm Value Mediated Through The Financial Performance, Agustina, Linda; Niswah Baroroh	2016	no	Empirical	ERM has no significant influence on firm value and profitability.	ERM assessment: ERM measures based on guidelines of risk management for commercial banks Performance: Data from annual reports and Indonesia Capital Market Directory, Price to Book Value, Return on Equity
Does Enterprise risk management Create Value, Norlida Abdul Manab, Zahiruddin Ghazali	2013	no	Questionaire with quantitative analysis	Risk management practices as well as corporate governance compliance have an effect on shareholder value. ERM was not the main factor that led to value creation.	ERM assessment: size of company Performance: Earnings per share, total debt over total asset, cost of financing and taxation, net profit margin, returns on asset, returns on equities in current year, cash and securities in hand, total intangible asset, error terms
A Study of the Relationship bet-ween a Successful Enterprise Risk management –system, a Performance Measurement System and the Financial Performance	2014	no	Questionaire with quantitative analysis	ERMS and PMS have only a weak positive correlation with the financial performance considering return on assets (ROA), return on equity (ROE) and earnings per share (EPS).	ERM assessment: answers to questions to assess the level of ERM Performance ROA, ROE, EPS

of Thai Listed Companies, Kittipat Laisasikorn, Nopadol Rompho					
Does Enterprise risk management Create Value for Firms?: Evidence from Nordic Countries, Sekerci Naciye	2013	no	Questionaire with quantitative analysis	Value creation of ERM is not supported.	ERM assessment: a survey with questions of the level of ERM implementation Performance: Tobin's Q, ERM, Size, Leverage, Profitability, Growth Opportunities, Dividends, Geogr. Diversification, industrial diversification
McShane, M. K., A. Nair, and E. Rustambekov (2011), "Does Enterprise risk management Increase Firm Value?", Journal of Accounting, Auditing and Finance 26(4), 641-658.	2011	(yes)	Empirical	A positive relationship were found between increasing levels of traditional risk management capability and firm value but no additional value for firms which achieved a higher ERM rating.	ERM assessment: ERM Rating and score based on Standard & Poor Performance: Tobin's Q, Size, Financial Leverage, Systematic Risk, Profitability, Cash-Flow Volatility, Growth Opportunities, Complexity (diversification)
The Impact of Enterprise risk management on Firm Performance: Evidence from Malaysia,Teoh Ai Ping, Rajendran Muthuveloo	2015	yes	Questionaire with quantitative analysis	A significant influence on firm performance through ERM implementation was found.	ERM assessment: 103 questionnaires with an analysis of ERM level based on the components of COSO framework consisting of risk management implementation, influence factors as Board of Directors, firm size and complexity firm performance: 6 financial values, 6 non-financial values
A Proposed Model of the Relationship between Enterprise risk management and Firm	2014	n.a.	Literature reserach	This paper proposes a model that links ERM to both financial and non-financial performance	The proposed models suggests that ERM can be measured not only in financial figures but also in customer satisfaction, learning and growth, and internal business processes

				through balanced scorecard (BSC).	
Performance, Parvaneh Saeidi,Saudah Sofian, Siti Zaleha Binti Abdul Rasid					
Conceptual Framework for Enterprise risk management performance measure through Economic Value Added, Kashif Shad, Lai Fong Woon	2015	n.a.	Literature reserach	This paper proposes a model that links ERM to Shareholder-value creation by proposing that the dimensions structure, governance, and process relate to EVA: Operating Margin, Cost of Capital, and Capital Employed.	The three dimensions are structure, governance and process with 14 elements have impact on operating margin, cost of capital, and capital employed
Panel Data Analysis on the Effect of Establishing the Enterprise risk management on Firms' Performance, Roslida Ramlee, Normah Ahmad	2015	no	Empirical	There is no significant relationship between ERM and firms' performances.	ERM assessment: ERM establishment is measured by ERM index based on the COSO frameowork and firms' performances: ROE , ROA and Tobin's Q, data taken from ThomsonOne.com database, OSIRIS database and corporate annual reports
An Empirical Investigation into the Association between Enterprise risk management and Firm Financial Performance, Ballantyne, Ryan	2013	no	Questionair e with quantitativ e analysis	ERM adoption is not associated with financial performance. Additionally, the authors find no prove that ERM maturity is associated with capital efficiency, profitability, total shareholder return, or firm value.	ERM assessment: COSO framework variables financial performance: capital efficiency, profitability, total shareholder return, and firm value
Enterprise risk management: A process for enhanced	2012	(yes)	Questionair e with quantitativ e analysis	It is suggested that use of ERM leads to increased management	ERM framework: COSO elements incl objective setting, identification, risk reaction, oversight,

management and improved performance Stephen Gates, Jean-Louis Nicolas, Paul L. Walker				consensus, better-informed decisions, enhanced communication of risk taking, and greater management accountability.	information and communication, internal environment, management performance performance measurement: benefits of meeting strategic goals, reducing earnings volatility, and increasing profitability based on answers of questionaire
The Effect of Enterprise risk management Implementation on the Value of Companies Listed on the Nairobi Stock Exchange, Nelson Waweru,Eric Kisaka	2013	no	Questionair e with quantitativ e analysis	No relationship between level of ERM implementation and industry of operation, level of board independence, size of the firm, and growth rate of the firm. But a significant relationship between a company's level or Enterprise Risk Management implementation and the company's value were found.	ERM assessment: Many different factors, e.g. ERM Level (based on research by the Economist Unit Intelligence Ltd 2009) size, industry, ownership, chief risk officer etc., Performance: TobinQ, Size, Leverage, Profitability, Dividend paid, Growth opportunities
Does ERM (Enterprise risk management) Help Firm's Performance in Times of Crisis?, Liao, Shin-Wie	2012	no	Empirical	An average firm with ERM program only performed slightly better than the other firms did.	ERM assessment: S&P's ERM rating of insurers between 2007-2012 Performance: Firms size, firms value, ROE, earnings Volatility, Share Return volatility
Enterprise risk management and business performance during the financial and economic crisis, Quon Tony K.	2012	no	Empirical	ERM information has no effect on business performance	ERM assessment: 156 non-financial firms on the Standard & Poor's Toronto Stock Exchange (TSX) Composite Index during 2007 and 2008, their ERM variables takes from annual reports Performance: Tobin Q, Sales, EBIT

Enterprise risk management Program Quality: Determinants, Value Relevance, and the Financial Crisis, Baxter Ryan, Bedard Jean, Hoitash Rani	2013	(yes)	Empirical	Higher ERMQ is associated with the following according to the authors: greater complexity, less resource constraint, better corporate governance - associated with improved accounting performance. The authors do not find a relation between ERM quality and market performance prior to and during the market collapse.	ERM assessment: Ratings of financial companies by Standard & Poor's, finer definitions of that ratings, complexity, values of the market Performance: ROA, Tobin's Q, cumulative abnormal returns, buy-and-hold abnormal returns, and several other values
Enterprise risk management and Performance in Malaysia, Shima Nickmanesh, Mahmood zohoori, Andira Musriyama Musram, Akbar Akbari	2013	(Yes)	Empirical	The Number of independent non-executive members and the size of the risk management committee positively impact ROA. Board Size and number of independent non-executive directors positively impact Turnover. But there is negative relationship between the existence of risk management committee and ROA.	ERM assessment: board size, number of independent non-executive directors, Number of directors with financial expertise, existence of risk management committee, Size of risk management committee, and Separateness of risk management and audit committee, Age of company, Total assets, Number of Foreign subsidiaries, and Type of Industry as controlling variables. Performance: ROA, Turnover

Summary of ERM-studies between the years 2011 and 2015 (Source: own elaboration based on the results of own research)

Appendix C: Number of certificates of international standards ordered by country (Source: ISO, 2018)

Top 10 countries for ISO/TS 16949 certificates - 2016		
1	China	28830
2	Korea, Republic of	5352
3	India	5289
4	United States of America	4293
5	Germany	3460
Top 10 countries for ISO 9001 certificates - 2016		
1	China	350631
2	Italy	150143
3	Germany	66233
4	Japan	49429
5	United Kingdom	37901
Top 10 countries for ISO 14001 certificates - 2016		
1	China	137230
2	Japan	27372
3	Italy	26655
4	United Kingdom	16761
5	Spain	13717
Top 10 countries for ISO/IEC 27001 certificates - 2016		
1	Japan	8945
2	United Kingdom	3367
3	India	2902
4	China	2618
5	Germany	1338

Top 10 countries for ISO 50001 certificates - 2016		
1	Germany	9024
2	United Kingdom	2829
3	Italy	1415
4	China	1015
5	France	759
5	India	570

Top 10 countries for ISO 20000-1 certificates - 2016		
1	CHINA	1666
2	INDIA	442
3	JAPAN	285
4	UNITED KINGDOM	217
5	SPAIN	215

Top 10 countries for ISO 13485 certificates - 2016		
1	United States of America	5298
2	Germany	4107
3	Italy	2980
4	China	2244
5	United Kingdom	2083

Summary of the international use of ISO standards

Overview ISO 9001

Year	2013	2014	2015	2016
TOTAL	1022877	1036321	1034180	1105937
Africa	9816	10143	12154	13378
Central and South America	52466	50165	49509	52094
North America	48579	41459	46938	44252
Europe	458814	453628	439477	451415
East Asia and Pacific	387543	414801	422519	480445
Central and South Asia	44847	44790	40822	41370
Middle East	20812	21335	22761	22983

Regional share - in %

Year	2013	2014	2015	2016
TOTAL	100%	100%	100%	100%
Africa	1,0%	1,0%	1,2%	1,2%
Central and South America	5,1%	4,8%	4,8%	4,7%
North America	4,7%	4,0%	4,5%	4,0%
Europe	44,9%	43,8%	42,5%	40,8%
East Asia and Pacific	37,9%	40,0%	40,9%	43,4%
Central and South Asia	4,4%	4,3%	3,9%	3,7%
Middle East	2,0%	2,1%	2,2%	2,1%

Annual growth - absolute numbers

Year	2013	2014	2015	2016
TOTAL	5598	13444	-2141	71757
Africa	142	327	2011	1224
Central and South America	1007	-2301	-656	2585
North America	9993	-7120	5479	-2686
Europe	-10925	-5186	-14151	11938
East Asia and Pacific	-8855	27258	7718	57926
Central and South Asia	12474	-57	-3968	548

Middle East	1762	523	1426	222

Annual growth - in %

Year	2013	2014	2015	2016
TOTAL	1%	1%	0%	6,9%
Africa	1,5%	3,3%	19,8%	10,1%
Central and South America	2,0%	-4,4%	-1,3%	5,2%
North America	25,9%	-14,7%	13,2%	-5,7%
Europe	-2,3%	-1,1%	-3,1%	2,7%
East Asia and Pacific	-2,2%	7,0%	1,9%	13,7%
Central and South Asia	38,5%	-0,1%	-8,9%	1,3%
Middle East	9,2%	2,5%	6,7%	1,0%

Overview ISO 14001

Year	2013	2014	2015	2016
TOTAL	273861	296736	319496	346147
Africa	2519	2545	3024	3551
Central / South America	9890	10084	10097	10444
North America	8917	8185	8712	8438
Europe	115764	119072	119754	120595
East Asia and Pacific	126760	145877	165616	189505
Central and South Asia	6577	7187	7708	8612
Middle East	3434	3786	4585	5002

Regional share - in %

Year	2013	2014	2015	2016
TOTAL	100%	100%	100%	100%
Africa	0,9%	0,9%	0,9%	1,0%
Central / South America	3,6%	3,4%	3,2%	3,0%
North America	3,3%	2,8%	2,7%	2,4%
Europe	42,3%	40,1%	37,5%	34,8%
East Asia and Pacific	46,3%	49,2%	51,8%	54,7%

Central and South Asia	2,4%	2,4%	2,4%	2,5%
Middle East	1,3%	1,3%	1,4%	1,4%

Annual growth - absolute numbers

Year	2013	2014	2015	2016
TOTAL	13009	22875	22760	26651
Africa	435	26	479	527
Central / South America	1688	194	13	347
North America	344	-732	527	-274
Europe	3957	3308	682	841
East Asia and Pacific	4390	19117	19739	23889
Central and South Asia	1608	610	521	904
Middle East	587	352	799	417

Annual growth - in %

Year	2013	2014	2015	2016
TOTAL	5%	8%	17%	17%
Africa	21%	1%	19%	17%
Central / South America	21%	2%	0%	3%
North America	4%	-8%	6%	-3%
Europe	4%	3%	1%	1%
East Asia and Pacific	4%	15%	14%	14%
Central and South Asia	32%	9%	7%	12%
Middle East	21%	10%	21%	9%

Overview ISO 27001

Year	2013	2014	2015	2016
TOTAL	21604	23005	27536	33290
Africa	99	79	129	224
Central / South America	272	273	347	564
North America	712	814	1445	1469
Europe	7952	8663	10446	12532

East Asia and Pacific	10116	10414	11994	14704
Central and South Asia	2002	2251	2569	2987
Middle East	451	511	606	810

Regional share - in %

Year	2013	2014	2015	2016
TOTAL	100%	100%	100%	100%
Africa	0,5%	0,3%	0,5%	0,7%
Central / South America	1,3%	1,2%	1,3%	1,7%
North America	3,3%	3,5%	5,2%	4,4%
Europe	36,8%	37,7%	37,9%	37,6%
East Asia and Pacific	46,8%	45,3%	43,6%	44,2%
Central and South Asia	9,3%	9,8%	9,3%	9,0%
Middle East	2,1%	2,2%	2,2%	2,4%

Annual growth - absolute numbers

Year	2013	2014	2015	2016
TOTAL	1984	1401	4531	5754
Africa	35	-20	50	95
Central / South America	69	1	74	217
North America	160	102	631	24
Europe	1573	711	1783	2086
East Asia and Pacific	-306	298	1580	2710
Central and South Asia	334	249	318	418
Middle East	119	60	95	204

Annual growth - in %

Year	2013	2014	2015	2016
TOTAL	10%	6%	20%	21%
Africa	55%	-20%	63%	74%
Central / South America	34%	0%	27%	63%
North America	29%	14%	78%	2%

Europe	25%	9%	21%	20%
East Asia and Pacific	-3%	3%	15%	23%
Central and South Asia	20%	12%	14%	16%
Middle East	36%	13%	19%	34%

Overview ISO 16949

Year	2013	2014	2015	2016
TOTAL	**53723**	**57950**	**62944**	**67358**
Africa	479	480	506	522
Central / South America	1585	1621	1602	1582
North America	5592	5928	6316	6389
Europe	11263	11848	12500	12786
East Asia and Pacific	29831	32728	36174	39986
Central and South Asia	4260	4618	5035	5329
Middle East	713	727	811	764

Regional share - in %

Year	2013	2014	2015	2016
TOTAL	**100%**	**100%**	**100%**	**100%**
Africa	0,9%	0,8%	0,8%	0,8%
Central / South America	3,0%	2,8%	2,5%	2,3%
North America	10,4%	10,2%	10,0%	9,5%
Europe	21,0%	20,4%	19,9%	19,0%
East Asia and Pacific	55,5%	56,5%	57,5%	59,4%
Central and South Asia	7,9%	8,0%	8,0%	7,9%
Middle East	1,3%	1,3%	1,3%	1,1%

Annual growth - absolute numbers

Year	2013	2014	2015	2016
TOTAL	**3652**	**4227**	**4994**	**4414**
Africa	15	1	26	16
Central / South America	4	36	-19	-20

North America	182	336	388	73
Europe	246	585	652	286
East Asia and Pacific	2846	2897	3446	3812
Central and South Asia	443	358	417	294
Middle East	-84	14	84	-47

Annual growth - in %

Year	2013	2014	2015	2016
TOTAL	7%	8%	9%	7%
Africa	3%	0%	5%	3%
Central / South America	0%	2%	-1%	-1%
North America	3%	6%	7%	1%
Europe	2%	5%	6%	2%
East Asia and Pacific	11%	10%	11%	11%
Central and South Asia	12%	8%	9%	6%
Middle East	-11%	2%	12%	-6%

Overview ISO 50001

Year	2013	2014	2015	2016
TOTAL	4826	6765	11985	20216
Africa	36	18	40	58
Central / South America	34	63	92	81
North America	34	77	77	73
Europe	3.993	5.526	10.152	17.102
East Asia and Pacific	478	693	1.035	2.086
Central and South Asia	189	299	459	663
Middle East	62	89	130	153

Regional share - in %

Year	2013	2014	2015	2016
TOTAL	100%	100%	100%	100%
Africa	0,7%	0,3%	0,3%	0,3%

Central / South America	0,7%	0,9%	0,8%	0,4%
North America	0,7%	1,1%	0,6%	0,4%
Europe	82,7%	81,7%	84,7%	84,6%
East Asia and Pacific	9,9%	10,2%	8,6%	10,3%
Central and South Asia	3,9%	4,4%	3,8%	3,3%
Middle East	1,3%	1,3%	1,1%	0,8%

Number of countries / economies

Year	2013	2014	2015	2016
TOTAL	**78**	**80**	**97**	**97**
Africa	10	4	12	12
Central / South America	6	10	13	13
North America	3	3	3	3
Europe	35	37	40	40
East Asia and Pacific	13	15	16	16
Central and South Asia	4	3	4	4
Middle East	7	8	9	9

Appendix D: Comparison of agile principles (chapter 4)

Comparison of agile principles and agile strategies at Alibaba and traditional plan-based strategies

Cluster	Agile principles	Application of principle on strategy within highly adaptive and reactive sector	Evaluation of principle on strategy within "traditional" manufacturing sector
Example Agile Cluster	Software development (considering agile production & agile supply chain management aspects)	Business strategy of Alibaba (2008 – 2014)	Business strategy of automotive industry (2007 – 2015)
1. Flexibility to change	Working software is delivered frequently (weeks)	*Core principles:* Modulate, Shape, Modify	*Core principles:* Define, Follow, Achieve
	Accept and adapt to changing requirements, (even in late development stages)	After testing of business model options, scaling up the most promising ones and closing down or reabsorbing those that are less promising.	Longterm fixed strategic plans in line with defined cycle plans for products and fixed product development process preventing late changes to the product
	Close and regular cooperation of business and developers	Close connection of strategy and lower management levels via empowerement to generate and test business models.	Strategy is a top-management topic supported by consulters or dedicated departments
2. Execution based on continuous feedback	Customer satisfaction by early and continuous delivery of developments & Built-to-order and demand driven "pull-systems"	Experimenting with business models. Customer and demand decides which strategic path will be promoted	Strategic investments based on predictions and periodic data analysis
	Face-to-face conversation is favoured (co-location)	*Not examined*	*Not examined*
	Sustainable development, able to maintain a constant pace	Constant or increasing generation of business options (in order to avoid rigidity and generate options)	New business models and strategic orientations are adjusted periodically or according to need but scarcely proactive
3. Execution by the whole	The team continuously looks for efficiencies and adjusts accordingly (KVP)	„Keep resetting the vision" → At any time Strategy should be customized to environment; Focus is shifted every 1 -3 years; Self adjusting strategy;	Vision and strategy is fixed for 5 to 7 years. Adjustments in between are not common

	Projects are based on motivated and trusted individuals	Supporting and promoting managers to create business models	Relying on top-management decisions
	Decentralized decisions & Self-organizing teams support architectures, requirements, and designs	Decisions are pulled by the market / Neither centralistic nor time-point based but continuous; Management rotates frequently	Decisions have been mostly centralistic, but e.g. approaches into various drivetrains are and investments are according to market demands with modulation based on expected future demand. Management rotates in general every 3 years
4. Focus on working products	Working software is the principal measure of progress	Positive business cases for business models	Sales increase, Return on investment, operating margin matching planned values
	Continuous emphasis to technical excellence and good design	*Continuous improvement Included in high level business strategy*	*Not examined*
	Simplicity: The art of maximizing the amount of work not done, is essential (Lean principle)	*Not examined*	*Not examined*

(Source: Own representation based on Kompalla Andreas, Kopia Jan, Tigu Gabriela,(2016a), An application of agile principles on business strategies with-in it-based industries and automotive enterprises, Zeitschrift für interdisziplinäre ökonomische Forschung, vol. 01, no. (2016), pg. 112-122, ISSN 2196-4688)

Appendix E: Interview questions from chapter 6.4

List of questions for the interviews:

Q1. How do you measure performance in your department?

Q2. How do you measure performance at the corporate level?

Q3. Does the use of the BSC help the organization to align the operational processes with the strategic level?

Q4. Is corporate sustainability an issue in your organization? Is this reflected by the use of an SBSC?

Q5. How many performance indicators are you using for your BSC?

Q6. How is the MSS / IMS linked with the BSC or with the organizational strategy?

Q7. Is the MSS / IMS part of the BSC-Process?

Q8. Does the BSC increase performance (on the operational or organizational level)?

Q9. How many MSS do you use? Does the MSS / IMS increase performance (how is this measured)?

Q10. Is your (integrated) management system successful based on the defined goals?

R1. MPD = Rate the performance development of the organization over the last 5 years (1=negative, 5=neutral, 10=strongly positive)

R2. BU = Rate the level of your BSC use between the BSC as performance measurement tool only and the BSC as strategic planning system (1=performance management system only, 10=strategic planning system)?

R3. IMS = At what scale is the MSS(s) integrated into an IMS? (1=not integrated, 10=fully integrated into an IMS)

R4. IBSC = How would you rate the integration of the MSS / IMS into the BSC (10=not integrated, 10=strongly integrated)?

R5. YIMS = When did you implemented your first MSS? (1=10 years before and more, 10=1 year before)

R6. YBSC = When did you integrated the MSS / IMS into the BSC? (1=10 years before and more, 10=1 year before)

R7. FM = How often are performance indicators in the BSC evaluated? (1=every 3 years or rarer, 10=4 times and more per year)

Appendix F: interview results of chapter 6.4

Interview results of the verification

Question	Yes	No	Summary of the results
Q1			Most organizations use specific KPIs or separated BSC on the department level.
Q2			Performance measurement systems which are based on financial values with different factors of other dimensions which are weighted (including quality-oriented measures and the Trible Bottom Line).

Question	Yes	No	Summary of the results
Q3	29	8	A regularly performed linkage process is executed by most of the organizations. This is done between every six months (by 4 organizations) until up to five years (by 10 organizations) 12 organizations use BSCs on a business unit or department level and aggregated the results regularly to the organizational wide BSC.
Q4	23	11	Corporate sustainability plays an important role for 56% of the organizations. 13 created an SBSC. The other organizations use different approaches for the integration of this topic into their measurement and reporting system. The financial aspects play a big role for all companies. They all follow a more hierarchical BSC model (see above) with financial values as main output. Aspects of sustainability are weighted individually in each organization based on the importance of the specific topic.
Q5			28 companies use more than 10 indicators on their BSC on the corporate level (but less than 20). On the individual and business unit level the BSCs have up to 20 indicators, sometimes generated automatically using systems / IT.
Q6			16 organizations integrate their management systems into the balanced scorecard by including central elements of the measurement of the management system as KPI. This allows a continuous monitoring and the visibility on the top level.
Q7	15	25	35 organizations use Strategy Map. 15 also assess management systems within the strategic mapping. One organization sees the use of a management system and sustainability as a strategic topic but evaluates them separately.
Q8	25	16	61% of the interviewees identified a positive relationship between the balanced scorecard and organizational performance. Some organizations state an increased transparency through the BSC about the operational status. No link to performance enhancement because of BSC were mentioned.
Q9			26 organizations use more than one MSS, 6 operate one management system based on either ISO or TQM, 8 use one management system. 12 of the organizations neglected an impact on organizational performance. 20 could not define exactly how performance could have increased but identified a positive correlation between the execution of the management system and performance increase (48%). Most organizations measure their management systems with specific KPIs. These KPIs are also part of the BSC (see question 7 and 9). All of the organizations which use management system aspects within the BSC emphasize the importance of this aspect since this allows the visibility on the upper level and therefore managerial decision making.
Q10	20	5	The author did only count answers from the organizations of which there is valid data of KPIs which can be used to calculate the maturity. He also estimated the trend of the KPIs over the last years since there was not enough data to generate these values. This is the case for 25 organizations. 20 of the 25 organizations state that their management systems operate efficiently and effective based on their defined goals.

(Source: own elaboration based on the results of own research)

Appendix G Risk management process in the case study of chapter 4

The risk management process between departments at the example case

Area of risks	Aspects of risk management
Finance	The accounting department is responsible for the risks in that perspective. This include compliance risks regarding taxes, but also risks in credit status, liquidity, and other market-based risks.
	Financial risks report are generated weekly for the middle management of the departments including the financial risk committee. These reports are summarized on a regular basis for other stakeholders including the top management and used for standard reports which are required by laws or regulations. The risk committee uses financial risks to include it into a generic enterprise wide risk report
Production	Risks within the production department includes risks in quality, defect rate, problems in the supply and alike. The risk management is strongly connected to the quality management system (not specified by the employees) and the required reporting. Problems in quality incidentally creates an incident and a reaction in the form of a countermeasure previously defined by the risk owner of the process. The quality process is derived from TQM, therefore quality is important for every employee within the production. ABC supports an open communication, which also include the identification of risks and possible solutions and countermeasures for them. A risk-based approach is established within the department, which is part of the constant exchange with the customer and supplier regarding quality issues and other problems. Risk owner of certain areas are responsible for collecting risks and possible solutions and improvements and communicating them to the production risk committee, the local quality managers, and the upper management. Risks are mainly identified within the day-to-day business and the established measurement methods of quality, defects, and other monitoring elements within the production. These operational risks are mandatory for the production since a problem with the production line could lead to a quick loss in profitability. Risks in the production area are reported on a daily basis toward the risk committee in order to react as quickly as possible in case of emergency. Typical KPIs are quality problems, defect rates, customer complaints, efficiency, number of products – most of the values are separated by region and product line).

(Source: own elaboration based on the results of own research)

Annexes

Annex 1: List of author's publications

1. Monographs / books / manuals

No publications.

2. Published scientific articles

a. Literature published in scientific ISI magazines

[1] **Jan KOPIA doctorand**, Andreas Kompalla, Melanie Buchmüller, Bastian Heinemann, 4 – *Performance Measurement of management system Standards Using the balanced scorecard*, Amfiteatru Economic, "Amfiteatru Economic Journal", Vol. XIX, Special 11/**2017**, pp. 981 - 1002, Nov. 2017**,** Editura ASE, Bucharest (Romania), ISSN 1582 - 9146, revista este clasificată CNCSIS în categoria A, inclusă ISI Thomson Reuters Services: Social Sciences Citation Index®, Social Scisearch®, Journal Citation Reports/Social Sciences Edition. Factor de impact pe anul 2012: 0,953. Articolul este disponibil pe http://www.amfiteatrueconomic.ase.ro. IDS Number: 710QA, Accession number: WOS: 000286525100013

b. Literature published in ISI proceedings

Jan KOPIA doctorand, 1 – *Study on integration and leadership styles of management systems based on a high level structure,* ICMLG **2016** 4th International Conference on Management Leadership and Governance St Petersburg Russia , ICMLG 2016, 4/14/2016, St Petersburg , Rep. Central Africa, published in ICMLG 2016 4th International Conference on Management Leadership and Governance St Petersburg , pg. 431-441, ISSN , ISBN 978-1-910810-84-2, conference Internationala,

© Springer Fachmedien Wiesbaden GmbH, part of Springer Nature 2019
J. Kopia, *Effective Implementation of Management Systems*, Sustainable Management, Wertschöpfung und Effizienz, https://doi.org/10.1007/978-3-658-26509-0

http://www.academic-conferences.org/conferences/icmlg/, The conference proceedings have an ISSN (2049-6818) and will have ISBN on publication. They are submitted on publication to:

indexed in the Thomson Reuters ISI Web of Science (WOS) Conference Proceedings Citation Index, indexed in the Elsevier SCOPUS abstract and citation database, indexed by the Institution of Engineering and Technology in the UK, listed on the Proquest Database,

listed on Google Books, listed on Google Scholar

[2] A. Kompalla, **J. KOPIA**, G. Tigu, 3- *Limitations of business strategies and management systems within automotive industry*, 10th International Technology, Education and Development Conference, INTED**2016**, 3/7/2016, Valencia, Spania, published in INTED2016 Proceedings, pg. 3817-3827, ISSN 2340-1079, ISBN 978-84-608-5617-7, conference Internationala, https://library.iated.org/publications/INTED2016, publication will be sent to be reviewed for its inclusion in the ISI Conference Proceedings Citation Index

[3] Andreas Kompalla, **Jan KOPIA**, Gabriela Tigu, 3 - *Analysis of correlation between intellectual capital and traditional key performance indicators within the automotive industry*, International Business Information Management Conference, 27TH IBIMA, 5/4/**2016**, Milan, Spania, published in IBIMA Conference Proceedings, pg. 10-20, ISSN , ISBN 978-0-9860419-6-9, conference Internationala, http://www.ibima.org/ITALY2016/index.html, The Thomson Reuters ISI Index to Scientific and Technical Proceedings® (ISTP®), The Thomson Reuters ISI Index to Scientific and Technical Proceedings (ISTP/ISI Proceedings), The Thomson Reuters ISI Index to Social Sciences & Humanities Proceedings® (ISSHP®), The Thomson Reuters ISI Index to Social Sciences & Humanities Proceedings (ISSHP/ISI Proceedings), The Thomson Reuters Index for Conference proceedings Citation index, social Sciences, and Humanities edition (Web of Science)

[4] Wiebke Geldmacher, Vanessa Just, **Jan KOPIA**, Aykut Bussian, 4 - *Requirements towards sustainable future urban mobility in germany*, BASIQ INTERNATIONAL CONFERENCE, BASIQ**2016**, 6/2/2016, Konstanz, Germania, published in CONFERENCE PROCEEDINGS , pg. 50-59, ISSN 2457-483X, conference Internationala, http://www.conference.ase.ro/

[5] Bußian Aykut, Singer Klaus, **KOPIA Jan**, Geldmacher Wiebke, 4 - *Perspectives on big data and business intelligence technologies in the context of audit tasks*, BASIQ INTERNATIONAL CONFERENCE, BASIQ2016, 6/2/**2016**, Konstanz, Germania, published in BASIQ INTERNATIONAL CONFERENCE, pg. 10-20, conference Internationala, http://www.conference.ase.ro/

[6] Singer Klaus, Bußian Aykut and **KOPIA Jan**, 3 - Implication of the new eu directive for disclosing non-financial information on sustainability, environment and social aspects, 28th IBIMA Conference, IBIMA, 11/9/**2016**, Seville, Spania, published in Proceedings of the 28th IBIMA Conference, pg. 10-29, ISSN 2457-483X, ISBN 978-0-9860419-8-3, conference Internationala, http://www.i-bima.org/SPAIN2016/papers/bubi.html, The Thomson Reuters ISI Index to Scientific and Technical Proceedings® (ISTP®), The Thomson Reuters ISI Index to Scientific and Technical Proceedings (ISTP/ISI Proceedings), The Thomson Reuters ISI Index to Social Sciences & Humanities Proceedings® (ISSHP®), The Thomson Reuters ISI Index to Social Sciences & Humanities Proceedings (ISSHP/ISI Proceedings), The Thomson Reuters Index for Conference proceedings Citation index, social Sciences, and Humanities edition (Web of Science)

c. **Literature publishes in national non ISI-magazines**

B+

[1] A Kompalla, **J KOPIA**, G Tigu, 3 - *Characteristics of business strategies and management systems within automotive industry*, Ovidius University Annals, Series Economic Sciences, vol. 15, no. 2, **2015**, pg. 267-274, ISSN , Indexata in minim 2 baze de date internationale, http://stec.univ-ovidius.ro/html/anale/ENG/ EBSCO host, Cabell's Directories , RePEc, DOAJ, ULRICHS WEB, J- GATE, ERIH PLUS, INDEX COPERNICUS,

Scientific Indexing Services, INFOBASE INDEX, ResearchBib

[2] A Kompalla, **J KOPIA**, G Tigu, 3 - *An application of agile principles on business strategies with-in it-based industries and automotive enterprises*, Zeitschrift für interdisziplinäre ökonomische Forschung, vol. 01, no. **2016**, pg. 112-122, ISSN 2196-

4688, Indexata in minim 2 baze de date internationale, https://www.allensbach-hochschule.de/ Deutsche Nationalbibliothek, Max Planck Institute for comporative public law and international law, ECONBIZ, Wissenschaftszentrum Berlin für Sozialforschung, Leibnitz-Informationszentrum für Lebenswissenschaften, Deutsche Zentralbibliothek für Wirtschaftswissenschaften, Leibnitz Informationszentrum-Wirtschaft, Google Scholars, Abteilung überregionale Bibliographische Dienste

Staatsbibliothek zu Berlin

[3] **Jan KOPIA**, Vanessa Just, Wiebke Geldmacher, Aykut Bußian, 4 - *Organization performance and enterprise risk management*, Ecoforum, vol. 6, no. 1, **2017**, pg. 1-1, ISSN 2344-2174, Indexata in minim 2 baze de date internationale, http://www.ecoforumjournal.ro/index.php/eco/article/view/573

[4] **J KOPIA**, A Kompalla, I Ceausu, 3 - *Theory and practice of integrating management systems with high level structure*, Quality – access to success, vol. 17, no. 155, pg. 52-59, 2016, ISSN 1582-2559, Indexata in minim 2 baze de date internationale, http://www.srac.ro/calitatea/en/ Editura SRAC, Bucureşti (România), ISSN 1582-2559, **2016**, http://www.srac.ro/calitatea/en/arhiva/2016/ 2016_06-Abstracts.pdf,

revistă clasificată CNCSIS în categoria B+ şi inclusă în bazele de date internaţionale SCOPUS, EBSCO, CABELL'S şi PROQUEST http://www.srac.ro/calitatea/index.html, revistă clasificată CNCSIS în categoria B+ şi inclusă în bazele de date internaţionale SCOPUS, EBSCO, CABELL'S şi PROQUEST http://www.srac.ro/calitatea/index.html

[5] Andreas Kompalla, **Jan KOPIA**, 2 - *Evaluation of the agile manifesto within business strategies*, Journal of Economics and Public Finance, vol. 02, no. 02, pg. 227-239, **2016,** ISSN 2377-1038, Indexata in minim 2 baze de date internationale, http://www.scholink.org/ojs/index.php/jepf

[6] Nina GOLOWKO, **Jan KOPIA**, Wiebke GELDMACHER, Ulrike S. FÖRSTER-PASTOR, 4 - *Comparative Study on Quality Management at German Private Universities*, Calitatea: Acces la Success; Bucharest, vol. 18, no. 157, pg. 85-94, **2017**, ISSN 1582-2559, Indexata in minim 2 baze de date internationale, http://

www.srac.ro/calitatea/en/ journal indexed in international data bases Web of Science™ Core Collection - Emerging Sources Citation Index (ESCI), SCOPUS http://www.scimagojr.com/journalsearch.php?q=177001567 09&tip=sid&clean=0, EBSCO, CABELL'S and PROQUEST, edited by Romanian Society for Quality Assurance - SRAC. http://www.srac.ro/calitatea/en/index.html

[7] Bastian HEINEMANN, Ioana CEAUŞU, Melanie BUCHMUELLER, **Jan KOPIA,** 4 - *Quality management system certification and the continuous improvement process by the example of a training company in germany*, Quality-Access to Success , vol. 18, no. 156, pg. 97-101, **2017,** ISSN 1582-2559, Indexata ISI Thomson, http://www.srac.ro/calitatea/en/ Editura SRAC, Bucureşti (România), ISSN 1582-2559, http://www.srac.ro/calitatea/en/arhiva/supliment/2015/Q-asContents_Vol.16_S1_March-2015.pdf, revistă clasificată CNCSIS în categoria B+ şi inclusă în bazele de date internaţionale SCOPUS, EBSCO, CABELL'S şi PROQUEST http://www.srac.ro/calitatea/index.html

[8] **Jan KOPIA**, Vanessa JUST, Wiebke GELDMACHER, Aykut BUßIAN,4 - *Meaning and usage of a conceptual enterprise risk management framework –a case study*, Ecoforum, Volume 6, Issue 2(11), **2017,** ISSN: 2344-2174, www.ecoforumjournal.ro/index.php/eco/article/view/597, journal listed/ indexed in the 26 academic databases/directories and document sharing platforms, edited by „Stefan cel Mare" University of Suceava, Romania http://www.ecoforumjournal.ro/ index.php/eco

[9] Andreas Kompalla, **Jan KOPIA**, Ulrike Foerster, Wiebke Geldmacher, 4 - *Analysis of correlations between coprporate strategy and operational strategy considering management system standards*, Ecoforum, Volume 6, Issue 3 (**2017**), ISSN: 2344-2174, www.ecoforumjournal.ro/index.php/eco/article/view/678, journal listed/ indexed in the 26 academic databases/directories and document sharing platforms, edited by „Stefan cel Mare" University of Suceava, Romania http://www.ecoforumjournal.ro/index.php/eco

[10] Melanie Buchmüller, Thorsten Eidmüller, Andreas Mussmann, Jan Kopia, *THE STATUS OF MODULAR SOURCING COMPARED TO OTHER PROCUREMENT STRATE-*

GIES, Ecoforum, Volume 7, Issue 1 (2018), ISSN: 2344-2174, http://www.ecofo-rumjournal.ro/index.php/eco/article/view/717, journal listed/ indexed in the 26 academic databases/directories and document sharing platforms, edited by „Stefan cel Mare" University of Suceava, Romania http://www.ecoforumjour-nal.ro/index.php/eco

3. Citations published in scientific literature

[1] Andreas KOMPALLA, Wiebke GELDMACHER, Vanessa JUST, Steffen LANGE, *Tailored Automotive business strategies in the Context of Digitalization and Service-Oriented Models*, "February 2017, Quality - Access to Success 18(156):77

[2] Kompalla, Andreas; Studeny, Michael; Bartels, Andreas; Tigu, Gabriela. *Agile business strategies: How to Adjust to Rapidly Changing Environments?*
European Conference on Innovation and Entrepreneurship; Reading: 414-424. Reading: Academic Conferences International Limited. (Sep 2016)

[3] Pedro Domingues, Paulo Sampaio, Pedro M. Arezes, (2017) *Management systems integration: survey results,* International Journal of Quality & Reliability Management, Vol. 34 Issue: 8, pp.1252-1294, https://doi.org/10.1108/IJQRM-03-2015-0032

[4] Wiebke Geldmacher, Vanessa Just, Carsten Kirschner, Melanie Buchmüller, Katrin Marquardt, *The Correlation of Information and Knowledge in Regard to the Acceptance Level and Their Implication on Self-Driving Cars in Germany*, Ecoforum Journal 6 (3), 2017

[5] B Heinemann, I Ceausu, M Buchmüller, J Kopia, *Quality management system Certification and the Continuous Improvement Process by the Example of a Training Company in Germany*, Calitatea: Acces la Success; Bucharest Vol. 18, Iss. 156, (Feb 2017): 97-101.

[6] Лузина Виктория Андреевна, *показатели оценки hr-бренда организации*, Журнал «Human Progress» http://progress-human.com/

Том 2, № 1 (январь 2016), http://progress-human.com/images/2016/Tom2_1/ Luzina.pdf

4. **Articles presented at national and international scientific conference proceedings**

A.   **Published scientific studies in conference proceedings**

[1] *New Trends in Sustainable Business and Consumption*, BASIQ 2017, International Conference. 31 May -3 June, 2017, Graz

[2] Development of corporate reporting – Recent changes and a shift to non-financial information, BASIQ 2018, 11 – 13 June, 2018, Heidelberg

B.   **Unpublished scientific literature presented at conferences**

[1] The current state of knowledge on sustainability of commercial processes - sustainable processes of commercial distribution in sales support, 10TH JUNE 2016, BUCHAREST, ROMANIA. within Doctoral School Business Administration

[2] The importance of risk management when outsourcing logistics processes, BASIC2018

[3] Fraud risk assessment in regular financial statement audits: pathways to (semi-) automated solutions, tba

5. Own projects

A. Seminars

[1] Seminar, discipline Business Informatics, Prof. univ. dr. Prof. Dr. Reckenfeld-erbäumer, semester 1, universitary year 2016, Faculty MANAGEMENT.

B. Quality management audits and information security audits

[1] **Jan KOPIA**, 1 – more than 20 audits conducted during the recent months in the field of quality management and information security